Bluegrass Renaissance

Bluegrass Renaissance

The History and Culture of Central Kentucky, 1792–1852

Edited by James C. Klotter
and Daniel Rowland

UNIVERSITY PRESS OF KENTUCKY

Many of the essays in this volume were originally presented at a
conference that was made possible in part by a Challenge Grant from
the National Endowment for the Humanities.

Editorial and Sales Offices: The University Press of Kentucky
663 South Limestone Street, Lexington, Kentucky 40508-4008
www.kentuckypress.com

16 15 14 13 12   5 4 3 2 1

Library of Congress Cataloging-in-Publication Data

Bluegrass renaissance : the history and culture of central Kentucky, 1792-1852 /
edited by James C. Klotter and Daniel Rowland.
    p.   cm.
Includes bibliographical references and index.
ISBN 978-0-8131-3607-3 (hardcover : acid-free paper) —
ISBN 978-0-8131-3663-9 (pdf) — ISBN 978-0-8131-4043-8 (epub)
  1. Lexington (Ky.)—History—18th century. 2. Lexington (Ky.)—History—
19th century. 3. Lexington (Ky.)—Social life and customs. 4. Lexington (Ky.)—
Intellectual life. 5. Lexington Region (Ky.)—History—18th century. 6. Lexington Region (Ky.)—History—19th century. 7. Lexington Region (Ky.)—Social life and customs.
8. Lexington Region (Ky.)—Intellectual life. I. Klotter, James C. II. Rowland, Daniel B.
(Daniel Bruce), 1941– III. Title.
  F459.L6B55 2012
  976.9'47—dc23

                    2012019013

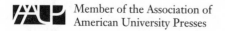

Contents

Part 3. Science, Arts, and Education

Introduction

What causes a city to be termed *great* in a moment in time? Why is a town seen as a place of progress and modernization in a specific region? What features create an environment that produces leadership in a variety of fields? What forces give birth to advancements in one area after another? And what elements combine to change the history of a place from one of betterment and hope to one of pessimism and despair? Finally, what aspects of the past, real or imagined, remain in that place, as parts that continue to form a new future?

To answer these and other questions, Daniel Rowland organized the 2007 symposium at which most of these essays were first presented.[1] As director of the Gaines Center for the Humanities at the University of Kentucky and head of the university's Marshall-Rhodes Selection Committee, Rowland had his historical interest in those queries stimulated through his work on the project to restore the Senator John and Eliza Pope Villa, built in 1812 in Lexington, and designed by the foremost architect of the period, Benjamin Henry Latrobe. Latrobe, the father of the architectural profession in the United States, is generally recognized as the greatest American architect before the age of Louis Sullivan and Frank Lloyd Wright.

Patrick Snadon, one of our essayists, established in a magisterial book he wrote with Michael Fazio on the domestic architecture of Latrobe that the Pope Villa is probably the most important of all Latrobe's domestic buildings, built or unbuilt, standing or demolished, in England or America. That would make the Pope Villa arguably the most important federal-period building in America from a strictly architectural point of view. Snadon's essay elaborates on Latrobe's surprisingly numerous commissions in Kentucky.[2]

Why was this amazing villa built in Lexington in 1812? This was the question that Rowland heard again and again over two decades, from both native Kentuckians and visitors, as he gave tours of the Pope Villa. Similarly, James C. Klotter had heard even broader questions along the same lines, in his role as the state historian of Kentucky.

A response to those experiences was the symposium "The Idea of the Athens of the West: Central Kentucky in American Culture, 1792–1852," sponsored by the Gaines Center, with Transylvania University, the University of Kentucky's College of Arts and Sciences, and the National Endowment for the Humanities. Most of the essays included in the present volume were given in preliminary form during that conference. (The dates chosen marked Kentucky's achievement of statehood and the death of Henry Clay, the close of an era.)

This collection attempts to answer the queries so often posed by visitors to the Pope Villa by examining the impressive cultural achievements (and problems) created by central Kentuckians in the first half of the nineteenth century and by addressing the questions raised earlier.

We have grouped the essays under headings to help readers understand this context. The first section is the most general. Klotter gives a concise overview of central Kentucky during the period under discussion, highlighting both the remarkable achievements of Kentuckians and the major problems (including slavery) that their society faced. Stephen Aron's memorable essay suggests that historians and the public make a mistake when they imagine European migration into Kentucky, and the West more generally, as proceeding from east to west. He examines the movements of Frenchmen, Spaniards, and others to show that it was a multidimensional affair. Finally, the late Shearer Davis Bowman compares central Kentucky as the "Athens of the West" with the original Athens of fifth-century BCE Greece.

The middle section of the book has a more sociological focus. Gerald L. Smith examines the history of slavery in central Kentucky and the attempts of antislavery advocates to change that institution. Randolph Hollingsworth outlines images of womanhood held by Kentuckians and describes some remarkable women. Maryjean Wall describes the development of horse breeding and racing. She searches for the advantages that allowed Kentucky horsemen to dominate their industry, particularly compared to their colleagues in Tennessee. Finally, Mark V. Wetherington goes beyond the usual (but important) narratives of the national importance of Kentucky politicians, including Henry Clay, to examine the influence of Kentuckians on the politics of other areas, particularly Texas.

The final section deals with culture defined broadly to include science, the arts, and education. There, John R. Thelin investigates the tight relation between education and civic pride and civic ambition, a theme crucial to the economic and cultural success of early Lexington. Tom Eblen and Mollie Eblen detail the rise and fall of perhaps the most important and influential cultural figure of the period, Transylvania's president Horace Holley. In so doing, they highlight the tension between religious orthodoxy and liberal thinking that has been a feature of Kentucky culture virtually since statehood. Matthew F. Clarke uses the remarkable and eccentric career of Constantine Rafinesque of Transylvania to uncover the surprising links between archaeological investigations of Native American mounds and the growth of American national consciousness and pride.

Three essays on culture more narrowly defined conclude the volume. Estill Curtis Pennington gives us a detailed picture of the visual arts in central Kentucky, often illuminating the links between Kentucky painters and those who trained them in eastern cities. Nikos Pappas reveals for us a world even less known: that of musical composition and performance in early Kentucky. A remarkable recording was made during the symposium: it contains performances by soloists and a twenty-piece symphony orchestra of music composed in antebellum Kentucky, much of it not heard since the Civil War.[3]

Finally, Snadon examines in detail each of the Kentucky architectural projects in which Latrobe had a hand. Most of these projects have received little or no scholarly attention before; Snadon's essay contains remarkable new evidence about both America's premier architect of the time and the cultural sophistication of Latrobe's Kentucky clients.

The discussions at that conference and the ensuing essays in this book did not emerge suddenly out of a vacuum. Authors have been telling the story of Lexington and its environs for some 140 years.

In 1872, the first general history of the city appeared. A year earlier, George W. Ranck had retired as editor of the *Lexington Observer and Reporter*, and he had used the time since then to prepare his history. Ranck's viewpoint appeared early in the book's preface: "Built up by daring man in the heart of an almost boundless wilderness, [Lexington] was the Jamestown of the West; the advance-guard of civilization; the center from which went forth the conquerors of a savage empire."[4] With heavy emphasis on those early years (and with virtually no mention of the recent Civil War), Ranck still presented a great deal of information, often gleaned from his newspaper's files. He wrote of education, artists, religion, military matters, politics, inventions, journalism, transportation, and much more. Subsequent writings would lean heavily on his fact-finding.

A decade later, Ranck helped prepare the second major study of the city, the larger 1882 *History of Fayette County, Kentucky*, authored by William H. Perrin. Part of the Perrin history came from the pen of Dr. Robert Peter, and those sections, in particular, added to the story that Ranck had told earlier and had revised since. Still, the overall tone remained the same—one filled with heroic settlers, few African Americans, many individual white male accomplishments, and little overall interpretation in the many fact-filled pages.[5]

Not for another ninety years would an overall study of the city appear again. In 1972, the prolific local gentleman-scholar "Squire" J. Winston Coleman Jr. delved into his considerable knowledge of municipal matters to compile *The Squire's Sketches of Lexington*. Its slightly more than one hundred pages unfolded in a year-by-year episodic chronology. Once more, numerous factual matters filled the book, but little interpretation intruded. Coleman, who had written a solid, if flawed, history of slavery in Kentucky, did bring in a few black faces to the mostly all-white pictures up to that time, but not many. Other topics, such as women's history, continued to remain still mostly absent.[6]

A decade later, the first modern history of the city came out, and it remains the most comprehensive study. Written by the Transylvania University history professor John D. Wright Jr., *Lexington: Heart of the Bluegrass* gave a balanced, more interpretive history, one that spoke of the Athens of the West but also of slavery, one that told of the frontier era but also of the Civil War and the twentieth century, one that presented the lives of the leaders but also of the wide spectrum of citizens in the city. Wright's account properly stressed the "remarkable" first decades but also noted "a degree of smugness" and "indifference" and "lethargy" that had occurred on occasion since then. It remains a fine study of the city.[7]

In 2004, Randolph Hollingsworth updated the story, adding material on often-ignored subjects, and presenting a fresh interpretation of the old city. Using the Wickliffe-Preston family papers, which had formed the basis for much of her dissertation, she also emphasized, more than any other author, the contributions made by women and African Americans to the Lexington story. By bringing the account into the twenty-first century, she could also note that, at the time of writing, Lexington stood sixth among U.S. cities in the percentage of the population having completed sixteen or more years of schooling.[8]

In addition to these general histories of Lexington and of Kentucky, other works have placed Lexington and its surroundings in the context of state, region, and nation. Some of those simply provided more depth to various facets of the Athens of the West story. For example, some books looked at the founding of the first settlement or of the pioneer city, while others focused on the college and intellectual world or the horse history of the Bluegrass. Fine works pictured the slave experience or examined the architectural or cultural life of the city as well. A whole series of biographies included the setting in which their subjects lived and worked, with the best perhaps being Bernard Mayo's account of the early life of Henry Clay.[9]

Even more focused on placing Lexington in its early Kentucky setting are a series of more recent books, well informed by solid scholarship. In 1982, an article surveyed the state of Kentucky history and noted the need for a new examination of frontier and antebellum history. Since that time, a number of historical studies have emerged. Many of them have brought in elements that help show Lexington's evolution in the context of the era and the place. Stephen Aron particularly focused on the transformation of land and commerce, Elizabeth Perkins on the society of the frontier, Ellen Eslinger on the religious world, and Craig Friend on the changes over time, just to mention a few.[10]

Other books put the city in a broader urban context. Allen Share's brief look at urban life in the commonwealth concentrated on Lexington and Louisville and emphasized themes of rivalries, problems, cultural life, and race. Placing Lexington's past even more in the regional urban framework was Richard C. Wade's still excellent 1939 *The Urban Frontier: The Rise of Western Cities, 1790–1830*. By comparing the cities of Pittsburgh, St. Louis, Cincinnati, Louisville, and Lexington, Wade showed the differences and similarities in their development, the richness and variety of the early urban experience, and the differing histories and what that meant for each.[11]

Unfortunately, not a large number of historians have followed that pathbreaking lead and added new urban history elements to the Lexington study. Since many histories of the urban South omit Kentucky and studies of the Midwest almost always do so, the city often finds itself in a historiographic wasteland, forgotten by regional scholars. Some historians, such as Lawrence H. Larsen and David Goldfield, do bring in Lexington examples, particularly from the antebellum era. But the field remains fertile ground even yet, for only a few have scratched the surface history of the antebellum city.[12]

Yet, from Ranck's work in 1872 to the present, a series of books—as well as articles, theses, and dissertations—have provided a mass of information and, more recently, interpretation. Those all sow the intellectual seeds that could bring forth a fresh crop of studies of the long-examined Athens of the West. This collection represents an initial harvest of that history.

Notes

1. This attempt to answer such questions also grew from Rowland's experiences as chair of the University of Kentucky Marshall-Rhodes Selection Committee not directly connected to the project. In the early years of the twenty-first century, a Kentucky student was in Chicago competing for a Rhodes scholarship. Like most Rhodes candidates, he was both ambitious and extraordinarily talented. One of two candidates selected statewide by the Kentucky Rhodes Committee, he was in the final round of interviews. The selection committee invited the students to a cocktail party, in an attempt to get acquainted informally despite the rigorous circumstances. The student introduced himself to two members of the interview team at this event, and they, of course, asked where he went to school. When he replied, "The University of Kentucky," the committee members looked at each other and rolled their eyes.

Over the years, Rowland had also found that many bright Kentucky students underestimated their abilities and skills and often assumed that they could not compete at the highest level with the nation's best students. Kentucky and its citizens often fall victim to the prejudices that arise from external stereotypes. Much more harmful, however, are the internalized stereotypes that insidiously burrow into the psyche of Kentuckians. They lead many, including young Kentuckians, to underestimate their talents, which inevitably undermines both their confidence and their prospects.

2. Michael W. Fazio and Patrick A. Snadon, *The Domestic Architecture of Benjamin Henry Latrobe* (Baltimore, 2006).

3. Available at www.kentuckypress.com.

4. George W. Ranck, *History of Lexington, Kentucky* (Cincinnati, 1872), n.p. (preface).

5. William H. Perrin, *History of Fayette County, Kentucky* (Chicago, 1882).

6. J. Winston Coleman Jr., *The Squire's Sketches of Lexington* (Lexington, 1972).

7. John D. Wright Jr., *Lexington: Heart of the Bluegrass* (Lexington, 1982), 223.

8. Randolph Hollingsworth, *Lexington: Queen of the Bluegrass* (Charleston, SC, 2004), 187.

9. Carolyn Murray-Wooley, *The Founding of Lexington, 1775–1776* (Lexington, 1975); Bettye Lee Mastin, *Lexington, 1779* (Lexington, 1979); Charles Staples, *The History of Pioneer Lexington, 1779–1806* (Lexington, 1939); Kolan Thomas Matlock, *Taking the Town: Collegiate and Community Culture in the Bluegrass, 1880–1917* (Lexington, 2008); Mary E. Wharton et al., *The Horse World of the Bluegrass* (Lexington, 1980); Gerald L. Smith, *Lexington Kentucky*, Black America Series (Charleston, SC, 2002);

Clay Lancaster, *Vestiges of the Venerable City: A Chronicle of Lexington, Kentucky* . . . (Lexington, 1978); James Duane Bolin, *Bossism and Reform in a Southern City: Lexington, Kentucky, 1880–1940* (Lexington, 2000); Gregory A. Waller, *Main Street Amusements: Movies and Commercial Entertainment in a Southern City, 1896–1930* (Washington, DC, 1995); Bernard Mayo, *Henry Clay* (Boston, 1937). Numerous excellent studies exist of the colleges and universities in the area as well.

10. James C. Klotter, "Clio in the Commonwealth: The Status of Kentucky History," *Register of the Kentucky Historical Society* 80 (1982): 67–74; Stephen Aron, *How the West Was Lost* (Baltimore, 1996); Elizabeth Perkins, *Border Life* (Chapel Hill, NC, 1998); Ellen Eslinger, *Citizens of Zion* (Knoxville, TN, 1999); Craig Friend, *Along the Maysville Road* (Knoxville, TN, 2005), and *Kentucke's Frontiers* (Bloomington, IN, 2010). For a more recent reexamination of the status of Kentucky historical writing, see James C. Klotter, "Moving Kentucky History into the Twenty-first Century: Where Should We Go from Here?" *Register of the Kentucky Historical Society* 97 (1999): 83–112.

11. Allen J. Share, *Cities in the Commonwealth* (Lexington, 1982); Richard C. Wade, *The Urban Frontier: The Rise of Western Cities, 1790–1830* (Cambridge, MA, 1959).

12. Lawrence Larsen, *The Rise of the Urban South* (Lexington, 1985), and *The Urban South: A History* (Lexington, 1990); David R. Goldfield, "Pursuing the American Dream: Cities in the Old South," in *The City in Southern History*, ed. Blaine A. Brownell and David R. Goldfield (Port Washington, NY, 1977), 52–91.

Part 1

Overview and Comparisons

❧ 1

Central Kentucky's "Athens of the West" Image in the Nation and in History

James C. Klotter

Percy Shelley wrote in 1821:

> Another Athens shall arise,
>   And to remoter time
> Bequeath, like sunset to the skies,
>   The splendour of its prime;
> And leave, if nought so bright may live,
> All earth can take or Heaven can give.[1]

In Kentucky, citizens and outside observers alike indicated that they had found a new Athens, one rising from the wilds of America's First West, from a frontier society "baptized in blood," from this new heaven on earth. The Massachusetts-born and Harvard-educated clergyman Timothy Flint visited the area in 1816 and wrote later of what he found in the Bluegrass. "Lexington," he said, "is a singularly neat and pleasant town . . . [that] has an air of leisure and opulence. . . . In the circles where I visited, literature was most commonly the topic of conversation." "The window seats," he continued, "presented the . . . covers of the new and most interesting publications. The best modern works had been generally read. . . . There was generally an air of ease and politeness in the social intercourse of the inhabitants of this town, which evinced the cultivation of taste and good feeling. In effect Lexington has taken the tone of a literary place, and may be fitly called the Athens of the West." Four years later, a Cincinnati newspaper concluded that Lexington "is unquestionably the Athens of the West."[2]

Was that image based on firm reality, or was it only some traveler's transitory observance? What did contemporary writers, both at home and from abroad, say about all that? And what does history now tell us regarding that society, that culture, that world? An overview of the Athens of the West image in the nation and in history reveals much.

Aspects of the story appear clear. As the first English-settled area beyond the endless mountains, Kentucky initially toyed with the idea of independence but finally settled into the Union as the fifteenth state. From that moment in 1792 until Henry Clay's death sixty years later, in 1852, the commonwealth took its place as one of the nation's most important states.

At a time when agriculture provided much of the wealth of a people or of a commonwealth, by 1840 Kentucky stood first in the nation in the production of hemp and wheat, second in tobacco and corn, and fourth in rye. Its diversified crops made it a breadbasket for the young nation. Moreover, it ranked first in good horseflesh and second in the number of mules and hogs. From the earliest times, that agricultural wealth, plentiful livestock, and good land attracted a large and diverse population. Strangers in the state might hear not only English but also African words from some slaves or the occasional Native American voice. Walking down the streets of Lexington, visitors could listen to an Irish brogue, or a Scotch-Irish accent, or individuals speaking German or French or Welsh. From all over, people seeking a better life in a new land surged to the commonwealth.[3]

The state's population reflected that influx of people. By 1840, Kentucky's 780,000 souls stood sixth in population among the then thirty states. In fact, perhaps the best way to stress the state's importance is to look at the presidential elections between 1824 and 1860. In those ten contests, a Kentuckian was on the ballot for either president or vice president in eight of the ten races. (And even that does not include Zachary Taylor, who lived most of his life in Kentucky, or the native-born Abraham Lincoln, both of whom represented other states when elected president.) In short, antebellum Kentucky formed a very important part of the federal union.[4]

And at the core of that state was its symbolic heart—Lexington and the Central Bluegrass. The first capital of Kentucky had been Lexington, but the city had lost that status when Frankfort outbid it. It also did not help that Lexington's member of the legislative committee making the decision on the location of the capital refused to vote for his hometown since that might seem dishonorable and unseemly. By that one-vote margin, the decision went to Frankfort.[5]

But, even without the capital, Lexington remained the largest city in Kentucky for almost the first four decades after statehood. It had 1,795 people in 1800—more than Pittsburgh and twice as many as Cincinnati. The city had more than doubled in size to 4,326 a decade later and increased more slowly to 5,279 by 1820—still the largest place in the state. By 1830, Louisville had taken that title. But, through all those decades before the Civil War, the Central Bluegrass continued to tout its strengths as the Athens of the West. But was it?[6]

Looking at travel accounts from that time can show how outside observers—many of them from across the ocean—viewed the area in the context of America and even the larger Western world. And, in fact, their words usually painted a very positive word picture of a new Eden, a land of milk and honey, a place of promise.

Almost all commented favorably on the beauty of the land and the fertility of the soil. Even before statehood, an English observer had noted the "fertile country . . . unequalled in the progress of population," which would make the region "among the first in the union." In his influential, London-published *A Description of Kentucky in North America* (1792), Harry Toulmin could barely find words to praise the land, calling it "a country beyond description," an "extensive garden" with no forbidden fruit, a place so rich "it is impossible that we can experience any thing like poverty, for no country . . . upon this globe is so rich in the comforts and necessaries [*sic*] of life." An 1806 traveler called the country "equal in beauty and fertility to anything the imagination can paint."[7]

When the New England–born and Dartmouth-educated Amos Kendall came to Kentucky, as he rode from Georgetown to Lexington he found it "one of the most beautiful spots I ever beheld." Another observer from that same area visited in 1816 and noted that "the scenery around Lexington, almost equals that of the elysium of the ancients," while Frances Trollope wrote in 1831 that she had "rarely seen richer pastures than those of Kentucky." Still another traveler from the Northeast stressed the "fine and ornamental rural mansions" that surrounded the town. A decade later, James Stuart similarly emphasized the "comfortable-looking villas" near the city. "There is an air of wealth about the place," he concluded. Even a usually critical Englishman found the region's farms well cultivated and well cleared, much as in England, though he admitted that Kentucky had "the finest . . . land in the known world."[8]

In fact, numerous observers compared the Bluegrass to England. Travelers from Great Britain saw the parklike forests, the well-fenced land, and the agrarian ethos of the people and felt at home. One young diarist called Lexington "the Bath of America, a very handsomely built town," while a woman from England said after her visit to the city: "It really looks quite English." An English-born engineer indicated that, of all the states, it was Kentucky in which an Englishman would feel most at home. After all, he wrote, "a Kentuckian is an Englishman with a little more pride."[9]

And, if the countryside and the rural ethos enthralled visitors, the city itself often enchanted them. The Scotsman John Melish had been prepared to find a fine place, but Lexington, with its wide and airy streets and brick homes, "did exceed my expectations." An English barrister called it "the neatest country town I had yet seen in the United States" and pointed to its spacious roads and "delightfully shaded" streets. Americans had similar reactions. *Niles' Register* predicted in 1815 that Lexington would be "the greatest inland city in the western world." Later, the Reverend Flint called the town buildings "handsome and some . . . magnificent." "Few towns," he wrote, "are more delightfully situated. . . . The town wears an air of neatness, opulence, and repose, indicating leisure and studiousness. . . . The main street is a mile and a quarter in length and 80 feet wide; well paved." The *Emigrant's Directory* of 1817 also praised the city's chief thoroughfare, noting the twelve-foot sidewalks on each side of the street. The author saw in the houses and stores "as much wealth, and more beauty than can be found in most of the atlantic cities."[10]

When the Yale-educated Horace Holley made his first trip to Lexington to become Transylvania University's president, he found: "The town is handsomer than I expected, and has a more comfortable and genteel aspect. It has not the pretension without the reality, that so many . . . towns have." A Savannah, Georgia, newspaper story compared Lexington with Boston and Philadelphia and found society similar in all. It concluded of the Bluegrass place: "The population is large; the style of living magnificent. . . . The architectural elegance of the buildings is not surpassed . . . by the Eastern cities."[11]

But, more than the strengths of the city itself, observers stressed again and again the positive aspects of the people and their culture. Visitors pictured a cosmopolitan, exciting, vibrant city and region, with strengths in business, education, religion, science, medicine, society, and culture.

In area after area, central Kentucky stood, not just on the cutting edge, but on the edge of the ledge. Here, Edward West operated a steamboat in 1801, before Fulton, and also patented a nail-cutting machine.

View of Main Street in Lexington in the 1850s. (Coleman Collection, Transylvania University Library.)

Thomas Barlow invented a rifled cannon and constructed a remarkable planetarium that won first prize at an exposition in Paris—France, not Kentucky. In Danville, Ephraim McDowell performed the first successful removal of an ovarian tumor on record.[12]

Lexington also pioneered institutional innovations in the New West. It had the most advanced police system and by 1815 had the only public lighting system among the cities beyond the mountains. That same year it also featured three fire engines, the most of any western urban area. The city became the home for the second hospital for the mentally ill in the entire nation—what is now Eastern State Hospital. Visitors described what was then called the lunatic asylum as a place "conducted with regularity and cleanliness." One traveler seemed amazed at the city and concluded: "Even the lunatic asylum . . . has a pleasant aspect." In nearby Danville, the Kentucky School for the Deaf was established in 1823, the first such state-supported school in the nation, and the first establishment in the West, of any kind, to educate the hard of hearing. Kentucky cared.[13]

At the beginning of the nineteenth century, the state also stood at the center of a new national religious rebirth—the Great Revival. Forged from Western Kentucky origins, the fires of evangelical excitement spread across the state in 1801, reaching their visual apex at Cane Ridge, near Paris—Kentucky, not France. There, as many as twenty thousand people gathered—a tenth of the commonwealth's population—to be part of what one historian has called "the most important religious gathering in all of American history."[14]

An aspect of the Second Great Awakening in America, the Cane Ridge Camp Meeting helped usher in a new revival style that "offered escape, renewal, and recreation." It espoused a more egalitarian Christianity, a new social equality, and a more inclusive, less structured worship service. Out of the extraordinary physical and emotional exercises and excesses of the great revival, a fresh democratic culture emerged, as did a more welcoming spirit for new religions. The Shakers soon after found a home in Kentucky, and in 1832 an entirely new denomination, the Christian Church, first formed in Lexington. Black churches also sprang up, with one having the largest congregation of any church in the state. A Scotsman who visited in 1811 called the "high-spirited, independent, and republican" people "very liberal on the subject of religion." In that area, as in others, central Kentucky seemed to be at the forefront of change.[15]

At the same time, the state showed its continuing ability to reconcile religion with racing, red-eye whiskey, and retailing. The antebellum Market Revolution found a happy home in old Kentucky. An 1811 traveler found shops "piled with goods," while another noted the numerous "men of enterprise" in this new Athens. City papers printed the currency exchange rates in New Orleans, New York, and London, for Lexington revolved around a global economy. Newspaper advertisements in the 1810s and 1820s offered consumers books from London, dinner plates from Liverpool, tea from India, rum from Jamaica, iron from Sweden, brandy or wallpaper from France, and linens from Ireland, all found in "great profusion" in Lexington shops.[16]

Merchants had first begun to gain considerable wealth by selling supplies to the armies on the frontier, and the area soon grew to become a distribution center for Kentucky and the West. As one historian notes, in contrast to many of their Virginia brethren, many Kentucky merchants reinvested their profits in their businesses, not in displays of wealth. In fact, the city's remoteness "served virtually as a protective tariff for the infant industries of the town." As a result, it developed markets, industries, and businesses that thrived—and that made numerous men, such as James Morrison and John Wesley Hunt, very wealthy.[17]

When the city's first directory appeared in 1806, it showed that the town of some three thousand people had access to twenty-one merchants, sixteen shoemakers, eleven tailors, and seven hatters as well as six physicians, five attorneys, five teachers, four silversmiths, three printers, a bookbinder, and a portrait painter. A second directory over a decade later included a midwife, several businesses operated by women, and some occupations conducted by African Americans. The 1838 city directory showed the great growth in commerce, for it included eighteen hemp factories (employing over a thousand people), five woolen manufacturers, three cigar factories, two cotton producers, a flour mill, and an iron foundry, among other enterprises. The city also featured two bathhouses, a lottery office, and a brewery.[18]

Some thus found this New West liberating and argued that it judged entrepreneurs and immigrants more on their actions than on their class or religion or past. The traveler Toulmin said that a newcomer to Kentucky would embark "in designs he never would have thought of in his own country." An 1825 visitor called the area "the best theatre for the boundings of the aspiring genius."[19]

Yet of all the aspects of central Kentucky that travelers and observers praised—the land, the town itself, the inventions, the businesses, and more—almost all most applauded the society, culture, and education in this Athens of the West. One who grew up there in that time titled a section of his memoirs "A Reading Population." And so it was. Citizens formed a library as early as 1796—almost two decades before Cincinnati did—and placed in it some four hundred volumes. At the end of the War of 1812, it had gathered over twenty-five hundred tomes. The 1838 city directory called it the "most cheaply accessible library in the United States" with its two dollar per year fee for reading privileges in its then seven thousand books. In fact, a broadened definition of central Kentucky shows that seven of the top fifty southern libraries at midcentury, and five of the top twenty-five, were in Kentucky.[20]

A bookstore had opened a year after statehood, and soon buyers could purchase the works of the Americans Franklin, Jefferson, and Paine but could also peruse titles bearing the names of Plutarch, Voltaire, Rousseau, Hume, and Chesterfield, for example. Inventories of estates further support the view that, among some at least, this public read widely. Books found in homes included those by Boswell, Gibbon, Johnson, Shakespeare, Swift, and Adam Smith as well as Cicero, Euclid, Homer, Virgil, and others.[21]

Nor did citizens confine themselves just to books. One visitor went to a reading room in a coffeehouse and found that it subscribed to forty-two different newspapers, many of them from overseas. There club members also played billiards, chess, and backgammon. The state's—and the West's—first newspaper, the *Kentucke Gazette*, started in Lexington in 1787 under John Bradford, "the Franklin of the West," and it would be joined by others as well as several literary and scientific magazines. Moreover, in literary society meetings or at lyceums, people met to discuss scholarly and public matters. One historian also called the number of people who could read and speak French "astonishing and revealing." Little wonder that a Cincinnati paper in 1820 called the city "the headquarters of science and letters in the western country" or that the English traveler J. Lewis Peyton wrote of his time in the area in the 1840s: "The more I saw of Kentuckians, the more agreeably was I impressed by them." "Remarkable for intellectual activity," he noted, "they are eminent in urbanity and real politeness."[22]

Society valued education and reading, honored intellectual pursuits, and praised public discussion of issues—and all that combined to produce a host of men and women of talent and skill. Artists such as the Gilbert Stuart–trained Matthew Jouett, Oliver Frazer, Joseph Bush, Edward West, and the Englishman George Beck all left their mark. Architects such as Gideon Shryock, sculptors such as Joel Tanner Hart, silversmiths such as Asa Blanchard, poets such as Theodore O'Hara (the author of the famous "Bivouac of the Dead"), political leaders such as Henry Clay, Richard M. Johnson, and John C. Breckinridge, all operated in central Kentucky in the antebellum years.[23]

Theatrical productions began as early as 1790, and the promoter Luke Usher opened his theater in 1808, appealing to patrons with such verse as:

Who's not been in Kentucky hath not seen the world;
'Tis the state in which Freedom's own flag is unfurl'd!
It is plenty's headquarters—'tis misery's grave;
Where the ladies are lovely, and the men are all brave!

By 1810, a production of *Macbeth* brought Shakespeare to a Kentucky theater for the first time, and within a decade Samuel Drake had made Lexington the center of western stage activity. Even before statehood,

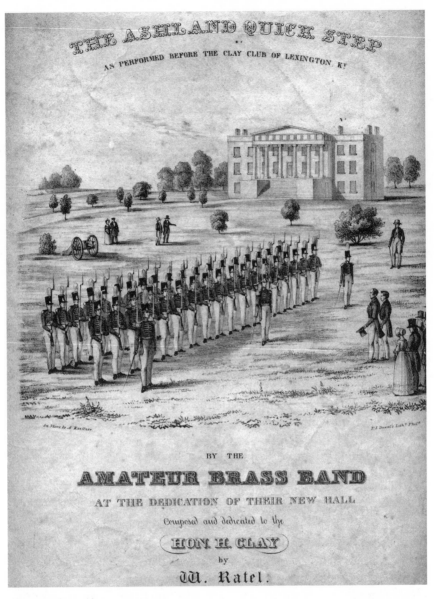

The combination of classical Lexington, the militaristic spirit, and politics all came together in *The Ashland Quick Step* sheet music. (Henry Clay Collection, Transylvania University Library.)

dancing schools and music teachers won support, with many of them later featuring instructors from France, Italy, Germany, and England. And the less musically inclined might go to a wax museum, or magic show, or animal display, or balloon ascension. It was a society and a place that offered much.[24]

Educational strengths and achievements formed the axis around which so many of those societal strengths revolved. For Transylvania University was, during a part of the antebellum era, one of the best schools in the nation. In its golden age under President Horace Holley, people called it the "Harvard of the West"; Holley sought to create an Oxford in the wilderness. With a law school, medical school, and undergraduate program, the institution received city and state support and became the early center of western and southern education. By the 1820s, students from fourteen states attended classes there; some of its 1830s medical class graduates included more from beyond the commonwealth than from within it. In fact, its medical library and the instruction offered in the medical school placed it among the elite. When Lafayette visited in 1825, his secretary wrote that the establishments for public instruction in Lexington "rival the most celebrated colleges and universities in the principal towns of Europe." Those eager to learn flocked to the Athens of the West. By the time one of Transylvania's former students, Jefferson Davis, went to Congress, he found that seven other senators—13 percent of the total—had graduated from there. With the addition of other good schools in that period, such as Centre and Georgetown, central Kentucky had become the educational heart of the South and West.[25]

Moreover, the region's female academies often offered education beyond the norm for women of that era. One traveler even asserted that "Kentuckians never dreamed that there was any intellectual inferiority" between the sexes. Whether in Mrs. Mentelle's famous school or the Lexington Female Seminary or others, young women could take, not only the gender-traditional courses, but also ones in such fields as natural history, algebra, geometry, chemistry, and logic, among others. Little wonder that Mary Todd Lincoln's biographer calls her one of the best educated women of her generation. The state's public school system was also considered one of the best in the South by the 1850s, largely owing to the efforts of Robert J. Breckinridge of Lexington and Danville, a man still called "the father of public education in Kentucky."[26]

All those varied elements combined to produce a cultured society that won praise from numerous observers from outside the state and beyond the seas. *Niles' Register* viewed the region in 1814 and concluded, to its

The main building, 1816–1829, Transylvania University, symbolized the academic stature of the city. (University Archives, Transylvania University.)

surprise: "Society is polished and polite and their balls and assemblies are conducted with as much grace and ease as they are anywhere else. . . . Strange things these in the 'backwoods.'" Just a few years before, another visitor from Scotland had written how the city "can boast of men who do honour to science, and of females whose beauty and amiable manners would grace the first circles of society." In fact, women garnered much attention from the mostly male travel writers. An 1818 narrative, for example, praised them as "the most spirited women in the world," even though they had grown "exceedingly fond of dress."[27]

But the "well-dressed" citizens brought forth comments, no matter what their sex. The *Emigrant's Directory* concluded: "The inhabitants are as polished, and I regret to add, as luxurious as those of Boston, New-York or Baltimore; and their assemblies and parties are conducted with as much ease and grace, as in the oldest towns of the union." At almost the same time, a more critical Englishman concluded of Lexingtonians: "They are gay and voluptuous to a proverb."[28]

Visitors loved to come to Lexington because Kentucky hospitality proved to be very real and very welcoming. The city featured excellent inns but even more excellent company. The theaterman Drake noted when he first arrived in 1815: "I have never found a more kind and hospitable people than those in Kentucky, generally, and I have travelled in most all States of the Union. . . . Kentucky . . . could boast of more high-minded men and beautiful women than any I had ever been in." The Reverend Flint agreed, finding the people "cheerful, intelligent, conversable, and noted for their hospitality to strangers." No town in the West, he concluded, had "more beauty and intelligence . . . [and a more] polished and interesting society." Almost more of a Paris than an Athens when it came to society, Lexington—according to one student—"is a fun place for amusements, to get into frolicks, visit the girls, and all such things." A minister's son indicated that "there is no place in the world like Kentucky for real enjoyment." Perhaps the only exception to the hospitable spirit came from an 1818 traveler, who noted: "A Kentuckian suspects nobody but a Yankee, whom he considers as a sort of Jesuit."[29]

Whether in rural retreats where one man kept a hundred deer and several elk in his woodland pastures, or in farms like Robert Wickliffe's where he housed perhaps the last buffalo in the state by that time, or in elegant city mansions and gardens, or even at nearby springs where the elite went "to flirt, freshen, and fatten," hospitality and high society flourished. In his still-excellent *Urban Frontier*, Robert Wade compared various western cities and concluded that Lexington "was not only the mercantile center of the West but its social and cultural leader as well." The most exciting place, with the most talented people, it seemed to him "like a Renaissance city of Italy" whose creativity stimulated minds and produced an era that could be rightly called "Lexington's enlightenment."[30]

Quite a picture. But that portrait of a city conceals as much as it reveals. Like an artist's canvas that has been painted over, another picture lurks beneath the Athens of the West image so admired and so praised in its time. That hidden view has darker hues and fewer bright points of light. Yet, in many ways, that other image better represents the real Athens of old, a place with deep flaws and dark secrets as well. Only if the surface picture is merged with the more hidden one can the era be seen in full. A few observers at that time noted the many sides of the city. Numerous historians have since done so. For, in truth, the Athens of the West was a land of many contrasts and contradictions.

For example, this place of such fertile land, this region that offered so much promise to those who came, this area of so much wealth, represented something else to so many. Some may have migrated and discovered a liberating and open West, but others soon found the best land rapidly taken, their hopes shortly ended, their promise quickly destroyed. In 1800, fewer than half the people in Kentucky owned any land—approximately the national average. In the state, over a hundred individuals held more than ten thousand acres each. Some 1 percent of the people controlled one-third of the total acreage. Fayette and surrounding counties showed similar trends. The rich had gotten richer, while many of the poor remained poor. Some did achieve their dreams, and their stories would be trumpeted abroad. But too many remained landless and voiceless.[31]

Kentucky was the first state in the Union to grant universal white male suffrage, free of the requirement to own property, and citizens touted their democratic spirit. Yet this learned society, this place open to change, this Athens in spirit, firmly embraced slavery, provided few legal rights to women, and employed young children in hard labor. The region may have been economically strong, but it also proved morally weak. Few listened to the voices of protest around them. Most could not cast off the racial and gender blinders and endorse changes in their society.[32]

While the state and the city initially seemed to support some views favorable to the abolition of slavery, such an action never voluntarily occurred. In 1810, half the white families in Fayette, and three-fourths of those in the city of Lexington, held people in slavery. Ads for runaway slaves, sales of divided families, the cries of the oppressed, reminded people daily of the system and what it did to all those it touched. A few travelers noted that. One commented critically on the "slave merchants" who sold humans. Another saw slaves being whipped and wrote: "Their screams soon collected a numerous crowd—I could not help saying to myself: 'These cries are the knell of Kentucky liberty.'"[33]

A few whites such as Robert J. Breckinridge, Cassius M. Clay, Calvin Fairbank, Delia Webster, and John G. Fee continued to work against the slave system in various ways; a few slaves, like Lewis Hayden and Lewis Clarke, made their way to freedom and lent their voices to the gradually rising chorus for freedom. But for the majority of the people in Fayette, Woodford, and Bourbon Counties—where over half the 1850 population lived as enslaved persons—opportunity and liberty seemed distant. It would take a devastating war and federal action to end the existence of the "peculiar institution."[34]

As the violence against slaves showed, this educated and cultured society could also be a very violent one. Henry Clay might be "the Great Compromiser," but, like others of the elite, he fought duels. Deadly personal encounters killed some leaders; wars with the British and then with the Mexicans killed others, including Clay's son; simple brawls ended the lives of a few.

Almost all the travel accounts praised Kentuckians' bravery and daring. Elias Fordham in 1818 called them "the best warriors of the United States, as far as courage." But, he noted, when they quarreled—usually over politics—"the pistol used to be the universal resort." Fordham also indicated that they enjoyed jokes, but, if they were offended by one of them, "a knife or a dirk is drawn." An English traveler praised the "irascible but generous" Kentuckians but noted that the habits of command inbred in slavery tended to give "unbridled indulgence in every passion . . . where resistance, or reluctance is unknown, or unpardoned." Charles Murray wrote about the "brave" Kentuckians, but he also stressed their propensity "for gambling, horse-racing, and etc." and their "quarrelsome" nature, one that could quickly turn deadly since even the well-dressed man could be seen picking his teeth with a dirk knife. In that same year of 1835, James Hall praised the state as "the cradle of courage and the nurse of warriors," but one whose reputation had long been as a place of "fighting, drinking, and gouging." He found the "amiable" people undeserving at that time of such a reputation but admitted that such had not always been the case. Elizabeth Steele's 1841 book reiterated all that, emphasizing that the people of the Bluegrass "have long been celebrated for their valor." But reason, caution, and compassion all too often failed to win out over rash actions, violence, and sudden death.[35]

If a society of violence, economic disparities, and racial and gender inequities, the Athens of the West did produce significant positive accomplishments in such areas as education, culture, religion, politics, science, and more. Its sophistication, cosmopolitan spirit, and cultural strengths were real. Yet, at the same time, it had a soft underbelly of narrow views and reactionary responses that could quickly become exposed.

Transylvania's president, Horace Holley, quickly discovered the existence of such outlooks. He had made the university great. But he had also incurred the wrath of important people and groups in doing so. His political stands angered the governor, and state aid would end by 1826. His Unitarian views brought forth religious attacks. His city's educational successes encouraged rising rival Louisville to strike out at him. His urbanity produced antipathy from several quarters. A journal in 1823 criticized him, saying: "The theatre, Ballroom, the Card table, and all those places to which the vain and dissipated resort . . . are places to which he resorts." Under siege for going to "large parties and to the public races," the unhappy leader resigned in 1827. Within a decade, a visitor noted that the college "does not seem to be in a very flourishing state," and a Virginia paper described it as a "now languishing institution." The medical department and law school both closed before the Civil War, and what had once been the jewel of education in Kentucky and in the South stood as only a faint glimmer of its former self.[36]

Holley's resignation marked the beginning of a period of decline from the earlier days of glory. In the three and a half decades after statehood, the city had deserved its title as the Athens of the West. But a series of events, some of which Lexington could control and some of which it could not, began to have an effect. Lexington's death knell did not toll loudly. Symbolic death came in stages, softly, over time—with the quiet whisper of Holley's quill pen as he wrote his resignation, the distant whistle of a steamboat on the Ohio, the dying sighs of cholera victims, the muffled sobs of slaves on the auction block, the sounds of businesses closing their doors in a depressed time. Each of these chipped away at the columns of past glory, leaving increasingly tarnished artifacts of fading grandeur and lost greatness.

The first crack in the facade came with the Panic of 1819, which seriously damaged the economic health of the region. Speculators lost fortunes, and property values still had not reached their predepression level even a decade and a half later. Henry Clay had property worth $75,000 before the panic; four years later his holdings were worth only $28,000. He never again got back to that 1818 level. And his story was repeated over and over. Another panic in 1837 just added to the problems.[37]

By the time that first depression hit in 1819, steamboats already had begun to ply the Ohio. As that mode of transport increasingly became important, Lexington's lack of a navigable watercourse made it more and more vulnerable. What was the agent of progress for so much of America instead became for Lexington "the agent of the disaster." Very early, the city tried to compensate by advocating turnpikes, but Andrew Jackson's veto of the Maysville Road project stunned the city and slowed that effort. Lexington also supported construction of a railroad to Frankfort and then to Louisville, one of the first such roads in the United States. But it progressed only slowly, and that option helped little in the antebellum years. In addition, as canals in the state of Ohio tied that populace more to the East, the river that had once united the West increasingly became a dividing line, now between North and South, further isolating Lexington. And so the riverboat bypassed the Athens of the West, and the city settled into a waterless economic backwater. When an English barrister visited in 1832, he said that the city stood as the "only place of note in the United States, whose prosperity, for several years, has been on the decline."[38]

Events the next year added to the decline. A cholera epidemic struck in June 1833, and, before it ended two months later, as many as five hundred citizens had died in a population of six thousand—one of every twelve people. In one family of nineteen, seventeen had perished. A person who lived through it all remembered that "it came like a sudden and awful clap of thunder upon us—the whole community was stunned and paralyzed." Travel stopped. Businesses closed. Schooling ceased. Henry Clay, Mary Todd Lincoln, Jefferson Davis, and John C. Breckinridge all were in the city then, and all survived, but others died so fast that not enough coffins could be built and not enough labor could be procured to bury the bodies fast enough. Part of the cholera problem had resulted from the city's rapid and unbridled development. Urban growth in the early years had not been matched by an adequately operating water supply, and the disease flourished under those conditions. So many children had lost parents as a result of the scourge that an orphan asylum had to be created to care for them all. It took in additional children after another epidemic struck in 1849 and left nearly 350 more dead.[39]

All that took its toll on the city in so many ways. As one 1833 newspaper story noted: "Yesterday the City was the Eden of the western world—there, there was an union of all the comforts of life . . . a people hospitable in their houses, accomplished in manners. . . . Look at her today. Gloom, and sorrow, and mourning is in every habitation." By 1835, a book praised the city's wide streets but noted that "two thirds of their width is at present overgrown with grass from the want of adequate use." As potential new leaders moved to the better promise of the trans-Mississippi West, as the economy stagnated, as the educational institutions declined, as the spirit of innovation faded, the Athens of the West lost some of its luster. Yet it continued to show real strengths. Still, in 1852, the death of Henry Clay would represent, not only the beginning of the end of the Whig Party so identified with him, but also a symbolic end to the Athens of the West image in the Central Bluegrass as well. Clay had first come to Kentucky five years after statehood; he and Lexington had matured together. Its image died in part with him, but it had already died a series of slow deaths over the previous three decades.[40]

Lord Byron once asked: "Ancient of days! august Athena! where, / Where are thy men of might? thy grand in soul?" He answered: "Gone—glimmering through the dream of things that were."[41] Yet, if the Athens of

The Henry Clay Monument in the Lexington Cemetery was dedicated in 1861, almost a decade after Clay's death and at the start of the divisive Civil War he sought to avoid. (Clay Lancaster Slide Collection, Special Collections, University of Kentucky.)

the West image had become almost only a dream and the leaders of its past were now gone and its grand soul seemingly forgotten, it did still remain in the historical consciousness to influence, at times, later generations.

Within a decade of Clay's death, the Civil War started, tearing through his beloved Bluegrass as the Brothers War. Yet his conciliatory spirit and his support for the idea of union lived on just enough to keep Kentucky from joining the Confederacy. Given the state's sizable population, rich agricultural stores, and natural Ohio River defense line, its decision would prove vital for the eventual success of the United States. The old image, the old ideas of leadership, the old nationalism, still resonated enough to make a difference.[42]

Hopes continued to run high in education, as well, that what once was might be again. In the 1860s, John Bowman told of his dream for what would become the University of Kentucky: "We want ample grounds and buildings, and libraries . . . and endowments and Prize Funds, and Professors of great hearts and heads. . . . Indeed, we want everything which will make this Institution eventually equal to any on this continent." In the 1920s, a Lexington editor repeated his hopes that the city would one day have "a great university," the rival of Oxford and Cambridge. Each advocate in his time could point to history and to Transylvania's once-vaunted status to support such ambitions. But what history, whose memory, which past did most people remember? Was it simply recalling the antebellum era as a kind of Camelot? Would individuals learn from the past or just live in the past?[43]

One of the dangers in remembering is that individuals often do so only selectively or imperfectly. They may recall an invented past, rather than one more faithful to reality. Their imagined image may drive them just as forcefully as a historical one can. But their memory may narrowly focus on a story of greatness based on the wrong assumptions. Their account may be cloaked in the golden shrouds of nostalgia, and the distant threads of past achievements may be recalled fondly, without the attendant weakness or the underlying faults. Such perceived traditions may guide actions or even give comfort in a modern world. But they offer little for those who seek to learn from the past in order to influence the future.[44]

In those memories, and in some later historical accounts, the Athens of the West image continued to shape—and perhaps still shapes—the mind-set of the Central Bluegrass. Some looked at their era and told themselves that fundamental problems all around them were only temporary and that the gilded past better reflected the real city than did the one of their present.

View of Lexington, 1857. (Clay Lancaster Slide Collection, Special Collections, University of Kentucky.)

But a much better guide to creating a stronger future is the historical Lexington as Athens, not some mythical one. Recognizing the flaws in the system, understanding the human weaknesses of those involved, seeing the mistakes made, allows individuals to become better heirs of the tradition. The worst parts of that society should be admitted and discarded—the harsh inequality of wealth, the racial divides, the deadly violence, the ever-present death and disease, the reactionary mind-set.

But the best parts of that reality and that image must remain, to inspire and provide a model to emulate as new generations seek their own symbolic Athenses—of the mind, of the intellect, of the spirit. They should recall what made the Athens of the West of the early years so appealing and so exciting to citizens and visitors alike—the sense of innovation, the enthusiasm for enterprise, the devotion to education, the emphasis on culture and beauty, and the stress on history. And, in doing that, they can then use the past to challenge their society—and themselves—to do better. The image can serve as a foundation for the beginning of a rebirth, one based on the best aspects of that time—its sense of creativity, its spirit of inquiry, its remembrance of traditions.

In that way, the Athens of the West image and history can still influence generations of the present and of the future. It stresses that the region once tottered on the cutting edge. It reminds of a time when central Kentucky stood high in national prominence. It tells of achievement and promise. But the image and the reality also show that living in a world of past glories can blind whole generations to the needs of the society around them in the present. That history demonstrates the fragileness of success. That past warns that each generation must craft its own new history, built on the past, but also free of it. Yet as one leader said: "It is history that teaches us to hope." In short, the hope and the history of the Athens of the West still speaks to us today, and we cannot—must not—ignore that voice.[45]

Notes

1. Percy Bysshe Shelley, "Hellas: Chorus," http://rpo.library.utoronto.ca/poem/1888.html. See also Patrick Lee Lucas, "It's All Greek to Me: Re-Examining the 'Athens of the West' Claim of Lexington, Kentucky, 1820–1829" (M.A. thesis, University of Kentucky, 1998), vii.

2. Bernard Mayo, *Henry Clay: Spokesman of the New West* (Boston, 1937), 48; C. Hartley Gratton, introduction to Timothy Flint, *Recollections of the Last Ten Years*, by Timothy Flint, ed. C. Hartley Gratton (New York, 1932), vi–vii; Timothy Flint, *Recollections of the Last Ten Years* (Boston, 1826), 67–68; *Cincinnati Liberty Hall*, May 27, 1820, quoted in Richard C. Wade, *The Urban Frontier: The Rise of Western Cities, 1790–1830* (Cambridge, MA, 1967), 330–31.

3. William E. Connelley and E. Merton Coulter, *History of Kentucky*, ed. Charles Kerr, 5 vols. (Chicago, 1922), 2:739; Mary E. Wharton and Edward L. Bowen, *The Horse World of the Bluegrass* (Lexington, 1980), vii, ix, 13–15, 19, 27–30; William Leavy, "A Memoir of Lexington and Its Vicinity," *Register of the Kentucky Historical Society* 40, no. 131 (1942): 107–31; 40, no. 132 (1942): 253–67; 40, no. 133 (1942): 353–75; 41, no. 134 (1943): 44–62; 41, no. 135 (1943): 107–37; 41, no. 136 (1943): 250–60; 41, no. 137 (1943): 310–46; and 42, no. 138 (1944): 26–53; Elizabeth A. Perkins, *Border Life: Experience and Memory in the Revolutionary Ohio Valley* (Chapel Hill, NC, 1998), 84, 94–99; Craig Thompson Friend, *Along the Maysville Road: The Early American Republic in the Trans-Appalachian West* (Knoxville, TN, 2005), 32–35, 209; Lee Shai Weissbach, "The Peopling of Lexington, Kentucky: Growth and Mobility in a Frontier Town," *Register of the Kentucky Historical Society* 81 (1983): 119; Lindsey Apple, "The French in Central Kentucky," *Border States* 4 (1983): 5–9; Huntley Dupre, "The French in Early Kentucky," *Filson Club History Quarterly* 15 (1941): 78–104; Thomas L. Purvis, "The Ethnic Descent of Kentucky's Early Population," *Register of the Kentucky Historical Society* 80 (1982): 253–66. For a general overview of the entire period under discussion, see Lowell H. Harrison and James C. Klotter, *A New History of Kentucky* (Lexington, 1997), 65–178.

4. J. D. B. DeBow, *Statistical View of the United States* (Washington, DC, 1854), 40; James C. Klotter and Freda C. Klotter, *A Concise History of Kentucky* (Lexington, 2008), 102. The eight contenders were Henry Clay (three times) and John C. Breckinridge (once) for president and Richard M. Johnson (twice), Breckinridge (once), and W. O. Butler (once) for vice president.

5. John D. Wright Jr., *Lexington: Heart of the Bluegrass* (Lexington, 1982), 18.

6. Wade, *Urban Frontier,* 170, 20. Friend (*Maysville Road,* 57) notes that, from 1790 to 1810, Lexington grew six times faster than the nation did overall.

7. Alexander Fitzroy, *The Discovery, Purchase, and Settlement of the Country of Kentuckie in North America* . . . (London, 1786), 15; Harry Toulmin, *A Description of Kentucky in North America* (London, 1792 [1793?]), 17, 93; Josiah Espy, "A Tour in Ohio, Kentucky, and Indiana Territory, in 1805," in *Ohio Valley Historical Series Miscellanies* (Cincinnati, 1871), 8. For overviews of travelers' accounts, see Samuel E. Allen Jr., "Observations of Travellers in Kentucky, 1750–1850" (M.A. thesis, University of Kentucky, 1950); J. Winston Coleman Jr., "Lexington as Seen by Travellers, 1810–1835," *Filson Club History Quarterly* 29 (1955): 267–81; and Raymond F. Betts, "'Sweet meditation through this pleasant country': Foreign Appraisals of the Landscape of Kentucky in the Early Years of the Commonwealth," *Register of the Kentucky Historical Society* 90 (1992): 26–44.

8. *Autobiography of Amos Kendall,* ed. William Stickney (Boston, 1872), 109; Samuel R. Brown, *The Western Gazetteer; or, Emigrant's Directory* (Auburn, NY, 1817), 91; Francis Trollope, *Domestic Manners of the Americans* (1831), ed. Donald Smalley (New York, 1949), 35; Timothy Flint quoted in Coleman, "Lexington," 276; James Stuart, *Three Years in North America,* 2 vols. (New York, 1833), 2:271; William Faux, *Memorable Days in America* . . . (London, 1823), in Reuben Gold Thwaites, ed., *Early Western Travels,* 32 vols. (Cleveland, 1904–1907), 11:188, 190.

9. Thomas H. Appleton Jr., "An Englishman's Perception of Antebellum Kentucky: The Journal of Thomas Smith, Jr. of Lincolnshire," *Register of the Kentucky Historical Society* 79 (1981): 61; Mrs. Basil Hall quoted in Betts, "Sweet Meditation," 30; Elias Pym Fordham, *Personal Narrative of Travels* . . . , ed. Frederic A. Ogg (Cleveland, 1906), 169. For a more recent comparison that makes the same point, see Carl B. Cone, "The English Connection," *Louisville Courier-Journal Magazine,* August 1, 1976, 10–14.

10. John Melish, *Travels in the United States of America* . . . , 2 vols. (Philadelphia, 1812), 2:184; Godfrey T. Vigne, *Six Months in America,* 2 vols. (London, 1832), 2:27, *Niles' Register,* January 28, 1815, quoted in Wade, *Urban Frontier,* 49; Timothy Flint, *The History and Geography of the Mississippi Valley,* 2nd ed., 2 vols. (Cincinnati, 1832), 1:354; Brown, *Emigrant's Directory,* 92.

11. John D. Wright Jr., *Transylvania: Tutor to the West* (Lexington, 1975), 62; *Savannah Georgian,* November 22, 1819, cited in Niels Henry Sonne, *Liberal Kentucky, 1780–1828* (1939; Lexington, 1968), 137. See also John Wilson Townsend, "Horace Holley . . . ," *Proceedings of the Mississippi Valley Historical Association for the Years 1914–15* 8 (1916): 123–24.

12. Leavy, "Memoir of Lexington" (no. 133), 374; "Samuel D. McCullough's Reminiscences of Lexington," *Register of the Kentucky Historical Society* 27 (1929): 412, 420–24; George W. Ranck, *History of Lexington* (Cincinnati, 1872), 183–86; Wright, *Lexington*, 26; James Thomas Flexner, *Doctors on Horseback: Pioneers of American Medicine* (1937; New York, 1969), 111–48.

13. Wade, *Urban Frontier*, 88, 90, 94; William H. Polk, *History of the Police and Fire Departments, Lexington, Kentucky* (Lexington, 1911), n.p.; Julius P. B. MacCabe, *Directory of the City of Lexington . . . for 1838 & '39* (Lexington, 1838), 25; Wright, *Lexington*, 59–60; Ronald F. White, "Custodial Care of the Insane at Eastern State Hospital in Lexington, Kentucky, 1824–1844," *Filson Club History Quarterly* 62 (1988): 303–35; Charles A. Murray, *Travels in North America*, 3rd rev. ed., 2 vols. (London, 1854), 1:189; Frederick von Raumer, *America and the American People*, trans. William Turner (New York, 1846), 445; Calvin Morgan Fackler, *Early Days in Danville* (Louisville, 1941), 143–45.

14. Stephen Aron, *How the West Was Lost: The Transformation of Kentucky from Daniel Boone to Henry Clay* (Baltimore, 1996), 171; John B. Boles, *The Great Revival, 1787–1805* (Lexington, 1972), 55–63; Ellen Eslinger, *Citizens of Zion: The Social Origins of Camp Meeting Revivalism* (Knoxville, TN, 1999), 193–97; Paul K. Conkin, *Cane Ridge: America's Pentecost* (Madison, WI, 1990), 58–62, 3.

15. Eslinger, *Citizens of Zion*, 214, 226, 239; Conkin, *Cane Ridge*, 115, 87, 132, 171, 149; Marion B. Lucas, *A History of Blacks in Kentucky*, vol. 1, *From Slavery to Segregation* (Frankfort, 1992), 122; Melish, *Travels*, 2:189. On the other hand, Josiah Espy in 1805 found the citizenry "immersed in infidelity and dissipation, while the more illiterate were downright fanatics and zealots in religion" ("Tour," 24). When she visited in 1835, Harriet Martineau commented that "a religion of hatred is preached" (John S. Gatton, "'Mr. Clay & I got stung': Harriet Martineau in Lexington," *Kentucky Review* 1 [1979]: 52). That same year, James F. Clarke called it "a horribly bigoted place" (John W. Thomas, ed., *Letters of James F. Clarke to Margaret Fuller* [Hamburg, 1957], 95). My thanks go to Harold Tallant for calling my attention to the last source.

16. Alexander Wilson quoted in Coleman, "Lexington," 268; Fordham, *Personal Narrative*, 177; Lucas, "It's All Greek to Me," 153, 101; Mary Jean Elliott, "Lexington Kentucky, 1792–1820: The Athens of the West" (M.A. thesis, University of Delaware, 1973), 26; E. MacKenzie, *An Historical, Topographical, and Descriptive View of the United States of America*, 2nd ed. (Newcastle, 1819), 233.

17. Leavy, "Memoir of Lexington" (no. 133), 373; Charles R. Staples, *The History of Pioneer Lexington, 1779–1806* (1939; Lexington, 1996), 31; Wade, *Urban Frontier*, 20; Clement Eaton, *Henry Clay and the Art of American Politics* (Boston, 1957), 10; Kim Gruenwald, *River of Enterprise: The Commercial Origins of Regional Identity in the Ohio Valley, 1790–1850* (Bloomington, IN, 2002), 88. Morrison's estate was valued at $488,320 and Hunt's at $891,294. See Lucas, "It's All Greek to Me," 138; Elliott, "Lexington," 32; and James A. Ramage, *John Wesley Hunt* (Lexington, 1974), 1.

18. Staples, *Pioneer Lexington*, 260; J. Winston Coleman Jr., *Lexington's Second City Directory* (Lexington, 1953), 3–19; MacCabe, *Directory for 1838*, 30.

19. Friend, *Maysville Road*, 34; Earl G. Swem, ed., *Letters on the Condition of Kentucky in 1825* (New York, 1916), 40.

20. Leavy, "Memoir of Lexington" (no. 137), 320, and "Memoir of Lexington" (no. 135), 129–33, 137; MacCabe, *Directory for 1838*, 18; Staples, *Pioneer Lexington*, 127–28; Michael O'Brien, *Conjectures of Order: Intellectual Life and the American South, 1810–1860*, 2 vols. (Chapel Hill, NC, 2004), 1:513–14. I thank Glen Taul for his reference to the last source.

21. Wade, *Urban Frontier*, 140; Mayo, *Henry Clay*, 59; Friend, *Maysville Road*, 88; Lucas, "It's All Greek to Me," 186–91.

22. F. Cuming, *Sketches of a Tour of the Western Country* . . . , in Thwaites, ed., *Early Western Travels*, 4:188; Apple, "The French in Central Kentucky," 7, 5; Wade, *Urban Frontier*, 115, 131; MacCabe, *Directory for 1838*, 18–19; Ranck, *History of Lexington*, 303; J. Lewis Peyton, *Over the Alleghanies and Across the Prairie* (London, 1870), 99. The *Kentucky Reporter* (Lexington), February 21, 1827, also called Lexington "the capital of science and letters."

23. Wright, *Lexington*, 37–38; Randolph Hollingsworth, *Lexington: Queen of the Bluegrass* (Charleston, SC, 2004), 34–36. See also the individual entries in John E. Kleber, ed., *The Kentucky Encyclopedia* (Lexington, 1992).

24. West T. Hill Jr., *The Theatre in Early Kentucky* (Lexington, 1971), 9, 24, 4, 108, 5, 7; Wright, *Lexington*, 35; Leavy, "Memoir of Lexington" (no. 137), 346; Elliott, "Lexington," 10. See also Mabel T. Crum, "The History of the Lexington Theater from the Beginning to 1860" (M.A. thesis, University of Kentucky, 1956).

25. Wade, *Urban Frontier*, 236; F. Garvin Davenport, *Ante-Bellum Kentucky: A Social History, 1800–1860* (1943; Westport, CT, 1983), 46; Ranck, *History of Lexington*, 45–48; Sonne, *Liberal Kentucky*, 191n; John R. Thelin, *A History of American Higher Education* (Baltimore, 2004), 46–47; Coleman, "Lexington," 278; *Kentucky Gazette* (Lexington), March 21, 1839; Robert Peter, *The History of the Medical Department of Transylvania University* (Louisville, 1905), v; James C. Klotter, "Promise, Pessimism, and Perseverance: An Overview of Higher Education History in Kentucky," *Ohio Valley History* 6 (2006): 54.

26. Peyton, *Over the Alleghenies*, 112; Leavy, "Memoir of Lexington" (no. 137), 345; *Kentucky Gazette* (Lexington), January 4, 1838; Jean H. Baker, *Mary Todd Lincoln* (New York, 1987), 37; Clement Eaton, *The Growth of Southern Civilization, 1790–1860* (New York, 1961), 117; James C. Klotter, *The Breckinridges of Kentucky, 1760–1981* (Lexington, 1986), 58–60.

27. *Niles' Register* quoted in Wright, *Lexington*, 30; Alexander Wilson quoted in Coleman, "Lexington," 269; Fordham, *Personal Narrative*, 168. An unidentified Virginian in 1825 found the women "easy, candid and unaffected," with "fashionable" clothes and "lively and interesting" conversation. The men were described as "courteous, well informed and cordially hospitable." Swem, ed., *Letters*, 49–50. A woman from the area commented that, while men in America usually did not like "wives, wiser or more enlightened than themselves," that was not the case in Lexington, "where no such danger exists." She concluded that "the ladies are not afraid to overstep or overreach their future partners." *Western Minerva* 1 (1821): 78.

28. Brown, *Emigrant's Directory*, 93; Faux, *Memorable Days*, in Thwaites, ed., *Early Western Travels*, 11:193. On the material culture, see Mary Jane Elliott, "A Background to Decorative Arts in Lexington: 1792–1820," *Kentucky Review* 7 (1987): 42–62.

29. Brown, *Emigrant's Directory*, 93; Friend, *Maysville Road*, 238; Coleman, "Lexington," 273; Hill, *The Theatre in Early Kentucky*, 116; Flint, *History and Geography*, 1:354; Wade, *Urban Frontier*, 236; Fordham, *Personal Narrative*, 223.

30. Richard L. Troutman, "Plantation Life in the Ante-Bellum Bluegrass Region of Kentucky" (M.A. thesis, University of Kentucky, 1955), 20; *Lexington Observer and Reporter*, October 10, 1838; John A. Jakle, *Images of the Ohio Valley: A Historical Geography of Travel, 1740 to 1860* (New York, 1977), 43; Wade, *Urban Frontier*, 21, 233, 240.

31. Lee Soltow, "Kentucky's Wealth at the End of the Eighteenth Century," *Journal of Economic History* 43 (1983): 620, 624. See also Joan Wells Coward, *Kentucky in the New Republic* (Lexington, 1979), 55; Fredrika J. Teute, "Land, Liberty, and Labor in the Post-Revolutionary Era: Kentucky as the Promised Land" (Ph.D. diss., Johns Hopkins University, 1988), 263, 275; Perkins, *Border Life*, 85; Aron, *How the West Was Lost*, 203; and Friend, *Maysville Road*, 107, 284.

32. Matthew Schoenbachler, "The Origins of Jacksonian Politics: Central Kentucky, 1790–1840" (Ph.D. diss., University of Kentucky, 1996), 60; Lowell H. Harrison, *Kentucky's Road to Statehood* (Lexington, 1992), 121; Coward, *Kentucky in the New Republic*, 27.

33. Toulmin, *Description of Kentucky*, 121; Appleton, "Journal of Thomas Smith, Jr.," 62; John David Smith, "Slavery and Antislavery," in *Our Kentucky: A Study of the Bluegrass State* (2nd ed.), ed. James C. Klotter (Lexington, 2000), 112–19; Aron, *How the West Was Lost*, 89–95; Wade, *Urban Frontier*, 125; Vigne, *Six Months in America*, 2:34; Brown, *Emigrant's Directory*, 92.

34. Lucas, *From Slavery to Segregation*, xviii.

35. Fordham, *Personal Narrative*, 163, 177, 180; E. S. Abdy, *Journal of a Residence and Tour in the United States of North America . . .* , 3 vols. (London, 1835), 2:354–55; Murray, *Travels*, 1:176–77; James Hall, *Sketches of History, Life, and Manners in the West*, 2 vols. (Philadelphia, 1835), 2:88, 70–71; [Elizabeth R.] Steele, *A Summer Journey in the West* (New York, 1841), 251.

36. Sonne, *Liberal Kentucky*, 205; *Paris (KY) Literary Pamphleteer* 1 (1823): 15; *Lexington Western Luminary*, February 10, 1825; Leavy, "Memoir of Lexington" (no. 138), 53, and "Memoir" (no. 135), 120–21; Murray, *Travels*, 1:189; *Richmond (VA) Chronicle* quoted in *Lexington Observer and Reporter*, October 13, 1838; Wright, *Transylvania*, 174–75. The law school would later reopen, but then closed again in 1895.

37. Wade, *Urban Frontier*, 182, 170; James F. Hopkins et al., eds., *The Papers of Henry Clay*, 10 vols. and suppl. (Lexington, 1959–1992), 2:665; Hollingsworth, *Lexington*, 71. See also Thomas F. Kiffmeyer, "Ideology Portrayed in Jacksonian Lexington: Popular Culture and 'Conscious' Language," *Register of the Kentucky Historical Society* 100 (2002): 37.

38. Wade, *Urban Frontier*, 53, 169–70, 84; Wright, *Lexington*, 51–52; "Samuel D.

McCullough's Reminiscences," 422–25; Gruenwald, *River of Enterprise*, 121; Vigne, *Six Months in America*, 2:28.

39. *Lexington Observer and Kentucky Reporter*, June 22, July 19, 1833; Andrew Reed and James Matheson, *Narrative of the Visit to the American Churches . . .* , 2 vols. (New York, 1835), 1:129; Leavy, "Memoir of Lexington" (no. 138), 26–28; Friend, *Maysville Road*, 277; Ranck, *History of Lexington*, 325–26; W. Harrison to Jillson Harrison, July 12, 1833, Harrison Family Papers, Kentucky Historical Society, Frankfort; Nancy D. Baird, "Asiatic Cholera's First Visit to Kentucky," *Filson Club History Quarterly* 48 (1974): 230–33; MacCabe, *Directory for 1838*, 22–23; Wright, *Lexington*, 45, 84; Robert Letcher to Orlando Brown, July 31, 1849, Orlando Brown Papers, Kentucky Historical Society. See also Orphan Society of Lexington Record Book, 1833–1859, Special Collections, King Library, University of Kentucky.

40. *Frankfort Commonwealth*, June 18, 1833; Reed and Matheson, *Narrative*, 1:129.

41. "Childe Harold's Pilgrimage," canto 2, stanza 2, http://www.rc.umd.edu/editions/sceptic/Pilgrimage.html.

42. On the importance of Kentucky to the Confederacy, see, e.g., William W. Freehling, *The South vs. the South: How Anti-Confederate Southerners Shaped the Course of the Civil War* (Oxford, 2001), 23, 52–54, 61; and James Lee McDonough, *War in Kentucky: From Shiloh to Perryville* (Knoxville, TN, 1994), 61–63.

43. Wright, *Transylvania*, 198; *Lexington Herald*, January 9, 1922.

44. Lucas, "It's All Greek to Me," 24–25, 25n; David Blight, *Race and Reunion: The Civil War in American Memory* (Cambridge, MA, 2001), 4.

45. Robert E. Lee quoted in Charles P. Roland, *Reflections on Lee* (Baton Rouge, 1995), 114.

2

Putting Kentucky in Its Place

Stephen Aron

What place does Kentucky hold in American history? A brief one, at least judging from the indexes of U.S. history textbooks. Typically, these surveys mention the settlement of Kentucky by pioneers like Daniel Boone and sometimes cite it being the home of Henry Clay or the birthplace of Abraham Lincoln. These references all occur during the period when Kentucky occupied first place among western states and when it, or at least the Inner Bluegrass region in and around Lexington, claimed the mantle of the "Athens of the West." Kentucky's Athenian moment, however, proved short-lived, as did its position at the front rank of western states. After the War of 1812, Lexington surrendered its economic and cultural preeminence, and Kentucky lost its demographic leadership in the trans-Appalachian region. Once passed by, Kentucky pretty much drops out of American history textbooks—save perhaps a paragraph or two about its uncertain allegiance during the Civil War.[1]

Equally problematic have been efforts to fix Kentucky's place in America's regional geography. If Kentucky reigned at the end of the eighteenth century and the beginning of the nineteenth as the Athens of the West, it soon shed that title and ceased to be considered part of the West as well. But, if not an Athens and not a West, then what? Most often, historians of nineteenth-century America move Kentucky into the South. Yet, in the early decades of the nineteenth century, Kentucky's southern orientation was incomplete. At midcentury, politicians from the Deep South doubted Kentucky's allegiance to their cause, and, sure enough, when the war came, Kentuckians split, but Kentucky stayed in the Union. True, after the Civil War, the state arguably turned more southern, but even then it did not fully share in the legacy of the Confederacy.[2]

Once West, but West no more, in but not fully of the South, Kentucky and its historians have had trouble finding a comfortable regional home and difficulty slotting the state's history into the appropriate broader context. Putting Kentucky in its place, then, presents a real challenge. But it is one worth taking up, for on this placement rests the significance of Kentucky's past, the explanation for its present, and the possibilities for its future.

The problem of placement—in history and geography—is not unique to Kentucky. Missouri's historical and regional trajectory closely followed that of the Bluegrass State. Indeed, in some respects, Missouri's experience was a sequel to Kentucky's. But the juxtaposition of the frontier histories of Kentucky and Missouri also provides a different angle on historical significance and regional placement. In particular, the comparison with Missouri better explains Kentucky's situation as a West, as a South, and as a land whose history has fallen between.

As West

The reconsideration of Kentucky's place begins with the title of one of my books, *How the West Was Lost: The Transformation of Kentucky from Daniel Boone to Henry Clay*. Over the years, some critical readers, blinded by current geography, have refused to see how a book about Kentucky could be about the West. It is true that how historians speak about the historical West can be bewildering. Kentucky is generally seen as part of what is sometimes called the *First West*. In the late eighteenth century and the early nineteenth, that West, stretching from the Appalachians to the Mississippi and nominally transferred to the United States as a result of the Revolution, was also designated as the *New West*. New it was to the just-born American nation, but the designation came to be a problem with the transfer of the Louisiana Territory to the United States in 1803. Thereafter, the United States gained a farther West, though that West, reaching ultimately from the Mississippi to the Pacific, has come to be known as the *Old West*—despite the fact that it was newer than the New West. Would that Americans had applied the appellations *Near West* and *Far West*. How sensible that would be, with perhaps the Midwest in between. But instead we are stuck with the confusion of Kentucky being part of the New West, which is older than the Old West, but is West no more, and in the minds of most Americans today was never West at all.[3]

How the West Was Lost and several articles published in the 1990s argued that the American conquest, colonization, and consolidation of

Kentucky constituted a seminal chapter in the westward expansion of the United States. What happened in Kentucky mattered to the history of the wider West because this was the nation's first of many Wests. What happened in Kentucky set a pattern for ensuing expansionist processes across that vast domain stretching from the Appalachians to the Pacific, which, to add one more term to the mix, nineteenth-century Americans referred to as the *Great West*. In Kentucky in particular and the Ohio valley more generally, the United States and its westering population learned to conquer—and understood or as often misunderstood the costs of colonizing lands and consolidating control over territory.[4]

This accent on the lessons that the trans-Appalachian West held for subsequent American Wests beyond the Mississippi River got me labeled a *neo-Turnerian*—and that usually was not meant as a compliment. Certainly, the link I drew between developments in the First West and later Wests echoed one of Frederick Jackson Turner's most often-quoted lines: "Stand at Cumberland Gap and watch the procession of civilization, marching single file—the buffalo following the trail to the salt springs, the Indian, the fur trader and hunter, the cattle-raiser, the pioneer farmer—and the frontier has passed by. Stand at South Pass in the Rockies a century later and see the same procession with wider intervals between." Thus did Turner blaze a historiographic trail across the Great West, neatly encapsulating the parallelism of eighteenth- and nineteenth-century American westward expansions. In his sketch of America's westward movement, the cavalcade into Kentucky repeated itself across the continent.[5]

While concurring with his judgment about the primacy of Kentucky, I agreed with critics who pointed out how many of the details Turner got wrong. Had he actually stood at Cumberland Gap and South Pass, he surely would have been less impressed by their similarities: the former lies amid wet, dense woodlands, while the latter is situated in a semiarid, treeless terrain. On this and other obvious discontinuities between trans-Appalachian and trans-Mississippi geography has risen the new western history—with its emphasis on the regional distinctiveness of the arid and semiarid western half of the North American continent. In addition to overturning Turner for missing the differences between Cumberland Gap and South Pass, historians have also pointed out that his neat parade of frontier types bore little relation to the messier process by which Kentucky and the Great West came to be American. Through Cumberland Gap and elsewhere, no carefully orchestrated sequence governed westward migrations. Instead, the people who headed west and the processes of conquest, colonization, and consolidation that they initiated overlapped. Moreover, the ejection of Indian peoples, the resettlement of expropriated lands, and the construction of a new national and industrial, capitalist order, which all were cause for celebration in Turner's time, no longer look so wonderful to recent generations of historians. And, though the title of my book did not suggest a story of paradise lost, my own take, accenting possibilities lost, made clear my distance from Turner and any triumphalist narrative of westward expansion. Yet my work did stand with Turner in holding to the idea that the coincident processes of conquest, colonization, and political and economic consolidation more or less repeated themselves and that this remained the foundation for the history of the Great West, or a "greater western history."[6]

Readers should notice that this discussion about my book on Kentucky and related articles has occurred in the past tense. That is in keeping with the advice given to my students: when writing about the past, best to stick with the past tense, and that applies as well to writing about what historians have written. After all, historians can—and do—change their minds. And, in the ten years since *How the West Was Lost* appeared, I have changed some of my views about the placement of Kentucky and the configuration of western American history, changes that can be discerned by readers of my subsequent book on frontier Missouri.[7]

Focusing on the Missouri frontier would, I thought, buttress my claims about Kentucky and for a greater western history. The original prospectus for the book proposed to trace how the area that became the state of Missouri emerged from its precolonial origins, how a frontier opened when colonists contested with natives for occupancy, and how its development led to its admission as one of the United States, the expulsion of Indian peoples, and the closing of the Missouri frontier. Telling the history of frontier Missouri that way appealed to me, for it made the book an obvious sequel to the one that I had written on frontier Kentucky. After all, the westward migrations of Kentuckians had landed many in Missouri, including Daniel Boone, who had, in *How the West Was Lost*, served as a synecdoche for pioneers moving across the Appalachians. Initially, the Missouri book would be the next chapter of a greater western history. Since my conception of a greater western history posited that patterns of conquest, colonization, and consolidation repeated themselves as American expansion proceeded westward, Missouri seemed the perfect place to look for a replay of what had happened to the east in Kentucky.[8]

Indeed, Missouri's standing in American history and regional geography corresponds closely with Kentucky's. It, too, tends to make an appearance in U.S. history textbooks at the time of its initial American settlement and its tumultuous entrance into the Union, then gets noted in a subsequent chapter as the staging ground for westward expansion and a focal point of sectional conflict in the 1850s. Thereafter, the "Show Me" state does not show up at all either. Also like Kentucky, Missouri's regional affiliations have been shifting and uncertain—it, too, was once clearly West, but is now not so, and is sometimes southern, but not wholly of the South.[9]

The journey from frontier Kentucky to frontier Missouri turned out to be more problematic than was first supposed, however. Unlike the Ohio River, whose course connects the two states and which became the primary route of pioneer migration from Kentucky to Missouri, the links between Kentucky and Missouri, it became clear, flowed in more than one direction. Rather than a simple sequel, the history of Missouri in the eighteenth and nineteenth centuries forwarded lessons of its own, including ones that have led me to rethink how we place Kentucky.

Crucial to this reframing was my collaboration on a world history textbook. From the perspective of world history, the area that became the state of Missouri—or, for that matter, the area that became Kentucky—had little significance if it is only one of fifty such chapters in the expansion of the United States. In world history, what made Missouri (or Kentucky) matter were the connections between the experiences of its peoples and those who occupied frontiers, not just within the present-day United States, but across the Americas and beyond. No longer just a contribution to a greater western history, the Missouri project became an opportunity to explore what the historian Herbert Bolton termed a *greater American history* and to put North American history in a hemispheric and even transoceanic context. Thus, the history of one state (within the history of one nation-state) evolved into a more complicated contemplation, involving multiple polities and overlapping colonial regimes, and speaking to a comparative and common history of the Americas and a consideration of how this chapter in the history of colonialism fit in a global scheme. Framed this way, patterns and repetitions that moved from east to west lost their exclusivity. Instead, processes of conquest, colonization, and consolidation traveled along multiple trajectories, running north, south, east, and west.[10]

Indeed, the geography of Missouri and its environs suggested a more fundamental reorientation of American history. Rather than a greater western history that unfolded as almost all U.S. histories do from east to west, I imagined a history of the continent from the perspective of the center out. Strictly speaking, Missouri does not lie at the geographic center of North America, but the defining geographic features of the region, the rivers that come together around it, long made it the heart of North America. Here were the confluences of the most important interior waterways, the Missouri, the Ohio, and the Mississippi. In fact, centuries before there was a place called *Missouri*, the conjoining of these waters saw more traffic from points near and far than any other locale in North America. For thousands of years, these rivers functioned more as corridors than as borders, bringing peoples and goods to and through from points north, south, east, and west, and facilitating the development of precolonial North America's greatest urban center. This was Cahokia, located near the east bank of the Mississippi just below its junction with the Missouri. At its peak in the eleventh century, Cahokia was home to between ten and twenty thousand persons spread across a five-square-mile metropolis. Its influence as a trading and ceremonial center reached far beyond these boundaries; from archaeological sites around Cahokia, digs have recovered at least nineteen different kinds of marine shells that originated in the Gulf of Mexico and the Atlantic Ocean, with the Mississippi, Missouri, and Ohio Rivers serving as the primary corridors of long-distance exchange. Even after Cahokia went into decline (and was eventually abandoned in the fourteenth century), the confluence of rivers ensured the primacy of the area. Certainly, from the vantage point of precolonial North America, there was nothing manifestly destined about the east-to-west axis.[11]

In the eighteenth century, Europeans arrived to colonize the region and presumed to turn arteries into borders, but their overlapping designs kept this hub a contested borderland. The junctions of the Ohio, Missouri, and Mississippi Rivers, an area that I came to designate the *American Confluence* or the *confluence region*, became the ground on which all North America's major colonial regimes converged, making it a unique vantage point from which to view the interplay of empires and frontiers.[12]

Particularly fascinating about the confluence region (and what I had not appreciated in Kentucky) was how the overlap of colonialisms—French, Spanish, British, and, finally, American—had decisively shaped the character of frontiers and the contours of North American history. At least through the eighteenth century, the convergence of colonial regimes had encouraged the construction of accommodationist frontiers. Pressured by the power of Indian peoples, and fearful of the designs of imperial rivals, French, Spanish, English, and American "invaders" adjusted their earlier frontier policies to reach accommodations with the confluence region's "indigenes." Under these borderland conditions, the

Spanish, English, and Americans perpetuated what they considered to be the "French" model of frontier relations.[13]

So the book *American Confluence* pursued a polycolonial history in which the east-to-west story line represented only one of many. True, later chapters tracked how westering Americans came to substitute their exclusive occupations for earlier traditions of inclusive relations. These forced relocations, which today we might designate as *ethnic cleansing*, had their parallels in Kentucky and the Ohio valley. But the Missouri book turned out not to be a sequel, for what happened in Kentucky prefigured little of what happened in Missouri.[14]

In fact, rather than drawing precepts from Kentucky to apply in Missouri, the frontier history of the confluence region has lessons to teach historians of Kentucky, starting with the Missouri book's central metaphor. What is a frontier, after all, but a confluence, a coming together of two or more streams of people? In some cases, the confluence, like the meeting of the Missouri and Mississippi Rivers, was a turbulent one, at least before the construction of dams tamed these waters. The crash of these still wild waters unleashed immense forces of destruction. Above the mouth of the Missouri, as numerous European explorers noted, the Mississippi ran relatively calm and clear; below the confluence, the joined rivers took on a murkier and rougher cast. So, too, frontiers within the confluence region (and elsewhere) sometimes engaged cohabiting peoples in violent conflict, and minglings almost always muddied cultural waters. By contrast, the Ohio's union with the Mississippi was a gentler one. And, in keeping with that model, frontiers within the confluence region (and elsewhere) have also been notable for the creative adaptations and constructive accommodations that allowed peoples to mix and meld more peacefully.

Nowhere was the record of collisions and collusions so apparent as in and around the American Confluence, though this mix also played out farther up the Ohio River. True, the upper Ohio valley did not witness the full set of overlapping colonial regimes that occurred downriver at its confluence with the Mississippi. In part for this reason, the common ground between Indian and European cohabitants, the hallmark of eighteenth-century frontiers in the confluence region, was not so easily found in Kentucky and its environs.[15]

Similarly, just as one cannot make sense of the history of the American Confluence by waiting for Americans to arrive or by treating it as a place that had to be an American West, so, too, the whole Ohio River valley, and what became the first American West, cannot be understood if it is seen only as a West in the making. For millennia of human history, the

Ohio valley was no more a West than it was a North, a South, or an East. Through the centuries, along with much of North America, it was the site of population movements from various directions. Even in the late eighteenth century, when the British and then the Americans claimed it as a western country, the Ohio valley and the expanse from the Appalachians to the Mississippi was not west at all for many of the people who lived there or moved there. It was, then, the focus of intensive rivalries between European empires; its future status—whether it would be a West, a South, a North, an East, or perhaps its own center or set of centers—remained very much up for grabs. True, the 1783 Treaty of Paris granted Kentucky, as well as the lands from the Appalachians to the Mississippi, to the new United States, but Britain had not really reconciled itself to the loss of its American colonies. In the decades after the Revolution, authorities in London plotted how to reconstitute the former realm, beginning by detaching the western country from the American nation. So, too, Spanish and even French officials conspired with disgruntled (or simply opportunistic) Americans to expand their influence and, perhaps, their imperial domains at the expense of the United States. Through the 1780s, and into the early 1790s, the weakness of the American nation—its inability to consolidate control over its western country and the discontent that this generated among westerners—made it anything but certain that Kentucky would stay a West as opposed to becoming part of a British South or a Spanish North. Making the first American West—and subsequent ones too—required breaking the claims of these rivals.[16]

It also involved the subjugation of Indian peoples, some of whom were long settled in the region, others of whom were themselves more recent arrivals. Through the eighteenth century, Indians in the Ohio valley pursued a variety of paths to resist dispossession and dependency. For a time, especially so long as one or another European power lent support to their cause, they enjoyed considerable success in checking American expansion. For a moment in the early 1790s, it appeared that a confederation of Indians, supported by the British, might wrest back control, if not of Kentucky, then at least of that portion of the western country north of the Ohio River. Unfortunately for Ohio valley Indians, European politics intruded, leading Britain to withdraw its backing. And, once imperial rivals withdrew, Indian options narrowed. In the 1790s, the United States turned from negotiating with the Ohio valley Indians to dictating to them. But, while by century's end Kentucky's place in an American western country was secured, much of the region retained its condition as Indian country for several more decades.[17]

With the breaking of claims of imperial competitors and of the military power of Indian inhabitants, the United States secured its first West, including Kentucky. Still, in retrospect, what is most striking about the making of the first American West is how long it took, particularly when compared with the more compressed chronologies of subsequent westward expansions. Indeed, never again would Indians contend on such even terms with Americans as they did when Kentucky was truly the West.

As South

To this point, I have addressed Kentucky's place as a frontier and as a West, a situation that applies primarily to the eighteenth century. But what of its identity after its frontier closed? What did Kentucky become when it ceased to be a West? The most common answer is to shift its placement from the New West to the Old South. In that vein, I once thought of titling my book *How the West Was Lost and the South Was Won*. By that addition, I would have called attention to the centrality of slavery to the world of Henry Clay. Clay had entered Kentucky's political scene in the late 1790s as a democratizing radical and a fervent opponent of slavery. In that decade, antislavery sentiment ran high in the newly admitted state. But proslavery forces turned back emancipationist demands at both Kentucky's first and its second constitutional conventions, and, by the early nineteenth century, the enfranchised part of the population strongly backed the continuation of slaveholding. For his part, Clay made a remarkably quick transition from opponent of slavery to holder of scores of slaves, establishing himself as a leading planter and as the political champion of the Bluegrass gentry.[18]

Yet I chose not to add *and the South Was Won* to the title then, and, in retrospect, I think that was the right decision. Though important to Clay's personal economy, slavery was not a centerpiece of his political economy. Clay owned up to fifty slaves at one time, but he remained a critic of the "peculiar institution." "No man," he asserted, "is more sensible of the evils of slavery than I am, nor regrets them more." That sense of evil and of regret spurred him to accept the chairmanship of the newly organized American Colonization Society in 1816. For more than a decade, he spearheaded the society's drive for the gradual emancipation and deportation of free blacks to Africa. At the same time, he always insisted that his "American System" did no harm to slave owners. His program, he maintained, harmonized the interests of all sections and all classes. Still, had slave owners across the South embraced his program of federally supported internal improvements and tariff protections for domestic industries, Clay would have been president, and the course of nineteenth-century American history would have been very different.[19]

Clay was not the favored political son of the South, and, despite the predominance of Virginians and North Carolinians in its pioneer population and the influence of Tidewater planter styles in the Bluegrass of Henry Clay, Kentucky was not fully in the South either. Yes, slavery was well entrenched in antebellum Kentucky. Already in 1800, slaves accounted for a quarter of the population in Fayette and neighboring counties. By the historian Allan Kulikoff's calculation, Kentucky received more than fifty thousand black migrants between 1790 and 1810, more than any other state in the nation. The destination of most of these slaves was the Inner Bluegrass region, where unfree laborers constituted more than one-third of the census in 1820. In the early nineteenth century, slavery also extended its base in other regions of the state, particularly in the Green River country. When Kentucky got around to revising its constitution again in 1849, the chance that emancipation, gradual or otherwise, might be enshrined had long disappeared. To the contrary, that convention made clear how unwelcome abolitionists were in Kentucky. By then, however, the percentage of Kentuckians who were slaves had gone into decline, falling from 24 percent in 1830 to 21.5 percent in 1850, as more and more Kentucky masters sent their chattel to territories to the south and west. Thus, despite the hostility to abolitionism, Kentucky, where slave percentages were diminishing and were much smaller than in the Cotton Kingdom, was viewed with suspicion by proslavery radicals in the Deep South. In the 1850s, its attachments to the South's cause were not certain. Sure enough, when the test of southern nationalism came, Kentucky failed by staying in the Union, though, of course, this decision was bitterly contested, and the state was truly a house divided during the Civil War.[20]

In many ways, Kentucky's southern history paralleled—and influenced—Missouri's. When white Kentucky pioneers first moved across the Mississippi River in the last decade of the eighteenth century, many brought African American slaves with them. After the Louisiana Purchase, the territory borrowed many of the provisions in its slave code from Kentucky ordinances. As in Kentucky, Missouri's admission to statehood was accompanied by controversies over slavery. True, in the case of Kentucky, these battles were generated from within, while, in that of Missouri, they resulted from the agitations of outsiders. Only through the efforts of Henry Clay was a compromise reached that allowed Missouri to gain statehood and the nation to avoid (or, as it turned out, delay) division.

The years immediately before and after the Missouri Crisis witnessed a mass migration of Kentuckians, both slave owners and slaves, bound for Missouri. The chief destination of these migrants was the Boon's Lick country (named for the salt works pioneered by two of Daniel Boone's sons). For transplants from Kentucky, the Boon's Lick country replicated the fine climate and soil for growing tobacco and hemp found in the Blue-grass region. As in Kentucky, most settlers in Missouri's expanding core of tobacco and hemp cultivation owned only a few slaves. A small number, however, arrived with, or built up, substantial holdings. During the 1820s, planters on arrival or by ambition replicated what had happened in central Kentucky, plowing tobacco and hemp profits into larger land- and slave-holdings, and replacing log cabins with two-story brick houses. These new showplaces lent an air of aristocratic distinction to their owners and to the surrounding countryside. With the establishment of hemp planta-tions and the expansion of slavery, the Boon's Lick country came to look more and more like the Kentucky Bluegrass. Its nickname also changed, becoming Missouri's *Little Dixie*, a sobriquet that accented the southern flavor of that part of the state.[21]

But Little Dixie did not make Missouri fully Dixie, any more than the Bluegrass region, with its strong inflections of the gentry culture of the Virginia Tidewater, made Kentucky wholly southern. That was readily apparent to any traveler through St. Louis, where the prominence of Eu-ropean immigrants and Yankees looked away from Dixie. Across Missouri, the population and percentage of slaves compared with Kentucky's, which again fell well short of states to the South.[22]

Making the case for Kentucky's influence on the history of slavery in Missouri does return to an east-to-west framework. But, as with my ear-lier reconsideration of the multiple points of entry and multiple directions of frontier histories, I would emphasize that the history of slavery did not *only* move from east to west across an *American* South. In the Louisiana Territory, slavery predated the migrations of Americans by nearly a cen-tury. While first French and later Spanish officials had tried to outlaw trade in and the holding of Indians as slaves, these regimes had planted and provided for African slavery in the territory. Elaborate regulations, building on the 1685 Code Noir, governed the treatment and punishment of slaves. After the United States purchased Louisiana, territorial officials attempted to put an American stamp on these laws. American authori-ties insisted that the new rules were more protective of slave welfare than French or Spanish codes had been. In practice, however, the importation of Kentucky statutes deprived slaves in the confluence region of various privileges. Under the new laws, slaves in the Louisiana Territory lost the right to testify against whites in court, while masters were released from legal obligations to safeguard the health and well-being of their chattel. Still, as with frontiers where the French influence lingered over intercultural relations for decades after the French king surrendered his North American claims, so the importation of Kentucky laws and the migration of Afro-Kentuckian slaves did not immediately erase the heritage of the prior regime. At least in St. Louis, it remained audible after the War of 1812, as evidenced by a resident who observed that "the negroes of the town all spoke French."[23]

In the years after the War of 1812, the sounds of French were increasingly muffled amid the flood of migrating English speakers, the majority of whose accents bore the imprint of their southern origins. First in the battle over statehood, and then in the decades leading up to the Civil War, Missouri, even more than Kentucky, moved to the front lines of the conflict between American North and American South. Like Kentucky, Missouri straddled the divide between sections. When the Civil War came, it also did not secede, though it, too, was a house bitterly and bloodily divided.[24]

It is, of course, ironic, not to mention tragic, that both Kentucky and Missouri remained part of the North during the Civil War but turned more toward the South after it. Significant numbers of white Kentuckians and white Missourians embraced the South's "lost cause" with great fervor—after it was lost. In both states, slavery died hard, and white supremacists waged a reign of terror. In Kentucky, lynchings claimed more than one hundred blacks between 1867 and 1871, while, in Missouri, as the most recent biography of Jesse James underscores, the most famous of western outlaws was primarily an unreconstructed Confederate.[25]

Finally, both Kentucky and Missouri shared in the relative decline that characterized the postbellum South. St. Louis saw its star eclipsed by Chicago, which stole its place as gateway to the Great West. Lexington and Louisville were similarly surpassed and faded into the second rank of cities. Population growth in both states lagged well behind national averages, and economic opportunities were more easily found in other places. So, while Kentucky and Missouri may have joined the South, it would be strange to describe this as a win—and that legacy very much shapes what these states are today.[26]

The beginning of this essay noted that putting Kentucky in its historical and regional place determines how we interpret its past, account for its present, and imagine its future. What I hope this brief exegesis has made clear is that the state's placement has never been that clear. There was nothing foreordained about Kentucky as West or as South. These regional affiliations were the product of contingent historical processes. Kentucky was not *born* West or South. It *became* these, as it might have become something else. Moreover, these identities were never fully realized or forever fixed. Kentucky became a West and subsequently shed that mantle. It moved toward the South but remained on the borders of that region. To put Kentucky (or Missouri) in its place requires that we embrace a history of becoming but not ever wholly being, that we probe its record as borderland and as border state, and that we appreciate the possibilities that follow from being between.

To be sure, being between may not be as comfortable a place as being safely in one camp or another. So, too, inhabiting shifting ground—and I write this as a resident of California, a state where we know well what happens when ground shifts—can be hazardous to one's health and one's sense of history. But the dangers (and confusions) that come with life on a fault line are compensated by the excitement of being where history happens—where natives and newcomers vie, where colonial regimes converge, where the forces of slavery and antislavery collide, and where people can find their place because no one knows their place.

Notes

1. An annotated scorecard of entries for *Kentucky* from the indexes of recent textbooks: John Mack Faragher et al., *Out of Many: A History of the American People*, 2nd ed. (Upper Saddle River, NJ, 1997), 186 ("in American Revolution"), 191 ("population of" in pioneer era), 242 ("admitted to Union"), 266 ("slavery issue in"), 276, 277 ("voting rights in" as established in early state constitutions), 313 ("settlement of"), 476, 481 ("in Civil War"); David Goldfield et al., *The American Journey: A History of the United States* (Upper Saddle River, NJ, 1998), 177 ("in American Revolution"), 212 ("in post-Revolutionary era"), 233, 350 ("settlement of"), 233 ("slavery in"), 234 ("admitted to Union"), 476–77 ("in Civil War"); Pauline Maier, *Inventing America: A History of the United States* (New York, 2003), 209 ("settlement of"), 256, 284, 362 ("statehood"), 272 ("land claims in"), 285 ("trade routes to"), 313 ("mining in"), 319 ("population of" in pioneer era), 381 ("farming in"), 498, 514 ("and slavery"), 498–99 ("and secession"), 502, 514 ("and Civil War"); Jacqueline Jones et al., *Created Equal: A Social and Political History of the United States* (New York, 2003), 312ff. ("voting rights, late 18th century"), 466, 469 ("in Civil War").

2. Lowell H. Harrison and James C. Klotter (*A New History of Kentucky* [Lexington, 1997], 195–271) provide the best overview of Kentucky's orientation during and after the Civil War. Dated, but still valuable for its interpretation of Kentucky's southward turn after the Civil War, is E. Merton Coulter, *The Civil War and Readjustment in Kentucky* (Chapel Hill, NC, 1926).

3. Stephen Aron, *How the West Was Lost: The Transformation of Kentucky from Daniel Boone to Henry Clay* (Baltimore, 1996). In choosing my title, I really did not want to confound readers; I did mean to pick a fight with self-proclaimed "new western historians." The late 1980s and early 1990s had seen the rise of this revisionist cavalry, who, led by Patricia Nelson Limerick, had sought to erase the traces of Frederick Jackson Turner's frontier thesis and replace it with an updated interpretation better suited to understanding the West where it is and as it is today. Accordingly, new western historians confined their attentions to the present-day boundaries of the American West, which, to make matters just a little more perplexing, more or less aligned with the so-called Old West. In the process of staking out a regionalist interpretation of western American history, new western historians turned against Frederick Jackson Turner's notion of a West born from a series of shifting frontiers and excised the First West, that is, the old New West, from their story line. For sterling examples of the new western history, which emphasize the centrality of region and which take their understanding of western boundaries from present-day understandings of where the West is, see Patricia Nelson Limerick, *The Legacy of Conquest: The Unbroken Past of the American West* (New York, 1987); Richard White, *"It's Your Misfortune and None of My Own": A New History of the American West* (Norman, OK, 1991); Patricia Limerick, Clyde Milner, and Charles Rankin, eds., *Trails: Toward a New Western History* (Lawrence, KS, 1991); and Donald Worster, "New West, True West: Interpreting the Region's History," *Western Historical Quarterly* 18 (1987): 141–56.

4. See esp. Stephen Aron, "Lessons in Conquest: Towards a Greater Western History," *Pacific Historical Review* 63 (1994): 125–47.

5. Frederick Jackson Turner, "The Significance of the Frontier in American History," in *The Frontier in American History* (New York, 1920), 12.

6. For a survey of the voluminous literature on the old (Turnerian) western history, see Ray A. Billington, *The American Frontier Thesis: Attack and Defense* (Washington, DC, 1958). For a more updated review of the Turner thesis and its continuing place in American historical scholarship, see John Mack Faragher, "The Frontier Trail: Rethinking Turner and Reimagining the American West," *American Historical Review* 98 (1993): 106–17. With Robert Hine, Faragher has coauthored a survey of western American history that, in contrast with the regionalist approach favored by new western historians, follows Turner in treating all North America as having once been a West. See Robert V. Hine and John Mack Faragher, *The American West: A New Interpretive History* (New Haven, CT, 2000).

7. Stephen Aron, *American Confluence: The Missouri Frontier from Borderland to Border State* (Bloomington, IN, 2006).

8. This view of the relationship between Kentucky and Missouri and between the generations of the Boone family informed my "The Legacy of Daniel Boone: Three Generations of Boones and the History of Indian-White Relations," *Register of the Kentucky Historical Society* 95 (1997): 219–35.

9. The annotated scorecard of index entries for *Missouri* from the same textbooks cited in n. 1 above: Faragher et al., *Out of Many*, 254 ("admitted to Union") 478, 481

("in Civil War"), 772 (agricultural problems during the Great Depression); Goldfield et al., *The American Journey*, 280, 351 ("admitted to Union"), 476–77, 487 ("in Civil War"); 313, 332–33 ("statehood of"), 313 ("lead deposits in"), 313, 566 ("agriculture in"), 319 ("population of"), 349 ("constitution of"), 333, 381, 498, 514 ("slavery in"), 499 ("and secession"), 631 ("home rule in"); Jones et al., *Created Equal*, 329 ("Lewis and Clark in"), 466, 469 ("in Civil War").

10. Jeremy Adelman, Stephen Aron, Steven Kotkin, Suzanne Marchand, Gyan Prakash, Robert Tignor, and Michael Tsin, *Worlds Together, Worlds Apart: A History of the Modern World from the Mongol Empire to the Present* (New York, 2002). For the call for a hemispheric history of the Americas, see Herbert E. Bolton, "The Epic of Greater America," *American Historical Review* 38 (1933): 448–74.

11. On Cahokia, its trading orbit, and related Mississippian culture sites in the Ohio valley, see William R. Iseminger, "Culture and Environment in the American Bottom: The Rise and Fall of the Cahokia Mounds," in *Common Fields: An Environmental History of St. Louis*, ed. Andrew Hurley (St. Louis, 1997), 49–57; Thomas E. Emerson and R. Barry Lewis, eds., *Cahokia and the Hinterlands: Middle Mississippian Cultures of the Midwest* (Urbana, IL, 1991); and James B. Stoltman, ed., *New Perspectives on Cahokia: Views from the Periphery* (Madison, WI, 1991).

12. Excellent general histories of precolonial and colonial Missouri (and the middle Mississippi valley) include William E. Foley, *The Genesis of Missouri: From Wilderness Outpost to Statehood* (Columbia, 1989); Carl J. Ekberg, *French Roots in the Illinois Country: The Mississippi Frontier in Colonial Times* (Urbana, IL, 1998); and James Davis, *Frontier Illinois* (Bloomington, IN, 1999).

13. This argument about how the overlap of colonial regimes shaped the character of frontier relations is made at greater length in Jeremy Adelman and Stephen Aron, "From Borderlands to Borders: Empires, Nation-States, and the Peoples in Between in North American History," *American Historical Review* 104 (1999): 814–41. Among the most notable of studies of English, French, and Spanish frontiers in North America are Richard White, *The Middle Ground: Indians, Empires, and Republics in the Great Lakes Region, 1650–1815* (New York, 1991); David J. Weber, *The Spanish Frontier in North America* (New Haven, CT, 1992); W. J. Eccles, *The Canadian Frontier, 1534–1760*, rev. ed. (Albuquerque, 1983), 1–59; and James Axtell, *The Invasion Within: The Contest of Cultures in Colonial North America* (New York, 1985). For an overview of the literature on the different colonial regimes, see Jay Gitlin, "Empires of Trade, Hinterlands of Settlement," in *The Oxford History of the American West*, ed. Clyde A. Milner II, Carol A. O'Connor, and Martha Sandweiss (New York, 1994), 79–113.

14. Aron, *American Confluence*, 106–243. The term *ethnic cleansing*, which emerged in the 1990s to describe the conflicts that accompanied the breakup of Yugoslavia, has now been profitably and provocatively applied to the North American frontier in a number of recent studies. See, in particular, John Mack Faragher, "'More motley than mackinaw': From Ethnic Mixing to Ethnic Cleansing on the Frontier of the Lower Missouri, 1783–1833," in *Contact Points: American Frontiers from the Mohawk Valley to the Mississippi, 1750–1830*, ed. Andrew R. L. Cayton and Fredrika J. Teute (Chapel Hill, NC, 1998),

304–26, and *A Great and Noble Scheme: The Tragic Story of the Expulsion of the French Acadians from Their American Homeland* (New York, 2005); and Gary Anderson, *The Conquest of Texas: Ethnic Cleansing in the Promised Land, 1820–1875* (Norman, OK, 2005).

15. Among the landmark studies of intercultural relations in various parts of the Ohio valley are John Mack Faragher, *Daniel Boone: The Life and Legend of an American Pioneer* (New York, 1992); Colin Calloway, *The American Revolution in Indian Country: Crisis and Diversity in Native American Communities* (New York, 1995); and Andrew Cayton, *Frontier Indiana* (Bloomington, IN 1996).

16. I offer more details about the competition between imperial rivals and the confederation of Indians in the Ohio valley, as well as a fuller bibliography, in my "The Making of the First American West and the Unmaking of Other Realms," in *A Companion to the American West*, ed. William Deverell (Boston, 2004), 5–24.

17. See esp. White, *The Middle Ground*, 413–68; Gregory Dowd, *A Spirited Resistance: The North American Indian Struggle for Unity, 1745–1815* (Baltimore, 1992), 90–122; and Wiley Sword, *President Washington's Indian War: The Struggle for the Old Northwest, 1790–1795* (Norman, OK, 1985).

18. Joan Wells Coward (*Kentucky in the New Republic: The Process of Constitution Making* [Lexington, 1979]) details the fights over slavery that animated Kentucky politics and constitution making and revision in the 1790s. The best treatment of Clay's early years in Kentucky remains Bernard Mayo, *Henry Clay: Spokesman of the New West* (Boston, 1937).

19. Henry Clay to John Sloane, August 12, 1823, in James F. Hopkins et al., eds., *The Papers of Henry Clay*, 10 vols. and suppl. (Lexington, 1959–1992), suppl.:149. For a study of Clay's political economy, see Maurice Baxter, *Henry Clay and the American System* (Lexington, 1995). For general works that place Clay's American System in the context of his times, see Charles Sellers, *The Market Revolution: Jacksonian America, 1815–1846* (New York, 1991); Sean Wilentz, *The Rise of American Democracy: Jefferson to Lincoln* (New York, 2005); and Daniel Walker Howe, *What Hath God Wrought: The Transformation of America, 1815–1848* (New York, 2007).

20. Allan Kulikoff, *The Agrarian Origins of American Capitalism* (Charlottesville, NC, 1992), 238–45; Marion B. Lucas, *A History of Blacks in Kentucky*, vol. 1, *From Slavery to Segregation, 1760–1891* (Frankfort, 1992), 1–50, 84–100; Aron, *How the West Was Lost*, 89–101, 143–49, 164–66; Lowell H. Harrison, *The Anti-Slavery Movement in Kentucky* (Lexington, 1978); Karolyn E. Smardz, "'There we were in darkness, here we are in light': Kentucky Slaves and the Promised Land," in *The Buzzel about Kentuck: Settling the Promised Land*, ed. Craig Thompson Friend (Lexington, 1999), 243–58; Harrison and Klotter, *A New History of Kentucky*, 167–94; Frank Mathias, "Kentucky's Third Constitution: A Restriction of Majority Rule," *Register of the Kentucky Historical Society* 75 (1977): 1–19; William W. Freehling, *The Road to Disunion*, vol. 1, *Secessionists at Bay, 1776–1854* (New York, 1990).

21. R. Douglas Hurt, *Agriculture and Slavery in Missouri's Little Dixie* (Columbia, MO, 1992), 1–151; Harrison Anthony Trexler, *Slavery in Missouri, 1804–1865* (Baltimore, 1914).

22. Jeffrey S. Adler, "Yankee Colonizers and the Making of Antebellum St. Louis," *Gateway Heritage* 12 (1992): 4–21; Hurt, *Agriculture and Slavery in Missouri's Little Dixie*, 215–72.

23. John F. Darby, *Personal Recollections of Many Prominent People Whom I Have Known, and of Events—Especially of Those Relating to the History of St. Louis—during the First Half of the Present Century* (St. Louis, 1880), 5. For more on the evolution of slavery in French and Spanish Louisiana, see Winstanley Briggs, "Slavery in French Colonial Illinois," *Chicago History* 18 (1989–1990): 75–81; Gilbert C. Din, *Spaniards, Planters, and Slaves: The Spanish Regulation of Slavery in Louisiana, 1763–1803* (College Station, TX, 1999); and Russell M. Magnaghi, "The Role of Indian Slavery in Colonial St. Louis," *Bulletin of the Missouri Historical Society* 31 (1975): 264–72.

24. Perry McCandless (*A History of Missouri*, vol. 2, *1820–1860* [Columbia, 1972]) provides a solid survey of Missouri history in the decades leading up to the Civil War. Michael Fellman (*Inside War: The Guerilla Conflict in Missouri during the American Civil War* [New York, 1989]) examines the bitter and bloody warfare in that theater.

25. Harrison and Klotter, *A New History of Kentucky*, 237; George C. Wright, *Racial Violence in Kentucky, 1865–1940: Lynchings, Mob Rule, and "Legal Lynchings"* (Baton Rouge, 1990); Marion B. Lucas, "Kentucky Blacks: The Transition from Slavery to Freedom," *Register of the Kentucky Historical Society* 91 (1983): 403–19; Hambleton Tapp and James C. Klotter, *Kentucky: Decades of Discord, 1865–1900* (Frankfort, 1977); T. J. Stiles, *Jesse James: Last Rebel of the Civil War* (New York, 2002).

26. Jeffrey S. Adler (*Yankee Merchants and the Making of the Urban West: The Rise and Fall of Antebellum St. Louis* [Cambridge, 1991]) and William Cronon (*Nature's Metropolis: Chicago and the Great West* [New York, 1991]) explore the causes of St. Louis's relative decline (and Chicago's ascent).

3

Kentucky's "Athens of the West" Viewed in a "Distant Mirror"

Shearer Davis Bowman

In 1853, en route from Baltimore to Texas, the landscape architect and antislavery journalist Frederick Law Olmsted took a brief detour to Lexington via a horse-drawn coach from Cincinnati. Olmsted had heard "glowing descriptions" of the town and wished especially to visit "a spot haunted by a man who had loomed so high upon our boyhood." The spot was Ashland, the home of the Whiggish-Unionist icon Henry Clay, who had died early in the summer of 1852. Olmsted observed that Lexington "is the centre of no great trade, but is the focus of intelligence and society for Kentucky, which, however, is not concentrated in the town, but spread on its environs." At that time, Clay's Ashland estate, purchased by his son James at his father's request, belonged to the town's Fayette County suburbs southeast of the city center. North of downtown lay the oldest university west of the Appalachian Mountains, Transylvania University, the principal source of Lexington's reputation as the leading font of intellect and culture in the Bluegrass State. The school's roots extended back to a 1780 charter from the Virginia General Assembly establishing a board of trustees and an endowment for a "public school or Seminary of Learning" on its trans-Appalachian frontier. In 1793, a year after Kentucky became the Union's fifteenth state, a group of Lexington boosters offered the trustees a brick house and the real estate known today as Gratz Park if the trustees would locate their institution permanently in the rapidly growing town. Six years later, the trustees merged their school with the nearby Kentucky Academy to form Transylvania University, which included departments of law, liberal arts, and medicine. Local luminaries, including the attorney Henry Clay, taught classes in these departments. When

Olmsted visited Lexington in the early 1850s, he took note of its "university, well attended, and ranking among the highest Western schools in its departments of Law and Medicine. Its means of ordinary education are also said to be of the best."[1]

As early as the mid-1820s, according to G. W. Ranck's *History of Lexington* (1872), the city's "literary and educational advantages" had led to its being "spoken of far and wide as the 'Athens of the West.'"[2] During the first half of the nineteenth century in America, the popular appeal of such a claim to fame reflected several influences: the strong emphasis on things Greek and Roman in higher education; the identification of classical antecedents for the young republic, even as it became more self-consciously "democratic" during the Jacksonian Era; and the popularity of Greek Revival architecture for both public buildings and private estates. By the mid-1830s, Lexington had a prominent architectural symbol for its claim to being Athens reborn in Kentucky—Morrison Hall at Transylvania University, designed in the Greek Revival style by Gideon Shryock to evoke the grandiose and idealized historical memory of the classical world. Just as Athens had assumed preeminence among the self-governing city-states of classical, Hellenic Greece during the fifth-century BCE, so Lexington sought to gain comparable status among urban communities in early national and antebellum Kentucky.

Far to the northeast, an older and larger city, Boston, placed an even bolder claim to the title "the 'Athens of America,' a city of statesmen and philosophers, artists, and writers." Prominent and proud Bostonians of literary bent, the sort of men who formed a club named the Anthology Society in 1803, could point, not only to the Boston Latin School and Harvard University, but also to the Bay City's commercial and financial prominence in the early republic as warrant for labeling their metropolis the *American Athens*.[3] As for the lesser title *Athens of the West*, other town boosters would, at different times during the nineteenth century, challenge Lexington's appropriation of the Athenian imprimatur: for example, Evanston, Illinois, in the 1850s and Berkeley, California, at the turn of the century.[4]

Even so, Lexington during the first half of the nineteenth century, more than Boston then or Evanston and Berkeley later, offers a particularly apt historical comparison to Athens during its mid-fifth-century heyday. The reason is the basic economic and social system that underlay the city's reputation as an oasis of cultural and intellectual sophistication in the trans-Appalachian West. In both the Athens of Pericles and the Lexington of Henry Clay, the contours of political, social, and cultural

Greek influences abounded in antebellum Lexington. Morrison Hall, Transylvania University. (Special Collections, University of Kentucky.)

life could hardly be divorced, or examined in isolation, from a working world pervaded by slavery. Just as Athens was the urban center of Attica (or Attika), so Lexington was the urban center of the Inner Bluegrass. The Inner Bluegrass of Henry Clay's day, like Periclean Athens and its Attican hinterland, warrants the influential distinction posited by Moses Finley: "slave societies, as distinct from societies in which there were slaves." In the former, as opposed to the latter, slave labor was essential rather than peripheral to the community's economic life.[5] In both Athens and Lexington, chattel slavery made foundational and unmistakable contributions to the business prosperity and cultural prominence of each city. The ownership of slaves was generally viewed as "an expression of status and power,"[6] even as slavery itself also stood as a concrete and pervasive model of life without the inestimable blessings of liberty and independence. The aim of this essay is not to provide a balanced and systematic comparative-contrastive study between antebellum Lexington and Bluegrass Kentucky, on the one hand, and Hellenic Athens and the peninsula in eastern Greece, Attica, over which it presided, on the other. Instead, the goal here is to gain a fresh comparative perspective on Lexington and its environs in the early nineteenth century as a society analogous to the fifth-century Athenian city-state, in that each combined chattel slavery for a substantial minority of the population with a patriarchal form of "political democracy." To borrow a phrase from Barbara Tuchman, the Athens of Pericles can serve as a "distant mirror," distant in both time and space, in which to examine Henry Clay's Lexington as Kentucky's Athens of the West.[7]

Kentucky's slave population reached its peak as a percentage of the state's total population in 1830: 24 percent, or 165,000 slaves out of the commonwealth's 688,000 inhabitants. In Fayette, the most populous county in the commonwealth, the slave percentage was about 42 percent in 1830. By 1850, the percentage for the state as a whole had declined to less than 22 percent, but that year in Fayette County, the heart of the Bluegrass, the absolute number of whites was exceeded by the number of slaves and free blacks. Just to the west, Woodford was the only county in Kentucky where slaves outnumbered whites. For the entire Bluegrass region, including Inner counties like Fayette and Woodford as well as Outer counties like Mason, Jefferson, and Boyle, the slave percentage remained over 40 percent at midcentury.[8]

The commonwealth's third constitution, written by a Frankfort convention in 1849, was among the stronger proslavery state constitutions in the United States. On the motion of the lawyer Garrett Davis of Bourbon County (within the Inner Bluegrass), who later became a pro-Union U.S. senator from Kentucky in late 1861,[9] the convention delegates added a proslavery amendment to the third section of the bill of rights. This amendment declared that "the right of property is before and higher than any constitutional sanction; and the right of the owner of a slave to such slave, and its increase, is the same, and as inviolable as the right of owner, of any property whatsoever."[10] It ensured that Kentucky could not implement any plan of gradual emancipation that did not include financial compensation for slaveholders.

During the Civil War, from March to July 1862, Republican president Abraham Lincoln, a Kentucky native supported by the Republican-controlled U.S. Congress, made a remarkable offer to the representatives of border slave states like Kentucky, those states that had not officially seceded from the Union. He proposed that these states accept a plan of state-managed, gradual, and compensated emancipation. Significantly, the plan did not include the mandatory deportation of ex-slaves outside the United States—something that southern luminaries from Thomas Jefferson to Henry Clay had always seen as the sine qua non of gradual emancipation. Instead, it offered federal support only to those freed slaves who *volunteered* for colonization outside the United States. At that point, in mid-

1862, Lincoln was not going to make former slaves leave the country any more that he was going to compel the slave states to free them. But the border-state representatives in Congress rejected the proposed plan emphatically, many of them expressing skepticism that the government could afford it. According to one Kentucky congressman: "I utterly spit at it and despise it."[11] Hence, slavery continued in Kentucky until the Thirteenth Amendment, ratified at the end of 1865, decreed abolition without any financial compensation. However much economic historians may debate questions about slave labor's efficiency and profitability, there is no doubt that the uncompensated abolition of chattel bondage left entrepreneurial white Kentuckians with far less investment capital after than before the Civil War. In retrospect, border slave states' politicians refusal to accept Lincoln's 1862 proposal seems a perfect example of what Barbara Tuchman in 1984 called historical "folly"—that is, stubbornly pursuing a policy that proved contrary to one's own long-term self-interest.[12]

The territory of Attica, or the city-state of Athens, encompassed some one thousand square miles and was, therefore, about two-thirds the size of the six counties that make up the Inner Bluegrass. A reasonable estimate for the population of Athens and Attica in the fifth century BCE is between 250,000 and 300,000, including between 80,000 and 100,000 slaves; that is, slaves composed about 30 percent of the inhabitants.[13] Slave labor worked at the marble quarries at Mount Pentelicum/Pentelikon in northeast Attica and proved absolutely crucial to the silver mine at Laurium/Laurion in the southeast. Although mines for precious metals were owned by the state, they were operated by private lessees employing slaves.[14] "Much of the spectacular cultural grandeur of Athens" was financed by the labor of miners, including boys, whose iron fetters have been found by archaeologists.[15] Female household slaves produced woolen textiles and bakery goods. Male slaves—very often working alongside free men and metics (resident aliens)—not only labored in the construction of public buildings (e.g., the Acropolis) but also fabricated swords, shields, furniture, and—most important economically—pottery. The famous Attic vases, formed from the region's excellent clay, were often filled with locally produced olive oil or, perhaps, wine for export. The soil of Attica was too thin to produce sufficient wheat, but olive oil and pottery paid for grain imports, much of it from the shores of the Black Sea (to the northeast of Greece by way of the Aegean, the Hellespont, and the Dardanelles). This Black Sea region also provided some slaves for the Greek market.

Compared to Attica, Kentucky's Inner Bluegrass had much deeper soil, rich in calcium and phosphorous because of its limestone foundation.

Even so, in both societies the majority of adult male citizens were small but independent landowners whose households might include one, two, or three slaves, which meant that their owners probably did manual labor alongside the slaves. In the agricultural Bluegrass and other rural parts of the slave South, lesser slaveholders have often been included in the category of *yeomen* farmers; in Attica, they belonged to the ranks of the men affluent enough to provide their own armor and weapons and fight as hoplites (named after the shield they carried, the *hoplon*) in the tightly packed military formation known as the *phalanx*. The ownership of slaves generally served to enhance the slaveholder's social status and honorable reputation in the community. As we would expect, slaveholdings, including retinues of household slaves, were larger among the genteel and well-to-do in both classical Athens and the antebellum Bluegrass. Moreover, the division of labor among lower-income groups and among slaves was not so strictly along gendered lines as it was among the upper classes. In elite families, men and women were thought to have distinct but complementary roles in promoting the welfare of the household: men in the public sphere, women in the private sphere. Agricultural vocations and skilled craftsmanship were generally deemed quite respectable, in large part because most voters, free men, followed such vocations in both Attica and the Bluegrass. But domestic work and intense physical labor done at the command of a superior were generally held in low regard by the middling and upper classes, in large part because it seemed to preclude that manly independence so crucial to the political and cultural worlds of Pericles and Henry Clay.

Slaves in classical Greece need not be, and seldom were, what would be termed in the modern world *racially* distinct from free citizens. Throughout the ancient world, victors in war had reduced captured losers to bondage and might sell their human chattel to purchasers elsewhere. Although some dramatists in fifth-century Athens might mock the idea that slaves were necessarily inferior to their masters, there was no egalitarian "natural rights" ideology to suggest the logical incompatibility of liberty for some with slavery for others. However, in post-Enlightenment Christian America, unlike the classical Greece of Plato and Aristotle, the institution of chattel slavery could inspire ideological discomfort, personal distaste, and even, sometimes, apologetic soul-searching and feelings of guilt. By 1805, every state north of the Mason-Dixon line and the Ohio River had either prohibited slavery or provided for gradual emancipation. In 1808, the federal government had made participation in the international slave trade illegal, but this legislation also served to increase the market value of slaves already in the United States. The closing of the U.S. market to foreign imports, in conjunction with the westward march of the Cotton Kingdom in the Lower South, served to promote a profitable interstate slave trade that had no equivalent among the city-states of Hellenic Greece. In Kentucky, a state colonization society was organized in 1829 to promote the voluntary manumission and deportation of freed slaves. More unusual, from 1833 to 1850, the Bluegrass State had on the books a nonimportation act that banned bringing slaves into the state for the purpose of selling them outside the state, generally to cotton and sugar planters in the lower Mississippi valley.[16] Such legislation testifies to moderate antislavery sentiments that, together with the emotional attachments that might develop within slaveholding households between members of the master's family and those they called their *servants*—and sometimes these servants had been fathered by male members of the extended family— could lead to the eventual emancipation of slaves like Milly and Alfred by "Mrs. Polly" Wickliffe.[17]

Antebellum Kentucky, unlike classical Greece, was home to a decidedly vocal, albeit small, antislavery movement, personified in the Bluegrass by "conservative emancipationists" Robert Jefferson Breckinridge and Cassius Marcellus Clay.[18] It is important to keep in mind the distinction between their moderate antislavery stance—which advocated gradual emancipation combined with the colonization abroad of freed slaves— and the more radical, color-blind abolitionist stance of the Berean John G. Fee, who endorsed a much quicker end to bondage and insisted that the ex-slaves should remain in an integrated America. More conservative antislavery spokesmen such as Cassius Clay, like his even more cautious distant cousin Henry Clay, stressed the alleged economic inefficiencies of bondage and also saw dependence on slave labor as undermining the free white man's republican virtues of self-discipline and independence. Although a coterie of outspoken, color-blind, and controversial abolitionists emerged in parts of the American Northeast during the 1830s, antebellum antislavery was seldom racially egalitarian. The predominant antislavery sentiment in the nation and Kentucky represented a post-Enlightenment but still Negrophobic discomfort with slavery as incompatible with the powerful principles of both natural rights and free labor.

After Solon's reforms early in the sixth century BCE, Athenians reached a point in their social and cultural development analogous to that reached by the English even before they began to colonize the Western Hemisphere. That is, both classical Athenians and colonial Englishmen assumed that you did not and should not enslave your fellow citizens, that slavery should be reserved for what were deemed uncivilized outsiders, those the Greeks called *barbarians* and white Americans usually termed *savages*. Kentuckians, as part of Virginia until 1792, were direct heirs to a cultural and legal tradition that people of European ancestry could be short-term indentured servants, who provided most of the labor on Virginia tobacco plantations in the seventeenth century. At the same time, the condition of permanent enslavement as chattel property was appropriate only for savage peoples, which could include some Indians but was especially appropriate for black Africans, the ultimate outsiders in colonial North America.[19]

In pre–Civil War Kentucky, slave labor could be and was assigned to many tasks, from transportation to prostitution. As in ancient Greece, slaves worked in both manufacturing establishments and in mines and were frequently hired out. Although some were permitted to purchase their freedom, in neither society could a former slave achieve the status of a freeborn citizen. The freedman in Athens received the noncitizen status of a metic; the freedperson in Lexington certainly did not achieve full equality before the law but remained the recipient of racial prejudice, unless he or she moved away and could "pass for white" because of obvious European ancestry. An especially memorable story related to mining and self-purchase concerns a slave who became "Free Frank" McWhorter, the son of a white man named George McWhorter and a slave woman named Juda. Frank managed his master's Fishing Creek farm in Pulaski County after his master moved to Tennessee in 1810 while also hiring himself out as a jack-of-all-trades.[20] Although the county seat of Pulaski lay some eighty miles south of Lexington and is not a part of the Bluegrass region, the fascinating story of Free Frank is nonetheless relevant to our focus on Lexington and its environs. As a slave, Frank earned enough money on his own time to purchase his wife's and then his own freedom from his master's heirs in the late 1810s for a total of some $1,600. He accomplished this feat just before leaving the commonwealth for the freer air of Illinois in 1830, where his family became part of the Underground Railroad to Canada. During the War of 1812, the slave who became Free Frank had taken advantage of higher demand and higher prices for saltpeter, necessary along with charcoal and sulphur for the production of gunpowder. He began mining crude niter, or saltpeter earth, in the caves of Pulaski County and set up his own saltpeter works in the Bluegrass town of Danville to produce crystals of potassium nitrate for shipment to gunpowder factories. There were six gunpowder factories in Lexington at the time. The major suppliers of saltpeter to those Lexington factories were miners at the "Big Cave" in Rockcastle County, just east of Pulaski. It seems quite likely that some of Frank's saltpeter also made it to Lexington. Lexington manufacturers purchased most of their sulphur from suppliers in Philadelphia, thus introducing another important theme in the economic development of Fayette County and the Bluegrass—the "Philly connection."

The individual most responsible for promoting this Philly connection was apparently John Wesley Hunt, a remarkable entrepreneur who received the foundation of his business education in his father's mercantile establishment in Trenton, New Jersey. After unsuccessful ventures in Virginia, he moved to Lexington in 1795, at just the time when the Battle of Fallen Timbers and the Treaty of Greenville signified the end of significant Indian attacks on settlers in the Ohio valley. Therefore, Hunt arrived at the right moment to take advantage of Lexington's dramatic growth during the late 1790s and the early years of the nineteenth century. He opened a general store, making use of his cousin and fellow merchant Abijah Hunt's establishment in Cincinnati, to which he sent bacon and liquor from Fayette County. He established very profitable, if at times risky, commercial and financial ties to Philadelphia—risky because trade between Philadelphia and Lexington at this time had to traverse the 350 miles by wagon or coach between Philadelphia and Pittsburgh, another 400 miles by often-treacherous river between Pittsburgh and Limestone, or Maysville, on the south bank of the Ohio, and another 65 miles by wagon from Maysville to Lexington. Despite the long and risky journey, the Lexington markup on goods that made it safely from the East Coast would be 75–100 percent.[21]

This was the rough-and-tumble presteamboat era, memorialized in the tales of Mike Fink, the era of the downriver flatboat and the upriver keelboat—on the lower Kentucky River, the Ohio River, and the Mississippi River. The rivermen included both black and white Kentuckians, just as the crews on Athenian ships included both slaves and free men. Most of the free white men working on riverboats prided themselves, said one observer, "on the roughness and rudeness of their manners" and "their half-horse, half-alligator" way of life.[22] In the words of W. F. Axton, such a man was "fiercely if insecurely proud of his equality with any man in any station anywhere, as contemptuous of formal culture as he was ignorant, and crude and vulgar to the last degree." This was also what Axton called "the heyday of the 'chaw'" among laboring men on both water and land, a chaw being a piece of tobacco bitten off from a rope of twisted tobacco leaves "about a foot long . . . and back-braided upon itself into a neat package." A chaw would become a twist of "sweet plug" if the tobacco was "liberally

John Wesley Hunt, Hunt Morgan House Photographs. (Special Collections, University of Kentucky.)

laced with any handy sweetening agent, preferably alcoholic." The visual effect included "the ochre-stained beard, the dark ground-down teeth, and the arching brown trajectory of expectoration leaping through the air." From a practical rather than an aesthetic point of view, chaw had the distinct advantage of not requiring the fire necessary for smoking tobacco before the invention of the safety match. Its other advantages? "Because tobacco is a powerful salivant, chewing kept a hot, sweating hand-laborer's mouth moist; it provided an instant antiseptic in case of a cut; and, because of its appetite-suppressing properties, it made the long stretch from breakfast at dawn to dinner at noon a little more endurable."[23]

The strenuous working world of the docks and the fields made possible the career trajectory of a shrewd entrepreneur like John Wesley Hunt. By 1801, he owned eleven slaves and raised hemp and grains, cattle, pigs, mules, and, of course, horses on his farm located about a mile outside Lexington on the Leestown Pike. Between 1803 and 1813, he operated a factory producing hemp bagging for cotton bales in partnership with the Scotsman John Brand, owning in 1812 a total of seventy-six slaves, forty of them boys sixteen and younger. He was among the first to ship hemp fiber and yarn up the Ohio River bound for Philadelphia and made an early connection with the rising Henry Clay. During the War of 1812, Clay worked as an agent for his father-in-law's hemp manufacturing company, Thomas Hart and Son, while also becoming a national politician and speaker of the House working to protect and promote Bluegrass hemp. Both Clay and Hunt hoped that profit from hemp products would come, not only by way of selling bale bagging and rope to the expanding Cotton Kingdom of the Deep South and the lower Mississippi valley, but also by way of the U.S. Navy's purchasing cloth and cordage to outfit its masted warships. Their recurring hopes for navy contracts were ultimately frustrated, partly by foreign competition (Russian hemp, grown in a climate better suited to dew rotting), partly by the high cost of transportation to East Coast shipyards. Attempting to enhance commercial efficiency and flow, Clay and his fellow National Republicans (especially entrepreneurs in Mason County) succeeded by 1830 in gaining state legislative support for constructing a "macadamized" turnpike, its roadbed paved with crushed rock, whose boosters hoped it would stretch from Maysville, on the Ohio River, to Washington, then on to Paris and Lexington. President Andrew Jackson slowed the project down when he issued his "Maysville Road Veto" of a federal bill that would provide national funds for the turnpike's completion. During the early 1830s, Maysville (incorporated as a city in 1833) turned its attention to steamboat connections with the downriver port of Cincinnati. Clay's National Republicans became interested in building a railroad that would connect Lexington and the Queen City, whose boosters envisioned an Athens of the West on the north bank of the Ohio River.[24]

John Wesley Hunt was hardly the first Lexingtonian to invest in hemp manufacturing, and the ongoing importance of slave hiring to both agricultural slaveholders and hemp manufacturers is evident in the papers of John Breckinridge, the Virginia native who came to Kentucky in the 1790s and founded one of the important political dynasties in U.S. history. As James Klotter has informed us, in 1801 Breckinridge decided that he had six slaves who were not really needed at his farm, Cabell's Dale, some sixteen hundred acres about six miles from town, and therefore he rented them out to the "ropewalk," or hemp cordage and rope factory, operated by a Peter January.[25] January was an early settler from Pennsylvania who, like Hunt, became a merchant in Lexington. His two-story house, built in the 1780s, is reputed to have been among the very first brick homes in Lexington. Randolph Hollingsworth tells us that his son and business partner, Thomas January, operated ropewalks and bagging factories that "took up much of the inner city area near Transylvania University."[26] His philanthropic activities included promoting the establishment by 1816 of the Lunatic Asylum of Lexington (which became Eastern State Hospital), the second public institution of its kind in the United States. Another important example of local philanthropy made possible in part by the hemp business involved the architectural product of a $70,000 bequest to Transylvania University by the manufacturer James Morrison, after whom the neoclassical Morrison Hall is named.

Let us step back for a moment and attempt a concise overview of the general evolution taken in the Bluegrass by the market economy and its working world after Kentucky entered the Union as an independent slave state in 1792. A very helpful guide is James F. Hopkins.[27] He reports that farmers and planters who left the Atlantic coastal plains of Virginia and the Carolinas and moved across the mountains to "Kentuck" in the late eighteenth century expected to, and in fact did, raise some tobacco. But they found that tobacco cultivation in the Bluegrass was not a sufficiently profitable use of their land and slaves. Hence, they turned to a more diversified regime of livestock, grains, and hemp as their major crops. Settlers from north as well as south of the Mason-Dixon line recognized early the economic potential of cultivating hemp and processing the harvest. Hemp in particular came to be known in Kentucky as a "nigger crop" because the work required to harvest and process the plant was physically demanding, if seasonal, and also very dirty. It was often said that no one could develop as much expertise in handling the crop as a healthy male Negro slave, motivated to greater exertion under a weekly task system of labor. The former Lexington slave Milton Clarke recalled in the mid-1840s that working in a spinning and weaving factory was "the worst kind of slavery in Kentucky." Business managers often hired boys ages ten to fifteen, whose owners might then sell them downriver to Louisiana between the ages of eighteen and twenty.[28]

The hemp business suffered a severe downturn in the Bluegrass after the War of 1812 and the Panic of 1819. But John Wesley Hunt did not suffer because he had been shrewd enough to sell his factory and sixty slaves in 1813. He invested much of his money in the profitable stock of the new Second Bank of the United States, chartered in 1816, and became one of only thirty-three investors in the country with more than one thousand shares. The president of the national bank's branch in Lexington was none other than James Morrison.

Hemp returned to profitability with the cotton-based "flush times" of the mid-1830s. By midcentury, over half the nation's hemp crop came from Kentucky and its more than 3,500 hemp plantations. Among Fayette County's 844 farms and plantations, 508 produced fiber, some linen, but mostly hemp. To be sure, hemp was quickly supplanted by burley tobacco after the Civil War. As a 2005 master's thesis at the University of Kentucky in the discipline of historic preservation observes: "Hemp faded as an industry [during the latter decades of the nineteenth century], [and] the culture of hemp died out and left no residue of its once-vast presence in Lexington. Tobacco, the crop that replaced hemp, is undergoing a similar fate today as many tobacco-related buildings are disappearing and leaving no trace of their existence."[29] But we have a clear and concise description of hemp factories from Randolph Hollingsworth: "Like the textile factories built around the same time in Lowell, Massachusetts, the Lexington rope and bagging factories were long and multistoried. Usually the first floor consisted of a ropewalk and a room for combing the hemp. On the second floor was a spinning room and sometimes sleeping quarters for the slaves; the third floor held the looms for weaving the bagging, and the fourth floor was where twine was spun."[30]

Bluegrass Kentuckians at midcentury continued to stress the importance of hemp to their region's economy. In 1849, a delegate to the state constitutional convention—his name William C. Bullitt, representing the Outer Bluegrass county of Jefferson—insisted: "The free states do not, and will not raise hemp and tobacco. Kentucky and Missouri have the monopoly of this great article hemp. This, as long as slavery remains must be the case." At the same time, Bullitt argued, Kentuckians did not have to worry about the prospect of having too many blacks in the state because the market demand for slaves from Deep South cotton and sugar plantations, aided and abetted by the commonwealth's easy access to that market by virtue of the Ohio and Mississippi Rivers, had the effect of keeping the population of slaves at what Bullitt called "a healthy point."[31] Most slaveholders, following the time-honored lead of Thomas Jefferson, may not have known the exact dimensions of this "healthy point," but they harbored real fears that, once this point had been exceeded, their society would become increasingly prone to slave revolts and the terrifying prospect of a bloody "race war" between vengeful blacks and retaliating whites.[32]

As long as strong demand for slaves from the Deep South continued, slavery in the Bluegrass remained a solid investment. The ongoing
importance of both slavery and hemp in the 1850s can be seen in the
career of John Hunt Morgan, who became a legendary Confederate cavalry commander during the Civil War. His father, Calvin Morgan, married John Wesley Hunt's daughter Henrietta, who inherited the mansion
Hopemont at Gratz Park after her father's death in 1849. As James A.
Ramage has suggested, John Hunt Morgan seems to have learned from
his mother's family that "property ownership was the key to honor," or
a gentlemanly reputation; from his father's family he learned about the
importance of the manly martial virtues to that same honor, whether on
wartime battlefields or on the dueling ground.[33] After serving as an officer
in the Mexican War, in 1848 Morgan married Rebecca Bruce, the daughter of Sanders Bruce, a partner with Benjamin Gratz in the hemp business.
With financial help from his mother, he bought sixteen slaves for rental
to hemp manufacturers. In 1853, he and his brother became partners in a
hemp factory located on West Main Street near the Lexington Cemetery.
By 1859, he owned thirty-three slaves, and the hemp factory also hired
both free blacks and other slaves. He also became involved with the slave
trader Lewis Robards, active at the Cheapside auctions, and a noted pur-
veyor of light-skinned "fancy girls."

John Hunt Morgan, like his grandfather John Wesley Hunt, became
a prominent member of what can be termed the *slaveholding gentry* of
Lexington and its environs. A few early settlers of the Inner Bluegrass
migrated as ready-made "landed gentlemen," the most notable example
probably being Robert Carter Harrison, a member of the so-called first
families of Virginia who arrived in Fayette County in 1805 with just over
one hundred slaves.[34]

To be sure, fifth-century Athens had a decidedly more authentic aristocratic tradition than did early nineteenth-century Kentucky, which had
made the transition from a frontier district of the Old Dominion to independent statehood only in the 1790s. The Athenian orator and politician
after whom the Age of Pericles (ca. 461–429) is named was descended
through his father, Xanthippus, from the noble family of the Alcmae-
conids.[35] However, we also find in classical Athens parvenus whose rise
to political prominence reflected "new money" made in manufacturing
with slave labor: to wit, the late fifth-century "demagogues" Cleon, whose
wealth came from his family's tannery business, and Cleophon, whose
family's affluence depended on its lyre-making slaves.[36] Lexington's obvious counterpart to Pericles, Henry Clay, could not claim descent from an

aristocratic family, but, when he arrived from the Old Dominion in 1797, at age twenty, he possessed both a license to practice law and helpful connections to members of the Virginia elite like George Wythe and Robert Brooke.

The importance of slavery and slaveholding to the economic and social worlds of both antebellum Lexington and classical Athens was, as we would expect, reflected in political life during the eras of Pericles and Henry Clay. Donald Kagan's evaluation of Pericles as "a politician of the rarest talents" could well be applied to Henry Clay.[37] The oratory of both leaders offered paeans to freedom and independence; for them and their voting citizens, the slaves in their communities highlighted the clear and concrete distinction between the virtues of independent liberty and the perils of dependent servitude. The best-known speech by Pericles, his famous funeral oration of 431 BCE (as reported by Thucydides), praised Athens as "the school of Greece," an independent, self-governing city-state whose free, honorable, and versatile citizenry participated in a "democracy," so-called because "its administration favors the many instead of the few." The fallen soldiers whom Pericles memorialized had "thought fit to act boldly and trust in themselves. Thus choosing to die resisting, rather than to live submitting, they fled only from dishonor, but met danger face to face."[38] Among Henry Clay's half dozen favorite speeches was one delivered to the House of Representatives in January 1824 in support of the revolt of "christian Greece" against the tyrannical "dominion" of the imperial Ottoman Turk and its "fanatical and inimical religion." Denouncing those political opponents in the House who did not support sending a commissioner or agent of the U.S. government to "suffering and bleeding Greece," he exclaimed: "My lips have not yet learned to pronounce the sycophantic language of a degraded slave!" To those fearful of antagonizing the counterrevolutionary European powers of the Holy Alliance, he proclaimed that the United States "can bring into the field a million of freemen, ready to exhaust their last drop of blood, and to spend the last cent in defence of the country, its liberty, and its institutions." He exclaimed: "Men only become slaves who have ceased to resolve to be free."[39]

When Clay delivered this speech in early 1824, the "Virginia dynasty" of U.S. presidents was about to end with the retirement of James Monroe. Both Kentucky and the nation were well into the political transition from the relatively deferential republicanism of the founding fathers to the more raucously democratic era symbolized by Andrew Jackson. Two millennia earlier, Pericles had presided over what may have been the world's first democratic form of government. We need not dwell at length on the differences between the "direct democracy" exercised by citizens in the fairly compact Athenian city-state and the representative republicanism of the dramatically larger commonwealth of Kentucky. For our purposes, it is sufficient to understand the ways in which chattel slavery pervaded the social and economic worlds of Attica and the Inner Bluegrass while at the same time recognizing its connections with political and intellectual life in the two communities.[40]

In October 1842, Henry Clay delivered another memorable speech, this time in Richmond, Indiana. Here, on his way to Indianapolis, he was presented a petition asking that he set an example by freeing the slaves at his Ashland estate. Like most of his fellow slaveholders in the Bluegrass, and following the lead of many of the founding fathers, including Jefferson, Clay refused to defend slavery in the abstract. He called American slavery "a great evil" but insisted that "greater evils" would "inevitably flow from a sudden, general, and indiscriminant emancipation." The greatest evil would be the "revolting admixture" of blacks and whites, "alike offensive to God and man." Without the colonization of free blacks abroad, Kentuckians would face a racial "civil war," which would result in "the ultimate extermination or expulsion of the blacks." Clay, like Jefferson in 1776, sought to exclude his society from moral condemnation by insisting that slavery was "introduced and forced upon the colonies by the paramount law of England."[41] In so doing, he illustrated how different his own post-Enlightenment, post–natural rights cultural and political values were from those of classical Athenians like Plato and Aristotle. For ancient Greeks and Romans, slavery was simply one aspect of "an assumed hierarchy of the natural moral order, rather than a problem demanding moral scrutiny."[42]

Nonetheless, Clay insisted in 1842 that Kentucky law clearly and unambiguously recognized "the right of property in slaves" and condemned "the unfortunate agitation of the subject" by monomaniacal abolitionists. He reported owning about fifty slaves, worth some $15,000, and asked whether the abolitionists were willing to pay him that sum for the freedom of his slaves. Near the close of his speech came a wonderful piece of rhetoric: "Go home, and mind your own business, and leave other people to take of theirs."[43]

Clay devoted much of his long political career in Washington, DC, to defusing sectional conflict between the slave South and the free North, hoping thereby to preserve what he and most of his fellow citizens saw as a glorious American republic bequeathed to them by the founding fathers.

Nonetheless, less than a decade after his death, southern Confederates and northern Unionists began a long and lethal war over the perpetuity of both the U.S. Constitution and chattel slavery in America. The uncompensated abolition of human bondage between 1863 and 1865, something envisioned by precious few Americans in 1861, did far more than the rising commercial supremacy of Louisville at midcentury to mark the end of Lexington as Kentucky's Athens of the West. Two millennia earlier, Pericles' death did not presage the end of either democracy or slavery in classical Athens. However, the often-ironic law of unintended consequences did have its say in post-Periclean Athens, just as it did in Bluegrass Kentucky after Clay. The Peloponnesian War with Sparta, over whose beginnings Pericles presided before his death in 429, weakened the independence and power of the very city-state he loved and glorified.

Notes

1. Frederick Law Olmsted, *A Journey through Texas; or, A Saddle-Trip on the South-western Frontier* (1857), with a foreword by Larry McMurtry (Austin, TX, 1978), 17–18; and James D. Wright and Eric H. Christianson, "Transylvania University," in *The Kentucky Encyclopedia*, ed. John E. Kleber (Lexington, 1992), 894–96.

2. George W. Ranck, *History of Lexington, Kentucky: Its Early Annals and Recent Progress* (1872; Lexington, 1970), 303. One of the first people to describe Lexington as the "Athens of the West" seems to have been the New England clergyman Timothy Flint in 1816. See James C. Klotter, "Central Kentucky's 'Athens of the West' Image in the Nation and in History" (in this volume).

3. A member of the Anthology Society "is credited with making the first reference to Boston as 'the Athens of America.'" He was William Tudor, "an enterprising merchant who soon became involved with his brother Frederick in the ice trade." Thomas H. O'Connor, *The Athens of America: Boston, 1825–1845* (Amherst, MA, 2006), 115.

4. In 2002, the public relations office of Northwestern University, just north of Chicago, publicized on its Web site an exhibit celebrating the 150th anniversary of the founding of Northwestern and Evanston; the exhibit identified *Athens of the West* as the label "used to attract students, faculty and residents to the growing North Shore community" beginning in the 1850s. Two years later, in 2004, the Web site of the University of California, Berkeley, announced a publication that used the same moniker, *Athens of the West*, to describe the Berkeley community of the late nineteenth century and the early twentieth.

5. M. I. Finley, *Ancient Slavery and Modern Ideology* (New York, 1980), 79. For the importance of this distinction to recent historians of the Old South, see Ira Berlin, *Generations of Captivity: A History of African-American Slaves* (Cambridge, MA, 2003), 8–9; and S. D. Bowman, "Synthesizing Southern Slavery: A Review Essay," *Register of the Kentucky Historical Society* 103 (2005): 736. According to one recent classicist, "slave

economies" are "those in which the contribution of a large number of unfree persons to the totality of wealth production is so substantial that a society's overall production, distribution, and consumption is highly dependent on slave labor." Edward E. Cohen, *The Athenian Nation* (Princeton, NJ, 2000), 130–31.

6. Keith Bradley, "Europe: Ancient World," in *An Historical Guide to World Slavery*, ed. Seymour Drescher and Stanley L. Engerman (New York, 1998), 193. In the words of Randolph Hollingsworth, Lexingtonians viewed "possession of slaves" as "evidence of wealth, class, and prestige." Randolph Hollingsworth, *Lexington, Queen of the Bluegrass* (Charleston, SC, 2004), 42–43.

7. Barbara Tuchman, *A Distant Mirror: The Calamitous Fourteenth Century* (New York, 1979).

8. See Marion B. Lucas, *A History of Blacks in Kentucky*, vol. 1, *From Slavery to Segregation, 1760–1891*, 2nd ed. (Frankfort, 2003), xv–xxii; Hollingsworth, *Lexington, Queen of the Bluegrass*, 42–43; and Lowell H. Harrison and James C. Klotter, *A New History of Kentucky* (Lexington, 1997), 99–100.

9. Harrison and Klotter, *A New History of Kentucky*, 117–18. On Garrett Davis and his antebellum career as a proslavery nativist and Unionist, the best study is Stephen Pickering, "The Disunion of Garrett Davis: Nativism, Slavery, and the Transformation of Kentucky Politics" (doctoral seminar paper, Department of History, University of Kentucky, 2008).

10. Harold D. Tallant, *Evil Necessity: Slavery and Political Culture in Antebellum Kentucky* (Lexington, 2003), 155–58.

11. Quoted in Stephen B. Oates, *Abraham Lincoln: The Man behind the Myths* (New York, 1984), 101–2. See also James M. McPherson, *Abraham Lincoln and the Second American Revolution* (New York, 1991), 32–34; Philip Shaw Paludan, *The Presidency of Abraham Lincoln* (Lawrence, KS, 1994), 125–28; Lowell H. Harrison, *Lincoln of Kentucky* (Lexington, 2000), 227–33; and Robert Murray, "The Ideal Society: Lincoln's Call for Gradual Emancipation and the Kentucky Delegation" (doctoral seminar paper, Department of History, University of Kentucky, 2008).

12. Barbara Tuchman, *The Pursuit of Folly: From Troy to Vietnam* (New York, 1984).

13. We do not have nearly as reliable statistics for the population of classical Athens and Attica, especially the slave population, as we do for antebellum Kentucky. See Finley, *Ancient Slavery and Modern Ideology*, 35–35, 80; Paul Anthony Cartledge, "Slavery, Greek," in *The Oxford Companion to Classical Civilization*, ed. Simon Hornblower and Anthony Spawforth (Oxford, 1998), 670–71; Cohen, *The Athenian Nation*, 17; N. R. E. Fisher, *Slavery in Classical Greece*, 2nd ed. (London, 2001), 35–36; and Paul Woodruff, *First Democracy: The Challenge of an Ancient Idea* (New York, 2005), 42–43. My thanks to the University of Kentucky classicist and my colleague Bruce Holle for recommending Fisher's valuable book to me and for offering helpful comments on an early draft of this essay.

14. See esp. Fisher, *Slavery in Classical Greece*, 47–53; and Woodruff, *First Democracy*, 43.

15. Bruce Thornton, *Greek Ways: How the Greeks Created Western Civilization* (New York, 2000), 68.

16. The law of 1833 could be and was easily circumvented. From the 1830s to the 1850s, "an estimated 2,500 slaves a year were exported from Kentucky." Hollingsworth, *Lexington, Queen of the Bluegrass*, 42.

17. Ibid., 48–53.

18. The label *conservative emancipationists*, as distinct from *radicals and abolitionists*, comes from Harold D. Tallant, "Slavery," in Kleber, ed., *The Kentucky Encyclopedia*, 828. Again, the antislavery movement in the nation and Kentucky represented the post-eighteenth-century discomfort with slavery as incompatible with the powerful principles of both natural rights and free labor; only seldom was it racially egalitarian.

19. On both continuities and discontinuities between ancient and "modern" slavery as fundamentally "dehumanizing," see esp. David Brion Davis, *Inhuman Bondage: The Rise and Fall of Slavery in the New World* (New York, 2006).

20. Juliet E. K. Walker, *Free Frank: A Black Pioneer on the Antebellum Frontier* (Lexington, 1983). See also Lucas, *From Slavery to Segregation*, 112, 115; and James C. Klotter and Freda C. Klotter, *A Concise History of Kentucky* (Lexington, 2008), 96–97.

21. See James A. Ramage, *John Wesley Hunt: Pioneer Merchant, Manufacturer, and Financier* (Lexington, 1974).

22. Matthew Carey (in 1828) quoted in William E. Ellis, *The Kentucky River* (Lexington, 2000), 8–9.

23. W. F. Axton, *Tobacco and Kentucky* (Lexington, 1975), 55–59.

24. See Craig Thompson Friend, *Along the Maysville Road: The Early American Republic in the Trans-Appalachian West* (Knoxville, TN, 2005), 251–69. My thanks to my graduate student Will Stone for calling my attention to this book.

25. James C. Klotter, *The Breckinridges of Kentucky, 1760–1981* (Lexington, 1986), 136–41.

26. Hollingsworth, *Lexington, Queen of the Bluegrass*, 27.

27. James F. Hopkins, *A History of the Hemp Industry in Kentucky* (1951), updated ed. (Lexington, 1998).

28. *Narratives of the Sufferings of Lewis and Milton Clarke, Sons of a Soldier of the Revolution, during a Captivity of More Than Twenty Years among the Slaveholders of Kentucky, One of the So-Called Christian States of North America. Dictated by Themselves* (Boston, 1846), 126–29.

29. Amanda Lee Schraner, "The Demise of Lexington's Historic Industrial Tobacco Landscape: A Study of the City's Vanishing Built Environment and Recommendations for Its Preservation" (master's project in historic preservation, University of Kentucky College of Design, 2005), 1. My thanks to Rachelle Green at the University of Kentucky for bringing this thesis to my attention.

30. Hollingsworth, *Lexington, Queen of the Bluegrass*, 43.

31. Bullitt quoted in Hopkins, *History of the Hemp Industry in Kentucky*, 29–30.

32. On the fears of Jefferson and later slaveholders, often focused on the example

of the slave revolution in Haiti at the turn of the century, see Davis, *Inhuman Bondage*, 170–74, 270–71.

33. James A. Ramage, *Rebel Raider: The Life of General John Hunt Morgan* (Lexington, 1986), 14–18.

34. Philip D. Morgan, *Slave Counterpoint: Black Culture in the Eighteenth-Century Chesapeake and Lowcountry* (Chapel Hill, NC, 1998), 669.

35. Christian Meier, *Athens: A Portrait of the City in Its Golden Age*, trans. Robert and Rita Kimber (London, 1998), 5–6. Again, my thanks to Bruce Holle for recommending this volume.

36. Fisher, *Slavery in Classical Greece*, 50; and Sarah B. Pomeroy, Stanley M. Burstein, Walter Donlan, and Jennifer Tolbert Roberts, *Ancient Greece: A Political, Social, and Cultural History* (New York, 1999), 294–95, 315.

37. Donald Kagan, *The Peloponnesian War* (New York, 2003), 97–98.

38. Kenneth J. Atchidy, ed., *The Classical Greek Reader* (New York, 1996), 106–10. With regard to the tyrannical power that imperial Athens exercised over other parts of the Greek world, Pericles referred only "to the empire which we now possess." See also Pomeroy et al., *Ancient Greece*, 291–92; Cohen, *The Athenian Nation*, 94–99; and Meier, *Athens*, 400–420.

39. Daniel Mallory, ed., *The Life and Speeches of Henry Clay*, 2 vols. (Hartford, CT, 1855), 1:488–95; Robert V. Remini, *Henry Clay, Statesman for the Union* (New York, 1991), 222–25.

40. For studies that emphasize the connections between black slavery and white male democracy in the antebellum South, see George M. Fredrickson, *The Black Image in the White Mind: The Debate on Afro-American Character and Destiny, 1817–1914* (New York, 1971); J. William Harris, *Plain Folk and Gentry in a Slave Society: White Liberty and Black Slavery in Augusta's Hinterlands* (Middletown, CT, 1985); and S. D. Bowman, *Masters and Lords: Mid-Nineteenth-Century U.S. Planters and Prussian Junkers* (New York, 1993).

41. Mallory, ed., *Life and Speeches of Henry Clay*, 2:595–600.

42. Seymour Drescher, "Moral Issues," in Drescher and Engerman, eds., *Historical Guide to World Slavery*, 283.

43. Speech in Richmond, Indiana, October 1, 1842, in *The Papers of Henry Clay*, ed. James F. Hopkins et al., 10 vols. and suppl. (Lexington, 1959–1992), 9:781.

Part 2

Facets of Life

❧ 4

Slavery and Abolition in Kentucky
"'Patter-rollers' were everywhere"

Gerald L. Smith

On June 15, 1902, the *Owensboro Messenger* published an interview with an African American named Daniel Daly, believed to be the oldest resident of Daviess County, Kentucky. Known as Uncle Dan to the community, Daly was described as a "very intelligent old fellow" with "a splendid memory." He claimed to be "at least ninety-nine years old possibly one hundred." While sitting on his son Amos's front porch at 917 Lewis Street, Daly vividly shared his memories of west Kentucky during the period of slavery. He described an unsettled region occupied by an abundance of large wild animals, the experience of seeing the first steamboat on the Ohio River, and personal encounters with Native Americans. "Numerous bands of Indians roamed around," he said, "but they were for the most part friendlies [*sic*], and generally behaved themselves if given a drink of whiskey, and we had a cellar full of wines and brandy." The hunting skills of the Indians especially impressed Daly. "I have seen, many a time, an Indian shoot a deer through and through with his bow and arrow with his horse on the dead run."[1]

Daly's recall of a wild region offers a rare insight into the relationship between Kentucky slaves and Native Americans, but it was his raw discussion of the "old slavery days" that sheds light on both slavery and abolition in the state. "The slaves in those days that had good masters and mistresses," recalled Daly, "were generally happy and well-provided for and had good medical attention when they were sick, for a nigger was worth something in those days." "All the money we could make working for other people during the Christmas week," continued Daly, "we were allowed to keep, but some of our neighboring masters were not so good, and wouldn't even allow their slaves any holiday." However, "at Christmas time we were sometimes allowed to visit the neighborings [*sic*] farms, but the 'patter-rollers' were everywhere, and it was 'run, nigger, run or the patter-roller catch you.'"[2]

Nearly forty years after the demise of slavery, the song associated with patter-rollers was apparently still etched in Daly's memory:

Run, nigger, run de patteroll catch you,
Run, nigger run fo' it's almos day,
Massa is kind an' Missus is true,
But ef you don' mind, de patteroll catch you.[3]

The patter-rollers—the white slave patrol of the South—constituted an integral part of a deeply rooted system designed to preserve the institution of slavery and protect whites from black insurrection. South Carolina created a patrol in 1704, Virginia officially established its patrol in 1727,[4] and, in 1799, the Kentucky General Assembly passed an act authorizing county courts to divide into a maximum of five districts and hire a company of patrollers for each district. Each company would have a captain and not exceed four patrollers. While the court determined how many hours each patroller would work each month, the number could not be less than twelve hours for each month of service. The captain received "four shillings" per twelve hours of service, and the other patrollers three shillings for the same period. To earn those funds, the men searched out unlawful gatherings of slaves. Slaves "strolling about" without permission could "receive any number of lashes on his or her bare back, at the discretion of the captain of the patrol, not exceeding ten." Slaves brought before the magistrate could receive "any number of lashes at the discretion of such magistrate, not exceeding thirty-nine, on his or her bare back."[5]

Living in a border state situated on the Ohio River, whites constantly had to guard their property from the liberating works of abolitionists, free blacks, and other runaway slaves. Because slavery and antislavery sentiments evolved simultaneously in Kentucky, an ongoing tug-of-war took place between those who viewed slavery as a "necessary evil" and those who appreciated its personal and economic benefits. Trapped in the middle of the political and ideological debates on slavery were the slaves themselves, men and women who wanted to be treated with respect as human beings and not counted simply as a piece of property.

As early as the mid-eighteenth century, African Americans had been brought to Kentucky as slaves. They accompanied the early explorers, long hunters, and settlers who were mesmerized by the beauty of the land. Kentucky possessed a fertile soil and abundant wildlife during the frontier years. Rivers and streams flowed with catfish, bass, trout, and bluegill. Walnut, oak, maple, and beech trees filled the forests. Attracted to this land of opportunity, white settlers came down the Ohio River or across the Wilderness Road, from Virginia, Maryland, North Carolina, and Pennsylvania. It was not an easy trip. The Wilderness Road extended across the Allegheny Mountains through the Cumberland Gap. The path had originally been laid by herds of bison and other animals, but there was not a preexisting path to the Bluegrass region.[6] Black slaves were forced to make this treacherous journey. For them, the "buzzell about Kentuck" meant very little.[7] They had no choices to make, no opportunities to pursue. They were chattel, property, expected to ease the transition for white families moving west by providing cheap labor. They were brought by their masters and mistresses to clear the land, pack supplies, prepare meals, build forts, erect fences, construct homesteads, and help defend white families from imminent attacks by Indians. Some settlers, like John Breckinridge, hired overseers to lead their slaves to Kentucky in advance to prepare for the family's arrival. Breckinridge's overseer, John Thompson, reported on the difficulties of the trip: "Our Negroes [were] Every day out of heart & sick." He further added: "When the Negroes were wet & almost ready to give out, then I came forward with my good friend whiskey & Once every hour unless they were Sleep I was Oblige[d] to give them whiskey."[8] The hardship of the trip to Kentucky did not dissuade the determination of white emigrants. In the 1790s, Daniel Drake, who settled in Maysville, recalled noticing the "caravans of travelers, mounted on horseback, and the gangs of negroes on foot."[9]

Not all slaves willingly accompanied their owners to Kentucky. Some made difficult choices to be with family members. Newspaper advertisements reported slaves from Virginia who ran away before the journey. Others refused to be separated from their families and made huge sacrifices to come to the state. In 1794, the *Winchester Advertiser* reported that a slave named Tom had been given permission to visit his wife in another county. Her owner, a man named Botts, had left for Kentucky. "I very much suspect," wrote Tom's owner, "that he intends pursing his rout [*sic*] to Kentucky where the above mentioned Botts is about to carry his wife."[10] Some slaves sought to negotiate with their owners regarding the trip. For example, John Breckinridge's sister-in-law, Mary Cabell, reluctantly did not send a slave child named Sarah because of the pleas of the child's slave mother: "I did my best to send little Sarah there to go with them but Violet would not agree to part with her so I proposed for her to go with her daughter." Cabell described Violet "as good a slave Ever was born . . . how ever she said she would not go to Cantuckey nor let Sarah until I deye'd unless Stephen her Husband could go with them." Because of Violet's negotiations, the Cabell family began to make arrangements to purchase Stephen from the neighbor planter. The Cabells understood the value of having cooperative slaves joining them in Kentucky.[11]

As whites and black slaves settled into frontier Kentucky, their dependence on one another for protection and defense evolved as a result of the violent encounters they had with Native Americans. Daniel Boone, Kentucky's most noted frontiersman, was forced to negotiate with a black slave named Pompey over the surrender of Fort Boonesborough in 1778. The slaves who lived at Boonesborough defended the fort and helped keep it from being seized. In 1782, when Indians attacked a white women and her daughter in Crab Orchard, Kentucky, a crippled slave fought with one of the Indians who entered the cabin until the young girl killed the attacker with an ax.[12]

But the most distinguished slave of the frontier years was Monk Estill. Originally owned by John Estill, who founded Estill Station in Madison County, Monk played a major role in protecting and rescuing settlers from Indian attacks. He was a musician and hunter who taught Daniel Boone the art of making gunpowder. And he also fathered the first black child born at Boonesborough.[13] The early years in Kentucky called for unlikely measures of unity. A consistent level of interdependence existed between slaves and whites on the frontier, but this relationship was not based on mutual respect and equality. It was a matter of survival and opportunity. For blacks, it centered on survival. For whites, it involved both survival and opportunity. African Americans, thought to be biologically inferior to whites, were a convenient source of free labor and an investment in their future. "In essence," writes the historian J. Blaine Hudson, "enslaved African-Americans were the farm machines and the household appliances of this era which whites believed necessary both for their comfort and for the productivity of their lands and other enterprises."[14]

Slavery grew rapidly in Kentucky. As of 1790, there were 11,830 slaves in the state and 114 free blacks. African Americans constituted a little more than 18 percent of the population. Over the next forty years, the Kentucky African American population grew at a steady rate, higher than that of whites. As of 1830, 165,213 slaves and 4,917 free blacks constituted 24.7 percent of the Kentucky population. The historian Todd H. Barnett posits: "The experiences of settlers to Kentucky reveal that these borderland southerners were interested in maintaining slavery, their wealth, their peculiar households, and their status as slaveholders, but without the pressing labor requirements of a staple crop, slavery was, for a time at least, becoming more vulnerable."[15] He notes that Virginia migrants of the late eighteenth century and the early nineteenth engaged in more diversified agricultural practices that included corn, grains, thread fibers, and livestock. Planting tobacco posed a risk to the soil, and it, along with hemp, seemed initially too expensive to transport. Spanish control of the Mississippi interfered with potential profits. Drawing on the experiences of John Breckinridge, who brought a large slave labor force to Kentucky in the 1790s, Barnett claims that Breckinridge operated like other Fayette slaveholders who used their slaves to work in a diverse agriculture system: "The value of his slaves' labor was not being fully used, but the bondsmen were equally important to him as symbols of his own wealth and property and as inheritances for his children." According to Barnett: "In the state of Kentucky generally, bondmen were present and used in the fields, but there is a little evidence to suggest that slavery was a crucial form of labor to the economy of early Kentucky." He continues: "Slaveholders had brought bondmen into the state from Virginia and elsewhere, but without specific labor designs in mind. For them slavery was a traditional, inherited facet of their families lives and their culture generally. They had no particular plans for their slaves, they brought them anyway because of their value as investments or symbols of wealth, and because they could perform whatever odd jobs that were necessary in creating new farms and plantations in the frontier wilderness." In sum, Barnett argues that slavery in Kentucky "had matured, and it represented a quite different less crucial labor system and was no longer the institution it had been in its infancy in North America." To substantiate his argument, he notes the slavery debate surrounding the formation of Kentucky's first state constitution in 1792, the religious opposition to slavery, and the passage of moderate slave codes.[16] But slave-population statistics, slave-hiring practices, and the actual enhancement of slave codes within the first decade of the state's founding raise other factors regarding the vulnerability of slavery in Kentucky before 1800.

To be sure, initial uncertainty existed about slavery in the state, but the large numbers of slaves brought to it by their masters seemed to resolve the question. Even though the vast majority of whites in Kentucky did not own slaves, they, nevertheless, realized the tangible and intangible values of preserving the institution of slavery in a border state like Kentucky. Clearly, the pervasiveness of slave patrols in Kentucky counties reveals the determination of slaveholders to protect and monitor slavery. James Farley, who had been enslaved in Virginia and Kentucky, noted how the worship activities of slaves were subject to the permission of the slave patrol. "One time when they were singing, Ride on King Jesus, No man can hinder Thee," recalled Farley, "the padderollers told them to stop or they would show him whether they could be hindered or not."[17] Patrollers rode horses and walked the roads inspecting slave passes and questioning slaves who were outside their master's property. These defenders of slavery confiscated items slaves were not supposed to have, such as guns and horses.[18] Their objective was clear: *protect and serve* in both rural and urban environments. Given Kentucky's geographic location, defenders of slavery relied on the work of patrols throughout the state. As the antislavery movement garnered nationwide momentum, it became necessary to closely monitor slave activities. In January 1833, George Payton was appointed captain of the patrol in the Washington district of Mason County, with three men under his command. In November 1837, four men were appointed to the patrol in Fayette. In December 1859, Thomas Thompson was appointed to patrol the first and second wards of the city of Lexington. In January 1861, Richard P. Mitchell of Mason County and two other men were appointed as "a special patrol to guard the Ohio River." Daviess County appointed forty-two men to patrol the Knottsville district during May 1861.[19] And on and on. By the eve of the Civil War, the need to defend slavery was entrenched in the state's social and political fabric.

The defense of slavery in Kentucky is rooted in the 1792 state convention. George Nicholas, a Virginia lawyer who had migrated to Kentucky, argued that the Virginia Compact, the Bible, the expense of freeing and purchasing slaves, and the threat of racial miscegenation provided enough reason to protect the existence of slavery in the state constitution.[20] Opposition to slavery comprised two ideologies: those who wanted to end slavery immediately and emancipationists who favored a gradual end to the institution. The Reverend David Rice led the antislavery delegation during the 1792 state convention. A Presbyterian minister, Rice considered slavery an immoral and unjust institution. Writing the first antislavery publication in Kentucky, entitled *Slavery Inconsistent with Justice and Good Policy*, he proposed a gradual emancipation of slaves, an end to the importation of slaves into the state, and the education of black men and women in order to prepare them for freedom. "As creatures of God, we are, with respect to liberty, all equal," he declared.[21] Nevertheless, Rice and his colleagues in the clergy could not garner enough support to abolish slavery in the commonwealth. Convention delegates voted to establish slavery in the state when they passed article 9 of the state constitution by a vote of 26–16.[22] Rice continued to own slaves, despite his writings and sermons seeking to abolish the institution in Kentucky.[23]

By 1800, slavery clearly was going to be a permanent social, political, and economic fixture in Kentucky. The number of slaves in the state increased more than 240 percent during the 1790s.[24] A traveler to Kentucky made an interesting observation about the new state: "The fertility of the lands generally vastly exceed any thing I ever saw before. But, O Alas! Here, as in Virginia, the slavery of the human race is unfortunately tolerated. Here the cries of the oppressed are heard."[25] Owners continued to find new ways to exploit black labor. For example, masters found slave hiring to be a useful means of getting the most out of their human investment. Slaves were leased to work as domestics, manufacturing laborers, and farmhands. Poor farmers who could afford only short-term labor welcomed the practice. John Breckinridge leased nineteen of his slaves during his term in Congress.[26] Slave owners took advantage of opportunities to advertise their slaves for hire. In Virginia, the *Winchester Gazette* advertised in 1794: "A very likely, lively, and healthy NEGRO MAN not more than twenty years old. He has been used to plantation work only. . . . I believe he would suit a person moving to the Western Country, as well as any Negro whatever."[27]

Slave hiring was available on a daily, weekly, or monthly basis. The practice was common in large Kentucky cities and was profitable for masters with a surplus of slaves both before and after 1800. Agents and traders made commissions from hiring slaves to work in hotels and restaurants and on railroads and ships. A firm in Louisville publicized the availability of "100 women and boys for brick-yards, draymen, etc., 40 men and boys for ropewalks, 40 men and boys for hotel waiters, and 50 Boys and Girls for tobacco stemmeries."[28]

As the number of slaves increased, whites adopted the state's first slave code in 1798. The law stipulated that slaves away from their residences more than four hours were required to have a pass in their possession. Employers, overseers, or slave family owners were the only persons authorized to issue these passes. Penalties were charged to those who violated the law. A slave without a pass was to receive "ten lashes on his or her bare back." White citizens could arrest slaves for "unlawful assemblies." City ordinances also restricted slave mobility. Under a Louisville ordinance, no more than three blacks were allowed to assemble in public or at the market. In Henderson, Kentucky, slaves who violated a 10:00 P.M. curfew were given twenty lashes. Paris, Kentucky, officials prohibited slaves from coming in the city unless they had a pass. And Lexington authorities forbade large crowds of blacks gathering on the weekends.[29] In 1811, the state legislature declared four crimes warranted the death penalty when committed by slaves. They included "conspiracy and rebellion, administering poison with intent to kill, voluntary manslaughter, and rape of a white woman." By 1860, burglary, robbery, arson, and wounding a white person with intent to kill had been added to the list.[30]

While slave prices and moral convictions kept the vast majority of white Kentuckians from owning slaves, these reasons did not discourage others from seeking opportunities to profit from slave labor. The largest concentration of enslaved African Americans existed in the Bluegrass region, where the soil was rich for agricultural production. By 1810, African Americans in Fayette, Jessamine, Jefferson, Scott, and Woodford Counties constituted 30 percent of the population. Western Kentucky had the next largest percentage of blacks. Henderson, Daviess, Christian, Warren, and Trigg Counties had steadily rising black populations throughout the antebellum period. Eastern Kentucky and the Jackson Purchase (the region west of the Tennessee River) had the lowest populations of blacks.[31] The land, the slow development of the towns in the region, and perhaps their location near the river determined the growth of slavery.

Since the early twentieth century, scholars have written about slavery in Kentucky. Most of these early studies described black enslavement in the state as mild, benign, and humane. In 1918, Ivan McDougle published *Slavery in Kentucky, 1792–1865*. According to McDougle: "In this commonwealth slavery was decidedly patriarchal. The slave was not such an unfortunate creature as some have pictured him. He usually had set apart for himself and his family a house which was located near the master's mansion. While this home may have been a rude cabin made of small logs, with a roof covered with splits and an earthen floor, likely as not the master's son was attending school a few weeks in the year in a neighborhood log cabin which boasted of no more luxuries than the humble slave dwelling. The servant and his family were well fed and had plenty of domestic cloth for all necessary wearing apparel." To emphasize this point, he cited the description of the quality of clothing worn by runaway slaves in newspaper advertisements. Aside from housing and clothing, he noted the Saturdays, Sundays, and holidays that slaves had off from work and the religious instruction they received as further evidence to support his interpretation of slavery in Kentucky.[32]

Additionally, McDougle claimed that slavery in Kentucky was not profitable to Kentucky planters. "As has often been said of the Kentucky situation," he wrote, "the program was to use negroes to raise corn to feed hogs to feed negroes, who raised more corn to feed more hogs."[33] Mc-Dougle was not alone in his interpretation of slavery in Kentucky.

By 1940, when J. Winston Coleman Jr. published his exhaustive study *Slavery Times in Kentucky*, the basic interpretation of Kentucky slavery had changed very little. Coleman noted how masters and slaves labored along-side one another in the fields, fought together against Indians, and were buried together in family cemeteries. He posited that slavery in Kentucky "was the mildest that existed anywhere in the world."[34] Drawing on the diaries and travel journals of whites, Coleman concluded that slaves in Kentucky received better housing, clothes, and food and engaged in bet-ter working conditions than northern white workers and slaves farther south.[35] "Generally speaking," he wrote, "the slaves were a happy, con-tented and carefree race; well-fed, as their looks testified, well-lodged and not overworked."[36]

Within the last two decades, scholars have begun to examine more closely the topic of slavery and abolition in Kentucky. Marion Lucas's 1992 general history of the black experience during the nineteenth century pro-vides a solid and impressive source of material on slavery that challenges earlier interpretations. He writes: "Kentucky slaves seemingly had little to look forward to but the 'setting of the sun.'"[37] Amy Young and J. Blaine Hudson's study "Slave Life at Oxmoor" focuses on the treatment of slaves on a plantation near Louisville. Using primary and secondary sources, Young and Hudson "deconstruct the biases" that have led to "inaccuracies in interpretations." Instead of relying solely on the perceptions that slave owners had of their slaves, they examined what slaves and masters were actually doing on the plantation.[38] Their research, along with that of other scholars writing on slavery in Kentucky, reveal the complexity of the slave experience in the state during the antebellum period. To interpret slavery in Kentucky merely as more humane and less harsh than other parts of the south clearly oversimplifies and misrepresents the realities of the very "peculiar institution."[39]

To be sure, slavery in Kentucky was, in the words of scholars, "dif-ferent" from slavery in the Lower South. Most slaves worked alongside their masters on farms that housed an average of five bondsmen. Only 20 percent of Kentucky's enslaved blacks worked in an agricultural environ-ment of more than twenty slaves. Kentucky did not have a climate condu-cive for the production of labor-intensive crops such as cotton, rice, and sugar; however, Kentucky slaves did work hard for their masters. They built and repaired barns and fences, tended livestock, plowed fields, planted gardens, and cut tobacco and hemp. In the Bluegrass area, hemp was dependent on slave labor and constituted the most important cash crop. Kentucky ranked second in hemp production in 1840. In 1849, the state produced 17,787 tons of hemp, more than half the nation's production. By 1852, more than three thousand Kentucky farms were growing hemp, which served as the raw material for rope and cloth. Slaves often suffered from "hemp pneumonia," as a result of the particles they inhaled while performing the dirty and labor-intensive task of using a hemp-breaking machine to separate the fibers from the stalks. According to James F. Hopkins: "Without hemp slavery might not have flourished in Kentucky, since other agricultural products of the state were not conducive to the extensive use of bondsmen."[40]

Slaves worked in a variety of capacities besides agriculture. They cared for the sick, cooked, cleaned, and washed the clothes of their white owners. They worked on riverboats that flowed down the Kentucky, Ohio, Barren, Green, and Tennessee Rivers. They moved freight in Maysville, Covington, and Paducah, Kentucky. They worked in the saltworks of Mason County and the iron furnaces of Montgomery, Bath, and Clark Counties. Nor was slave labor reserved for adults. Henry Bibb, born a slave in Shelby County, recalled working as a youth polishing furniture, preparing the kitchen fires, and shooing flies away from his mistress while she slept. He never forgot that she was "too lazy to scratch her own head."[41]

Despite the various uses of slave labor, the percentage of slaves in Kentucky gradually declined after 1830. By 1860, Kentucky was home to 225,483 slaves, 19.5 percent of the total population. This was 5 percent less than in 1830. One of the factors that explained the decline was the growing demand for slaves "down the river." Healthy slaves in the prime of their life commanded the best prices. Male slaves in Kentucky cost anywhere from $400 to $700. Slave women ranged from $350 to $450. The demand for labor on cotton, sugar, and rice plantations in the Deep South afforded Kentucky slaveholders and slave traders the opportunity to maximize their investments. The firm of Hughes and Downing took thirteen slaves to Natchez, Mississippi, in 1843. Having purchased the slaves in the Bluegrass for a little more than $5,200, they sold them in Natchez for more than $8,000. Such profits drew slave dealers to Kentucky. While Louisville and Lexington housed the largest slave-trading firms, smaller dealers gathered slaves in Madison, Nelson, and Mason Counties as well.[42]

Kentucky slaveholders also invested in young, attractive, mulatto female slaves, identified as fancy girls or choice stock. These women were purchased to be prostitutes or mistresses for prominent whites. The Lexington slave market had a reputation for supplying slave owners with fancy girls. Their prices ranged between $1,000 and $2,000. In 1833, the state passed a nonimportation act that prohibited bringing slaves into the state for resale. The act sought to curtail the number of slaves in the state instead of gradually removing slavery or completely outlawing the domestic slave trade. Throughout the antebellum period, rumors of slave insurrections throughout Kentucky and the South had elevated the fears of whites. In 1810, a number of Lexington slaves were arrested on suspicion of planning a "dangerous conspiracy." In 1848, E. J. Doyle, an abolitionist and student at Centre College, sparked an uprising of slaves in Fayette and Bourbon Counties. Up to seventy-five reportedly armed slaves ran away through Harrison and Bracken Counties before being apprehended. Doyle was convicted and sent to prison for twenty years for his role in the disturbance, while three slaves named Presly, Shadrock, and Harry Slaughter were convicted and then pardoned by Governors William Owsley and J. J. Crittenden. In 1856, white citizens in Hopkinsville became alarmed when rumors spread that their slaves were joining forces with a band of slaves in a nearby community to fight their way to freedom in Indiana. More than thirty black suspects were arrested after they confessed to the plot. Like slaves in the Deep South, Kentucky slaves had a history of resistance.[43]

Over the years, slaves grew tired of the false promises of freedom, the separation of their families, the demands on their labor, and the punishment they received. In response to this mistreatment, they destroyed farm tools, burned buildings, worked at a slow pace, and sometimes resorted to measures that included self-mutilation. In Boone County, a group of slaves stole merchandise from their owners and traded it to buyers across the Ohio River in Indiana before being caught by the slave patrol and whipped for their actions.[44] But slaves were not merely victims of their condition. They also personally attacked slaveholders. In 1844, Richard Moses got tired of the abuse he received from his Lexington mistress and strangled her to death. Five years later, a young slave woman in Fayette County was sentenced to die for mixing glass into the food of the family that owned her. In 1862, slaves on a Henderson, Kentucky, farm choked their overseer with his suspenders because of the whippings they had received from him.[45]

Still, the most disruptive and apparent form of resistance exhibited by the slaves was expressed in their decision to run away. Some left for a short period of time, while others made their escape across the Ohio River into the North and Canada, as a permanent protest of enslavement. Robert Kirtley, a slave patroller in Boone County, gave his slave Ben a "cowhiding" when he was caught without a pass.[46] Slave patrols nevertheless could not prevent other slaves from pursuing their freedom. Henry Morehead, an escaped slave from Louisville, was interviewed in Canada in 1856 about his successful journey north with his wife and three children: "I left because they were about selling my wife and children to the South. I would rather have followed them to the grave, than to see them go down." He continued: "With all the sufferings of the frost and the fatigues of travel, it was not so bad as the effects of slavery." Lewis Richardson was originally from Lexington but escaped to Canada because of beatings he had received. In an address at an antislavery meeting, he declared: "I am free from American slavery, after wearing the galling chains on my limbs for 53 years, 9 of which it has been my unhappy lot to be the slave of Henry Clay. It has been said by some, that Clay's slaves had rather live with him than be free, but I had rather this day, have a millstone tied to my neck and be sunk to the bottom of the Detroit River, than go back to Ashland and be his slave."[47]

Given the brutality of slavery, antislavery efforts did gradually expand in Kentucky. According to a popular legend, the term *Underground Railroad* had its origins in Kentucky when a slave named Tice Davids escaped from Maysville to Ohio across the river. Davids's owner supposedly said that he "must have gone off on a underground railroad." Considering that the Ohio River flowed along Kentucky's six-hundred-mile northern border, slaves heading north had to cross over the state's borderland. The geographic location of the state kept the Underground Railroad busy and also elevated the suspicion of antislavery activities in the states.[48]

While slaves incorporated a number of different strategies to escape bondage, the role of free blacks in assisting their getaway was an ongoing concern for slaveholders. A newspaper announcing the search for a pregnant slave woman from Louisville reported that "she has been conveyed away by some free negro, with whom she may attempt to pass as his wife." In Carrollton, Kentucky, a "free man of color" was accused of attempting to "run off a couple of slaves" near the mouth of the Kentucky River. To be sure, free blacks did interact frequently with slaves. Living in both rural and urban areas, with their largest number residing in the Bluegrass region of Kentucky, they could own property, operate businesses, teach schools, purchase slaves who were members of their families, and establish churches. Yet, according Marion Lucas, "the free black family lived a precarious existence." Crimes carrying the death penalty when committed by slaves also carried the death penalty when committed by free blacks.

Additionally, free blacks faced harassment and had to carry their papers with them at all times in order to avoid being arrested.[49]

However, the abolitionist work of free blacks was not the only concern of slave owners, for white opponents of slavery also assisted blacks in escaping slavery. Forty slaves almost escaped from Woodford County with the aid of whites in November 1848. Once the plot was discovered, it was learned that some white men had "furnished them free passes." In August 1852, Charles Armstrong of Louisville offered a $500 reward for the return of four of his slaves, who were last seen with two white men. Armstrong suspected they had "stolen the negroes."[50] Some white abolitionists in Kentucky were bold and courageous enough to assist slaves via the Underground Railroad's secret escape network. But other whites expressed their discontent with slavery in other ways.

For example, some whites freed their slaves by deeds of emancipation. In 1790, John Barber of Lexington freed his slaves because of "the injustice and criminality of depriving my fellow-creatures of their natural right."[51] James Birney of Danville freed six of his slaves in October 1834, and John G. Fee, who later founded Berea College and the city of Berea, worked as a longtime abolitionist. Rather than allow his father in Bracken County to sell an old faithful slave named Julett, Fee borrowed money to purchase her. He then gave her a "perpetual pass," declaring her a free woman.[52]

The most visible expression of antislavery activity in Kentucky came through in the works of the Kentucky Abolitionist Society (KAS) and the Kentucky Colonization Society (KCS). The KAS was founded in 1808 and advocated gradual emancipation. It declared slavery "a system of oppression pregnant with moral, national and domestic evils, ruinous to national tranquility, honor and enjoyment." By 1827, the society had organized eight local societies and briefly published the *Abolition Intelligencer and Missionary Magazine*. The KCS was organized in 1829 and had thirty-one local societies within three years. The KCS was a branch of the American Colonization Society (ACS), which advocated colonizing free blacks. The distinguished political statesmen Henry Clay served as president of the ACS from 1836 to 1852 and served as its strong advocate in Kentucky. But Kentuckians gave more verbal than financial support to the mission. Kentucky in Liberia, with a central town named Clay Ashland, was established, but the state society still sent only 661 black Kentuckians to the colony. Some free blacks agreed to make the trip, while others were forced to leave once they gained their freedom.[53]

In his book on slavery and political culture in Kentucky, Harrold Tal-lant concluded that whites "thought of slavery as an evil to their state, but one whose burdens must be born patiently until some safe and practical solution to the problem could be found." He added: "To them, slavery was a necessary evil."[54] The antislavery movement in Kentucky did not fulfill the expectations of outside opponents of slavery. As one antislavery advocate wrote: "The very general confession of the evil of slavery, and the oft-repeated wish that we were clear of it, is often to be understood as we understand the drunkard, when he condemns drunkenness and wishes he was delivered from the habit, while he would quarrel with the man who would hide his bottle."[55]

By the 1850s, Kentucky opponents of slavery were clearly split be-tween emancipationists and abolitionists. Some, like Cassius Clay, were emancipationist, favoring a gradual abolition of slavery, while others, like John G. Fee, called for immediate abolition. In Fee's view: "Prejudice, unholy prejudice, is at the bottom of the whole of it."[56] Fee believed in the power of moral suasion and his Christian convictions to erase slavery. The churches he organized in northern Kentucky and Berea considered slavery a sin, withheld fellowship from slaveholders, and opposed drink-ing, secret societies, and caste systems. In describing services at his Glade church in Berea, Fee noted: "We make no distinction at our Communion, because of the color or condition of members: we know our Savior would not."[57] Kentuckians eventually forced Fee to leave Berea in the 1850s for his radical idea to establish a college for black and white students. His work, however, reinforced the efforts of proslavery advocates to guard slavery in Kentucky even more closely.

Clearly, the presence of antislavery sentiment in Kentucky through-out the frontier and antebellum years generated concern among slave-holders. Slave patrols were organized to watch black activities, especially at night. The patrols visited African American living quarters, disbanded unlawful assemblies of slaves, and arrested slaves who did not have passes. Those slaves caught without passes were whipped and taken to a slave jail for their masters to reclaim.[58] According to Sally Hadden: "Slave pa-trols were both similar and different from expert slave catchers, private citizens who claimed slave-recapture rewards, overseers, and constables who controlled the slave population in cities." "The titles, obligations, and methods of operation among these authority figures varied widely," she added, "but they were all part of the collective community effort to control slaves and prevent them from acting like free men." That slave patrols were appointed by the counties they served placed them in a better position to monitor local activities. When necessary, masters hired slave catchers to travel to hunt specific slaves. These professional slave catchers used dogs to locate the whereabouts of fugitive slaves even though owners did not want their property to "be bruised and torn by the dogs."[59] But W. D. Gilbert of Franklin in Simpson County advertised a poster announcing that he had "a splendid lot of well broke NEGRO DOGS, and will attend at any reasonable distance to the catching of runaways, at the lowest possible rates."[60]

Despite the appointments and presence of slave patrols, not all whites were pleased with the services they provided. In January 1849, D. L. Price of Fayette County published a resolution drafted by a committee intended to petition the General Assembly to repeal the county's patrol law. According to the preamble: "Numerous disorders and irregularities exist amongst the slaves of Fayette County, and many persons in violation of law, traffic with them to the great detriment of the slaves themselves." The resolution called for a seventy-five-cent tax on slaves sixteen and older in the county, the funds to be used for "efficient police in the county to preserve quiet and order amongst the slaves, and suppress illegal traffic with them."[61] This kind of resolution reveals two important realities about antebellum slavery in Fayette County and the state. First, not all slaveholders were pleased with the services they were receiving. Second, slaves did not totally fear the presence of slave patrols. Disorders were evidently quite common in Fayette County, but this was an issue in other parts of the state as well. Harriet Mason of Garrard County recalled how one white woman would not let the "Padarores" come to dances at her home: "If they did come, who would get her pistol and make them leave."[62] Clearly, African Americans despised the patrollers, whom they considered "pore [sic] white trash." One Madison County slave described them as "the offscouring of all things, the refuse, the ears, and tails of slavery, the wallet and satchel of pole-cats, the meanest and lowest and worse of all creatures." In retaliation for patter-roller activities, slaves sometimes stretched a waist-high rope or grapevine across a dark road at night in order to throw patrols from their horses as they strolled down these unsuspecting paths. This act of retaliation and rebellion inclined some patrollers to travel on foot rather than risk being a victim of this kind of slave practice.[63]

As Daniel Daly recalled in the *Owensboro Messenger* more than thirty years after slavery: "The 'patter-rollers' were everywhere." But so were opponents of slavery. They were black and white, slave and free, rural and urban, in state and out of state. Few opponents of slavery were as brave and bold as the Reverend John G. Fee, who pressed for the end of slavery and asked for racial equality. But, as committed as Fee was to work to end slavery in the state, he did not wield enough influence to defeat an institution deeply rooted in Kentucky history. Patter-rollers served as an important means of enforcing, protecting, and preserving white supremacy. While they did not make speeches, write books, or pass laws, they were a strong constituency in a state that depended on their presence to help keep African Americans in their place. These local officials appointed to carry out state laws ultimately kept the controversial issue of slavery a divided subject in a border state. The movement of slave patrols throughout the state served as a daily, visible reminder of the depth of the African American freedom struggle in Kentucky and the South. As one self-proclaimed antislavery man wrote in an article published in the *National Era* in June 1847, slavery was maintained in Kentucky because it was "too intertwined with all the habits of the people." He further observed "that whites, accustomed from childhood to have the attendance of servants, know not how to make the attempt to do without them."[64] Ironically, in the end, the slave patrol was an agency for both abolitionist and proslavery advocates in Kentucky. Even though he expressed himself differently, Dan Daly shared the same observation: "A nigger was worth something in those days."

Notes

1. John T. Higdon, "Uncle Dan Daly: Memories of the Early Days of Western Kentucky," *Daviess County Historical Quarterly* 8 (1990): 16–17.

2. Ibid., 18.

3. J. Winston Coleman Jr., *Slavery Times in Kentucky* (Chapel Hill, NC, 1940), 97. See also Higdon, "Uncle Dan Daly," 16–17.

4. Patrols were also known as the *patrole*, *padaroe*, and *paderole*. See Coleman, *Slavery Times in Kentucky*, 97; and Sally E. Hadden, *Slave Patrols: Law and Violence in Virginia and the Carolinas* (Cambridge, MA, 2001), 19–20, 30.

5. *Acts Passed at the Fifth Session of the Eighth General Assembly for the Commonwealth of Kentucky* (Frankfort, 1800), 36–37.

6. For the settlers who came down the Ohio River, Limestone (Maysville) was the most convenient place to dock their boats. Ellen Eslinger, ed., *Running Mad for Kentucky: Frontier Travel Accounts* (Lexington, 2004), 8, 18.

7. Craig Thompson Friend, ed., *The Buzzell about Kentuck: Settling the Promised Land* (Lexington: University Press of Kentucky, 1999), 1.

8. Eslinger, ed., *Running Mad for Kentucky*, 36.

9. Ibid., 37.

10. Ellen Eslinger, "The Shape of Slavery on the Kentucky Frontier, 1775–1800," *Register of the Kentucky Historical Society* 92 (1994): 6–7.

11. Ibid., 6.

12. Marion B. Lucas, *A History of Blacks in Kentucky*, vol. 1, *From Slavery to Segregation, 1760–1891* (Frankfort, 1992), xi–xiii.

13. Ibid., 15; Marion B. Lucas, "African Americans on the Kentucky Frontier," *Register of the Kentucky Historical Society* 95 (1997): 126–27.

14. J. Blaine Hudson, "Slavery in Louisville and Jefferson County, 1780–1812," *Filson Club History Quarterly* 73 (1999): 262.

15. Eslinger, "The Shape of Slavery on the Kentucky Frontier," 6; Todd H. Barnett, "Virginians Moving West: The Early Evolution of Slavery in the Bluegrass," *Filson Club History Quarterly* 73 (1999): 224.

16. Barnett, "Virginians Moving West," 233.

17. Hadden, *Slave Patrols*, 108.

18. Ibid., 109–10.

19. Fayette County Order Book, March 1836–April 1840 (November Court, 1837), 20, Fayette County Order Book (December 13, 1859), 74, Mason County Order Book R, 1859–1865 (January Term), 215, and Daviess County Court Order Book, 1859–1863, vol. G (May Term 1861), 263, all in Kentucky Department for Libraries and Archives, Frankfort.

20. Lowell H. Harrison and James C. Klotter, *A New History of Kentucky* (Lexington, 1997), 62–63.

21. John David Smith, "Slavery and Anti-Slavery," in *Our Kentucky: A Study of the Bluegrass State*, ed. James C. Klotter (Lexington, 1992), 114.

22. Harrison and Klotter, *A New History of Kentucky*, 63.

23. Smith, "Slavery and Anti-Slavery," 114.

24. Harrison and Klotter, *A New History of Kentucky*, 71.

25. James C. Klotter and Freda C. Klotter, *A Concise History of Kentucky* (Lexington, 2008), 92.

26. Barnett, "Virginians Moving West," 238–39.

27. Eslinger, "The Shape of Slavery on the Kentucky Frontier," 13.

28. Lucas, *From Slavery to Segregation*, 101–3.

29. Ibid., 29–30.

30. Ivan E. McDougle, *Slavery in Kentucky, 1792–1865* (Westport, CT, 1918), 38.

31. Lucas, *From Slavery to Segregation*, xvii–xxii.

32. McDougle, *Slavery in Kentucky*, 71, 72, 74, 81.

33. Ibid., 26.

34. Coleman, *Slavery Times in Kentucky*, 15.

35. Ibid., 51–56, 66.

36. Ibid., 53.

37. Lucas, *From Slavery to Segregation*, 28.

38. Amy L. Young and J. Blaine Hudson, "Slave Life at Oxmoor," *Filson Club Historical Quarterly* 74 (2000): 189–219.

39. Labor organization, housing, and diet varied in Kentucky because of the presence of farms and plantations and the personal preferences of owners.

40. Smith, "Slavery and Anti-Slavery," 109–11 (including Hopkins quotation).

41. Several publications discuss slave labor. The best general description can be found in Lucas, *From Slavery to Segregation*, 2–11.

42. Ibid., 84–100.

43. Ibid., 59–60, 86. See also Governor William Owsley Papers, Petitions for Pardons, Remissions and Respites, boxes 27 and 28, Governor Owsley, Executive Journal, September 6, 1848, 235, and Governor J. J. Crittenden, Executive Journal, October 9, 1848, 13, all in Kentucky Department for Libraries and Archives; Harrison and Klotter, *A New History of Kentucky*, 98; and Lucas, *From Slavery to Segregation*, 73.

44. Merrill S. Caldwell, "A Brief History of Slavery in Boone County, Kentucky" (paper presented at the meeting of the Boone County Historical Society, Florence, KY, June 1957), 4 (a copy is held in the collection of the Filson Historical Society, Louisville).

45. Harrison and Klotter, *A New History of Kentucky*, 51–52, 57–59.

46. Caldwell, "A Brief History of Slavery in Boone County, Kentucky," 5.

47. J. Blaine Hudson, *Fugitive Slaves and the Underground Railroad in the Kentucky Borderland* (Jefferson, NC, 2002), 57.

48. Ibid., 12, 72.

49. Ibid., 74–75; Lucas, *From Slavery to Segregation*, 108–13.

50. Hudson, *Fugitive Slaves*, 75.

51. Steve Moreland, "Straddling the Fence of Freedom: The Free African-American Community of Antebellum Lexington" (M.A. thesis, University of Kentucky, 1996), 17.

52. Lucas, *From Slavery to Segregation*, 54.

53. Harrison and Klotter, *A New History of Kentucky*, 176.

54. Harold D. Tallant, *Evil Necessity: Slavery and Political Culture in Antebellum Kentucky* (Lexington, 2003), 3; Lucas, *From Slavery to Segregation*, 53–54.

55. Tallant, *Evil Necessity*, 18.

56. Ibid., 32.

57. Richard Sears, *The Kentucky Abolitionists in the Midst of Slavery, 1854–1864: Exiles for Freedom* (Lewiston, NY, 1993), 8.

58. Coleman, *Slavery Times in Kentucky*, 26–27, 96.

59. Hadden, *Slave Patrols*, 79–80.

60. Abraham Chapman, ed., *Steal Away: Stories of the Runaway Slaves* (New York, 1971), 6, 1.

61. *Lexington Observer and Reporter*, January 13, 20, 1849.

62. George P. Rawick, ed., *The American Slave: A Composite Autobiography*, 41 vols. (Westport, CT, 1972), 16:31.

63. Coleman, *Slavery Times in Kentucky*, 98.

64. Hudson, *Fugitive Slaves*, 18.

≈ 5

"Mrs. Boone, I presume?"
In Search of the Idea of Womanhood in Kentucky's Early Years

Randolph Hollingsworth

Searching for evidences of women in the history of Kentucky is like pushing through the lush Kentucky cane, taller than a woman on horseback, in the beautiful Bluegrass. Reasonably, many resources exist—but most show evidences of men's lives and thoughts. Where are the women? Just as Henry Stanley found David Livingstone in Ujiji, an ancient town in western Tanzania, we can find only glimpses of Rebecca Bryan Boone and other women of Kentucky's early years in the historical narratives published even during their lifetimes. The earliest and most influential portrait of her was in the 1833 *Memoir of Daniel Boone,*[1] largely written by Timothy Flint. Flint was the first to think about the role of Rebecca Boone since the 1784 publication of "The Adventures of Col. Daniel Boon,"[2] in which John Filson mentioned her only in passing. By the 1830s, writers described Rebecca as the Victorian Age's ideal woman: meek yet courageous and her husband's affectionate friend.

In 1852, Elizabeth Ellet's *Pioneer Women of the West*[3] dropped the meekness but emphasized the domestic skills, leaving readers to think that Rebecca worked near the hearth raising children. This image remains in the general public's mind, confronting us even as late as the 1960s. A mythical portrait of Rebecca Boone can be found on the dustjacket of a biography by Etta DeGering published in 1966 for young readers. The artist, Ursula Koering, a popular illustrator of children's books, seems to have relied on the stereotypical portraits of women popular since the nineteenth century. Boone is slim, neat, and clean, wearing a spotless white apron as she hovers over a campfire, one graceful hand holding back her dress from the sparks, checking on the stew since it seems she has nothing better to do (there is no spoon depicted in her hand to stir it) while her husband waits—manfully with his rifle at the ready—to be fed.

Yet surely there could be a different picture? We have long had documentation that Daniel said Rebecca was strong and independent. We forgot that her husband said she had "transported my family and goods, on horses, through the wilderness, amidst a multitude of dangers"[4] and that she hunted well enough to feed her large extended family and others (as her husband recounted). Many tell the same stories based on Flint and Ellet over and over with slight variations as evidence of her place more in revered legends of pioneer Kentucky than in history. Can we not do better for Rebecca Boone and other women in early Kentucky?

When historians choose to look for primary sources by or about women of Kentucky, many emerge: in letters, memoirs, and celebratory speeches; in tax records, store ledgers, and overseers' farm reports; in pamphlets, newspapers, and even the earliest printed books. But where would one find direct evidence of an illiterate woman of meager means? The daughter of a Welsh Quaker family without formal education, Rebecca Bryan moved from Virginia to the North Carolina backcountry with her grandparents Morgan and Martha (Strode) Bryan. There in the Yadkin River valley the young Daniel Boone's family also settled, and we can assume that the two families knew each other well. Rebecca and Daniel began their courtship in 1753 and married three years later on August 14, 1756.

Frontier women's lives were rough and violent, and Rebecca's was no different. From the first time the Boones fled trouble (during the Cherokee War in 1759) until her death, Rebecca set up house at least fifteen times. Her and Daniel's marriage lasted fifty-six years, and together they had ten children: six sons and four daughters. Rebecca moved many times during her lifetime. She created homes in North Carolina, Virginia, Kentucky, and, finally, Missouri, where she spent the last fourteen years of her life. We know that she died at the age of seventy-five on March 18, 1813, at her daughter Jemima Boone Callaway's home near the village of Charette (near present-day Marthasville). She was buried at the Bryan family cemetery nearby overlooking the Missouri River, disinterred, and buried again in Frankfort, Kentucky. Her children later told that she was an experienced midwife, leather tanner, sharpshooter, and linenmaker— resourceful and independent in the isolated areas in which she and her large combined family often found themselves.[5]

Try finding illiterate, rural Kentucky women in the history books— perhaps a few women are portrayed as pioneers, some slaves, and more belles. The same stories about Rebecca told long ago filter through to the current-day history books, each time resurrected often without question. As a result, readers lose the chance to see history from the perspective of more than half the population. The task then is to look more carefully at the way in which the early documentation portrays women—to examine the lens of history used by those who recorded women's deeds and aspirations of their time.

Particularly intriguing about the late eighteenth century and the early nineteenth in Kentucky's history is that women were caught between two historical periods: the revolutionary pioneer era and the early national era. Women who came from the East during this time period to start a new life in Kentucky brought with them certain cultural expectations for women—or the ideal of womanhood, both white and black. For white and free black women, the political and cultural messages of the earlier part of this time period reflected the ideal of what historians today call a *republican motherhood*. Later, as villages grew into towns and the Era of Good Feelings transformed into the Age of the Common Man, women in Kentucky experienced the same pressures as their eastern and southern sisters to conform to a specific form of domesticity that emphasized submissiveness and piety.[6] Illiteracy—since too many families moving into the southern frontier did not choose to or have the opportunity to teach their girls to read—bound most women in Kentucky to an even more dependent status.[7] However, the women of central Kentucky during the years 1792–1852 participated in crafting a social, economic, and political world that was noteworthy in a new nation.

Female heads of household in Kentucky had wealth and sociopolitical standing from the earliest days of settlement, and legal records show that they were increasingly visible in central Kentucky's socioeconomic world. Many frontier homes were mere shacks clustered together for military support during attacks and quickly abandoned once the conditions in the station or fort worsened. Since most men served in the local militia and did not stay at home for very long, their wives had to manage their economic futures on the farm. Sketches of stations or forts showed evidence of women's presence, even when the written records did not. One good example of this, a sketch of Constant's Station in 1785 as remembered by one of its residents, shows where fields included hemp for women to process for clothing and cordage.[8] In the 1780s, the frontier women of Strode's Station (nearby what is now Winchester, Kentucky) worked together to produce thirty yards of hemp linen for an old widower—this was recorded in an oral history interview of William Clinkenbeard by the

Ann McGinty blockhouse at Fort Harrod, a 1920s reconstruction of an eigh-teenth-century blockhouse at Fort Harrod on the Wilderness Road establish-ing the first permanent British settlement west of the Alleghenies. Anne Ken-nedy Wilson Poague Lindsay McGinty was, according to early records, highly esteemed and given one of the Fort Harrod blockhouses for her family of seven children to inhabit. She was said to be the first to bring her spinning wheel to Kentucky, crafting linen from the lint of local nettles and linsey-woolsey with buffalo wool. She died on November 14, 1815, and was buried at Fort Harrod, having outlived four husbands. (Photograph from C. Frank Dunn Photographs Collection, 1900–1954, bulk 1920–1940, 1987PH2. Kentucky Historical Society, Special Collections and Archives, Frankfort, Kentucky.)

Reverend John Dabney.[9] Pioneer families often planted flax and hemp right away for the domestic production of clothing, cordage, bagging, and paper for family consumption or for barter. Women traditionally man-aged the textile production in the rural home. The richer the pioneer, the more hemp could be grown, manufactured, and sold for a hefty profit—and women, whether black or white, took advantage of this opportunity in the new frontier. Enslaved women on Kentucky farms in the 1790s worked long past their task rate and earned extra money producing bolts of jean cloth for sale both locally and to ship downriver.[10] Tax lists for the

1780s and 1790s show that a surprising number of early pioneer women as well as men owned slaves or had indentured servants who could do the backbreaking work in the hemp and flax fields. With the opening of the Mississippi River in the late 1790s, hemp became an important export commodity, and manufacturers of good quality hemp products on a reliable basis made more money by shipping large quantities downriver to New Orleans.

The violence of the frontier meant that there were many young widows, but they rarely stayed single. A frontier woman succeeded economically and socially if she married at some point in her life. The Virginia law of *coverture* continued on the frontier, and this meant that married women had few rights in property ownership or even in the guardianship of their own children. In practical terms, however, women often had strong personal control over their lands and family—and widows could serve as the heads of household. This power greatly increased if the woman had a strong kin network to support her.

Records of early Kentucky wills and land transactions show that women were able to accumulate great wealth and exercise a legal independence unknown in the former British colonies across the mountains (see table 1). Of the thirty-one names of women found in the six lists of recorded taxpayers from the period 1787–1791, seven were slave owners. These women owned an average of three to four slaves per household, putting them into a more wealthy rank than the majority of the Kentucky population. Four women paid taxes on their indentured servants (whose first names are recorded). Comparably, these thirty-one women held great wealth in a region where most families lived as tenants. In the 1790s, less than half the potential voters in Kentucky owned any land at all, while the rest of the nation saw property ownership in as much as 80 percent of the electorate.[11]

By 1838, Kentucky widows and female heads of household (*femme sole*) earned the right to vote in school-related elections[12]—a victory for women's suffrage long before Elizabeth Cady Stanton and others started their campaign at Seneca Falls, New York. Kentucky women joined together in voluntary associations, white and black separately, emphasizing religion, education, temperance, or the abolition of slavery. White women and women of color in central Kentucky took on roles with ever-increasing power so that, by the turn of the twentieth century, white males in the Kentucky legislature felt compelled to rescind white and black women's right to vote in local elections—a backlash against women as a whole class in society that came at a time when other states were beginning to succumb to the pressures of women's rights activists.

Table 1

Female Heads of Household: Women's Names in Personal Tax Lists of Fayette County, 1787–1791

Taxpayer Head of Household	1787 Tax List for Fayette County, VA	1788 Tax List	1789/90/91 Tax Lists
Ann Baker		√	Fayette 1/11/1790
Sarah Bush	√ (2 slaves)	√	
Joanne Campbell	√ (1 slave)		Fayette 6/30/1789 Woodford 5/29/1790
Eliz. Clemons	√		
Eliz. Curtner†	√		
Mary Davison		√	
Marget Drake	√ (5 slaves)		Fayette 1/11/1790
Eliz. Ewart	√		
Mary Gibson	√	√	Fayette 1/11/1790 Bourbon 3/1791
Mary Harper		√	
Rebecca Hunter	√		
Jane Huson		√	
Martha Johnson	√		
Eliz. Jones	√ (Elliot*)		
Grace Jones	√ (9 slaves; John and Francis*)	√	Fayette 1/11/1790
Eliz. Mair	√		
Mary McConnell		√	Fayette 3/19/1790
Ellizabeth McCorkle		√	
Marget McGuire	√ (John*)		
Rosanna Mitchell		√	?

The realities of women's lives in Kentucky thus intersected with and sometimes contradicted the ideals of womanhood expounded in their times and perpetuated by some historians. As women arrived in central Kentucky during the rise of Lexington in the 1790s, they had many opportunities for success. Scholars agree that most women moved West reluctantly. Yet Mary Coburn Dewees wrote in her journal of her arrival in Lexington in January 1788: "Since I have been here I have been visited

Table 1 (cont'd)
Female Heads of Household: Women's Names in Personal Tax Lists of Fayette County, 1787–1791

Taxpayer Head of Household	1787 Tax List for Fayette County, VA	1788 Tax List	1789/90/91 Tax Lists
Elizah Poage	√ (1 slave)	√	
Mary Richardson		√	
Mary Spaw	√ (Michael Capiday*)		
Jane Todd†	√ (5 slaves)		Fayette 1/11/1790
Jane Tompson‡		√	
Jane Venable		√	
Marget Ward	√		
Ester Wilson	√ (1 slave)		
Jane Wilson	√		Fayette 1/11/1790
Margaret Wilson			Fayette 2/26/1790
Mary Wilson	√		

Source: Part Second – State Enumerations of Heads of Families, Virginia & Kentucky. "First Census" of Kentucky 1790 (1940; Baltimore, 1993).

Note: This is an abridged version of the personal tax lists, focusing only on those names that seemed to be those of women.

† In 1783, the Lexington trustees distributed town lots to three women in addition to men: Jane Todd, "Widow McDonald," and "Widow Kirtner" (could be Curtner?).
* Additional white tithables.
‡ Maybe this is the same Jane Thompson listed in the Lexington Station Trustee Book (available on microfilm at the Lexington-Fayette Urban County Government Records Center and Archives, Lexington) as receiving a town lot on December 26, 1781. Also, a Jane Thompson married John Scott on September 11, 1792, at Walnut Hill Presbyterian Church in Fayette County, according to the Papers of Rev. James Crawford, in the Rev. John Dabney Shane Manuscript Collection of the Presbyterian Historical Association (Philadelphia), 28th reel, vol. 5.

by the genteel people in the place and receiv'd several Invitations both in town & Country. The Society in this place is very agreeable and I flatter myself I shall see many happy days in this Country."[13] The Kentucky frontier had begun its transformation in the 1790s into an economic locus for those journeying down the Ohio River or up through the Cumberland Gap and north into the rich Ohio valley lands. Lexington, even before Louisville or Cincinnati, served as an important point for families and adventurers going to western territories or to trade in the international markets of New Orleans. Kentucky women, slave and free, played key roles in the rise of central Kentucky, functioning as entrepreneurs, artists, farm managers, laborers, and artisans—as well as wives and mothers, sisters and daughters.

In the rhetoric of the postrevolutionary era, society fixated on women's sexuality. The question of white women's role in the building of a new nation took on particular importance. Called *republican motherhood* by historians today,[14] the ideal expected a good woman to use her sexual powers to lure wayward men into more pious and moral approaches to republican virtue—and to use her maternal influence and intellectual powers to teach her sons to become model citizens of the Republic. Certainly, the women of backcountry Virginia and Pennsylvania knew of these expectations and brought them down the Ohio River and then south to Lexington. Most pioneer farm women (especially those with extensive kin networks, as Rebecca Bryan Boone had) felt obligated to try to maintain the trappings of civilization in the midst of the complex and horrific violence of the Kentucky frontier—though they often did not succeed.[15]

One of the stories of the Boone family carefully handed down through the years leaves a clue. Rebecca insisted that her boy, caught on the Great Warriors Path, tortured, and finally killed by Indians (one of whom he had known), be buried wrapped up in one of her handmade linen sheets. Even though her son would never see home again, she encased him in one of her most precious domestic possessions as a sort of protection against the wilderness. The Daughters of the American Revolution in the late nineteenth century knew this trail had become important in the narration of the founding of the nation: the path where the frontier families led by Daniel Boone, the most famous of them all, came through to Kentucky.

For many, Daniel Boone remains an iconic figure in Kentucky history, and the impact of his Wilderness Road looms large. As his biographer John Mack Faragher wrote: "Before the end of the eighteenth century more than two hundred thousand people, most of them poor and many of them slaves, had come to Kentucky over the Wilderness Road, the route first explored, marked and laid out by Boone."[16] The earliest stories of Kentucky and the American frontier included biographies of Boone, and his wife was the pioneer woman venerated by all. During Governor Robert P. Letcher's administration, the Kentucky legislature appropriated money to move the remains of both Daniel and Rebecca Boone from Missouri to Frankfort. Nearly every county of the state, besides many southern and western states, were represented at the ceremonies in 1845. In

1852, George Caleb Bingham painted an epic portrait of Boone escorting settlers through the Cumberland Gap.[17] Rebecca Boone plays the part of the romantic Madonna, this time completed in interpretive ways with a faithful hunting dog and her husband leading the noble charger. She represented all pioneer women that the mid-nineteenth century idealized and celebrated.

On August 16, 1896, the Lexington chapter of the Daughters of the American Revolution erected a monumental wall around a famous spring, five miles out on Bryan's Station Pike. Said to be the first monument funded and erected "by women—for women," its inscription read: "In honor of the women of Bryan's Station who on 15th of August, 1782, faced a savage host in ambush and with a heroic courage and a sublime self-sacrifice that will remain forever illustrious obtained from this spring the water that made possible the successful defense of that station." The stories described the sixteen younger women at first as scared and reluctant but convinced in their heroic duties by the older women. Led by Jemima Suggett Johnson, twenty-eight girls and women made "the resolute march to the spring" and even—so they say—laughed as they passed within shooting range of the enemy, filled their buckets, and returned to the stockade.[18] This physical act of protest against the British and their Indian allies became a cherished moment in Kentucky history and places the *republican* in the ideal of republican motherhood.

Such bravery stands in the face of fear of rape and slavery in an Indian community. The Shawnee continued to raid Kentucky settlements and even threatened a pan-Indian uprising during the War of 1812. The antebellum stories of Daniel Boone inevitably included a version of the 1776 incident in which four Shawnee and Cherokee kidnapped his thirteen-year-old daughter, Jemima, and her girlfriends. In the 1852 lithograph *The Capture of the Daughters of D. Boone and Callaway by the Indians*, by Karl Bodmer and Jean-François Millet,[19] the image of the savage is clearly represented in terms of potential rape. The ensuing stories about that incident usually included an aura of this fear, with the storytellers emphasizing that the girls were not injured. A descendant of Jemima's remembered how embarrassed the girls said they were when their male relatives (and Jemima's future husband) found them with their skirts chopped off above the knees—despite the fact that the Shawnee had given them leggings and moccasins to hide their legs.[20]

Women who helped build the frontier forts, homesteads, villages, and cities of Kentucky, however, did not always remain tied to a domestic role as prescribed and valorized in the ideal of the republican mother. Records

Bryan Station Monument in Fayette County, a monument in Fayette County to the bravery of Kentucky pioneer women erected by the Lexington Chapter of the Daughters of the American Revolution on August 15, 1896. The inscription reads: "In honor of the women of Bryan's Station who on the 15th of August 1782 faced a savage host in ambush and with a heroic courage and a sublime self-sacrifice that will remain forever illustrious obtained from this spring the water that made possible the successful defense of that station." (Photograph from C. Frank Dunn Photographs Collection, 1900–1954, bulk 1920–1940, 1987PH2. Kentucky Historical Society, Special Collections and Archives, Frankfort, Kentucky.)

include stories of women evidencing military valor during their lives of constant warfare. Most women had to take on the role of frontier warriors but preferred to remain anonymous in the process, and a more acceptable role was publicly to shame men not adequate in their roles in the defense of the community. Women retained the responsibility, then, for turning the frontier into the civilization of domesticity they once knew or wanted to emulate. Mostly of the middle class and married (since poor or working-class women could not often afford the expensive trip to the West until after the 1780s), they brought with them or ordered from relatives or favorite stores back East the respectable white doilies, elegant china, and plated silver for their tables. While Kentucky frontier women kept having babies and working in the fields to clothe and feed their families, they also started up schools when living in forts and made sure that preachers held church services when they could. So it is difficult to see these women as simply one thing or another. Daniel Trabue remembered that some women traveling from Forts Harrod and Logan went on a shooting spree but transformed into "Ladys" when they celebrated in fancy dress at George Roger Clark's new Fort Nelson at the Falls of the Ohio in 1779.[21]

Kentucky women sent their men off to battle regularly throughout the early years, in the hopes of a safer, more civilized life. Colonel John Todd, who built the Lexington fort, had brought his Virginia wife and slaves to join him during these dangerous times. Jane Hawkins Todd held tea parties while still living in the fort, though, as one woman remembered her mother telling it, she had "nothing but tea and dried buffaloe [sic] meat."[22] Todd brought her genteel manners and worldview with her from Virginia and crafted her world of parlor politics even in the midst of frontier violence.

At the same time, the household economy of eighteenth-century farms in which women and men worked together to be self-sufficient changed with the rise of urban factories and a market economy. Sweatshops and the new age of the machine transformed American labor systems. Slater's Mill in Rhode Island, the first commercially successful cotton-spinning mill with a fully mechanized power system in America, started operating in 1793. Central Kentucky entrepreneurs had mechanized the carding and spinning of cotton, hemp, and linen within a decade. According to the 1806 Lexington directory, John Wesley Hunt, one of the first millionaires west of the Alleghenies, had a "Duck (canvas) manufactory" that employed forty to fifty "hands"—very likely young girls or boys between eight and sixteen years of age, enslaved and hired out to the factory or free children bound in apprenticeships. Society expected married women to perform domestic labor in their own or someone else's home—and this contribution to the labor force became less valued by the new nation, which focused on the new demands for labor in the new factories and offices.

Eighteenth-century depictions of liberty and independence relied on certain assumptions about white women in the new republic. For example, in the 1786 seal for the Philadelphia Society for the Promotion of Agriculture,[23] Liberty celebrates the agrarian citizen-soldier as he makes good

A piano was a critical component of an educated woman's household. This Clementi spinet, made in England in 1800 and imported to Staunton, Virginia, was given as a present to Martha Elizabeth Garber by her father when she married William Adam Menzies. Menzies brought it to Woodford County, Kentucky, in 1810. Her daughter, Mrs. George Nicholson Johnson, donated it to the Kentucky Historical Society in 1882. (Photograph from C. Frank Dunn Photographs Collection, 1900–1954, bulk 1920–1940, 1987PH2. Kentucky Historical Society, Special Collections and Archives, Frankfort, Kentucky.)

on the promise of independence, and, in a 1796 lithograph by Edward Savage,[24] Liberty stands under the liberty cap and flag as she nurtures the eagle symbolizing the victorious new nation. She was triumphant in her place as moral compass. With the rise of the new nation, white women's trousseaux, their dress, and their manners served as important watchwords for the new American identity separate from the royalist Europeans or the supposedly barbaric American Indians. As many a visitor to early Lexington noted, central Kentucky's elite white women dressed extravagantly and paraded themselves in the streets as well as in drawing rooms as living embellishments of a newly created civilization. These women, perceived as sitting passively on the sidelines with flowery accolades for the heroic republican, exhibited the feminine sensibilities of modesty, compassion, and decorum while at the same time functioning as standard-bearers of the virtuous new republic.

The role of the republican mother in teaching her son presupposes a formal education above and beyond what her colonial mothers knew. Southern families relied on social events in their homes, and with the rituals of hospitality came exposure to new ideas and politics.[25] Young ladies' academies became popular in this time period, and the practical value of women who knew history, empirical science, political theory, and moral philosophy lay in their ability to prepare their children for the new nation. At the same time, the academy's curriculum must include the fine arts so that the educated lady could soothe her husband and his friends on their return from the new battlefields of capitalism and electoral politics. "Thus, as postwar intellectuals urged their country-men and -women to acknowledge women's moral and intellectual capacities, they drew a tight circle around the space in which she would apply them: the home and family."[26]

Lexington had three schools for girls before 1800. Around 1793, Ann Walsh opened a school just for girls where they would learn spelling, reading, and needlework. In 1797, Lucy Gray established an academy at her country home four miles out from town where lessons included Italian and arithmetic. The next year, James W. Stevens rented the upper story of Montgomery Bell's storehouse to use as a young ladies' academy "in order to prevent an indiscriminate intercourse of the sexes so injurious to the morals, and incompatible with the delicacy of the 'fair' for the purpose of conferring the degree of a classical education."[27] The most famous Lexington schools in the early 1800s attracted girls from all over the nation: Beck's, Mentelle's (which Mary Todd attended), Dunham's (which was renamed Lafayette Female Academy after the beloved general visited there in 1825), St. Catherine's, and Sayre Female Academy.[28] As an article in the *Kentucky Gazette* trumpeted in July 1806 after the year-end exams at Mrs. Beck's School:

> Let the world be told, that young ladies from every part of the State, are here, not only made *perfect* in the elegant and useful arts of reading and spelling, and writing, and accounts, and drawing, and music, but that they have also infused into them, with *great care* the first principles of geography, and astronomy and logic, and rhetoric and natural philosophy. In the instruction, we hail the dawn of that day, when science shall establish her universal empire over the inhabit-

ants of the Western world—when *sisters* shall vie with their brothers in their knowledge of every useful part of literature, and when *Mothers* shall be able to judge for themselves, what progress their sons and daughters are making in the places of public education.[29]

The conscious effort to create an educated and enlightened society makes a case for perceiving the ideal of womanhood in Kentucky to be more active than passive, more literate and assertive in genteel company conversation than pliant and wallflower-like. Women's role in the building of Lexington's cultural identity becomes clearer by looking between the lines of documented events. In 1810, the fear of a local slave revolt modeled on Prosser's in Virginia launched an intense military action against the black population in Lexington.[30] In that same year, the Shawnee renewed their attacks from the north and along the Ohio River, and Lexingtonians took up the battle cry again. It was the passion of his fellow Lexingtonians that shone in Henry Clay's speeches when he was elected to the U.S. House of Representatives for the first time in 1811 to lead the famed "War Hawks" in bullying James Madison into war against Great Britain. Though hidden from view in historical accounts, Kentucky's women outfitted the men in six companies, including the Lexington Light Infantry, which paraded through Lexington on its way north to fight once more against the British and the Indians. Those same women must have listened enthusiastically when Clay boasted to his fellow congressmen: Kentucky men alone would conquer Canada. In February 1815, Lexington celebrated the victory at New Orleans and the Treaty of Ghent, and the churchgoing women of the city participated openly in the celebrations. A notice in the *Kentucky Gazette* announced a resolution passed by the trustees of Lexington: "Resolved, That the Citizens of the Town be requested to attend at their respective houses of Divine Worship . . . to render homage to the Supreme Ruler of the Universe, and to express their gratitude to Him for the signal success with which He has been pleased to crown the American arms under the command of Major-General ANDREW JACKSON."[31] Yes, women could attend public orations at the courthouse, fireworks displays, torchlight parades, and even some of the elegant dinners complete with long dramatic toasts. However, their public participation in churchgoing would also express their patriotism—upholding a womanly ideal for moral reform against excessive individual pride.[32]

Another public arena for women's active roles in creating the new nation and the state presented itself through the fervor of the Second Great Awakening. The great revivals of Kentucky started in the summer of 1800, but, even before then, frontier families would travel for miles to attend a Sunday preaching marathon that would last two to three hours. Few churches had pews, and most early churches segregated their congregations by sex and race. The service would end with a family picnic and important social and political interactions that served as "welcome relief from the toil and loneliness of frontier life."[33] During the in-migrations of the 1790s, the established frontier churches could not keep up, and the historical records emphasize the obsession with salvation and redemption in the white and black communities during this time of transition. Informal "fast and prayer" societies came into vogue, and religious tract publishers made big profits.

Little is known about the more informal activities in women's homes, but historians acknowledge that these then fueled the attendance at the camp revivals as well as the later, better documented temperance, abolitionist, and Sunday School movements. A good example is Margaretta Mason Brown, who came to Frankfort in 1801. The daughter of a Presbyterian minister from New York City, she married the Kentucky senator John Brown, a man who had read law with Thomas Jefferson. Influenced by Mary Wollstonecraft's *A Vindication of the Rights of Woman*, she was fiercely antislavery and a dedicated mother to her boys. She led study circles for young women in her home (often held in the lovely orchard behind the house) and in 1810 established the first Sunday School west of the Allegheny Mountains. Her work came to fruition with the formation of the First Presbyterian Church of Frankfort. On the death of her seven-year-old daughter (the second child of hers to die), she and her husband quit society and invited clergy to preach at her home at any time. Frankfort's citizens came to call her home "the Preachers' Hotel"—and when she knew a sermon was to be delivered she would send a servant through the streets ringing a cow bell to invite others to attend. Her religious fervor and continued mourning did not halt her political activities, however. She hosted visits from prestigious national figures, including President James Monroe (who came with General Andrew Jackson and Major Zachary Taylor) and General Lafayette.[34]

More examples of women's evangelism and self-efficacy can be found in the story of Milly Crawford of Lexington, the mother of Alfred Russell, an Episcopal minister and the tenth president of Liberia.[35] Milly, a light-skinned African American, was born into slavery in 1803 at the farm of Jane Hawkins Todd on the Boonesborough Road (now called Richmond Road) two miles east of the center of Lexington. Milly's mother, Anaka, had been brought to Lexington from Virginia to serve Jane but legally belonged to Jane's brother, James Hawkins. Thus, when Jane Todd married Colonel Thomas Irvine, Anaka and Milly stayed with her but never changed owners. When this second marriage soured, Jane, Milly, and Anaka moved to Crawford County, Illinois, to be with Hawkins relatives sometime after 1808. On August 17, 1817, Milly gave birth to Alfred Francis Russell. His skin was white and his dark hair softly curled. Jane and James Hawkins both died in 1822, and Milly and Alfred's fates fell into the hands of Littleberry Hawkins. On his way to Texas in 1825, Littleberry Hawkins sold Milly and Alfred to a slave trader, J. B. R. McIlwain, to settle James Hawkins's estate. Jane's daughter, Mary Owen "Polly" Todd Russell, bought Milly and the eight-year-old Alfred for $650 from the slave dealer on April 8, 1825, and brought them to her mansion, Glendower, in Lexington.

A very religious woman and an important founding member of the Market Street Presbyterian Church, Polly Russell served on the governing board of the Lunatic Asylum and helped start an orphanage for poor white children of Lexington. She sent her son, John Russell, to Eton and then Princeton for schooling even though she feared for his poor health. He died at twenty-two in 1822, the same year as his grandmother and uncle. In 1826, Polly married Robert Wickliffe, an ambitious lawyer and landowner, and went through a series of legal transactions to assure her continued ownership of her slaves. Only two years later, she became a member of the newly formed Kentucky Colonization Society. Charlotte Mentelle, a French teacher whose boarding school sat on the land donated by her friend Polly, wrote how Polly believed that she was bettering the world by sending freed slaves to Liberia. Polly's actions came from "benevolence and from her conception of the sense of the scriptures . . . ; what she wished and contemplated for the black part of the human race, was the recognition of what she thought its rights; and support by its labors in the freedom of enjoying it. . . . She thought colonization and industry the only ways to secure permanent good."[36]

Those may have been Polly's sentiments, but Milly's perspective remains undocumented. Perhaps Milly wanted her and her child's freedom so badly that she would travel to Africa for it, or perhaps she felt a calling to evangelize in the new African republic of Liberia, as her white patrons believed she should. Relatively few black Kentuckians, whether slave or free, chose the risky path of emigration, and free blacks continued to insist on acquiring full rights as American citizens.[37] Perhaps the family rumors were true: that she had been raped by Polly's son, John Russell, while he visited his grandmother in Illinois while on vacation from Princeton and she could no longer stand living with the bereaved mother.[38]

Either way, she and her child earned their freedom when they joined over a hundred other settlers traveling to Liberia under the sponsorship of the American Colonization Society. In March 1833, Milly and Alfred left Lexington with their cousin Lucy Russell and her four children, Sinthia, Gilbert, George, and Henry. Sometime later, George Crawford joined them. Milly wrote a long letter of thanks from their first stop in Frankfort, revealing her formal speech to be laced with references to her faith in God:

March 10 1833 Saterday night

My Dear Misstress we have all arrived at frankfort in safety and health little George Lucy and all the children are well. My dear Misstress how shall we thank you for all your kindness too us. We sometimes despond being all females and children haveing no male protecter of our own. but we try to put our trust in the Almighty and go on in his srength. whatever betide us. My Dear Mystress you have done your whole duty. and may the [Almighty] bless and reward you a thousand fold.[39]

They traveled on to Louisville to board the riverboat *Mediterranean*. From there, they sailed down the Ohio and Mississippi Rivers to New Orleans and boarded the brig *Ajax* on April 20. A bout of cholera, whooping cough, or bowel disorders forced the brig to put in for many days at a West Indian island, and 30 of the 146 new settlers (mostly children) died while anchored off the coast.[40] The *Lexington Observer and Reporter* noted the tragedy and in passing mentioned that one of the survivors was "a female slave brought up by Mrs. Wickliffe, who possessed a superior education and gifted mind, and was intended for a teacher in Liberia. With her was her son Alfred who was to become a minister."[41] The author of this article ensured that all readers knew of Milly's virtues and abilities as well as of the wealthy Mary Owen Todd Russell Wickliffe's role as an active abolitionist in a slave state. This small public notice is of particular significance since this is a time of great debate locally and nationally about women's roles and the rights of African Americans.

Milly and Alfred arrived in Liberia on July 11, 1833, after three months of being on the *Ajax*, and the authorities immediately put them under quarantine. Eventually, Milly and Alfred moved to Caldwell on the St. Paul's River (formerly Bassa country). Few houses stood ready for them to live in, little food could be bought, and no other doctors cared for the ill besides a Dr. Mechlin who was in charge of the whole colony. Milly started a garden right away—probably raising corn, potatoes, cassava, plantains, and bananas—and her husband, George, joined her in Caldwell.

Nearly half of all emigrants from the United States died within the year. According to letters from Alfred later in life,[42] Milly knew that "Mrs. Polly" had sent money to the colonization society for Milly to use in Africa. The white minister who was the colony agent, however, chose to purchase farming equipment for the community to use. When the equipment came by ship late and unattended, it was lost and probably stolen at the port. Lucy also never received any of the money that had been reserved for her use. Milly and George made a living probably from farming and trading, and they kept Alfred in school to be trained as a teacher. Eventually, Alfred was ordained as a minister, and he traveled inland as a missionary "on the Goulab and Pessa lines." While he was away, Milly died in 1845 of "dropsey"—a general swelling of the body due to kidney disorder. In 1877, Alfred Russell, by then a successful coffee and sugarcane planter, won election as vice-president of Liberia under President Anthony W. Gardner. When President Gardner resigned in 1883, Alfred became the tenth president of the country.[43]

While the evangelism of Polly Wickliffe and Milly Crawford played out in the rural villages of West Africa, other women fueled the religious fervor at home in Kentucky. Women traveled the rough trails of the backcountry for days to attend camp revivals. Some felt empowered by the gatherings to take up a new life of religious homosocial communalism. Some joined the United Society of Believers in Christ's Second Coming—the Shakers at South Union and at Pleasant Hill (near Harrodsburg). They promised to live a "virgin life" and abstain from any forms of lust, especially sex. For rural women who lived a life of endless work, constant pregnancy, and degradation in a violent world of men, the Shaker communal life must have seemed a haven.[44] There, they could learn a trade, become educated, worship ecstatically, and be a part of a community that respected them as human beings. The Shakers' simple, functional designs for household and farming tools and furniture, breed stock, specially hybridized seeds, music and dancing, and self-published books became popular in secular culture. These industries served not only as the sustaining income for the Shaker community but also as a form of recruiting and publicity. The idea of Mother Ann Lee as the second half of Jesus, the female form of Christ, must have been truly radical and empowering for those who routinely heard from their regular preachers of the evils of women as daughters of Eve and Jezebel. In the years before the Civil War, the Shakers reached their peak membership and had become a tourist attraction for outsiders to observe on Saturday evenings.[45]

For women dedicated to spiritual contemplation, higher education, and hard work, the Sisters of Loretto (in Marion County) and the Sisters of Charity of Nazareth (in Bardstown, then at St. Catherine's in Washington County) stood tall. In the early nineteenth century, these powerful Kentucky women chose a religious setting in order to fulfill their ambitions. In 1811, Mary Rhodes came from Maryland to visit her brother and sister in St. Charles (a little town today known as St. Mary). Angry that her nieces did not have basic skills in reading and arithmetic or know their catechism, she began to teach them daily. Neighbors soon began to ask if their children could join in the lessons. After receiving the approval of the local priest, Father Charles Nerinckx, Mary set up a school in an abandoned old log cabin and, with the help of two women who joined her effort, Christine Stewart and Nancy Havern, set up an unused cabin for their living quarters. They approached Father Nerinckx to ask for his support in taking the steps needed to form their own religious order. He agreed to observe them for three years and, as a test of their obedience, gave them a Rule to live by based on the teachings of the great Christian misogynist St. Augustine. Nellie Morgan and the young Ann Rhodes, suffering from tuberculosis, became the fourth and fifth members of the order. Finally convinced of the women's commitment, Father Nerinckx raised the funds and made the journey to Rome to submit the Rule with an additional request. The women's new order would be placed directly under the pope's jurisdiction and independent from bishops in Europe. The Vatican agreed, and, on April 25, 1812, the Sisters of Mary became the first order of nuns founded in America.

This organization of young Catholic women often drew criticism from church authorities threatened by female leaders.[46] However, news of the "American sisters for American children" spread, and people remembered that a girl walked all the way from the Missouri Territory to join them. By 1815, there were fourteen members of the community, and the order began to establish schools in other settlements. Five years later, the order began a program for teacher training, Mary chose to return to the rank of sister, and Christine Stewart was elected to be "Dear Mother." Today, the Loretto schools can be found in sixteen states, China, South America, and

Africa. The sisters' commitment to social justice continues, and they not only serve as social workers but also participate in protests against terrorism, torture, and the death penalty through the order's nongovernment organization status at the United Nations. In the early nineteenth century, however, many perceived these Catholic sisters as aberrant, not too much different in the eyes of the rural Baptist preacher from the Shaker women who spurned men's sexual advances.

Working women in central Kentucky were the norm, whether free or slave, so the hard work in women's religious orders was nothing new to their recruits. Though Lexington early on became an urban center, the rich farmlands around it served as a reminder of what most women in Kentucky experienced every day.[47] Women's lives in the rural southern backcountry of the nineteenth century meant isolation and loneliness, especially for black women, and the social gatherings that reinforced kin networks, religious beliefs, or political agendas served as wonderful diversions from the usual drudgery of subsistence farming.[48] Central Kentucky's industrial and financial growth relied on and profited from the agriculture around it. Though not much research has been done on the status of women in the Lexington environs, the topic is worth exploring.

Lexington's early industrial workforce included women and girls, both slave and free, on farms and in the city. The importance of hemp and other textiles to early Kentucky has been documented. Around 1810, for example, there were two steam mills processing both flour and cotton, two cut-nail factories, four hat factories, thirteen ropewalks, five bagging factories, two sail-duck factories, four cotton and two wool spinning factories, a spectacle factory that mounted glasses, soap- and candle-making industries, a tobacco factory, a piano manufactory, an oil mill, and a paper mill. Of the five wool-carding factories, the newly invented machinery run by horsepower was touted as being so simple that "any child could run it."[49] The Lexington Manufactory advertised in 1816 for women, girls, and children over nine years to work—alongside its call for twenty men and boys from fourteen to twenty-one years of age.[50] Ropewalks, bagging factories, and weaving factories needed the dexterous hands of women and children already knowledgeable in the mechanics of textile production.

Women's role in the northern U.S. textile industries has been well documented and analyzed, but the history of the urban Upper South's female workforce remains largely ignored. Lexington most likely attracted girls into the urban workforce for the better personal wages and different types of work available there than on the farm. Table 2 shows evidence of an extraordinary growth of businesses run by women in Lexington.

Professional women were listed in the first directory of 1806 (properly employed in professions considered evidence of their gentility), yet 12 of the 18 women listed (out of 266 names total in the directory) list no profession. By 1818, however, with the rapid population growth of Lexington during its ascendency as the "Athens of the West," more women appear as heads of household and owners of businesses, including an African American, Esther Underwood, who lived on Mulberry and is described as the "widow of Sam." Mrs. Underwood is in the 1818 Fayette County tax listing with two lots of land valued at $1,200, two horses, two cows, and a "cart"—a large one since it was valued at $40. She is also in the 1820 census as a "free colored person" with three members of her household. A brave and resourceful woman indeed. The MacCabe directory describing Lexington and Fayette County in 1838–1839 shows an exponential rise in the number of professional, independently wealthy women in Lexington (white and black), women with a great variety of skills.

The historian Wendy Gordon compared the "independent migration" of young, unmarried, and unchaperoned girls to the urban mills and marketplaces in England, Scotland, and the U.S. Northeast. Women's supportive networks in these manufacturing centers helped attract and retain women workers—though women alone and outside family relationships were viewed with suspicion. Gordon posits that women made the choice to move out of the home and migrate in order to transition to adult responsibilities. She notes that, in all three of her cases, by the 1850s the average age of women millworkers was between twenty-six and thirty-eight years and that most, though not all, were married.[51]

Women also took on important economic roles in the several marketplaces in early Lexington. There were at least six market houses in antebellum Lexington, and, in 1813, the watchman polled the town's housekeepers to determine their preferences for market days.[52] Women of all classes were important in early Lexington as consumers.[53] Besides employment in the regular market houses, women likely worked as street vendors and on-demand service providers such as laundresses, cooks, midwives, charwomen, and prostitutes. Likely places for successful women entrepreneurs were at the many stagecoach taverns and train depots in and around Lexington[54] and the county courthouse in the center of town.

One famous street vendor was Charlotte, who sold pies and cakes on the courthouse square. Her story was told in passing by the Lexington historian George Ranck in 1872,[55] and she is softened and romanticized as the iconic black mammy in the colorful stories of "King Solomon" by James Lane Allen in the 1880s.[56] The legends tell of a free black woman

Table 2
Female Heads of Household: Women's Names in Early Lexington Directories

Occupations	1806	1818	1838 & 1839	1859–1860
Asylum staff (matron attendant, etc.)				15
Boardinghouse		3	8	14
Boot/shoe trimmer			1	
Cart proprietor			1	
Confectioner and fancy goods			(1)	
Dressmaker			9	5
Embroideress				1
Fancy store			1	1
French teacher				1
Grocer		2	2	5
Hat trimmer			1	
Housekeeper				1
Laundress			(13)	1 (1)
Mattress maker			1	
Mantua maker				2
Midwife		1		
Milliner and millinery store	2	3	3	19 (1)
Morocco manufacturer			1	
Music teacher			1	1
Nurse				(1)
Schoolmistress	2	1	2	15
Seamstress	2	1	3 (2)	1

who saved the vagrant William Solomon from alcoholism and heavy labor. He was put up by the sheriff of Lexington to be hired out to the highest bidder at an "assembly concerning the poor,"[57] and, so the story goes, Charlotte paid the money to free him and sober him up in time for him to become the volunteer gravedigger during the terrible summer of

Table 2 (cont'd)
Female Heads of Household: Women's Names in Early Lexington Directories

Occupations	1806	1818	1838 & 1839	1859–1860
Servant				2
Shirt manufactory				1
Shoe binder			(1)	
Soap and candle manufactory				2
Tailoress			6	
Tannery owner				1
Weaver			(1)	
Women with no occupation listed or listed as "gentle-woman" or "widow of . . ."	12	23 (1)	67	315 (64)
Total	18 of 266 names (6.8%)	35 of 341 names (10.3%)	125 of 902 names (13.9%)	470 of 2,315 names (20.3%)

Source: Joseph Charless, *Lexington Directory, Taken for Charless' Almanack, for 1806* (Lexington, 1806); Julius P. Bolivar MacCabe, *Directory of the City of Lexington and County of Fayette for 1838 & '39* (Lexington, 1838); C. S. Williams, *Williams' Lexington [Kentucky] Directory, City Guide, and Business Mirror,* vol. 1, *1859–60* (Lexington, 1859); and William Worsley and Thomas Smith, *Directory of the Town of Lexington, for 1818* (1818; reprint, Lexington, 1953).

Note: Free black women are numbered in parentheses when identified as of color in the directory. The single black woman listed in the 1818 directory is Esther Underwood on Mulberry, "widow of Sam" (vs. such designations as "Mrs. Eliza Trotter," "southern suburb," and "widow of Gen George Trotter"). The 1818 Fayette County tax list shows "Underwood, heirs of Samuel (colored)," but no occupation is listed; the entry under sex is "ha"; also shown are two inlots valued at $1,200, two horses valued at $100, one cow valued at $10, one (4WH_N) valued at $150, and, under the Other Tax "cart" valued at $40, one house, one stable, one death, total blacks four, no specific address listed for the directory. The 1820 census identifies her in the list of "free colored persons residing in Lexington" as (En[r?]ster Underwood) with three in her household.

1833 when hundreds of Lexingtonians died during the cholera epidemic and thousands fled to the countryside to escape the disease (and the terrible medicines used by the local doctors to try and cure those afflicted). No legal or other historical records have been found to substantiate this favorite story of white Kentuckians in every century.[58] The journalist and local historian extraordinaire Burton Milward tried to find the historical Charlotte but did not succeed.[59] He surmised that a reference to "Free

Charlotte" in the Lexington Town Trustees Book might be the one of the King Solomon legends. On May 7, 1829, Lexington paid Free Charlotte $1.50 for cleaning the watch house—and she appears again on August 6 of that same year when she was paid an additional $0.75.[60] However, Milward did not find her in the list of cholera victims—and he did not say whether he looked in the deed books, census, or tax lists.

A search for Charlotte in the public records produced one "Charlotte Lewis col. wn" in the 1830 census. Listed as the head of her household, she lived with two free black men, one between thirty-five and fifty-four years of age and the other aged fifty-five or older. Her age is between thirty-six and fifty-five. Neither Charlotte Lewis nor William Solomon appears in the Fayette County Deed Books, where indentures are recorded, or in the Fayette County Order Book for 1833. Charlotte Lewis is not on the Fayette County tax lists for any year in the 1830s, nor is she in the 1820 or the 1840 census. Perhaps some still-extant church record includes her, but no other official records mention her again. Charlotte Lewis might be the famous "Aunt Charlotte."

The life of a black woman in Kentucky was hard and fraught with dangers, even if she were free. By 1798, Kentucky enacted its first slave code, requiring slaves to have a written pass if away from their residences for more than four hours, or suffer ten lashes if caught. In 1800, African Americans constituted just over 18 percent of Kentucky's population of nearly 221,000, and only a fraction of black Kentuckians (741) were free. The percentage of blacks in Kentucky's population reached its zenith in 1830 with over 24 percent.[61] The historian Marion Lucas tells of Julett, an older woman slave whose relationship with John G. Fee's mother was rocky enough that Kentucky's most famous abolitionist bought her and gave her a "perpetual pass." This was not enough for Julett; she wanted Fee to acquire her husband, Add, and their children, knowing they could be sold away from her at any time. Just before the Civil War, she and some of her younger children migrated to Ohio. When she heard that her children and grandchildren left behind as slaves were going to be sold South, she returned to help them escape. Patrollers caught her and her band of refugees before they reached the Ohio River and imprisoned her and her whole family. A slave trader sold them to southern slave markets.[62]

Black female domestic servants, almost always in the near vicinity of whites, had more chance of being subjected to racial violence. Whites feared black women's access to their food and used this to punish recalcitrant women. The famous abolitionist Cassius M. Clay accused one of his enslaved women of trying to poison his child, and the sentence would have been death had the proslavery jury believed him. A black woman by the name of Casilly was executed in Fayette County in 1849 for putting broken glass in the white family's food, and another woman known in the records only as "Harriet" was put to death after being convicted of "poisoning the master's coffee."[63] Women were flogged at the public whipping post in the courthouse yard, and their screams drew crowds.[64] Young black women in the new cities of Kentucky were most vulnerable to slave traders, who wanted to use them as "fancy girls." Whether for sale or just for manhandling, slave women of all colors, but especially the "high yellow" women, were highly desired by white men. According to Marion Lucas, enslaved women in the sex markets of Lexington, Frankfort, and Louisville could by the 1840s garner prices as high as—or higher than—male fieldworkers.[65]

Public auctions in the county courthouse yard at Cheapside gained greater notoriety than the private sales by slave traders or plantation owners.[66] A story told often is of the public sale of Eliza, "white with lustrous eyes, straight black hair and a rich olive complexion."[67] The climax of the story always comes with the slowdown of bids and the auctioneer ripping off the front of her dress and then lifting her skirts to her waist to show the curious crowd her body. A similar story is told of two white sisters who were attending Oberlin College and came home to attend their father's funeral. They were seized as part of his estate and auctioned off to a slave trader, who sent them to New Orleans for sale at the "fancy girls" market there. William Wells Brown, a refugee from Kentucky slavery, included the plight of a white slave girl on the auction block in his novel *Clotel; or, The President's Daughter.*[68]

The ultimate resistance to slavery was to run away, and women did. Of the several advertisements in Kentucky newspapers for women who ran away, most included references to the fugitives being with men, some even carrying children with them. In the slave narrative by William Wells Brown (unlike in that of Frederick Douglass, who writes almost dispassionately about the terrible treatment of female slaves in his youth), his mother tries in vain to protect her boy from being sold away by his biological father. In 1820, the *Lexington Public Advertiser* ran a $100 reward ad for the return to Nathaniel Prentiss or M. A. Giraud of three slaves, Ned, "his wife," Sukey, and a six-month-old baby girl. "Sukey is a very bright black woman, very large full eyes, her voice soft and fine."[69]

A famous runaway Kentucky woman was Margaret Garner, who killed her own baby rather than see him returned to slavery, a scene eerily similar to that in *Uncle Tom's Cabin* where the mother jumps into the river and drowns herself after being sold South and having her baby taken from her.[70] The abolitionist Harriet Beecher Stowe chastises white southern women for their heartlessness through the character of the southern belles: the passive Emily Shelby (who is later iconized in Stephen Foster's "My Old Kentucky Home" as the lady weeping as the family slaves are sold) and the spoiled, motherless Marie St. Clare. The southern slave owner St. Clare had married Marie because she was "the reigning belle of the season": "He became the husband of a fine figure, a pair of bright eyes, and a hundred thousand dollars." In one scene, the hypochondriac Marie complains that she does not get enough attention from her beloved Mammy. Saying that Mammy would mourn for her children and husband, from whom she was separated when she was sent to New Orleans with Marie on her marriage, Marie whines to the heroic Miss Ophelia (who stands in for all women abolitionists): "I believe that Mammy has always kept up a sort of sulkiness about this. . . . They are just so selfish, now, the best of them."[71]

Descriptions of woman's proper sphere in the antebellum era centered as they do today on this mythological southern belle. She flourished in an elite world of the sentimental adulation of female purity and the male code of honor. The historian Barbara Welter studied religious tracts, advice literature, and fashion magazines such as *Godey's Lady's Book* and wrote that these characters portrayed a "cult" of "true womanhood" with four cardinal virtues: domesticity, piety, submissiveness, and purity.[72] Though few of Welter's references included southern women, Kentucky women read similar literature. The Lexington Female Tract Society reported that it had distributed ten thousand tracts in 1821,[73] and records of customers seeking the latest in fashions from Philadelphia, New York, and Paris abound in Kentucky archives.

Mainstream assumptions about the white women of antebellum Kentucky can be found in contemporary literature: Bel Tracy in John Pendleton Kennedy's *Swallow Barn* (1832) is very similar to the women in the Kentucky novel *Woodburn*, by Rosa Vertner Johnson.[74] Bel is a sixteen-year-old marriageable daughter of a landed family who is doted on by her father and becomes exuberant, a little vain, and a little naive. Talented as a horsewoman, skilled in music, and proud of her aristocratic heritage, she wants not just a man but a "gallant cavalier." The literature describes a society that preferred its women to be charming coquettes who were swathed in yards and yards of material and bound tightly by corsets yet would never yield their purity to slim, aristocratic young swains.

In 1835, Thomas R. Dew proferred his advice to women in the *Southern Literary Messenger.* A woman must learn how to win men's protection, he said, as she is confined within "the domestic circle." A good woman must cultivate "those qualities which delight and fascinate—which are calculated to win over to her side the proud lord of creation, and to make him a humble supplicant at her shrine. Grace, modesty, and loveliness are the charms which constitute her power."[75] In her history of plantation women, Catherine Clinton decried: "Cotton was King, white men ruled, and both white women and slaves served the same master."[76] However, the historian Mary P. Ryan stressed the need to remember women's "multiple points of entry into the public life" in the nineteenth century and not simply reorganize those pieces of evidence within some artificially contrived boundary of "public" versus "domestic" spheres.[77]

In real life, belles functioned politically in multiple ways alongside and sometimes despite men—either as great entertainers in their homes, as letter writers, as powerful marriage brokers for their children, or as flamboyant widows free to spend their money on whatever political cause they wished. The antebellum American elite allowed for and expected women's power wherever they gathered together. Whether in the streets, in a tavern, in church, on a dueling ground, at a dinner table, or in a parlor salon, white elite women had prescribed spaces in which they could garner respect and admiration for their quick wit, their sophisticated arguments, and theatrical displays of their inherited wealth and power. Antebellum women's political acts might be found in wills dispensing valuable properties, in their carefully contrived utterances in a spa's parlor, in personal letters seeking patronage favors for their kin, or in relating economic or political information to their elite peers. These evidences are as important as records of their clubs and community service and their fund-raising for schools, asylums, orphanages, or missionary work. These more hidden evidences are, indeed, proof of their political work, yet this proof has been systematically made almost invisible today. Not until long after the Civil War did southern women venture into legislatures to present petitions signed by the hard door-to-door campaigns, and too many historians assume that these activities represent the first evidences of their political ideology.

How do we interpret the work of Lucretia Hart Clay, managing a huge plantation of sixty slaves and expensive animal stock with eleven children of her own? She sold produce, eggs, and chickens to downtown hotels, entertained presidents and other political notables, and saved her profligate husband from bankruptcy, as one writer put it, "again and again."[78]

Most elite politico women represented and preserved "the innate and indigenous conservatism of Kentuckians."[79] Rarely did those who threatened the social hierarchy of race and class acquire much political power in Kentucky.

Yet elite white women could garner much influence, even at the dinner table. Mary Todd Lincoln, the daughter of a wealthy Bluegrass banker, grew up a member of a large, politically savvy family in the center of Henry Clay's seat of power. Educated in Lexington, where girls' schools abounded since the eighteenth century, she "stood in no awe of great men, they were to her as much a matter of course as the air she breathed": "At fourteen she knew why she was a Whig and not a Democrat."[80] As a wife and mother, she found that her openly partisan politics worked most effectively in the parlor and in public assemblies. With the rise of her husband to the White House, she became an overnight celebrity and refused to seclude herself upstairs, as her predecessors had. Mary Todd Lincoln crafted a presidential household like none other before.[81] However, the Washington ladies' open rejection of her made her impatient and angry—assuring that she never gained the social insiders' approval. Even more damaging was her tendency to see these relationships as "extensions of politics," "her party being ever the Lincoln one of her marriage."[82] She demanded intense loyalty from her friends, and, as did her enemies, they felt her wrath when her husband or his legacy was in danger. Then, with the deaths of her sons and husband, any successes she may have had as First Lady took a back seat to the stories of her instability and lack of decorum. In the 1882 *The Ladies of the White House*, Laura Holloway spoke for her age when she said: "Mrs. Lincoln was not greatly inclined to observe the requirements of her social position, and she thereby lost opportunities of advancing her husband's interests of which she perhaps was unaware. She did not rightly estimate the importance of conciliatory address with friend and foe alike, and seemed not conscious of the immense assistance which, as the wife of a public man, she had it in her power to give her husband. And this was all the more singular for the reason that she was very ambitious."[83]

The same story of the rejection of an ambitious, educated woman must be told of Mary Austin Holley. A gifted musician and writer, the wife of the controversial president of Transylvania University did little to help his political chances for success as a liberal freethinker in the 1820s when Lexington society was fast imposing its own sense of conservative propriety. She never seemed to get the right level of social acceptance by her peers in those early years and probably even hurt his career by writing controversial essays in a local journal and holding soirees with extravagant delicacies, music, and dancing as if the clergy and church leaders invited to her home did not matter.[84]

By the 1840s, the up-and-coming of Kentucky society moved to the shiny new river cities of Louisville and Cincinnati. The famous Sallie Ward dominated men and women alike with her charm—and, when that did not work to her advantage, she used her family connections to keep her sociopolitical ascendancy. Born in 1827 in Georgetown, the eldest daughter of the planter and lawyer-politician Robert Ward, Sallie was brought up in Louisville in a mansion located in the fashionable area at Second and Walnut. She attended a French finishing school, and her doting parents gave her debut to southern society in May 1846; she traveled to extravagant parties in Newport, White Sulpher Springs, and New Orleans. Her poet/journalist admirer George Prentice of the *Louisville Journal* wrote: "Genius comprehends all the loveliness of woman, and to be a famous belle one must be a genius." According to the historian Thomas D. Clark, at the Harrodsburg Springs' huge dining table, a three-cornered "race" occurred among Sallie, Prentice, and old Dr. Christopher Columbus Graham: "No one else dared interrupt when Sally and George were exchanging thrusts with their flashing wits." Sallie's portrait by George Peter Alexander Healy (now housed in the Speed Museum, Louisville) shows idealized small hands and a rounded figure with auburn hair, blue eyes, and penciled brows. Clark wrote that Prentice said the girl "was intended for a princess, but by accident, lived under the flag of a republic."[85]

Her pranks and feats as a horsewoman became legendary in her own time and after her death, when memories of the Old South still sold profitably to an admiring audience. An early twentieth-century book on southern belles described how Sallie became bored with a gentleman suitor one afternoon while riding horses in a park. She galloped through the Louisville market house with a dare to "her patronizing riding companion" to follow, destroying market stalls as they went. The admiring author wrote that Sallie then taunted her gentleman suitor: "'Now, sir, you'll have a pretty fine to pay, $25 apiece, for that little stretch,' but when he went to pay, found she had already paid."[86] Sallie's independence and aristocratic air of extravagant wastefulness made her public adore her all the more.

At age twenty-two, in December 1848, she married Bigelow Lawrence, whose father sold cotton on the foreign market and became ambassador to England. The wedding party of four hundred was well described in the local papers, and the newlyweds spent their honeymoon at her father's home in Louisville. When they finally traveled to their own home in

Boston five months later, Sallie continued to live in the style to which she had grown accustomed—her own. She wore slippers on the street, leaving her ankles exposed to the horrified glances of the Boston ladies; she did not come down for company until after noon; and, when forced to come earlier by her mother-in-law, she arrived in her dressing gown. Even more unusual for Boston ladies, Sallie used cosmetics,[87] which led to arguments with her husband over what he considered a lack of wifely obedience. Her mother, a descendent of wealthy Huguenot immigrants who settled in Scott County, Kentucky, wrote: "Stick to it with some of your mother's spunk. . . . Determine one of two things—to give it up at once, or stick to it in defiance of all and everything that may oppose. You cannot live long as you are. Then, Sallie, be a woman, and act as one in future."[88]

Sallie left Boston in August, saying that the weather was too vigorous for her health, and the Lawrence family published open letters in Boston and New York newspapers denouncing her forwardness: "While every reasonable wish was gratified, some foolish whims were opposed, Till Mrs. Lawrence arrived in Boston, she had never learned to heed the wishes of others—the idol of the ballroom had always met with submission, and the secret of obedience had never been acquired by her. . . . We allude to the frequent and free use of paints and other cosmetics. . . . Such a habit could not be allowed, and Mr. Lawrence sought to exert the prerogative of a husband by forbidding its practice."[89] Lawrence Bigelow published a typical advertisement announcing his wife had left him and that he no longer held responsibility for her debts.[90] George Prentice rose to her defense in the *Louisville Journal*, insisting that the advertisement was

> uncalled for, wanton, and outrageous. . . . We have never known a parallel case . . . where a lady of such lofty standing . . . was posted by a husband who even professed to have a claim to the character of a gentleman. . . . There is not a lady in Kentucky more admired and beloved than Mrs. Lawrence . . . kind-hearted, beautiful, fascinating, accomplished, brilliant, . . . the idol and ornament of the society in which she lives. . . . Some of her early hopes have been blighted by her unfortunate matrimonial alliance, but her high heart is uncrushed, and her innumerable admirers and friends cling to her more affectionately than ever, and a thousand aspirations ascend to heaven that she may long continue, as now happy and giving happiness. . . . Our sympathies are entirely in the unfortunate lady's behalf.[91]

On May 25, 1850, Robert Ward appeared before Circuit Judge William F. Bullock, petitioning for a divorce on behalf of his daughter, and testified that Sallie's health was "too delicate for the Boston climate," that "she had always paid her own bills of expense," and that "the first intimation of Mr. Lawrence's dissatisfaction with his wife's residence in Louisville was the publication of the advertisement." The case went to the jury, which determined that "Mrs. Lawrence had been harshly and improperly treated by her husband, and that he had slandered her by his advertisement."[92] The divorce decree was granted to Sallie. Mr. Lawrence obviously did not know that the antebellum southern elite considered a discrete physical separation acceptable.[93] Sallie married three more times in her lifetime. She spent her money lavishly, remaining the belle of the ball with her frequent charity balls for the poor. She was a favorite of Napoléon III's, and Kentuckians seemed proud of the outgoing behavior that Bostonians deemed unwomanly. There were Sallie Ward livestock, steamboats, racehorses, children, and a Sallie Ward slipper and type of walk, even a Sallie Ward type of lavender. Usually, any woman who might stray from the expectation of the ideal woman would be ostracized by her female peers and slowly but surely destroyed by the leading men in the community. Southern white elite men relied heavily on the outward validity of their power over women, as an important component of their sense of honor and manhood.[94] Yet, in this case, her kin network supported Sallie in the divorce proceedings against a northerner, despite those who decried her behavior.

Kentucky's women constituted a vital part of the state's success in these early years all the way through the Progressive Era. Somehow, women lost this status in the mid-twentieth century, and the professional women of today continue to fight the same cultural prejudices. The future success of the commonwealth can best be measured by the status of its women. Today, the most negative stereotype—that of a Rebecca Bryan Boone—reigns over that of a Lucretia Clay, a Margaretta Brown, or even a Sallie Ward. The nation may see Kentucky women through the lens of the failed War on Poverty: poor, barefoot, disfranchised, pregnant from an early age, illiterate, and in ill health. Where is the visibility of the earlier, entrepreneurial Kentucky woman? Studying women's past can help young girls and boys of today create a better tomorrow. Gerda Lerner wrote that history should be seen as a necessity, and, in crafting good history, we must ask ourselves questions that can be answered only by including both men's and women's activities and ideas.[95] What were women doing while men were doing what the books tell us they were doing? What were women experiencing while men were doing what the textbooks highlight as important activities? In this transformative process, we open a vista of greater human experience and of a complexity that defies stereotypes. In this way, historians can improve the discourse of national history, and citizens can take their place as important agents in the nation's aspirations, instead of being victims of stereotyping. The future depends on an ability to be a "critical public" and write better, more inclusive, histories.

Notes

1. Timothy Flint, *Biographical Memoir of Daniel Boone, the First Settler of Kentucky* (Cincinnati, 1833).

2. John Filson, "The Adventures of Colonel Daniel Boone, Containing a Narrative of the Wars of Kentucke," appended to *The Discovery, Settlement and Present State of Kentucke* (Wilmington, DE, 1784).

3. Mrs. [Elizabeth Fries] Ellet, *Pioneer Women of the West* (1852; New York, 1856), 42–57.

4. Filson, *Discovery and Settlement of Kentucke*, 8.

5. See more on this in John Mack Faragher, *Daniel Boone: The Life and Legend of an American Pioneer* (New York, 1992).

6. My work is informed by such theorists as Patricia Hill Collins, bell hooks, Gerda Lerner, Joan Wallach Scott, and Elizabeth Spellman. Denise Riley reminds us, too, that the time period under study is a key part of an era starting in the late seventeenth century in which *woman* "as a category does undergo a broadly increasing degree of sexualization." She also reminds us that the concepts of this categorization shifted—not in "a merely sequential" way from one characterization to another but in a more fundamental way, in a "reconceptualization along sexed lines, in which the understandings of gender both re-order and are themselves re-ordered." Denise Riley, "Does a Sex Have a History?" in *Feminism and History*, ed. Joan Wallach Scott (Oxford, 1996), 17–33, 29.

7. Margaret Ripley Wolfe, *Daughters of Canaan: A Saga of Southern Women* (Lexington, 1995), 37.

8. Elizabeth A. Perkins, *Border Life: Experience and Memory in the Revolutionary Ohio Valley* (Chapel Hill, NC, 1998), 72.

9. Lucien Beckner, ed., "Reverend John Dabney Shane's Interview with Pioneer William Clinkenbeard," *Filson Club History Quarterly* 2 (1928): 119.

10. See the voluminous lists by overseers and farm managers at the many different farms owned by the Preston and Wickliffe families. For example, boxes 12 and 13 of the Wickliffe-Preston Family Papers (Special Collections, University of Kentucky Libraries, Lexington) contain primarily farm accounts and inventories.

11. Lee Soltow, "Kentucky Wealth at the End of the Eighteenth Century," *Journal of Economic History* 43 (1983): 617–33.

12. "Sec. 37. *Be it further enacted,* That any widow or *femme sole,* over twenty-one years of age, residing and owning property subject to taxation for school purposes, according to the provisions of this act, in any school district, shall have the right to vote in person or by written proxy." *A Digest of the Statute Laws of Kentucky . . .* (Frankfort, 1842), 282.

13. Ellen T. Eslinger, ed., *Running Mad for Kentucky: Frontier Travel Accounts* (Lexington, 2004), 145. Few women chose to come to Kentucky willingly. On black slave women, see Gail S. Terry, "Sustaining the Bonds of Kinship in a Trans-Appalachian Migration, 1790–1811: The Cabell-Breckinridge Slaves Move West," *Virginia Magazine of History and Biography* 102 (1994): 455–76. Terry uses the Cabell-Breckinridge records to observe ways in which enslaved people responded to forced separation from other family and kin. For the white women of that same kin network, see the anguished letters from Betsy Breckinridge Meredith quoted in Hazel Dicken-Garcia, *To Western Woods: The Breckinridge Family Moves to Kentucky in 1793* (London, 1991), 142–44. This interpretation based on letters from literate women may not be representative of most white women who came to Kentucky, however. Eslinger makes the case that most Kentucky settlements formed around kinship claims and that the migrations preserved interpersonal relationships rather than breaking them. See Ellen T. Eslinger, "Migration and Kinship on the Trans-Appalachian Frontier: Strode's Station, Kentucky," *Filson Club Historical Quarterly* 62 (1988): 52–66.

14. On the expectation for white women in the new nation to be good mothers in order to fulfill their citizenly duties, see Linda K. Kerber, *Women of the Republic: Intellect and Ideology in Revolutionary America* (Chapel Hill, NC, 1980); and Mary Beth Norton, *Liberty's Daughters: The Revolutionary Experience of American Women, 1750–1800* (Boston, 1980).

15. Wolfe, *Daughters of Canaan,* 69.

16. Faragher, *Daniel Boone,* 351.

17. George Caleb Bingham, *Daniel Boone Escorting Settlers through the Cumberland Gap* (1851–1852), oil on canvas 36.5 × 50.25 inches (92.7 × 127.6 centimeters), Washington University Gallery of Art, St. Louis. Image can be accessed at http://commons .wikimedia.org/wiki/File:Daniel_Boone_Escorting_Settlers_Through_the_ Cumberland_Gap_by_George_Caleb_Bingham_1851-52.jpg.

18. Reuben T. Durrett, *Bryant's Station and the Memorial Proceedings Held on Its Site under the Auspices of the Lexington Chapter, D.A.R., August the 18th, 1896, in Honor of Its Heroic Mothers and Daughters,* Filson Club Publications, no. 12 (Louisville, 1897).

19. *The Capture of the Daughters of D. Boone and Callaway by the Indians,* lithograph in Karl Bodmer and Jean-François Millet, *Annals of the United States Illustrated: The Pioneers, Nr. 1* (New York, 1852). See the digital image at http://commons.wikimedia. org/wiki/Image:Capture_of_the_Daughters_of_D._Boone_and_Callaway_by_the_ Indians.jpg.

20. Nathan Boone, *My Father, Daniel Boone: The Draper Interviews with Nathan Boone,* ed. Neal O. Hammon (Lexington, 1999), 47–51; and Michael A. Lofaro, *Daniel Boone: An American Life* (Lexington, 2003), 68–74.

21. Chester Raymond Young, ed., *Westward into Kentucky: The Narrative of Daniel Trabue* (Lexington, 1981), 55–56.

22. Quoted in Perkins, *Border Life*, 105.

23. Seal for the Philadelphia Society for the Promotion of Agriculture (1786), Annenberg Rare Book and Manuscript Library: Van Pelt–Dietrich Library Center, University of Pennsylvania. Image can be accessed at http://www.explorepahistory.com/displayimage.php?imgId=99.

24. *Liberty. In the Form of the Goddess of Youth; Giving Support to the Bald Eagle* (1796), stipple engraving by Edward Savage, Library of Congress, Popular Graphic Arts Collection, Prints and Photographs Division, LC-USZ62-15369. Digital image can be accessed at http://www.loc.gov/pictures/resource/cph.3a17616.

25. Cynthia A. Kierner, *Beyond the Household: Women's Place in the Early South, 1700–1835* (Ithaca, NY, 1998), 68.

26. Carol Berkin, *Revolutionary Mothers: Women in the Struggle for America's Independence* (New York, 2005), 155.

27. *Kentucky Gazette*, February 21, 1798.

28. See Gladys V. Parrish, "The History of Female Education in Lexington and Fayette Co." (M.A. thesis, University of Kentucky, 1932).

29. *Kentucky Gazette*, July 19, 1806.

30. Marion B. Lucas, *A History of Blacks in Kentucky*, vol. 1, *From Slavery to Segregation, 1760–1891* (Frankfort, 1992), 59.

31. *Kentucky Gazette*, February 20, 1815.

32. See, e.g., the chapter on Virginia women's work in staffing and supporting an evangelical "united front" dedicated to promoting piety in the early 1800s in Elizabeth R. Varon, *We Mean to Be Counted: White Women and Politics in Antebellum Virginia* (Chapel Hill, NC, 1998), esp. 23–25. For more on the importance of women in the male-dominated national period and beyond, see Nancy Isenberg, *Sex and Citizenship in Antebellum America* (Chapel Hill, NC, 1998), esp. chap. 1, "Firstborn Feminism."

33. John B. Boles, *Religion in Antebellum Kentucky* (Lexington, 1976), 15.

34. Nettie Henry Glenn, *Early Frankfort Kentucky, 1786–1861* (privately printed, 1986), 62–68, 86, 103–4. See also Page Putnam Miller, "Women in the Vanguard of the Sunday School Movements," *Journal of Presbyterian History* 76 (1998): 45–54.

35. I first made this connection between Alfred Russell of Kentucky, the subject of acrimonious debate between Robert Wickliffe and Robert J. Breckinridge, and Alfred Russell as president of Liberia in my "She Used Her Power Lightly: A Political History of Margaret Wickliffe Preston of Kentucky" (Ph.D. diss., University of Kentucky, 1999).

36. C[harlotte] Mentelle, *A Short History of the Late Mrs. Mary O. T. Wickliffe* (Lexington, 1850), 11 (available on microfilm at University of Kentucky Special Collections and Archives). For more on women's work in antislavery movements, see Beth A. Salerno, *Sister Societies: Women's Antislavery Organizations in Antebellum America* (DeKalb, IL, 2005).

37. For more on black Kentuckians' resistance to slavery and their attitudes toward the colonization experiment, see Lucas, *From Slavery to Segregation*, 54.

38. Other stories of Milly and Alfred can be found in William H. Townsend, *Lincoln and His Wife's Home Town* (Indianapolis, 1929); Lowell H. Harrison, *The Antislavery Movement in Kentucky* (Lexington, 1978); and James C. Klotter, *The Breckinridges of Kentucky, 1760–1981* (Lexington, 1986). For more on how black women resisted their enslavement, see Darlene Clark Hine, "Female Slave Resistance: The Economics of Sex," *Western Journal of Black Studies* 3 (1979): 123–27; and Darlene Clark Hine and Kathleen Thompson, *A Shining Thread of Hope: The History of Black Women in America* (New York, 1988), 79–81.

39. Milly C[rawford] to Polly Wickliffe, March 10, 1833, box 39, Wickliffe-Preston Family Papers. Spelling, capitalization, and punctuation are her own.

40. *Niles' Register*, April 13, 1833, 98.

41. *Lexington Observer and Reporter*, June 27, 1833.

42. Alfred F. Russell to Robert Wickliffe, July 3, 1855, box 50, Wickliffe-Preston Family Papers.

43. James Wesley Smith, *Sojourners in Search of Freedom: The Settlement of Liberia by Black Americans* (Lanham, MD, 1987); G. E. Saigbe Boley, *Liberia: The Rise and Fall of the First Republic* (New York, 1983); Alice Allison Dunnigan, *The Fascinating Story of Black Kentuckians: Their Heritage and Traditions* (Washington, DC, 1982).

44. Married women's lives in Kentucky's rural areas were rough and violent. See, e.g., Honor R. Sachs, "The Myth of the Abandoned Wife: Married Women's Agency and the Legal Narrative of Gender in Eighteenth-Century Kentucky," *Ohio Valley History* 3 (2003): 3–20.

45. See Karen Kay Nickless, "'A good faithful sister': The Shaker Sisters of Pleasant Hill, Kentucky" (Ph.D. diss., University of South Carolina, 2004); Edward D. Andrews, *The Community Industries of the Shakers* (Philadelphia, 1972); Thomas D. Clark and F. Gerald Ham, *Pleasant Hill and Its Shakers* (Harrodsburg, KY, 1983); and Flo Morse, *The Shakers and the World's People* (Hanover, NH, 1987).

46. Steven L. Baker, "Improvising on the Borderlands of Gender: The Friends of Mary at the Foot of the Cross, 1812–1834," *Filson Club History Quarterly* 71 (1997): 202–26.

47. For the importance of researching rural women's lives, see John Mack Faragher, "History from the Inside Out: Writing the History of Women in Rural America," *American Quarterly* 33 (1981): 537–57.

48. See Wolfe, *Daughters of Canaan*, 62–65. See also Richard Sears, "Working Like a Slave: Views of Slavery and the Status of Women in Antebellum Kentucky," *Register of the Kentucky Historical Society* 87 (1989): 1–39.

49. *Kentucky Gazette*, March 25, 1813.

50. *Kentucky Gazette*, February 12, 1816.

51. Wendy M. Gordon, *Mill Girls and Strangers: Single Women's Independent Migration in England, Scotland and the United States, 1850–1881* (Albany, NY, 2002), 2, 156–57.

52. *Kentucky Gazette*, August 3, 1813.

53. See Perkins, *Border Life*.

54. Not only were white, black, and Native American women employed in car cleaning and other domestic service jobs for the railroads in the 1830s, but they also served water to passengers and sold fruit to women traveling in ladies' cars. Nancy Levinson, *She's Been Working on the Railroad* (New York, 1997). See also the description of the amenities available at the Villa, a train rest stop in Versailles on the way from Lexington to Frankfort, advertised in the *Lexington Observer and Reporter,* May 23, 1833.

55. George W. Ranck, *History of Lexington, Kentucky: Its Early Annals and Recent Progress* (Cincinnati, 1872).

56. James Lane Allen first published the fanciful legends of the hero of the 1833 cholera epidemic, William Solomon, in *Harper's Magazine* in 1888 and again in his book of short stories *Flute and Violin, and Other Kentucky Tales and Romances* (New York, 1897).

57. Poor auctions were used frequently by rural towns throughout the United States in the antebellum years to clean up their streets or to deal with abandoned or orphaned children. See, e.g., the "bound apprentice indenture" for Lewis, "a negro boy" who was placed in a poor auction in 1803 and then formally apprenticed to John Robinson as a weaver. This apprenticeship served a very important purpose for this free black man since Robinson was bound to teach him not only the "art and mystery of a weaver in a masterly and workmanlike manner" but also "reading, writing and artithmetick [*sic*] including the rule of three with propriety" and, when he turned twenty-one, to give him a "decent new suit of cloathes [*sic*]" and three pounds ten shillings. Even more importantly, Robinson is directed to "observe towards the said apprentice a proper and becoming treatment and behavior and such duties as the law prescribes." Indenture, October 13, 1806, Fayette County Court, Book B, 304, Fayette County Court Records, Lexington-Fayette Urban County Government Records Center and Archives, Lexington.

58. Solomon died in 1854, and, according to the newspapers of the day, a large crowd gathered to honor him. See his obituary notice in the *Kentucky Statesman,* December 5, 1854. A stone monument was erected over his grave in 1897. *Lexington Herald,* June 27, 1897. In 1908, poems, an oil painting, and a new marble monument accompanied a large celebration honoring him. See the several articles in the *Lexington Herald* from May 19 to September 19, 1908, where the reburial ceremony is described. Articles in Lexington newspapers crop up nearly every decade thereafter to revisit the strange story of a white man being bought at auction by a black woman. Some black Lexingtonians did not find Charlotte to be such a heroic figure, however. In 1940, the Negro Civic League asked in vain that the new black housing projects not be named Charlotte Court. The slightly miffed journalist wrote: "According to the league, Lexington Negroes have shown a preference for a title honoring a person better known than Charlotte, the kindly Negro woman who, more than a century ago, befriended King Solomon, white hero of the cholera plague of 1833." *Lexington Leader,* June 24, 1940.

59. Burton Milward, *William "King" Solomon, 1725–1854* (Lexington, 1990).

60. Lexington Town Trustees Book III, 370, 379, Lexington-Fayette Urban County Government Records Center and Archives. Thanks to Robin Rader for her research aid regarding Charlotte.

61. Lucas, *From Slavery to Segregation*, xvi (fig. 1).

62. Ibid., 54. See also Deborah Gray White, *Ar'n't I a Woman?* (New York, 1985).

63. Lucas, *From Slavery to Segregation*, 6–7, 58.

64. J. Winston Coleman Jr., *Slavery Times in Kentucky* (Chapel Hill, NC, 1940), 105.

65. Lucas, *From Slavery to Segregation*, 86.

66. See, e.g., Coleman, *Slavery Times;* or Eloise Conner, "The Slave Market in Lexington, Kentucky, 1850–1860" (M.A. thesis, University of Kentucky, 1931).

67. Coleman, *Slavery Times*, 131–34. See also Dunnigan, *Black Kentuckians*, 49.

68. William Wells Brown, *Clotel; or, The President's Daughter: A Narrative of Slave Life in the United States* (London, 1853).

69. "$100 Reward," *Lexington Public Advertiser*, March 22, 1820.

70. Harriet Beecher Stowe, *Uncle Tom's Cabin; or, Life among the Lowly* (New York, 1900), 137–45.

71. Stowe, *Uncle Tom's Cabin*, 168, 184. For more analysis on this topic, see Marli F. Weiner, *Mistresses and Slaves: Plantation Women in South Carolina, 1830–80* (Urbana, IL, 1998).

72. Barbara Welter, "The Cult of True Womanhood: 1820–1860," *American Quarterly* 18 (1966): 151–74.

73. "Lexington Female Tract Society," *Kentucky Reporter* (Lexington), May 21, 1821.

74. John Pendleton Kennedy, *Swallow Barn; or, A Sojourn in the Old Dominion, in Two Volumes* (Philadelphia, 1832); Rosa Vertner Johnson, *Woodburn* (New York, 1864).

75. Thomas Roderick Dew [signed Z.X.], "Dissertation on the Characteristic Differences of the Sexes, and Woman's Position and Influence in Society, No. I," *Southern Literary Messenger; Devoted to Every Department of Literature and the Fine Arts* 1 (1835): 495.

76. Catherine Clinton, *The Plantation Mistress: Woman's World in the Old South* (New York, 1982), 35.

77. Mary P. Ryan, *Women in Public: Between Banners and Ballots, 1825–1880* (Baltimore, 1990), 4.

78. Helen Deiss Irvin, *Women in Kentucky* (Lexington, 1979), 34.

79. Hambleton Tapp and James C. Klotter, *Kentucky: Decades of Discord, 1865–1900* (Frankfort, 1977), 4–5: "Conservative thought, with some exceptions, had more or less prevailed in Kentucky since the beginning of statehood in 1792."

80. Katherine Helm, *The True Story of Mary, Wife of Lincoln* (New York, 1928), 41.

81. Jean H. Baker, *Mary Todd Lincoln: A Biography* (New York, 1987), 178–81.

82. Ibid., 150.

83. Laura C. Holloway, *The Ladies of the White House* (Philadelphia, 1882), 322.

84. Paul E. Fuller, "Women in Kentucky History: Mary Austin Holley," *Kentucky Cardinal* 40 (1969): 3–5. See also Kitty Thornton, "Women in Fayette County

History" (Lexington, 1974). Thornton insisted that Holley's parties so soon after the open letters in 1824 demanding President Holley's resignation only angered her husband's critics even more. It is not so clear in the full-scale biography by Rebecca Smith Lee, perhaps because she had not gathered much information from local Kentucky women's papers. See Rebecca Smith Lee, *Mary Austin Holley: A Biography* (Austin, 1962), 149–69.

85. Thomas D. Clark, *The Kentucky* (1942; Lexington, 1992), 241.

86. Virginia Tatnall Peacock, *Famous American Belles of the Nineteenth Century* (Philadelphia and London, 1901), 152.

87. Isabel McLennan McMeekin, *Louisville: The Gateway City* (New York, 1946), 108.

88. Quoted in "An Exposition of the Difficulties between T. B. Lawrence and His Wife Sallie Ward Lawrence Which Led to Their Divorce. Prepared by T. B. Lawrence and His Counsel" (Boston, n.d.). A copy is in the possession of the author thanks to Dr. Robert Ireland, University of Kentucky History Department.

89. Ibid.

90. *Louisville Daily Courier,* February 25, 1850: "Whereas my wife, Sallie W. Lawrence, has willfully and without cause deserted me, this is to caution all persons against harboring or trusting her on my account, as I hold myself responsible for no debts contracted by her."

91. George Prentice, *Louisville Journal* (1850?), quoted in Melville O. Briney, *Fond Recollection: Sketches of Old Louisville* (Louisville, 1955), 51.

92. Briney, *Fond Recollection*, 46–53. See also Clark, *The Kentucky*, chap. 15; Ella Hutchison Ellwanger, "Mrs. Sallie Ward Downs," *Register of the Kentucky Historical Society* 16 (1918): 8–14; Peacock, *Famous American Belles*, 148–60; "An Exposition of the Difficulties between T. B. Lawrence and His Wife Sallie Ward Lawrence"; and William Preston to Robert Wickliffe Sr., June 11, 1850, box 46, Wickliffe-Preston Family Papers.

93. See the change in English common law regarding women's rights (e.g., the husband giving up his privilege to his wife's physical body) in the chapter "Separate Maintenance Contracts" in Susan Staves, *Married Women's Separate Property in England, 1660–1833* (Cambridge, MA, 1990). Glenda Riley saw 1850 as a watershed and the rise of "the Great American Divorce Debate," in which Victorian respectability began to demand greater regulation of women's access to legal divorce. See Glenda Riley, *Divorce: An American Tradition* (New York, 1991), 54–61.

94. See Joan Cashin, *A Family Venture: Men and Women on the Southern Frontier* (New York, 1991); Elizabeth Fox-Genovese, *Within the Plantation Household: Black and White Women of the Old South* (Chapel Hill, NC, 1988), 203; and Clinton, *The Plantation Mistress*, 204–5.

95. Gerda Lerner, *Why History Matters: Life and Thought* (New York, 1997), 119.

❧ 6

"A richer land never seen yet"
Horse Country and the "Athens of the West"

Maryjean Wall

In the beginning was the soil. The soil made the land rich in minerals and abundant grass; the land, in turn, made the horse industry of Bluegrass Kentucky. The soil leeched calcium and phosphorus from layers of limestone rock lying below the surface; these minerals passed through spring water and the soil into the grass and other vegetation, with the result a verdant grazing land that explorers called the Great Meadow. Land scouts and settlers described this region as a land richer than anything they had yet seen, for these woodland meadows held the promise of great riches to be realized in farming and raising livestock. To early agriculturalists, the Bluegrass region appeared like a promised land.

Kentuckians of those early nineteenth-century decades when Lexington reigned as the "Athens of the West" could not possibly have predicted the global, multi-billion-dollar horse industry that would spring from this rich grazing land. They realized only that all stock, including racehorses, flourished in the Bluegrass and that nearly everyone in these parts appreciated a lively horse race. Yet it was during the Athens era that a pattern of horse production emerged on this mineral-rich land in anticipation of the commercial industry to evolve during the latter nineteenth century.[1]

The result was that Americans began to associate the idea of the Bluegrass as racehorse country from decades before the Civil War. This did not happen by accident. As Paul Peterson has suggested: "The natural systems of soil and topography, resulting from specific geological features . . . together with the inclinations of the region's human occupants, encouraged a 'pattern of land use' synonymous with a specialized livestock industry, a productive system of agriculture, and, more recently, a flourishing tourist business." The rich land enabled the rapid rise of a wealthy class of "gentlemen" farmers who modeled their lifestyle on that of Virginia's cavalier class and, ultimately, on the squires of English estates. Intrinsic to this lifestyle was a sophisticated appreciation of the racehorse. The "gentry" of the Bluegrass became highly skilled at breeding and raising strong, fast horses that won races throughout the South.[2]

Nearly a century following that period when Lexington was known as the Athens of the West, a new style of country gentleman began buying up enormous tracts of central Kentucky farmland. These newcomers generally resided in major American cities. They possessed enormous wealth and constituted an expanding class of multimillionaires that was emerging simultaneously with the nation's rapid industrial growth. These capitalists, industrialists, and Wall Street speculators invested heavily in the former Athens of the West, buying up thousands of acres of horse farm land. Men of their type already had shifted the center of horse racing from the South and from Kentucky to the Northeast after the Civil War; decades later, this new generation of capitalists further changed the face of the Bluegrass, building lavish Thoroughbred and Standardbred nurseries intended for the purpose of replenishing their eastern racing stables.

These new gentlemen farmers of the Bluegrass were not agriculturalists like the old class of gentry who had lived off the land. In fact, the majority of newcomers came in as absentee landowners. They frequented horse country but once or twice yearly, their visits usually coinciding with the racing season. All the same, they made an indelible imprint on the local community by altering the landscape with ostentatious expressions of their vast wealth. Horse country became the rural retreat for multimillionaires like one mining king, James Ben Ali Haggin, who built an outsized mansion he called Green Hills on his Elmendorf Farm. The millionaires also built lavish horse barns and replaced many of the venerable old stone fences with fancy new board fencing painted white. In doing so, they reorganized the physical landscape of the Bluegrass into acres of white-fenced pastures dotted with barns that appeared more like horse palaces. An iconography emerged with this fencing and these elaborate buildings to signify notions of racehorse country. Americans began to associate this iconography specifically with Bluegrass Kentucky and with the wealthy who assumed the persona of southern colonels or English squires while in residence at these farms.

The horse farms served a dual purpose. Their owners regarded these estates as suitable country retreats. But they also depended on their farms to refurbish their racing stables with young stock. The young racehorses went off to the centers of the sport as they existed during the early twentieth century—tracks in New York, New Jersey, Florida, and Maryland. Rarely did these young horses remain in Kentucky. In contrast to the previous fifty years and more, Kentucky no longer stood central to the racing end of the sport. Bluegrass Kentucky's significance continued to remain in the land and the minerals the land imparted to the water and the grass. Although racing of any significance other than the Kentucky Derby and the Blue Grass Stakes would not return to Kentucky until the latter twentieth century, the Bluegrass remained known worldwide as the cradle of the racehorse. The farms served their wealthy owners well as stations supplying a steady source of reinforcements for the best racing elsewhere.

During the interregnum before major-league racing returned to Kentucky on a regular basis, Bluegrass horsemen and outside capitalists developed a useful partnership that saw central Kentucky retain its position as the premier breeding center in the United States, if not the world. This synergistic relationship saw absentee farm owners supplying the capital while the locals supplied the expertise for managing the farms. In every phase of breeding and raising a horse, from determining which mares to breed to which stallions on to preparing young horses for the races or the sales, Bluegrass Kentuckians stood at the center. From this arrangement developed a new class of Bluegrass Kentuckians, a group of elite horse farm managers who formed their own regional aristocracy.

These professional managers enjoyed great freedom in operating the farms. The most successful among this group achieved a measure of wealth and some of them their own farms. They gained worldwide stature in their role of *hardboots*, a term that loosely defined a crafty native Kentucky horseman who could not be outdone in a horse deal because he possessed the innate knowledge known enviously by outsiders as *horse sense*.

Occasionally, but never too frequently, women held positions of significance and respect within this tight circle of the Bluegrass horse aristocracy. M. Louise Wilson served as secretary of the board of the Kentucky Association track in 1918, and Mary LeBus received public recognition in 1913 for organizing the Hinata Race Meet at Hinata, the country estate she shared with her husband, Clarence LeBus. When the world renowned Man o' War retired to stud in 1920, he went into the care of Elizabeth Daingerfield, a woman greatly respected in a man's world for her vast knowledge of Thoroughbreds.[3]

Women had long played an influential role in Thoroughbred racing simply by attending the races; their presence lent a legitimacy to the sport that it might not have realized otherwise. Articles in newspapers and sporting journals throughout the nineteenth century consistently mentioned the attendance of women at the racecourses, as though this feminine presence in the crowd signified a race meet favored by persons of high moral caliber. "This is the strongest index of the future success of racing at this point," *Wilkes' Spirit of the Times* remarked in 1865. "Wherever woman will lend the beauty of her countenance, there the gay and gallant of the opposite sex will be found." Female patrons at Saratoga in 1873 went beyond merely blessing the sport with their attendance: they demanded that backs be added to the grandstand seats they were expected to occupy. Early in the twentieth century, an African American held a highly unusual job for any woman, working as a "clocker," the individual who timed the workouts of racehorses. Speculation held that she worked as a scout for various bookmakers and players. People observed her working at the track in Memphis; they thought she might have ventured down from Lexington.[4]

Back in the Bluegrass, a handful of women managed farm operations, most notably Josephine Clay, the wife of the horse trainer and breeder John Clay, who was a son of Henry Clay's. Mary B. Kinkead received occasional notice up to 1875 in newspapers as the owner of a stock farm in Woodford County. Bluegrass horsemen credited Meta M. Hunt Reynolds of Frankfort with managing the well-known Fleetwood Stable headquartered at the farm she owned with her husband, J. W. Hunt Reynolds. Among her other achievements was advising the youths who worked in the stable, including the young Isaac Murphy. She taught them proper manners and how to read and write.[5]

In more recent times, another group of managers generally has replaced the local hardboots of the twentieth century. Those in this twenty-first-century group, many of them Irish born, are knowledgeable horsemen who have brought a global orientation to the Bluegrass as their roots have not been in local soil.

All these persons, regardless of their roots, benefit economically from Bluegrass land and soil, just as livestock breeders realized riches from the land when Lexington reigned as the Athens of the West. The soil and its reputation historically brought the best stallions from throughout the United States to stand at stud in Kentucky; the notion of the Bluegrass serving as the true source of the racehorse perpetuated the belief that here was the place to raise a good horse. Challenges to this notion have arisen from time to time, certainly. If history shows the way to the future, Bluegrass Kentucky will always need to reassert its claim as the racehorse capital of the world. All the same, it has a long running start over challengers who might assert that a good racehorse can come from anywhere. Kentuckians have been successful at discrediting that notion since the period of the Athens of the West.

Central Kentucky had begun building a reputation for its lush grazing land from the time the earliest European explorers made their way west through this Great Meadow, the place later called the Bluegrass. The verdant meadows and fertile soil, growing thick with cane and grass and dotted with hardwood trees, left a highly favorable impression on all those who happened on this land. These persons praised its qualities to any and all who would listen. Central Kentucky never lacked boosters and promoters, even from the start.

One of the earliest explorers to see central Kentucky, a trader named John Finley, spoke of this Great Meadow lying south of the Ohio River. George Rogers Clark, a revolutionary soldier and frontiersman, sent word about central Kentucky back to his father in Virginia in 1775, stating unequivocally: "A richer and more beautiful country than this I believe has never been seen in America yet." Finley and Clark were among many frontiersmen who painted glowing word descriptions of this region.[6]

To these early explorers who saw central Kentucky, the Great Meadow appeared like the paradise that agriculturalists dreamed about, at a time when East Coast Americans realized that poor practices had farmed out a considerable portion of land in the founding states. The historian Thomas D. Clark frequently wrote how Kentucky soon teemed with scouts seeking to locate fertile, well-watered lands rich in grass. As Clark suggested, they did not have to look far for good land in any direction on arriving in the Great Meadow, not even those who arrived late.

Settlers grew a wide variety of crops in central Kentucky, including wheat, rye, hemp, corn, and flax, but not yet tobacco; the latter would replace hemp as a major cash crop later in the nineteenth century. Grass grew easily and abundantly in fertile, thinly forested central Kentucky. Here, the trees stood wide apart, allowing sunlight to fall on the fields and air to circulate where settlers sowed grass. A magazine published in 1835 described the method settlers and subsequent residents used to enhance the grazing land, reporting: "The underwood and useless trees are removed, and the valuable timber trees are left, standing sufficiently wide apart. . . . The ground is then sown with grass, and extensive tracks . . . are thus converted into spacious lawns studded with noble trees." Such scenes constituted the early, pastoral iconography of the Bluegrass. More than two hundred years later, the Bluegrass landscape remains known world-wide for these woodland pastures, the same features that the early explorers valued so highly.[7]

People observed that livestock raised in central Kentucky grew fatter and healthier than livestock quartered on the swampy Atlantic coast or on rocky or worn-out agricultural land to the east. Animals are what they eat, as farmers know. If animal husbandmen of the late eighteenth century and the early nineteenth did not understand the nutritional process in purely scientific terms, they at least recognized that livestock thrived on the grass of the Great Meadow. Moreover, horses raised there gained renown for their strong limbs. *Hickory-boned horses* people called these racehorses bred in Kentucky. Only later, with the advancement of science, would people begin to understand that these hickory-boned horses drew their strength from a rather unusual combination of calcium and phosphorus that the grass absorbed from the limestone rocks and sediment beneath the soil.

Promoters of Bluegrass land recognized the value of the limestone-infused soil from at least 1865 and possibly earlier. The *Louisville Journal* noted that this land "seems to possess some rare fattening qualities, for the flesh of the beef cattle and the sheep of that region possess an exquisite flavor and tenderness unknown to the leathery meat of other States." The article ascribed these favorable qualities to "the stratum of blue limestone which underlies the whole country at the distance of from ten to twelve feet from the surface, and perhaps has some effect upon the grass."[8]

Among the earliest professionals to attribute the qualities of land in central Kentucky to the limestone rock beneath the soil was Professor Nathan Shaler, a geologist and nineteenth-century historian and observer of Kentucky culture. Shaler wrote in 1876 that Bluegrass land is "surpassed by no soils in any country for fertility and endurance." During that same decade, an article in the *London Daily Telegraph* cited the mineral benefits that horses in Kentucky (and also in Middle Tennessee, a land of similar geological characteristics) received from the soil.[9]

During the modern era, Professor Karl B. Raitz described the geography of the Bluegrass region as "a broad limestone plain which has been etched on a structural arch of Ordovician limestones and shales." He has written: "The gently rolling terrain is underlain by phosphatic Lexington and Cynthiana limestones which decompose into exceptionally fertile silt loam soils."[10]

Professor Frank R. Ettensohn believes that the calcium—in combination with a rare and unusual phosphatic content of the limestone—contributes to strong and healthy bones renowned in Kentucky-raised horses.

According to this geologist, people formerly believed that the limestone's calcium was singularly responsible for the hickory-boned horses of the Bluegrass. But the phosphates, as Ettensohn has stated, play an immense role in the process of raising a strong horse. Calcium-based limestone can be found in many places, Ettensohn has written. Yet a heavy concentration of phosphates within the same rock is a rare occurrence, one found in central Kentucky and in few other places. Ettensohn relates this rare accumulation of phosphates in the limestone to events occurring 460 million years ago during the Ordovician Age—a period of mountain building, of continent shifting, and of seas opening into a shallow, tidal shelf that brought these mineral deposits to the region now known as the Bluegrass. These paleo-occurrences accounted for the rich agricultural advantages that animal husbandmen of the Athens of the West reaped, millions of years later, with their livestock-breeding practices and horse racing programs.[11]

Precisely at what point the Bluegrass evolved more specifically into horse country remains to be identified since farms in this region did not identify themselves specifically as horse operations or even more specifically as farms raising runners (Thoroughbreds) or trotting horses. Bluegrass farmers raised prized herds of Shorthorn cattle as well as purebred horses and well-bred mules. They also raised herds of valuable sheep. After the Civil War, the farms raising horses increasingly took up the breeding of both Thoroughbreds and trotters for sale, capitalizing on the twin markets developing for these two different types of racehorse. Nonetheless, the culture, perhaps even more than the economy, of central Kentucky, intrinsically entwined itself specifically in horses almost from the beginning of settlement.

There was no doubt that settlers in central Kentucky were thinking of horses right from the start. Daniel Boone, Richard Henderson, and a small group of men constructed a fort at Boonesborough, organized an assembly in May 1775, and passed several laws for the governance of their community. Among those laws was "An Act for Improving the Breed of Horses." The meeting of this assembly, held outdoors under the shade of a pair of trees, was the first political expression that English civilization made in the western United States. Two months earlier, not far from Boonesborough, the group had suffered casualties and immense discouragement when Indians attacked. "Hope vanished from the most of us," Felix Walker wrote in a letter. But, once established at their new fort, the men had their minds on improving the breeding of horses.[12]

Kentucky's pioneers depended almost entirely on horses or mules for every phase of their daily lives; thus, they maintained close, familiar contact with these animals. Yet people in similar circumstances depended on these very animals in all newly settled regions of the United States. Something unique occurring in central Kentucky separated this culture from others and led to an early embrace of the racehorse. Arguably, the major influence was the settlement in the Bluegrass of a gentry class from Virginia and Maryland, a people who brought with them a cavalier culture that maintained a fondness for horse racing and other horse sports as signifiers of their upper-class status. Kentuckians closely associated their lifestyle with horses. A census taken in Lexington in 1789 showed that horses outnumbered humans 9,607 to 9,000. Culturally, these early Bluegrass Kentuckians began constructing their society around this animal that eventually would form a significant cornerstone in the Bluegrass economy.

Settlers of the Bluegrass relied greatly on what they could learn from English practices of horse breeding as disseminated in farm journals received from that country. Lewis Sanders, an early nineteenth-century agriculturalist in the Bluegrass, brought English practices to livestock exhibitions he held at his Lewis Sanders Gardens at Sandersville, just north of Lexington. A notice in the *Kentucky Gazette* in 1816 announced an upcoming exhibit of cattle, sheep, hogs, and horses at his gardens, where Sanders planned to present silver cups to the owners of the winning animals. Thomas Clark has commented: "If not actually the introduction of the julep cup, the prizes marked the popularization of this prestigious Kentucky vessel in association with fine livestock."[13]

Sanders wrote an 1836 letter to the editor of a weekly sporting journal in which he described how horses had been central to the settlement and early years of Kentucky culture. Said Sanders: "It should not be forgotten that Kentucky was settled pending and immediately after the Revolutionary War; that many of the chivalrous and gallant spirits of that day were among the first settlers; that having participated in the strife of the battle-field . . . when peace was declared they removed with their families to Kentucky, then a wilderness. . . . Gentlemen of respectability and wealth, emigrated from the State of Virginia; they brought their families, slaves and horses with them." He added: "The intercourse kept up between Kentucky and the old States, from its settlement up to the running of stages and steamboats, a period of nearly thirty years, was on horseback; the campaigns against the Indians were generally on horseback. To no people that ever lived was a good horse of more importance than to a Kentuckian of those times. Game, and good wind, stoutness and durability, were indispensable qualities—the breeder was directed to attain those qualities." Sanders also stated that almost all the mares brought to Kentucky early on were obtained in Virginia.[14]

Virginian and English influences on the culture of Bluegrass Kentucky became greatly apparent during the Athens period, when the elite class began to put its wealth on ostentatious display. Clark has written on this matter of class formation: "Where the soil was fertile and arable there early came into existence a rural gentry who looked proudly upon their way of life as Virginian and, back of that, English. From the more prosperous agricultural sections came early political leadership." The Bluegrass land and the fat, healthy livestock it produced made the region's farmers wealthy quickly—or wealthier, if they had brought family money with them into Kentucky. The leisure time their lifestyle afforded them allowed the people of this elite class to pursue their beloved horse sports. Bluegrass landowners also possessed the workforce needed to operate their horse stables, for virtually all of them kept slaves. Charles Kerr's history of Kentucky states that memories of horse racing in Virginia led to the establishing of a racecourse in Lexington as early as August 1789. Up to that time, racing took place informally on a spur-of-the-moment basis on city streets. This prompted a city ordinance in 1787 prohibiting racing on the "commons."[15]

The gentry class living on rural estates inhabited large, comfortable houses, a good number of them mansions bearing names in the English fashion, such as Cabell's Dale, Mt. Brilliant, Chaumiere du Prairie, Ashland, and Grassland. Houses of this elite class customarily were situated well back from the road, usually surrounded by trees, and generally built on natural elevations in the landscape. Some have interpreted this choice of rising ground as providing the occupants with a view all around or even opening these large houses to natural breezes. Dell Upton has interpreted their location as a status-driven practice, with the houses situated in such a way that their occupants could look down on the larger world of common folk.[16]

The culture bound up in racehorses and elegant homes expressed well-understood notions of cavalier ideals imported from Virginia and, ultimately, England. The great wealth that the gentry class of farmers realized from Bluegrass land made it possible to emulate these "country" practices: a life of horse racing, fox hunting, and rural retreats. James Silk Buckingham wrote that, on visiting Lexington in 1841, he observed that the rural environs of the city were "thickly studded with country residences." During the late eighteenth century and the early nineteenth, Kentuckians often built these large homes in the Georgian style, with a broad central hall and a stairway leading up to a landing, from which the stairway then proceeded on to the second floor. During the Greek Revival period, which began in the 1830s and was popular through much of the eastern portion of the United States, columns and front porticos appeared on many of these homes. Kentuckians were not out of touch with the eastern architectural fashion, led by Benjamin H. Latrobe, who initiated the Greek Revival style in the United States.[17]

Various outbuildings added to the functional operation of these antebellum rural estates in the Athens of the West. Behind the mansion were found the slave cabins, often with the overseer's house nearby. Describing these estates, the historian Richard L. Troutman has written: "Within easy distance of the mansion were the coach-house, stables or barns . . . , ice-house, smoke-house, dairy, stone spring-house, blacksmith and carpenter shop, and a hemp house."[18]

Not all Bluegrass Kentuckians possessed wealth and the elegant houses that visitors were so fond of describing. People of all classes populated this region, with wide gulfs separating the social and economic divisions. Kerr's history stressed that "created wealth widened the early classes that had tended to appear in Kentucky society almost as soon as a society could be said to have existed." Nineteenth-century Kentuckians became known for their rough qualities and especially for their pugnacity. But the large landowning class of the Bluegrass worked diligently to separate itself from any association with these types. The elite classes built their society around English and Virginian traditions of gracious living, cavalier manners, paternalism, and other signifiers of upper-class status, characteristics that similarly appeared in the culture of racehorse ownership. Class distinctions defined according to different regions of Kentucky also became recognized. As Clark has written, many Kentuckys existed. The culture of Bluegrass elites did not develop uniformly throughout the state, even though the vision of horse farms and white fences became iconic of the entire commonwealth.[19]

One example of class stratification was the distinction early historians made between the culture associated with Bluegrass life and the culture developing in Louisville. The latter city was "as rough as the roughest" of all the river towns catching the westward migration, according to Kerr's history. Louisville was a town of "350 people living in houses of boat planks and of logs, small but arranged in regular streets," where one of the popular sports was "gouging." This form of fighting, specific to the lower classes, engaged two men in a struggle in which they twisted their thumbs or fingers into the other's eye and pushed the eye from its socket until it fell on the cheeks. "There was, however, the beginnings of a refined and cultivated society evident in the Bluegrass Region by the time Kentucky had become a state," Kerr noted, adding: "Lexington early became the center of refinement, for the District and State, and for many years held first place in this respect throughout the whole western country." The racehorse culture of Bluegrass life remained demonstrative of these class differences.[20]

Central Kentucky (and also Middle Tennessee) became known as the Bluegrass sometime early in the nineteenth century, in reference to the type of grass that flourished in these similar limestone-based regions. On questions concerning the grass itself—whether it is really blue, where it came from, whether it was native to Kentucky—no one has ever produced definitive answers. The debate over the origin and precise color of the blue grass has entertained Kentuckians throughout much of their history, but the theories remain relatively unimportant. The grass made the reputation of the Bluegrass region as a result of the fast horses it produced. People have long credited the legume—the blue grass—with producing high-quality animals; more precisely, they believed that the mineral content of the soil initiated a nutritional process resulting in strong bone in livestock, most notably the region's racehorses. But it was the breeders who took the gift of the rich soil and developed the art and science of turning strong horses into a breed of ever-faster animals. They improved on the rich natural qualities of the land.[21]

Scholars of horse racing indicate that the first Thoroughbred to appear in Kentucky was a filly—a young female—brought to Lexington by John Stevenson Jr. in 1779. But those frontier times did not require that horses be Thoroughbreds to compete in a race. People had been breeding non-Thoroughbred horses for some time before the first representative of this breed stepped foot in the Bluegrass. Central Kentuckians had raced horses anywhere they could lay out a suitable path, either in the woods or on a main road within the urban area. All they needed to hold a horse race were fast horses, whatever their type or breed.

By the time the nineteenth century dawned, horse-related activities had become well established in central Kentucky. Lexington had a specially designated race path as far back as 1780, before statehood, close to the center of the city. The intention in designating this path for racing was to give horsemen somewhere other than Main Street to race their horses. Kentuckians did not refer to this or other race paths as *racecourses* at this time. The paths were the scene of many hotly contested match races set up between two horses that raced perhaps a quarter mile down a straight path. A racecourse apparently did come into use not long afterward in Lexington, and more of these courses, or tracks, began to appear in a variety of towns throughout the commonwealth.[22]

The beginnings of an infrastructure of ancillary services for supporting horse-oriented pursuits began appearing in Lexington during the early nineteenth century, albeit in a minor way. Among these pursuits was the practice of the advertising of breeding stallions in the local newspaper. The state's first newspaper, the *Kentucke Gazette*, published its inaugural issue in 1787 and carried its first advertisement related to horse breeding the following year. Significantly, the *Gazette* was publishing a special spring supplement beginning in 1805 to advertise breeding stallions. The Athens period existed as a formative time leading toward the development of the many businesses that would come to comprise the modern horse industry.[23]

Additional ancillary businesses closely associated with horse racing and breeding included the Phoenix Hotel and its predecessor, Postlethwait's Tavern. This famous landmark in the city center of Lexington drew much of its business from racing men; it had been attracting horse-racing enthusiasts from the time the tavern opened for business during the late eighteenth century. More businesses began catering to horse interests, including local silversmiths, who crafted cups intended as prizes for races and livestock shows. A few agricultural societies formed, and their activities consistently included the exhibiting of equine breeding stock. George Ranck's *History of Lexington, Kentucky* tells of a Kentucky Agriculture Society formed in 1814, a group that, Ranck wrote, held annual exhibitions at "Fowler's Garden" on the Maysville Road. In 1816, following a livestock show that Lewis Sanders organized, local agriculturalists formed a professional society that they named the Kentucky Society for Promoting Agriculture. In 1838, the Kentucky Agricultural Society formed in parallel to the increasingly popular practice of exhibiting livestock at fairs. Among the livestock exhibited were breeding stallions; the purpose of exhibiting these horses at the fairs was to attract the interest of owners of mares for the purpose of paying for breeding services.[24]

Bluegrass Kentuckians also began in disparate ways to learn how to turn the sport of horse racing into a business. For example, a house that Colonel Robert Sanders built in 1798 near Georgetown in Scott County became part of a complex that was said to include a five-hundred-bed hotel, a race track, and a farm for Thoroughbreds. Arguably, horse racing and breeding would not begin to evolve into an organized, commercial industry until after the Civil War, when the disparate enterprises began to focus in a larger, structured fashion on the expanding market in the Northeast. But, from the earliest years of Bluegrass settlement, Kentucky horsemen engaged in individual commercial activities that eventually would combine to make an industry.[25]

Lewis Sanders once told how his uncle, "the Colonel," had purchased and imported into Kentucky a horse from Virginia that stood at stud for only one season before its death in 1802. Despite the stallion's short time in the stud, his offspring proved to be a big boost to Kentucky's racehorses; according to Sanders, they "improved the blood stock of Kentucky more than that of any other horse." The horse was named Melzar, a bay who stood tall at sixteen hands. His sire, Medley, stood as one of the finest and most significant breeding stallions in Virginia. Lewis Sanders wrote that the offspring of Melzar became so highly prized that almost all the males were kept entire (i.e., not castrated) in order that they themselves could be put to stud. According to Sanders, the first sweepstake ever run in Kentucky was arranged by the breeders of Melzar's colts and fillies. Melzar is listed in one of the earliest versions of a stud book in the United States, *The Gentleman's New Pocket Farrier.* The notation next to his name notes that Melzar was "a bay horse by Medley. Went to Kentucky." By means of horses like Melzar, and also by expanding their expertise at breeding, Bluegrass Kentuckians during the Athens of the West period were laying the foundations for what would develop into the state's signature enterprise.[26]

While the majority of Thoroughbreds imported into Kentucky appear to have come from Virginia, a few also came from England since people then believed that English Thoroughbreds were superior to their American counterparts. The practice of importing Thoroughbreds from England to Kentucky began in 1797 with the stallion named Blaze, brought to Scott County. Later, educated Bluegrass breeders began to increase their knowledge of breeding by reading the *American Turf Register,* which John Skinner began publishing in 1829 in Baltimore. Through the pages of this journal, breeders became better informed on the latest practices. Consequently, they kept up-to-date with the current science in agricultural practices. This trend accelerated when the notable statesman Henry Clay brought the principles of "scientific" farming—an educated approach to agriculture—to his Bluegrass estate, Ashland. Clay, a leader in national politics, also stood as a leader to those Kentuckians who engaged in livestock breeding.[27]

Clay was a stalwart of the turf who helped guide the fortunes of Thoroughbred racing in early Lexington. Although he never kept more than perhaps thirteen mares at Ashland, he began a Thoroughbred breeding dynasty with one stallion, Yorkshire, and two mares, Margaret Wood and Magnolia, the mares a gift in 1845 from General Wade Hampton of South Carolina and Dr. W. N. Mercer of Louisiana, respectively. From these three Thoroughbreds descended twelve Kentucky Derby winners over 131 years following Clay's death in 1852. Although born in Virginia, Clay typified the stereotypical Kentuckian in that, on occasion, he gambled, drank, and swore. Most of all, he loved a good horse race. In that sense, he was a Kentuckian through and through.[28]

While Clay bred racehorses, he did not do so on the large scale of John Breckinridge at Cabell's Dale, situated about six miles northwest of Lexington. Breckinridge relocated to Kentucky from Virginia in 1793 and began to import English Thoroughbreds eight years later. When he died in 1806, his Cabell's Dale was home to 125 horses by one count, 200 by another. Either number, even in modern times, would be considered a fairly good-sized band of breeding stock.[29]

Perhaps the most significant event in laying the groundwork for a horse industry was the organizing of Bluegrass Kentucky's leading landowners and breeders into the Kentucky Jockey Club in 1797. The membership of this elite group included most of the major landowners and racehorse owners, all of them in agreement that racing must be conducted along the highest moral terms for the purpose of improving the breed. The Kentucky Jockey Club reorganized as the Lexington Jockey Club in 1809 and held annual race meets each autumn. These groups had founded an important tradition—racing on a high moral level for the improvement of the breed—a policy that generally progressed with succeeding generations of racing leaders in the Bluegrass.

When people enjoy a day of Thoroughbred racing at Keeneland in modern times, they should thank the early agriculturalists and sportsmen of late eighteenth-century Kentucky for laying the foundations for a racing tradition that continues to thrive more than two centuries later. These principles, embodying the highest standards for the sport, eventually led horsemen to found Keeneland in 1936. At Keeneland, the horse, more than the betting, was intended from the beginning to be the focus of the sport.

Early landowners like Henry Clay and John Breckinridge took great care that, when holding race meets in central Kentucky, they would uphold high standards and suffer nothing less. Although sporting bets made between gentlemen were a fact of the cavalier lifestyle in Kentucky, gambling as a practice in itself was never the underlying principle in promoting the sport in early Lexington. Not by accident did this same philosophy hold over to modern-day Keeneland, where for decades the only "exotic" or combination wagering offered was the daily double. The cornerstone of racing in the Bluegrass remained a constant: the improvement of the breed by determining which horses were superior on the racecourse.

The families associated with the earliest organized racing in Lexington also spread webs of power and control that enabled the Thoroughbred sport to flourish in the Bluegrass. The earliest organizers of this sport consisted largely of wealthy and respected landowners. In 1789, John Fowler, the first congressman to represent the new state of Kentucky in Washington, attended the taking of entries for racing in the Bluegrass. John Breckinridge, the founder of Cabell's Dale, served as attorney general for Kentucky, won election to the state legislature, and served as a delegate to Kentucky's 1799 constitutional convention before becoming a U.S. senator and the American attorney general. U.S. senator Henry Clay had powerful political connections throughout Kentucky and into Washington; he sought election to the U.S. presidency multiple times and for years was an active officer in the Kentucky Association track. During various time periods, the list of elected officials in Kentucky and at the state and national level included James T. Williams, who mentored the jockey Isaac Murphy when the famous African American was learning to ride in the early 1870s. State politicos also included members of the Kentucky Association track, such as Senators James B. Beck and J. C. S. Blackburn. John C. Breckinridge served as president of the racecourse at the same time that he won election as vice president of the United States.[30]

Persons who bred, raised, and raced horses also held considerable local power in the Bluegrass, including control of the earliest transportation systems. Dr. Elisha Warfield, the breeder of the great stallion Lexington (a horse originally named Darley), was among those who incorporated the earliest railroad in central Kentucky. Horse owners and their close associates eventually played key roles in the region's banking, political offices, merchant trade, and hemp and tobacco trade as well as oil, gas, and mineral exploration in eastern Kentucky. But, unlike the absentee horse farm owners who bought up Bluegrass land from the late nineteenth century on, these powerful landowners of the Athens era were local residents with a vested interest in the fortunes of the Bluegrass. Their power, influence, and wealth helped assure a friendly environment for the development of their racing interests.

Horse racing provided one of the greatest encouragements for improving the practice of horse breeding since the racecourse existed as a proving ground for the Thoroughbred and, later in the nineteenth century, the Standardbred: the breed that includes the trotter and the pacer. The fastest and most durable bloodlines on the racecourse consequently saw the most activity in the realm of breeding.

Everyone wanted a fast horse. Everyone also wanted a sound horse since it would have been most unfortunate for one's horse to suffer unexpected lameness with an important race scheduled on the calendar. The mineral-rich soils of Bluegrass land certainly remained the constant for producing these sound and hickory-boned horses. But the speed at which these horses could race and the endurance they needed to possess in order to race multiple "heats" of one to four miles within a single day was quite another matter beyond what the land alone could furnish.

Speed and endurance came from pedigrees that humans artificially manipulated to produce these highly sought-after qualities. Thus, horses' family trees began to prove increasingly important as the sport and the practice of breeding became more finely tuned during the Athens period. Central Kentucky was not yet a region of specialized horse farms. All the same, wealthy landowners began to move in that direction. They were becoming skilled at discerning which equine family trees, when brought together in the mating of a stallion and a mare, would increase their possibilities of developing the strong, fast horses they desired. As these wealthy, landed gentlemen refined their art, so grew Kentucky's reputation as a horse-breeding region known for locals who possessed specialized knowledge and skill in breeding fast Thoroughbreds and Standardbreds.

Despite their increasing ability to produce a superior racehorse, Kentucky breeders of the early nineteenth century shared a problem with all breeders of Thoroughbreds and trotters throughout the United States. This was the dearth of accurate pedigree information. As Lewis Sanders stated in his letter to the *Spirit of the Times:* "The value of blood stock rests mainly on the authenticity of its pedigree. An individual may possess a brood mare of pure blood, but if he cannot establish the fact, her offspring will sell for but little money."[31]

Unfortunately for all involved, breeders had lost a great amount of pedigree information during the time of the American Revolution. And, unfortunately, a good number of horse owners were not beyond embellishing or even fabricating the facts when reconstructing these pedigrees some years later. In an attempt to bring some order to this confusion, in the early nineteenth century John Skinner published in Baltimore his *English Stud Book*, which contained an appendix of "American Blood." But, as Lewis Sanders noted in Kentucky, this appendix was "scant, very scant."[32]

Sanders prevailed on the editor of the *Spirit of the Times* to encourage someone—anyone—to compile and publish an American stud book. "In fact we want a Kentucky stud book," Sanders wrote, "for which materials would now be collected. It is for the interest of breeders to take this matter in hand efficiently, and to carry it out completely." This eloquent appeal went largely unheeded, however. Kentucky racehorse breeders (and breeders from other states as well) continued their practice of handwriting the pedigrees of their own horses without always knowing or adhering to the facts. This system of writing one's own horse pedigrees required a considerable amount of trust on the part of others and did not do much to alleviate the confusion prevalent in the Thoroughbred breed. The situation would not begin to undergo serious correction until the business of breeding began to assume a much more defined commercial aspect during the later nineteenth century. But the system would remain flawed into the twentieth century.[33]

Other practices prevalent during the Athens period had a lasting effect on horse racing. These included slavery. Written histories of the sport largely overlooked how slaves assigned to the stables of horse breeders developed a major repository of horse knowledge. In fact, the slaves of the South and of Kentucky contributed greatly to the development of the racing sport and the horse industry that emerged from the sport. A slave who was talented and knowledgeable in the riding or training of racehorses was a prized possession on any estate. In fact, in the decades following the Civil War and emancipation, former slaves turned out to be the primary possessors of hands-on knowledge about the care and racing of Thoroughbreds. According to legend, one well-known slave jockey in Kentucky, named Cato, won his freedom by winning a challenge race, called a *match race*, that was of wide interest in 1839. He rode a horse named Wagner, defeating another called Grey Eagle. The contributions of African Americans in building and expanding horse racing and breeding in Kentucky have not been fully appreciated or explored.[34]

Following the Civil War, African Americans continued a long line of contributions to Thoroughbred racing and, to a lesser degree, to the sport of racing trotters. One reason the nascent commercial horse industry did not collapse in Kentucky after the Civil War was that the labor system did not collapse entirely. Former slaves rather soon agreed to return to the large estates. They came to this decision even as the agricultural system lay broken and in disarray after the labor force fled north or away from the country to Kentucky cities. This serendipitous development resulted,

Grey Eagle had run the fastest two miles in the United States before he met Wagner (representing his Maryland owner) in a famous match race at the Oakland course in Louisville in 1839. Wagner defeated Grey Eagle, but the event brought considerable nationwide attention to Kentucky racing. Among Grey Eagle's offspring was Traveller, Gen. Robert E. Lee's warhorse. (Keeneland Library.)

in part, because Bluegrass landowners offered to deed ownership of small sections of land, usually out of sight and at the rear of their estates, to former slaves as an inducement to return to work. African American agricultural workers, many of them experienced horsemen, agreed to purchase these plots of land, where they built houses, small gardens, and even general stores and churches, all within walking distance of the large farms. The situation resulted in a win-win scenario for the former slaves and the landowners. Horse production and other forms of farming resumed quicker in the Bluegrass than in the former Confederate South.[35]

    With slaves and the gentry class contributing simultaneously to the development of horse racing, the sport had made great progress in the Bluegrass during the early nineteenth century and the Athens era. Landowners and social leaders had overseen the organization of the sport in central Kentucky since 1785 and the beginnings of racing in and around

Bluegrass residents knew
Elisha Warfield as the Father
of the Kentucky Turf. He
was the breeder of the horse
called Lexington. (Keeneland
Library.)

Lexington. Formation of the Lexington Jockey Club followed in 1797,
continuing until 1826, when elites of central Kentucky formed the Kentucky Association for the Improvement of the Breeds of Stock. Among the
sixty charter members of the Kentucky Association were some of the region's most influential families, including Robert J. Breckinridge, Thomas
W. Clay, Robert Wickliffe, E. M. Blackburn, Elisha Warfield, William
Buford, Leslie Combs, and Willa Viley.[36]

For the first two years, the Kentucky Association held its race meets
in the west end of Lexington. Beginning in 1828, the meets moved to
property in the east end, at Fifth and Race Streets, on a site that Dr. Elisha Warfield personally selected. Here, the association built a clubhouse,
grandstand, betting pavilion, and racecourse, with prestigious and influential residents of Lexington lending their guidance and influence to this
sport that the elite class in the Bluegrass was taking special care to nurture
and develop.[37]

Following the example of John Breckinridge, Warfield became the
second Bluegrass turfman of consequence to devote his attention to his
bloodstock operation full-time. He became known as the Father of the

"The Home of Lexington" at Dr. Elisha Warfield's the Meadows. (Keeneland Library.)

Kentucky Turf, a title much deserved. Warfield retired in middle age from his professions of physician, merchant, and businessman to devote all his attention to breeding Thoroughbreds, a passion he continued to pursue until his death at age seventy-eight in 1859. He belonged to Lexington's upper class, his children married prominently, and he personally lent considerable support to Henry Clay, a man he greatly admired. For all the influence Clay would leave on Thoroughbred breeding with Yorkshire, Magnolia, and Margaret Wood, Warfield outdid him with the breeding of the most outstanding Thoroughbred of the nineteenth century, the horse called Lexington. Warfield called him Darley; subsequent owners changed the colt's name. He was a son of the prized stallion Boston out of a mare called Alice Carneal. Three years after Lexington's birth, Warfield sold the horse to a syndicate headed by the gambler, track owner, and racehorse owner Richard Ten Broeck; it was the syndicate that renamed the horse. As the breeder of this renowned horse, Warfield secured a place for all time in the annals of the sport's history, for Lexington's influence in bloodlines continued far into the twentieth century.[38]

While still named Darley, the horse began its racing career at age three. Warfield, seventy-two years old at the time, made the decision to lease Darley for racing purposes to an African American horseman named

Burbridge's Harry. All the same, Darley ran in Warfield's colors because the sport at that time was limited to white men and Burbridge's Harry thus could not enter a horse in a race. For this man known only as Burbridge's Harry, the horse whose destiny was to have a huge impact on racing and breeding won two stakes races at the Kentucky Association track. Then, quite suddenly, Warfield sold the colt to Ten Broeck's group, and Burbridge's Harry lost his racing rights to the horse.[39]

With his name changed, this splendid horse won a number of important stakes races and engaged in a rivalry with another well-regarded Thoroughbred from Mississippi named Lecomte. Their rivalry played out in New Orleans, which at that time reigned as the center of racing in the United States. Lexington lost one and won one in this rivalry, but he also became known as the world's fastest racehorse after setting a record against the clock in New Orleans. He raced through age four and retired to stud in Kentucky at Nantura Farm in Woodford County. Two years later, Ten Broeck sold the horse to Robert Aitcheson Alexander, the owner of Woodburn Farm, adjoining Nantura. In order to acquire Lexington, Alexander paid $15,000, a record price at that time for a Thoroughbred. Lexington soon justified the high price, for it was at Alexander's Woodburn that the horse ascended to prominence and achieved his greatest triumphs as a breeding stallion. He quickly became the nation's leading stallion in numbers of winners produced; he held that position for sixteen years. No stallion has ever matched this record. Historians traditionally have credited Lexington with having a major impact in launching the commercial horse-breeding business of the Bluegrass following the Civil War, for it was his offspring that horse owners throughout the United States paid dearly to own.[40]

The site of Lexington's winning races—the Kentucky Association track that Warfield and other elite landowners founded—was Keeneland's predecessor. Throughout much of the nineteenth century, and into the early decades of the twentieth, that track served a significant purpose as the proving ground for some of the best-known horses in the sport's history. No less than the brilliant Man o' War, a product of Kentucky but a horse who never raced in the state, made his farewell appearance prior to his stud career by galloping around the old track in a public exhibition in 1920. One iconic feature of the old Kentucky Association track was an iron gate and an entrance post with the initials *KA* in relief. Keeneland has incorporated copies of the post into both entrances along Versailles Road. The original iron gate and another copy of the post stand in Keeneland's clubhouse area. Many do not realize that the *KA* stamped on the posts

Lexington's fame as a sire, acquired during the nineteenth century, remains unequaled in the history of the turf. He led the sire list in number of winners among his offspring for sixteen years. On his retirement, he was purchased from the racetrack by Robert Aitcheson Alexander for a then record $15,000 and stood at stud at Woodburn Farm. (Henry William Herbert, *Frank Forester's Horse and Horsemanship of the United States and British Provinces of North America*, vol. 1 [New York: Stringer & Townsend, 1857], facing 386.)

stands, not for Keeneland Association, but for Kentucky Association, the old racecourse that once stood at Fifth and Race Streets. This iconography, as well as the enlightened philosophy of conducting racing in order to improve the breed, carried over from the old track to the new.

Central Kentucky's standing in the horse-breeding world increased with each decade as a result of well-founded practices initiated during the period of the Athens of the West. By perhaps 1840, the Bluegrass region of Kentucky had passed Virginia as the leading importer of English racehorses. This marked a significant turn, for it represented a passing of the torch from Virginia, the region recognized since colonial times as the mother of the turf in the United States. Virginians had been importing English Thoroughbreds since before explorers had ventured into Kentucky. But, by 1840, Bluegrass Kentuckians were demonstrating that they

The Kentucky Association racecourse. (Keeneland Library.)

were equally as serious as or more so than their Virginia forebears had been about improving their stock of racehorses.

Writing in *Horse World of the Bluegrass*, the historian Mary Wharton credited Kentucky's continued and steady importation of the best stallions from other states as the reason the commonwealth surpassed Virginia. She wrote that, while the most important racing during the 1850s was in New Orleans, the most significant breeding was taking place in the Bluegrass. She was partly correct. New Orleans was the center of racing. But, in breeding, both Tennessee and Kentucky had assumed preeminence in racehorse production in the United States. Belle Meade Plantation near Nashville produced top-quality Thoroughbreds, as did a handful of farms close by Belle Meade in Middle Tennessee: the southern portion of the Bluegrass. The Civil War did not completely obliterate the bloodstock in Middle Tennessee, and the breeding of Thoroughbreds resumed soon after the Civil War. But, at this critical turn, Kentucky's breeders joined the new racing market in greater numbers and with greater vision for the new version of the sport arising after the war. Central Kentucky was also the site of the most successful livestock-breeding operation of that period: Robert Aitcheson Alexander's Woodburn Farm in Woodford County, with the stallion Lexington the premier attraction.

Nineteenth-century Americans called Woodburn *the mother of all stock farms*. The ascendancy of Woodburn during the mid- to later 1850s made it a worthy rival to Belle Meade Plantation even before Woodburn surpassed Belle Meade in significance and production after the war. The two breeding operations respected each other's achievements and supported one another's stallions with their own mares. Woodburn eventually assumed greater significance, however, partly because Alexander had the stallion Lexington in his possession, and partly because Alexander followed "scientific" agricultural practices that Henry Clay had begun in the Bluegrass during that period known as the Athens of the West. In the tradition of Clay, Alexander brought an enlightened, organized approach to livestock breeding. Moreover, he possessed a personal fortune that enabled him to pursue agricultural practices he had observed in England and Europe while he was a youth living in Scotland.

Alexander is thought to be the first horse breeder, at least in the Bluegrass, to design how a horse farm should look—a model that other breeders began to follow. He held major livestock auctions at Woodburn, a practice that he began before the Civil War, with these sales drawing buyers from throughout the United States even prior to the war. Historians credit him as the first to publish a sales catalog listing the pedigrees of horses he planned to sell at the Woodburn sales. Alexander also supported the work of Sanders Bruce in compiling the first volumes of the *American Stud Book*. He had a vision for the future that helped secure the Bluegrass as the center of breeding for American Thoroughbreds and trotting horses. But he also followed in the tradition that others before him had initiated during the Athens of the West era.[41]

In the work of Bluegrass power brokers like Henry Clay, John Breckinridge, Elisha Warfield, and Robert Alexander and the Thoroughbred stallion Lexington can be seen the origins of Kentucky's vast commercial racing and breeding industries. During the enlightened period of the Athens of the West, the work of powerful men and significant horses began to assign specific meaning to the Bluegrass as horse country. Powerful, wealthy, and influential families, in conjunction with their slaves, seized the opportunities offered them in the raw material of Bluegrass land and soil. They turned these opportunities into a regional enterprise that, over time, achieved great standing as the leading agricultural industry in the commonwealth. Kentucky attained its position as the horse capital of the world by capitalizing on the rich soil of the Bluegrass. The payoff was not only in the horses but also in the global acknowledgment of the beautiful land that produced these animals. "Only in the hallucination of some strange form of insanity," wrote ex–Confederate general Basil W. Duke, "could he [i.e., a typical Kentuckian of Duke's era] believe that Kentucky is not the fairest land of the Creator, and the Bluegrass region its paradise."[42]

Notes

1. An early agriculturalist in the Bluegrass, Lewis Sanders, identified cattle production as an endeavor preceding the raising of Thoroughbred horses in central Kentucky. See Anna Virginia Parker, *The Sanders Family of Grass Hills: The Life of Lewis Sanders, 1781–1861* (Madison, IN, 1966).

2. Paul D. Peterson Jr., review of *Bluegrass Land and Life: Land Character, Plants, and Animals of the Inner Bluegrass Region of Kentucky, Past, Present, and Future*, by Mary E. Wharton and Roger W. Barbour, *Register of the Kentucky Historical Society* 1 (1993): 80–81.

3. *Lexington Leader*, June 30, 1938; *Thoroughbred Record*, April 26, 1913; "Her Success as a Horse Breeder," *New York Times*, July 16, 1922.

4. "The American Turf: Cincinnati Spring Meeting," *Wilkes' Spirit of the Times* 12 (July 15, 1865): 307; *Turf, Field and Farm*, August 15, 1873; *Lexington Leader*, April 6, 1903.

5. Henry Clay Simpson Jr., *Josephine Clay: Pioneer Horsewoman of the Bluegrass* (Louisville, 2005); "Report of the Sale of Mrs. Kinkead's Splendid Woodford Farm and Stock," *Kentucky Live Stock Record*, July 2, 1875, 3; "Horse Gossip: The Fleetwood Stable," *Turf, Field and Farm*, November 24, 1882, 347; Maryjean Wall, "Kentucky's Isaac Murphy: A Legacy Interrupted" (M.A. thesis, University of Kentucky, 2003), 11.

6. George W. Ranck, *History of Lexington, Kentucky: Its Early Annals and Recent Progress* (1872; Lexington, 1970), 270. See also Roger Longrigg, *The History of Horse Racing* (New York, 1972), 209.

7. Mary E. Wharton and Edward L. Bowen, *The Horse World of the Bluegrass* (Lexington, 1980), 5.

8. "Agricultural Resources of Kentucky," *Louisville Journal*, reprinted in *Turf, Field and Farm*, October 7, 1865, 149.

9. Thomas D. Clark, *Agrarian Kentucky* (Lexington, 1977), 5–6; *Kentucky Live Stock Record*, February 12, 1875, 24.

10. Karl B. Raitz, *The Kentucky Bluegrass: A Regional Profile and Guide* (Chapel Hill, NC, 1980), 1.

11. Frank Ettensohn, interview by Maryjean Wall, October 2, 2007. See also Frank R. Ettensohn, "Horses, Kentucky Bluegrass, and the Origin of Upper Ordovician, Trenton-Age Carbonate Reservoir and Source Rocks in East-Central United States," *Program with Abstracts, 2007, Eastern Section, American Association of Petroleum Geologists Annual Meeting*, and "Evidence and Implications of Possible Far-Field Responses to Taconian Orogeny: Middle-Late Ordovician Lexington Platform and Sebree Trough, East-Central United States," *Southeastern Geology* 41 (2002): 1–36.

12. E. Polk Johnson, *A History of Kentucky and Kentuckians*, 3 vols. (Chicago, 1912), 1:20–21.

13. Clark, *Agrarian Kentucky*, 38–40.

14. Charles Kerr, ed., *History of Kentucky*, 5 vols. (Chicago, 1922), 1:294–95.

15. Clark, *Agrarian Kentucky*, 76; "Lexington Is Foremost Horse City in U.S.," *Lexington Herald*, February 21, 1929, sec. 4, p. 2.

16. For more the interpretation of the mansions as situated on higher ground— *processional landscapes*, as he calls them—see Dell Upton, *Holy Things and Profane: Anglican Parish Churches in Colonial Virginia* (New Haven, CT, 1997).

17. Richard L. Troutman, "The Physical Setting of the Bluegrass Planter," *Register of the Kentucky Historical Society* 66 (1968): 367–77.

18. Ibid.

19. Kerr, *History of Kentucky*, 1:524.

20. Ibid., 294–95. See also Elliott J. Gorn, "'Gouge and bite, pull hair and scratch': The Social Significance of Fighting in the Southern Backcountry," *American Historical Review* 90 (1985): 18–43.

21. Carol Flake, *Thoroughbred Kingdoms: Breeding Farms of the American Racehorse* (Boston, 1990), 19; James Gill, *Bloodstock: Breeding Winners in Europe and America* (New York, 1977), 173.

22. Wharton and Bowen, *Horse World*, 16.

23. Ibid., 15.

24. Lowell H. Harrison and James C. Klotter, *A New History of Kentucky* (Lexington, 1997), 138.

25. "Rowland House Once Home for Col. Sanders, Famous Horseman," *Lexington Leader*, March 23, 1966.

26. *Spirit of the Times*, October 8, 1836, 270–71; Richard Mason, ed., *The Gentleman's New Pocket Farrier* (Richmond, 1835).

27. Wharton and Bowen, *Horse World*, 15.

28. Maryjean Wall, "Feats of Clay: Political Hero Had a Lasting, Little-Known Effect on Horse Racing," *Lexington Herald-Leader*, July 9, 2000, K1; "Henry Clay, Founder of Ashland Stud," *Thoroughbred Record*, May 7, 1921, 334.

29. Harrison and Klotter (*A New History of Kentucky*, 137) put the count of Breckinridge horses at 125. Wharton and Bowen (*Horse World*, 19) put it at 200, citing an article written by Breckinridge's son, Robert J. Breckinridge, "The Blood Horse in Kentucky," *American Turf Register and Sporting Magazine* 1 (1829): 170–72.

30. "City Always Has Bustled" (*Lexington Leader*, June 30, 1938) is a concise, helpful history of the Kentucky Association race track. See also "Kentucky Association," *Lexington Leader*, October 27, 1901.

31. *Spirit of the Times*, October 8, 1836, 270–71.

32. Ibid.

33. Ibid.; Timothy T. Capps, "He Wished to Set the Record Straight," *Thoroughbred Times*, October 1, 2005, 73–74.

34. Edward Hotaling, *The Great Black Jockeys* (Rocklin, CA, 1998), 128.

35. Peter C. Smith and Karl B. Raitz, "Negro Hamlets and Agricultural Estates in Kentucky's Inner Bluegrass," *Geographical Review* 2 (1974): 217–34; Peter Craig Smith,

"Negro Hamlets and Gentlemen Farms: A Dichotomous Rural Settlement Pattern in Kentucky's Bluegrass Region" (Ph.D. diss., University of Kentucky, 1972), 40.

36. "Kentucky Association" (n. 30 above).

37. Wharton and Bowen, *Horse World*, 17.

38. H. W. Smith and John L. Hervey, "Life of Lexington" (unpublished manuscript, n.d., Keeneland Library, Keeneland Race Course, Lexington). See also Kent Hollingsworth, *The Kentucky Thoroughbred* (Lexington, 1976), 20–32.

39. Gill, *Bloodstock*, 179.

40. *Horses in the National Museum Racing Hall of Fame* (Saratoga Springs, NY, [1970s]). See also Wharton and Bowen, *Horse World*, 29.

41. Dan M. Bowmar III (*Giants of the Turf* [Lexington, 1960]) provides a reliable overview of the Alexander family and Woodburn Farm.

42. Basil W. Duke, *Reminiscences of General Basil W. Duke* (New York, 1911), 19.

❧ 7

Three Central Kentuckians, the "Bone" of Political Office, and the Kentucky Exodus, 1792–1852

Mark V. Wetherington

In many respects—arts, architecture, and education—the early republic was the time and central Kentucky the place to ponder the idea of the commonwealth as a likeness of classical Athens. But ancient Athenians did not stay at home. They expanded their influence and power, particularly through the use of their navy, over much of the Mediterranean world. Kentucky's political leadership between 1792 and 1852 accomplished the same. The state's exodus sent explorers, politicians, soldiers, settlers, and enslaved African Americans from central Kentucky throughout the First West and, later, the trans-Mississippi West.

This was a remarkable achievement. Consider that, in 1792, the cutting edge of the western Euro-American settlement line touched the Falls of the Ohio, that settlement had slowed during the American Revolution, and that land-hungry people were ready to move again. In 1803, Meriwether Lewis and William Clark gathered the core of the Corps of Discovery from the commonwealth before heading up the Missouri to the Pacific Ocean. Moreover, Kentuckians played important roles in the conquest and settlement of the Old Northwest during the Revolutionary War and the War of 1812 as well as of the Southwest during the Texas Republic and the Mexican War. Long before Kentucky was thought of in terms of being a part of the South, it was a part of the West.

For, just as Virginia was in many respects the "mother" of Kentucky, then Kentucky fulfilled the same role for western settlements far beyond its present-day boundaries. Kentucky was the middle ground, not only between North and South, but also between the trans-Appalachian and the trans-Mississippi Wests. And, as middle grounders, the commonwealth's people imported the political customs and laws of Virginia and other eastern colonies. They then applied them to the enormous transfer of sovereignty represented by the defeat and removal of the French, English, and Indians and the establishment of the new republic's first postcolonial state. The surveying and remapping of this Ohio valley region fell to men such as Daniel Boone and William Clark who led a migratory wave beyond the Mississippi, carrying with them the political traditions of Kentuckians.[1]

Political life in this western country was not something that happened during congressional, gubernatorial, or presidential elections, only to lapse into dormancy until the next balloting. It took place daily on all levels—neighborhood, county, state, and nation. Most often, political life unfolded within the county context, for counties formed the organizational blocks of the political system. At every step of the way west, a workable system of government was established locally. And land—hundreds of small and mostly privately owned tracts—formed the counties. Each tract of land was, over time, surveyed, bought, traded, and inherited. Public acts of the legislature regulated the toll roads, ferries, and tobacco-inspection stations that appeared on early maps. Local political officeholders guided and recorded the process. More counties meant more "petty offices" for the would-be politicians who designed to make them their bailiwicks. Such politicos seemed constantly in search of the "bone of office," as one reform-minded journalist described the object of all their "growling and fighting" almost a century after statehood. He wistfully hoped that "the Legislature wipes out" the offending counties.[2]

One way in which to explore this idea of a central Kentucky exodus is by briefly examining the lives of three political leaders who lived in central Kentucky and its outer fringes. One of them—Isaac Shelby—remains well-known today. The other two—Peter W. Grayson and George A. Caldwell—although recognized as political leaders in their own time, seem virtually unknown today. Collectively, the public lives of these three men spanned the length of time between the birth of the commonwealth of Kentucky and the Mexican War.

Isaac Shelby (1750–1826) and the Northwest

In 1792, Kentucky became the fifteenth state, one of the first to work through the new political process of admitting states to the nation. By then, white Euro-Americans and their enslaved African Americans had settled "Caintuck" permanently for less than twenty years. Most of its newcomers were born east of the Appalachian Mountains and poured into the commonwealth, dispossessing the Indians of their lands in a protracted period of frontier warfare that lasted about two decades. Isaac Shelby, who became the first governor of the first postrevolutionary political state, was among the newcomers.

Shelby was born in Maryland in 1750. That year marked Daniel Boone's first long hunt and Dr. Thomas Walker's expedition through the Cumberland Gap. Isaac Shelby spent several years surveying and locating land in western Virginia and North Carolina, at times for the Transylvania Company, which also hired Boone to cut a road to its claims in Kentucky. By the early 1770s, Shelby and his father, Evan, had established a store at Sapling Grove among the North-of-Holston settlements along the present-day Tennessee-Virginia border.[3]

The encroachments on Indian lands by long hunters and settlers such as the Boones and the Shelbys resulted in a series of attacks and retaliations between Indians and whites that culminated in Lord Dunmore's War. In October 1774, Isaac Shelby, then twenty-four, took part in the defeat of the Shawnee and Delaware Indians at Point Pleasant, a battle he later described as "the hardest ever fought with the Indians." Subsequently, the Shawnee chiefs pledged to make peace and cease hunting south of the Ohio River if white settlers stayed south of the river.[4]

Despite the Proclamation of 1763, which prohibited settlement west of the Appalachian Mountains, speculators and surveyors fanned out across the countryside. Beginning in the summer of 1775, Shelby joined them as a surveyor "in the cane brakes of Kentucky for near twelve months," an experience that left him "unhealthy." In 1779, he was elected to the Virginia legislature but could not take his seat. In a preview of the surveying problems that plagued Kentucky for generations, it was determined that Shelby actually lived across the line in North Carolina. During the American Revolution, he served as a colonel in the North Carolina militia and participated in the battle at King's Mountain in October 1780, which gave him status as a military leader.[5]

In 1783, Shelby and his wife, Susannah Hart, moved to backcountry Lincoln County, Virginia, in present-day Kentucky. Like most of Virginia's remote backcountry counties, Lincoln was large and stretched from the Cumberland Gap area to the vicinity of present-day Paducah. It was also known as the Green River Military District, reserved for holders of Virginia land warrants distributed as a reward for Revolutionary War ser-

Isaac Shelby by Matthew Harris Jouett, ca. 1816. (The Filson Historical Society, 1995.15.)

vice. The Shelbys built their home, Traveler's Rest, a few miles south of Danville. After ten statehood conventions, in several of which Shelby participated, Kentucky officially became a commonwealth in 1792. Meeting in Lexington, forty electors chose Isaac Shelby as the first governor.[6]

Shelby doubted that his limited executive experience qualified him for high office but accepted the governor's job out of a sense of duty and responsibility to his fellow Kentuckians and the new commonwealth. Nine counties then existed: Bourbon, Woodford, Fayette, Madison, Mercer, and, to a lesser extent, Jefferson formed most of what we today would call central Kentucky. Most of the settlements were clustered in the Bluegrass and at the Falls of the Ohio. During his first administration (1792–1796), lingering Indian problems in the Northwest Territory preoccupied Shelby's time. To deal with the threat, the legislature's first session established military divisions within the commonwealth and made all free white men between the ages of eighteen and forty-five subject to military duty. The state militia became the training ground for both military and political leaders, who were often, like Shelby, one and the same.[7]

In 1792–1793, the Kentucky militia made several excursions north of the Ohio into Indian country. Early in 1793, after several years of sporadic attacks, Benjamin Logan wrote Shelby that "on the frontier the Indians have been every place" and pointed out the need for guards on some roads and settlements. But the attacks had pretty much ended by the end of his Shelby's term. As governor, he helped speed up the settlement of Kentucky by stationing militia on the Wilderness Road and commissioning improvements to Cumberland Gap, which became passable by wagon late in 1796, the final year of his term.[8]

Following his first term, Shelby retired to private life at Traveler's Rest. He owned over six thousand acres in the Bluegrass Region and enough slaves to be counted among the state's planters. As a member of the central Kentucky elite, he defended the institution of slavery and actively participated in the exchange of enslaved African Americans as property. His hemp plantation became an advertisement for the Kentucky good life with its horse and mule breeding, its cattle raising and whiskey making, and its constant gathering of family and guests around tables groaning with the bounty of his land. As Isaac and Susannah's sons grew older, he divided his real estate into generous plantations for them and theirs. And therein lay the problem. As Kentucky filled up owing to natural increase and immigration, the next generation needed more living room.[9]

Shelby was over sixty when, after a hiatus of about sixteen years, he came out of retirement for a second term. Why did he agree to serve when he had already outlived the average life expectancy? One reason involved the spirit of the times. Many Kentuckians supported U.S. representative Henry Clay and the "War Hawks" as they pressured President James Madison to declare war on Great Britain and remove British interference in the West once and for all. Indian troubles on the frontier, particularly Tecumseh's efforts to halt white settlement in the Northwest, made most Kentuckians eager for a campaign to make the Old Northwest safe for expansion and settlement. The Battle of Tippecanoe in November 1811 represented the opening battle, although the United States would not declare war for seven more months. William Henry Harrison, the territorial governor of Indiana, was pressured to open up for settlement land ceded by Indians along the Wabash River.

Like the nation, the state of Kentucky was ill prepared for war, despite the prevailing war fever. Selecting Shelby governor proved a wise move. He had the military reputation and responded once again out of a sense of duty. Moreover, the body politic, largely formed by militiamen, would volunteer and follow him. In May 1813, he wrote Henry Clay stating that he agreed to a second term "under the belief I should be able to render Services to my Country in the event of a war with the Savages, having had a long and intimate knowledge of Indian affairs." Thus, his leadership mattered both at home and in the field.[10]

Shelby, Clay, and other Kentucky leaders urged that more U.S. troops be sent west and succeeded in having Harrison named a major general in the Kentucky militia. He was placed in command of military forces in the Northwest. By the end of the war's first year, owing in part to Harrison's popularity, Kentuckians accounted for two and one half regiments. Over the course of the war, almost twenty-six thousand Kentuckians served as regulars, volunteers, and militia. Of the almost nineteen hundred Americans killed during the War of 1812, some 64 percent (about twelve hundred) were Kentuckians, more casualties than all other states combined.[11]

At a single engagement at the River Raisin in January 1813, for example, upward of 400 Kentuckians were killed outright or later by Indians while being held as prisoners. The following May, another "mournfull disaster" (Shelby's words) struck at Fort Meigs. About 500 Kentuckians were captured and another 150 killed when, against orders, they delayed their retreat after spiking enemy guns and were overwhelmed by a counterattack. Shelby wrote: "A more careless inconsiderate waste of Human blood cannot be found upon the Annals of North America." "Remember the Raisin" became the rallying cry for Kentucky militiamen.[12]

Despite such disasters, Isaac Shelby, Henry Clay, and Kentucky's citizens emerged from the war as leaders of westward expansion. Shelby believed that Kentuckians had earned this reputation by forming the bleeding edge of U.S. efforts to remove both Indians and British. The commonwealth's militia casualties were so high that Shelby's confidence in President Madison's ability to effectively manage the war "in the western country *has greatly abated,* and I feel but little inclination . . . to see a greater proportion of the best blood of Kentucky put to hazard in the General cause than what would be our equal share in the War."[13]

Kentuckians paid the price of territorial expansion with their "best blood" and formed first in line to cross the Ohio River into the Northwest Territory. There they carried their political customs into the southern tiers of new Indiana and Illinois counties, the "butternut" region, so-called because their plain homespun clothing was naturally dyed a yellowish brown by the butternut. Into this world Abraham Lincoln's father, Thomas, migrated in 1816, along with a host of Kentuckians over the coming years. Thomas had title problems with all three of his Kentucky farms. But, on this new frontier, Kentuckians had a major interest in good land titles surveyed under the systematic township system and busied themselves creating an entirely new landscape of counties with more political bones of office for the taking. Abraham Lincoln, surrounded by his new circle of family and friends, including the Speeds and the Todds, symbolized the steady political advancement that was possible beyond the Ohio River.[14]

Although almost seventy, Shelby was not finished with gaining new political sovereignty over lands neighboring the commonwealth. Along with Andrew Jackson, he helped bring about the so-called Jackson Purchase. At that time, 1818, Andrew Jackson was, as the hero of the Battle of New Orleans, in his ascendancy, but Isaac Shelby was a Revolutionary War hero, a field commander in the War of 1812, and twice governor (1792–1796, 1812–1816). Few leaders in the Ohio valley region could match his political and military background. Ratified by the U.S. Senate, and confirmed by President James Monroe in 1819, the Jackson Purchase resulted in Kentucky adding two thousand square miles, and Tennessee six thousand square miles, west of the Tennessee River. The Chickasaw Indians gave up all lands east of the Mississippi River and north of the present-day Mississippi state line in exchange for $300,000. Shelby had delivered another nearby West, easily accessible to white settlers and slave labor.[15]

To Isaac Shelby and Kentucky politicians like him, expansion and war in the Northwest were means of extending the field of settlement and county creation into a new western country. That job done, Shelby now planned to return to Kentucky to live out his life.

Peter W. Grayson (1788–1838) and Texas

But, for a younger generation, symbolized by William Clark, new lands in the West beyond the Mississippi became a place to settle permanently. And, for an older generation tired of the "buzzel" in Kentucky, symbolized by the iconic Daniel Boone, it became a refuge for retirement. Peter Grayson would join them in the trans-Mississippi phase of Kentucky's exodus.

Grayson was born in 1788 at Bardstown, then a backcountry Virginia town. His family was prominent in local politics. His father, Benjamin, served as clerk of court for Nelson County. Peter Grayson, like Isaac Shelby, served in the War of 1812. He enlisted for one month in a Kentucky Mounted Volunteer militia company in 1813 and served another stint in 1814 as an infantry sergeant in the Seventh Regiment, U.S. Army. He was not the only Grayson to volunteer. His older brother, Frederick W. S. Grayson, joined the fight a year earlier and served as captain of Grayson's company, Third Regiment, Kentucky Detached Militia, commanded by Lt. Col. Nicholas Miller. Following the war, Peter acquired a town lot in Bardstown, dabbled in trade, and served as the local agent for a Louisville newspaper. Early in 1822, he resigned as Bardstown's postmaster. Prosperity eluded him.[16]

Like many men seemingly stuck in rural communities as the frontier moved beyond Kentucky, Grayson joined a rural to urban migration to the commonwealth's larger towns. He chose Louisville. It was nearby and booming with trade and steamboat traffic. There, he sought a wider field for his ambitions and more success than he enjoyed in Bardstown. He could also count on the support of his older and more successful brother Frederick, who had already moved to the city and established a thriving law practice. By the mid-1820s, Frederick returned $12,500 in property for tax purposes, including 8 acres in Louisville and another 556 acres in Jefferson County. In 1825, he was appointed the commonwealth's attorney general. A half century later, Frederick Grayson's "quaint brick house" would be remembered primarily for its location at Sixth Street and Walnut, where it sat atop one half of an Indian mound, Grayson having "partly dug down" the other half to fill in "Grayson's pond." Thus, Frederick and his kin not only helped vanquish the Indians to the trans-Mississippi West but also claimed one of the earlier mound builder's monuments for the foundation of his new family home.[17]

Peter Grayson was not at the center of the material world enjoyed by his older brother. Although he advertised between 1824 and 1827 that he would practice law in Jefferson County, apparently not much business came to his office on Market Street. Indeed, it appears that he owned no real property in Jefferson County and returned a town lot at Bardstown valued at $500 only between 1826 and 1829. Furthermore, the failure of a previous business venture left him deeply in debt and dependent on Fred-

Peter Grayson by Matthew Harris Jouett, ca. 1827. (The Filson
Historical Society, 1995.13.2.)

erick. The mid-1820s found him trying to recover financially while he
practiced a little law and, like his older brother, wrote some poetry. This
did not mean that Peter was entirely without political or social standing.
For example, he served on a committee to prepare an act of incorpora-
tion for the city of Louisville in the fall of 1824. And, during the following spring, he was actively involved in a local arrangements committee
charged with welcoming General Lafayette to town with a barbeque.[18]

Then family disaster struck. On October 27, 1828, Frederick died. But
he had remembered Peter in his estate planning. Peter received his sib-
ling's law books and a release from all debts owed by him to Frederick, on
the condition that Peter pay off all the obligations incurred by his business

failures, thus restoring honor to his name. Moreover, the older brother directed that Peter pay "my dear Mother" $200 per year "during her life for her Separate use." Frederick did his best to give Peter a new start.[19]

The fresh start included a future in politics. Given his political bloodline—his great-uncle Col. William Grayson was an aide-de-camp to Gen. George Washington, received a seventy-thousand-acre patent signed by Isaac Shelby in 1795, and became a U.S. senator—it is not surprising that Peter entered the political arena. Although he had few financial resources of his own, he was brother-in-law to Sarah Ward Grayson, Frederick's "widow of high social position." In 1828, he ran for one of Jefferson County's seats in the state legislature as a Jackson Republican and rode Jackson's coattails to victory. Of that election the *Louisville Public Advertiser* wrote: "Our successes in electing a decided majority of Jackson men in the legislature, proves, that we are not only competent to contend with our adversaries in November next, but to triumph over them." Grayson benefited from the anti-Clay "corrupt bargain" press mobilized by Jackson's supporters.[20]

In the year prior to his election, Grayson, then almost forty, sat to have his portrait painted by Matthew Harris Jouett, among the last the Kentucky artist would attempt. In the unfinished likeness, Grayson sits with his right hand to his chin, his elbow resting on a table. Little in this painting indicates that beneath the surface he was struggling with mental illness, which made him "adverse to mental exertion of any kind," he later wrote, throughout the 1820s. This "fiend that pursued me," as he described the illness, may help explain why he was incapable of sustaining any profitable business endeavor at Louisville yet capable of hiding his disability from friends and voters. His mental instability, when combined with his indebtedness and the deaths of "his friend" Jouett and his brother Frederick, left him "a partially deranged man."[21]

By 1830, however, Grayson believed that his condition had improved and seemed ready for a fresh start. During the 1820s–1840s, a steady stream totaling a quarter of a million emigrants left Kentucky for new frontiers, some of them formerly peopled by the Ohio valley's original settlers—its Indians—and won by military leaders and rank-and-file soldiers such as Isaac Shelby and Grayson himself. Foremost among these destinations were tracts in present-day Indiana and Illinois. In the fall of 1828, for example, an Indiana newspaper reported that the return of autumn brought from twenty-five to thirty families through town each day on their way to the Wabash River country. Peter Grayson decided instead to put more distance between his troubled Ohio valley past and his future.[22]

Peter Grayson's name disappeared from the Jefferson County tax list in 1830. That same year he wrote to Stephen F. Austin, who had established a colony in remote northern Mexico, seeking information about land. Austin attended Transylvania University, and Grayson may have become acquainted with him during his Kentucky days. But Grayson was not the first Kentuckian to catch "Texas fever." Austin received hundreds of similar letters. As early as 1821, Elijah Noble of Lexington wrote on behalf of a group of Kentuckians regarding immigration to Texas, and the following year Benjamin Milam sought a colonization contract. But drought, Indian attacks, lawlessness, concerns about religious freedom, and shaky land titles slowed down settlement until the mid-1820s. Kentucky newspapers continued to print favorable reports from Texas, and by 1830 other letter writers joined Grayson. For example, the president of Centre College, the Reverend Gideon Blackburn, considered bringing up to a hundred families to Texas, where he planned to advance "the cause of literature and religion."[23]

Grayson's departure from Kentucky came at a point in time when political power in the governor's mansion began to shift from Jackson's supporters to Henry Clay's. But Grayson's political career was far from over. It is not clear how long it took Grayson to reach Texas or by what route. It is known that he claimed land certificates in Missouri and may have considered settling there. One source observed that he was, "if we mistake not, a very tolerable lawyer in Natchez," suggesting that he spent some time there on his way to Texas. Like many Upper South people troubled by debt during the 1830s, *gone to Texas* described Grayson's fate as well.[24]

Texas allowed Grayson to reinvent himself even as "this most delightful and fertile country" was being remapped by Anglo-American colonists. In his new environment, he blossomed. He practiced law at San Felipe de Austin, the Brazos River seat of Austin's colony, under contract with the Mexican government. In this small settlement, Grayson, after his arrival in 1830, became a confidant of Stephen Austin's. His personality at this time showed no hint of his deeper mental disability. People remembered him as possessing "a warm and enthusiastic temperament, strong in his friendships, chivalrously honorable in his private character, a most accomplished member of the bar, and in his manners a finished gentleman."[25]

Austin came to believe that "the local government of Texas ought to be organized, or that country ought to be transferred to the United States." He also maintained that "the Gothic politico-religious system set up by Rome and Spain to hold the people in subjection like beasts of burden" slowed Texas's development. Grayson agreed with Austin. He became involved in both the military and the political maneuvering that eventually resulted in the Anglo-American revolution against Mexico, including recruiting volunteers in the United States. When Mexican authorities arrested Austin in 1834, Grayson and another lawyer, Spencer Jack, traveled to Mexico to make a case for Austin's release. After being freed, Austin traveled to Kentucky in March 1836 to appeal for support for his "struggling country" now at war with Mexico. Speaking in Louisville, Austin recounted all the "difficulties and dangers incident to all new and wilderness countries infested with hostile Indians." Seeking to link Kentucky's past to the present and future of Texas, he declared that such "appalling" experiences could "only be appreciated by the hardy pioneers of this western country, who have passed through similar scenes." Moreover, former Kentuckians were now dying for the "holy cause of liberty" in Texas. During the storming of Mexican fortifications at San Antonio de Bexar, Benjamin Milam of the Texas militia led the storm and died, in the words of Austin, "as such a spirit wished to die, in the cause of liberty, and in the arms of victory. Texas weeps for her Milam; Kentucky has cause to be proud of her son." Meanwhile, Peter Grayson served as Austin's aide-de-camp, was elected president of the council of war by Texas soldiers, and, as attorney general of the Republic of Texas, signed the Treaties of Velasco in May 1836.[26]

After independence, Grayson again served as Texas attorney general, when President Sam Houston named him to that post in 1837. He traveled to Washington that year as a special envoy for Texas annexation by the United States. Late in 1837, Houston named him naval agent for the Republic of Texas to the United States. Leading Whigs back home in his native state were at odds with his position on Texas annexation. In January 1838, Henry Clay wrote that the annexation question should not be introduced during the war between Mexico and Texas and that he would not support the annexation in peacetime. Bringing Texas into the Union would only raise the question of the expansion of slavery. "I think it better to harmonize what we have," Clay wrote, "than to introduce a new element of discord into our political partnership, against the consent of existing members of the concern."[27]

Against his better judgment, Peter Grayson reluctantly agreed to run for the presidency of the Republic of Texas as the Houston Party's candidate. This proved to be his undoing. His supporters believed that, having learned of his troubled years of mental instability in Kentucky, his political enemies in Texas used "*slang* and *calumny*" (Grayson's words) to undermine his campaign. This was too much for Grayson, and his old fears of "the horrors of the madhouse" returned. On June 9, 1838, even as he campaigned for office, Grayson wrote his last will and testament, "feeling at the present moment particularly the uncertainty of life." One month later, as he traveled to Washington as the republic's minister plenipotentiary to the United States, Grayson passed through East Tennessee and stopped at Bean's station. There, on the night of July 8, the depression that he had held in check caught up with him at May's Inn. After asking for a room and complaining of pain in his forehead, he went upstairs, took half a vial of laudanum, put a pistol to his head, and pulled the trigger.[28]

Always the southern gentleman, Grayson left a letter to the innkeeper and apologized for the "frightful scene I have made in your house. . . . You will find money in my pocket-book to defray all my necessary expenses." He also left a suicide note: "*To my friends.* I go to my grave for the quiet the world can never give me. The fiend that pursued me for a long time previous to 1830, and then let me rest, ('twas when I went to Texas,) has started on me again with redoubled fury. To save myself from the horrors of the madhouse, I go to my grave. Farewell! To you and a few kindred of my particular affections I yield the last pulsations of my heart."[29]

Unlike Isaac Shelby, who helped expand the nation but returned home to Kentucky, Peter Grayson hoped to live out his life in a new land. Although he met a tragic end, his career illustrated the economic and political possibilities for an ambitious man willing to move west and remain there.

George Caldwell (1814–1866) and Mexico

George Alfred Caldwell, like Peter Grayson, is virtually unknown in Kentucky today. But in his own half century of life he helped expand the spatial and political influence of Kentuckians beyond Peter Grayson's Texas. He was born on October 18, 1814, in Adair County, Kentucky, even as Shelby and Grayson fought the British and their Indian allies on the northern borderlands. His life illustrates how rapidly the western edge of the new republic moved as it took in new land to be surveyed, sold, and governed. Consider that George was a child of the War of 1812 and a veteran of the Mexican War and that within a generation of his birth the boundaries of the current-day lower forty-eight states expanded to the Canadian and Mexican borders and to the Pacific.

Caldwell's father, William Caldwell (1777–1854), and his mother, Nancy Anne Trabue, were born in Virginia, became prominent members of the Adair County, Kentucky, community, and served as "faithful, pious and zealous members of the Baptist church." Present at the creation of

Adair County in 1801, William soon achieved a longevity in office that reflected his early role in the county. He was reelected clerk of court of Adair County for a half century, and he came close to leaving office feet first. One of those record keepers historians love, he amassed so many pieces of official county paper between 1802, when he was named clerk of court, and 1825 that his small office overflowed. County authorities permitted him to remove all the papers to a room in his home, which became his official office. This convenient combination of home and workplace meant that for a short time his children grew up in a site of county business. William also concurrently served as clerk of the circuit court. Keeping records for both offices forced the county in 1827 to buy a private dwelling and move papers there, and, in 1838, an even larger clerk's office was constructed. When this double duty became too much for William, his son Junius took over the office of clerk of the circuit court in 1841.[30]

During the 1840s, the Caldwell family's power and influence grew, in part because George's parents encouraged their children to seek an education beyond that offered in Adair County. George graduated from St. Joseph's College at Bardstown and received his law degree in Lexington in 1837. After returning to Columbia, he was admitted to the bar at the age of twenty-three. Following his younger brother Isaac's graduation from Georgetown College and his admission to the bar in 1847, the two practiced law together in Columbia. Their brother William graduated from Transylvania and practiced medicine in Columbia. Not to be outdone, Junius eventually gave up his clerk's post and became a lawyer. Moreover, George's was "a lucrative practice," and his "talents were rapid in their development and in their recognition by the people."[31]

The people soon rewarded George Caldwell with public office. Although later described as a man who preferred the "quiet of private life, and . . . the studies of the gentleman to the hurly-burly of public service and the dissipations of the politicians," he quickly overcame "the sensitiveness of his modest nature" and entered the political arena. He first ran for a seat in the Kentucky legislature in 1839 when he was twenty-five and won. In all likelihood, he used the same neighborhood- and kinship-based political network that allowed his father to keep a firm grip on the county clerk's office. He was reelected the following year, despite the county's strong Whig leanings.[32]

Caldwell soon moved on in search of a bigger political bone. Running as a Democrat in a district described as "strongly, overwhelmingly Whig," he won a seat in the Twenty-eighth Congress, by about five hundred votes. His victory was due in part to a split Whig ticket. In his first

George Caldwell by an unknown artist, ca. 1845–1866. (The Filson Historical Society, 1997.1.2.)

congressional term (March 1843–March 1845), he became the chairman of the Committee on Expenditures in the Department of the Treasury. A "strict States-rights Democrat," he rode the same groundswell that carried his fellow Democrat James K. Polk into the White House.[33]

In June 1846, George Caldwell volunteered for service in the war with Mexico. Wars offered excellent opportunities for county-level politicians to display their leadership skills, win some military glory, and use that fame to greater political advantage. Wars also provided ways in which to distribute political favors by issuing officers' commissions to political cronies. Governor William Owsley, a Whig like Henry Clay, was not particularly enthusiastic about the war, but, once it started, he got into step with most Kentuckians and supported it.

There was also a lot of political wheeling and dealing in the air when Governor Owsley revealed the results of his brand of selective service. The U.S. War Department asked for 2 infantry regiments and 1 cavalry regiment from Kentucky, but 105 infantry companies had eagerly volunteered. Owsley accepted only 30, most of them organized in counties that reflected his power base in the Bluegrass region and the more urban areas along the Ohio River. Understandably, Owsley usually selected companies organized and led by Whigs, his political bedfellows. Although Henry Clay opposed the war, his son Henry Jr. was one of those who found his way into Mexican War service through this reward system.[34]

Being a good Democrat, George Caldwell probably did not see his name show up on Governor Owsley's list of candidates for officer's commission. His commission may have come from President James K. Polk, as a result of recommendations from top Kentucky Democrats. In any event, he received a commission as a major and quartermaster of Volunteers in June 1846. One of his immediate regimental superiors was Lt. Col. Joseph E. Johnston, later on a leading Confederate commander. Caldwell followed in the footsteps of both Isaac Shelby and Peter Grayson in their War of 1812 service and of the latter in his revolutionary designs on Texas and Mexican territory. By April of the following year, he was a major in the infantry.[35]

At the Battle of Chapultepec, Mexico, George Caldwell "rendered particularly brave service" and was breveted lieutenant colonel. After the war's end in August 1848, he mustered out of the army and returned to Adair County, just at election time. He had been available for military service in 1846 because the finicky voters in his Fourth Congressional District had narrowly rejected his reelection bid in 1845. They chose a Whig instead. Imagine the horror of Whigs such as Governor Owsley when Caldwell returned to Columbia in 1848 a war hero and began campaigning for his old seat in Congress. He easily defeated his Whig opponent and joined the Thirty-first Congress (March 1849–March 1851). He even got back his old chairmanship of the Committee on Expenditures in the Department of the Treasury.

In 1851, at the end of his term, Caldwell decided not to run for reelection. Instead, he and his brother Isaac moved to Louisville, where they practiced law together from an office on West Jefferson St., where George also maintained his residence. George Caldwell lived to see the failure of the American political system when secession tore the nation apart in 1860–1861, one eventual outcome of the expansion of slavery into the landscapes that he and Peter Grayson came to know. He died in

1866, living just long enough to see the two sections take the first steps toward reunion. The *Louisville Daily Democrat* wrote: "Kentucky deplores the removal by death of a son who, in the halls of legislation, before the tribunals of justice, and in the mad charge and stern shock of battle, had few equals and superiors."[36]

Conclusion

Three generations fill the time between the formation of the commonwealth in 1792 and the death of Henry Clay in 1852. The lives of Isaac Shelby, Peter Grayson, and George Caldwell fill these years with some time to spare. In looking at their political careers, several themes emerge. Their early political activities took place daily in small rural places on the farm, town, and county levels. New land was the commodity in their political beginnings. Whether as state legislators, congressmen, governors, attorneys general, and diplomats, local office formed the foundation of careers that reached up from the county to Frankfort to Washington and beyond.

Second, those small places—counties, villages, and towns—expanded tremendously during the period: from east of the mountains (Shelby's birthplace), into the new commonwealth of Kentucky (the birthplace of Grayson and Caldwell), and beyond the Ohio and Mississippi Rivers. Generally, the direction was west. Each expansion created new counties and new bones of office to fight over. Remapping the territories by Anglo-Americans meant new naming opportunities. Shelby County was created in 1792 in honor of the commonwealth's first governor. In 1846, after the U.S. annexation of Texas, the Texas legislature created Grayson County in honor of Peter Grayson, a man they considered a "Texas patriot." George Caldwell seems to have missed out. The migration of the Caldwells to Louisville reminds us that the east-to-west migration represented by Isaac Shelby, William Caldwell, and Peter Grayson was not the only one at work. There was also a rural/small town to urban pattern represented earlier by Grayson's move from Bardstown to Louisville.

Third, Shelby and Caldwell were military men at some point in their lives and used their military reputations to advance their careers—Peter Grayson less so, but his War of 1812 service, his friendship with Stephen Austin, and his insider role in the Texas revolution carried him to high political office in a new nation. George Caldwell won reelection to the U.S. Congress in part because of his Mexican War record. The long-range consequences of these men's military operations are too numerous and complex to explore here, but decades of warfare in the East shaped a culture accustomed to conquest, expansion, and the dispossession of native populations farther west. The defeat of the British and their Indian allies during the War of 1812 made the Northwest Territory safe for continued settlement and sped up statehood for Indiana and Illinois, which before the war had a total of about thirty-eight thousand white settlers between them. "They came in swarms," wrote one historian. The same could be said of Texas. Its annexation by the United States in 1845 and the defeat of Mexico in the war that followed ultimately led to the Compromise of 1850 and California's admission as a free state. Between 1792 and 1852, the borders of the nation had moved from Kentucky to the Pacific Ocean in what Stephen Austin would have called "Americanizing . . . by filling it with a population from this country, who will harmonize in language, in political education, in common origin, in every thing, with their neighbors to the east and north." Well, almost everything, for the Old Northwest and the Southwest, in which Kentuckians had such a strong hand in colonizing, differed in one important way—one was free, the other was slave, and on that there would ultimately be no political compromise.[37]

And, finally, getting and keeping the political bone proved risky. Shelby realized this. Reluctant to accept office because he believed that he was not well qualified, he did so out of a sense of duty. He came out of retirement to help the commonwealth in time of war, but military disaster could have left him with a tarnished reputation. Caldwell's status as a Mexican War hero helped him overcome his previous political defeat, but he apparently tired of Washington and retired to a successful law practice in Louisville. Poor Grayson knew his past might catch up with him, even in distant Texas. In his suicide note he wrote: "The last trap to catch my soul, and send it to a hell of torture, was the *good feeling* of my friends, urging me and prevailing on me to be a candidate for the presidency of Texas! Oh, God!!"[38]

Notes

1. See John R. Hale, *Lords of the Sea: The Epic Story of the Athenian Navy and the Birth of Democracy* (New York, 2009); Stephen Aron, *American Confluence: The Missouri Frontier from Borderland to Border State* (Bloomington, IN, 2006), 106, 120; and Otis K. Rice, *Frontier Kentucky* (Lexington, 1993), 1–17.

2. Elizabeth A. Perkins, *Border Life: Experience and Memory in the Revolutionary Ohio Valley* (Chapel Hill, NC, 1998), 120–24. For quotations, see "The Kentucky Vendetta," *Frank Leslie's Illustrated Newspaper,* September 10, 1887, 55. I want to thank Mark Wetherington Jr. for bringing this article to my attention. For a discussion of

Kentucky counties, see Robert M. Ireland, *The County Courts in Antebellum Kentucky* (Lexington, 1972).

3. Sylvia Wrobel and George Grider, *Isaac Shelby: Kentucky's First Governor and Hero of Three Wars* (Danville, KY, 1974), 4–11, 68–76.

4. Meredith Mason Brown, *Frontiersman: Daniel Boone and the Making of America* (Baton Rouge, 2008), 65–67.

5. "Autobiography of Isaac Shelby," 1–2, Filson Historical Society photocopy of original in Reuben T. Durrett Collection, Special Collections, University of Chicago Library; Rice, *Frontier Kentucky*, 39; Lowell H. Harrison, "Isaac Shelby," in *The Kentucky Encyclopedia*, ed. John E. Kleber (Lexington, 1992), 815–16; Lowell H. Harrison and James C. Klotter, *A New History of Kentucky* (Lexington, 1997), 19–20, 65–66.

6. Harrison and Klotter, *New History of Kentucky*, 68–69; Harrison, "Isaac Shelby," 815. See also Joan Wells Coward, *Kentucky in the New Republic: The Process of Constitution Making* (Lexington, 1979).

7. Wrobel and Grider, *Isaac Shelby*, 89–91.

8. Benjamin Logan to Isaac Shelby, April 8, 1793, *Register of the Kentucky State Historical Society* 1 (January 1903): 33; Thomas L. Connelly, "Gateway to Kentucky: The Wilderness Road, 1748–1792," *Register of the Kentucky State Historical Society* 59 (1961): 130; Harrison and Klotter, *New History of Kentucky*, 49.

9. Wrobel and Grider, *Isaac Shelby*, 98–103.

10. James F. Hopkins et al., eds., *The Papers of Henry Clay*, 10 vols. and suppl. (Lexington, 1959–1992), suppl.:27; Harry S. Laver, *Citizens More Than Soldiers: The Kentucky Militia and Society in the Early Republic* (Lincoln, NE, 2007).

11. Harrison and Klotter, *New History of Kentucky*, 90–91, 94.

12. Ibid., 94; Hopkins et al., eds., *Papers of Henry Clay*, suppl.:26, 28.

13. Hopkins et al., eds., *Papers of Henry Clay*, suppl.:27–28.

14. Lowell H. Harrison, *Lincoln of Kentucky* (Lexington, 2000), 3, 26, 27; Stephen Berry, *House of Abraham: Lincoln and the Todds: A Family Divided by War* (Boston, 2007), 26–31.

15. Hunter M. Hancock, "Jackson Purchase," in Kleber, ed., *Kentucky Encyclopedia*, 460–61.

16. *Report of the Adjutant General of the State of Kentucky: Soldiers of the War of 1812* (Frankfort, 1891), 49, 337, 364; Lola Frazer Crouded, comp., *Early Louisville, Kentucky Newspaper Abstracts, 1806–1828* (Galveston, TX, 1995), 27; *U.S. Federal Census Index, Kentucky, 1820*, comp. Ronald Vern Jackson (South Jordan, UT, n.d.), 59 (listing Peter Grayson as still living in Nelson County).

17. "Benjamin Alsop, Commrs. Book for the Year 1826," 16, Kentucky Tax List, Jefferson County, microfilm box 188, Filson Historical Society, Louisville; J. Stoddard Johnston, ed., *Memorial History of Louisville . . .* , 2 vols. (Chicago, 1896), 1:33, 85.

18. Jefferson County Tax List, 1826, 15, and Jefferson County Tax List, 1829, 9, Filson Historical Society; *Louisville Public Advertiser*, October 20, 1824, May 7, 1825.

19. Grayson Family File, Filson Historical Society; *Louisville Focus,* October 30, 1828.

20. Johnston, ed., *Memorial History of Louisville,* 1:85; *Louisville Public Advertiser,* August 13, 1828; William Barrow Floyd, *Jouett-Bush-Frazer: Early Kentucky Artists* (Lexington, 1968), 68–69.

21. Floyd, *Jouett-Bush-Frazer,* 69. See "Death of Peter W. Grayson, Esq. of Texas," *Niles' Register,* August 18, 1838, 394–95.

22. Matthew Schoenbachler, "The Social Origins of Jeffersonian Democracy" (Ph.D. diss., University of Kentucky, 1996), 234–35; *Indiana Journal* quoted in *Olive Branch and Danville Advertiser,* November 1, 1828; Jefferson County Tax List, 1830, Filson Historical Society.

23. Eugene C. Barker, *The Life of Stephen F. Austin, Founder of Texas, 1793–1836 . . .* (1925; New York, 1968), 95–96, 148, 252–53; Mark E. Nevils, "Grayson County," in Kleber, ed., *Kentucky Encyclopedia,* 385; *Niles' Register,* August 18, 1838, 394–95.

24. Barker, *Stephen F. Austin,* 95–96, 148, 252–53.

25. Ibid., 131; *Daily National Intelligencer,* August 11, 1837; *Richmond (VA) Enquirer,* August 17, 1838.

26. Barker, *Stephen F. Austin,* 437, 429, 447. See the Grayson entry in "The Handbook of Texas Online," http://www.tshaonline.org/handbook/online/articles/fgr29; "Address of the Honorable S. F. Austin, Delivered at Louisville, Kentucky, March 7, 1836," 2, 13, Avalon Project at Yale Law School, http://avalon.law.yale.edu/19th_century/texind01.asp.

27. Henry Clay to Peter B. Porter, January 26, 1838, in Hopkins et al., eds., *Papers of Henry Clay,* 9:135.

28. Manuscript copy of will of Peter W. Grayson, June 9, 1838, Dorothy Sloan Books, Austin, TX, Auction no. 4, April 5, 1997; *Niles' Register,* August 18, 1838.

29. *Niles' Register,* August 18, 1838.

30. *Louisville Daily Democrat,* September 18, 1866; Christopher Waldrep, "Opportunity on the Frontier South of the Green," in *The Buzzel about Kentuck: Settling the Promised Land,* ed. Craig Thompson Friend (Lexington, 1999), 156–59; Michael C. Watson, comp., *An Adair County, Kentucky History* (n.p., 2001), 80, 303.

31. *Louisville Daily Journal,* September 18, 1866; William J. Morison, "Isaac Caldwell," in *The Encyclopedia of Louisville,* ed. John E. Kleber (Lexington, 2001), 155; Watson, comp., *An Adair County, Kentucky History,* 80, 303.

32. *Louisville Daily Democrat,* September 18, 1866.

33. Ibid.; *Biographical Directory of the United States Congress,* s.v. George Alfred Caldwell, http://bioguide.congress.gov/scripts/biodisplay.pl?index=C000031.

34. Harrison and Klotter, *New History of Kentucky,* 114–16.

35. *Biographical Directory of the United States Congress,* s.v. George Alfred Caldwell.

36. *The Louisville Directory and Annual Business Advertiser for 1855–56* (Louisville, 1855), 49; Morison, "Isaac Caldwell," 155; *Louisville Daily Democrat,* September 18, 1866.

37. Andrew R. L. Cayton, *Frontier Indiana* (Bloomington, 1996), 228–39; Ray Allen Billington, *Westward Expansion: A History of the American Frontier* (New York, 1974), 283, 508; "Address of the Honorable S. F. Austin, Delivered at Louisville," 15.

38. *Niles' Register,* August 18, 1838.

Part 3

Science, Arts, and Education

❧ 8

Jewels in the Crown

Civic Pride and Educational Institutions in the Bluegrass, 1792–1852

John R. Thelin

Building the Booster College: An American Tradition

At the start of the twenty-first century, American colleges and universities are hailed as a success story in large part because of their real and imagined role as economic engines that make a city or even an entire state prosperous.[1] Two centuries ago, however, the story had a slightly different inflection: the campus was embraced, indulged, and subsidized because various constituencies—ranging from mayors, state legislators, governors, merchants, and real estate promoters to clergy and citizens—saw the founding of a college as a source of civic pride. Yes, the college stimulated the local economy. More important, however, was the distinctively American belief that for a town to be home and host to a real college meant that it was bona fide—no less than a real city. The best counterpart to the American fondness for building colleges in 1800 now is found in the quest that mayors and city councils have to attract professional sports such as an NBA franchise or an NFL team to town. It is illustrated by the case of Atlanta, which in the 1970s lured the National League Milwaukee Braves baseball team to the South.[2] Whatever the expense in civic subsidies, it was a crucial event because, according to its advocates, it transformed Atlanta into a true "major league city." Although a college or a professional sports team might eventually bring income to a city, at the start it usually meant that taxpayers were going to pay dearly for the privilege of hosting the coveted institution.

And so it was with towns and cities in Kentucky from the late eighteenth century to the mid-nineteenth as every hamlet and crossroads vied with larger cities to attract or create its own homegrown college. The historian Daniel Boorstin called this the *booster college* phenomenon in the social history that characterized American westward expansion.[3] How important was a college to a town? It took priority over clean drinking water, paved roads, irrigation systems, and even the establishment of elementary schools. This latter oversight later would cause a few problems, as the local college officials soon discovered that they had little, if any, reliable source of students who could pass the college admissions examination. The usual solutions were tributes to American pragmatism in the face of adversity: first, be lenient in grading the admissions exam, and, second, have the college faculty also offer (for a tuition charge, of course) some preparatory classes.[4]

The market forces of civic competition for colleges led to bidding wars among communities and, then, a proliferation of new institutions. One reason this was able to take place was that, in the young United States, the ground rules of institution charters departed dramatically from the customs and statutes in England. Whereas in the mid-nineteenth century England had a large, dense population, it had only three chartered, degree-granting universities: Oxford, Cambridge, and the young University of London.[5] This was so because royal charters conferred by the crown were preceded by caution and thorough scrutiny. In England, one group applying for a college charter in the New World argued to the royal court that it was a wise venture because a college might ultimately help save souls. The beleaguered royal attorney general replied curtly: "Souls! Damn your souls! Raise tobacco."[6] Most kings and queens preferred to have colonial revenues coming in to Mother England rather than going out to the distant colonies. As a result, those few persistent and persuasive groups that were effective in persuading the crown's agents to grant a collegiate charter literally were well rewarded. This was because it meant that the monarchy accepted the obligation and commitment to provide annual and long-term funding for the fortunate universities that did receive a charter. It was a custom that held in the American colonies, where, for example, the College of William and Mary in Virginia had the double blessings of a royal charter granted in 1693 and generous income from such sources as taxes on tobacco, fees for licensing surveyors, and tolls from bridges along with subsidies from the royal exchequer. With the end of colonial status, the comforts of royal protection and financing halted abruptly. American colleges faced a new deal.[7]

In contrast to the provisions of the British Empire, with the advent of independence from England after the Revolutionary War colleges in the new nation were cast into a completely different political and economic environment. Henceforth, college charters were conferred by state legislatures—not by a national body or the federal government or Congress. What successful state politicians ranging from legislators to governors discovered by 1800 was that granting a college charter to a group of supporters or friends was an easy way to repay political debts. A college charter became a coin of the realm in the spoils system of statewide patronage, especially in the new states in the southern and western borders of the new, growing nation.[8] It meant that, by the mid-nineteenth century, the sparsely settled United States could boast of several hundred colleges and universities—along with a motley crew of medical schools, law schools, theological seminaries, academies, technical institutes, scientific schools, and even some engineering schools. The enduring legacy of this change in charters and government relations was that all colleges, including such historic institutions as Harvard, Yale, and Princeton, were dependent on year-by-year revenues—most of which came from students' tuition payments. Subsidies and private donations helped, but few colleges in the first half of the nineteenth century could boast of having substantial endowment or financial reserves that would allow them to be indifferent to enrolling a sufficient number of students who either could pay their expenses or brought with them tuition scholarships sponsored by such external interest groups as churches or missionary societies. Academic operations represented a hardscrabble existence that called for persistent attention to keeping operating expenses low and revenues adequate, if not abundant.[9] One way in which a college president and board could do this was to be vigilant in monitoring public demands for new educational programs.

The college consumerism of the era dictated that presidents be resilient—that is, daring to offer new degree programs and professional courses if there was student market demand. One consequence of this situation was that, from time to time, a college president, out of either desperation or confidence, might start a "scientific" track or course of study, a rough approximation of what we would today consider an engineering school. More typical, however, was a college's reliance on three degree programs—liberal arts, law, and medicine—as its staple offerings to prospective students. One irony of the academic marketing of the era was that presidents worked hard to keep tuition charges low, indicative of a lack of confidence that even a prestigious institution would be able to charge a relatively high price and simultaneously attract an adequate number of new students to fill recitation halls and dormitories. Sporadic appropriations or subsidies from state legislatures or other groups during prosperous years may have temporarily masked the precarious financial health, even of such established and attractive institutions as Transylvania. And any change in political fortunes or favor with a state government left a college vulnerable to operating budget shortfalls. In sum, higher education in the early nineteenth century was a booming field—but it was an unregulated enterprise subject to vacillations, not unlike ventures in mining or timber.

Concern for educational standards may have been important to dedicated founders who themselves were college graduates, but they were often not high priority to legislators and land developers. Contrary to our contemporary practices, chartering a medical school was the cheapest enterprise. One medical college in Indiana, whose founder later skipped one step ahead of the sheriff and moved to Ohio, conferred over three hundred M.D. degrees without having a faculty, a laboratory, or a lecture hall. Given this lean arrangement of physical plant and professional personnel, it was not surprising that the medical school provided certification without instruction or class work.[10] It was a model of efficiency for its founder and its alumni as its only expense was the founder's purchase of reasonably good quality sheepskin diplomas—an investment readily offset by the graduation fees required of degree candidates. Less certain was whether patients as consumers gained or lost when treated by physicians who were alumni of this medical school. Since the dead do not speak or fill out satisfaction questionnaires, the quality of professional education remains unclear at best. What this case in medical education shows is that nineteenth-century America was strong on enterprise and even hucksterism, with educational accountability and quality lagging far behind. Higher education was, in short, an entrepreneur's dream come true.

Fortunately for the good name and historical reputation of the commonwealth, the medical schools in antebellum Kentucky demonstrated a more responsible, serious commitment to professional teaching and learning than did this infamous counterpart in Indiana. The Medical Department of Transylvania University was highly regarded, in terms of both the prestige of its full-time professors and the number of enrolled students. The medical school in Louisville, hailed as the "first among medical schools of the West," did provide classrooms, lecture halls, and dissection rooms as integral facilities in the education of future physicians and surgeons. Yet, as with all professional education of the era, medical schools consistently displayed a pay-as-you-go character—probably bringing to mind what we today associate with for-profit and proprietary colleges. For example, typical practice was to require a medical student to purchase tickets to gain admission to a professor's announced medical lecture. One of the major sources of revenue for the self-supporting professors of medicine was to charge hefty examination fees for those students who wished to earn an M.D. degree. The format for final exams usually was an oral questioning by one or two faculty members. And, at the University of Louisville, the custom was for professors to require degree candidates to take their final exams twice.[11] Most likely, the faculty motive was enhancing their earnings, rather than assuring high-quality student achievement prior to certification. Medical schools literally sought bodies—but of two different types. Foremost, they needed applicants who could pay expenses. Not far behind, they faced an insatiable demand for corpses—essential to anatomy courses for aspiring young doctors. Little wonder, then, that a prime location for a medical college was a fairly populated area—and preferably near a river where malaria and cholera assured a steady supply of cadavers.

One hitch in this college charter sweepstakes was that the state legislators did not follow the English custom of pledging ample government support for chartered colleges. The charter provided essentially a license to operate, with no guarantee of state funding and certainly no guarantee that a college would survive. Each state legislature acquired its own signature style of college funding. Usually, it was uncertain, sporadic, cheap, and marked by unabashed political and religious partisanship. In New York State, for example, an upstate and largely rural state legislature gave generous support via lottery proceeds to the new Union College and showed its contempt for downstate New York City by giving Columbia University the consolation prize of worthless swamp land. Ironically, long after Union College had spent its annual lottery proceeds, Columbia benefited from its cheap land grant—more familiar to us today as the real estate known as Lincoln Center.[12] Such were the pleasures and pains and unexpected consequences of the halcyon days of the American booster college.

Compared to most states in the early nineteenth century, the commonwealth of Kentucky put into place some relatively generous provisions to encourage the establishment of educational academies and colleges. According to the historian James Klotter, the typical state practice was to give a new, proposed institution a land grant of about six thousand acres. Klotter elaborated: "Moreover, some schools received permission to levy local taxes, while others secured the right to operate a lottery."[13] Land grants provided some potential for raising money or creating an endowment but seldom reaped lasting or large returns for colleges. Indeed, since land was abundant, trustees often squandered fund-raising on bad deals. For colleges in Kentucky and other states, year-to-year operation usually meant having to appeal to two constituencies: potential donors and prospective students. It is important to note that American colleges of this era, including those in Kentucky, were limited and exclusionary. College attendance was confined to white men—and most colleges at least aspired to be the locus where future leaders were educated. Excluding women and racial minority groups limited the pool of potential students. This self-imposed restriction by colleges made their work of attracting academically able, paying students all the more difficult.

Whereas an American university of the twenty-first century is characterized by the administrative bloat that supports more vice presidents and administrators than a bank or an industrial corporation, the early nineteenth-century college's organizational chart was, to use the argot of contemporary business consultants, lean and mean. The college president, usually a minister, parlayed the tenacity of squeezing Sunday morning tithes from squirming members of the congregation to support for a college. Guilt proved a wonderful lever for extracting gilt from those pillars of the community who had claimed allegiance to a church and its denominational college. Apart from the college president, about the only expense allotted for an administrator was the "college agent." This indefatigable official, who cropped up pervasively across American higher education, went across nearby counties and towns to persuade merchants and farmers to make college donations, whether large or small. At the same time, the college agent combined fund-raising with admissions recruitment. The ultimate coup was to conscript a potential college student who could afford to pay tuition. When one missed that prize, the fallback tactic was to convince a potential donor to pledge a relatively modest amount of money that would provide him with a "perpetual scholarship." This meant that the donor's offspring and descendants were promised admission and no charge for tuition for perpetuity. It was an easy compact for the college agent to make since the future counted little for a college that was not certain it could meet its enrollment threshold and payroll for the coming academic year.[14]

Campus and Community: The Case of Kentucky

The ease of obtaining a college charter from a legislature created a boom-and-bust atmosphere in campus finances. Although hundreds of new colleges opened for instruction, many also soon went out of operation. Mergers and splinters prevailed as well as each constituency (usually along religious denominational lines) wanted its own college to educate the sons and daughters of a faithful congregation. A snapshot of this growth and denominational specialization is found in the comprehensive survey that Colin T. Burke presented in his ambitious 1984 *American Collegiate Populations*. And prominent in this nationwide college-founding frenzy one finds Kentucky! According to Burke, the commonwealth of Kentucky had fourteen colleges founded by the mid-nineteenth century.[15] The roster is as follows: Augusta College, Bacon College/Kentucky, University/ Collegiate Institute, Bethel College, Bethel College (again), Centre College, Cumberland College, Georgetown College, Paducah College, St. Joseph's College, St. Mary's College, St. Thomas Aquinas College, Shelby College, Southern College, Transylvania University.

Burke's roster is conservative in its estimates. As best as can be determined, each of these listed colleges was chartered by the state with the power to confer the bachelor's degree. Other, earlier scholars claimed some evidence of even more higher education institutions—with such designations *seminary* and *academy* as well as *college*. Some institutions we recognize today as universities were in this historic period confined to specialized programs, such as medicine, law, commerce, teacher training, engineering, or theology—and, hence, often not included in the list of colleges. In Kentucky, for example, prior to the Civil War, documents indicate the operation of the Louisville Medical Institute (regarded as a forerunner to the University of Louisville), the Kentucky School of Medicine (founded in 1850), the Medical Department of Transylvania University (opened ca. 1817), and, later, the Transylvania School of Dental Surgery. Law schools include Transylvania Law School, the University of Louisville Law School (1847), and the Western Military Institute Law School. Danville Theological Seminary and Western Baptist Theological Seminary represented Kentucky's specialized denominational seminaries. And, to add to the abundant educational enterprise, by the mid-nineteenth century a groundswell rose of newly founded educational institutions for women, which often offered academic work comparable to that of established colleges yet did not confer the bachelor's degree. Kentucky's college-founding tradition gained prominence in the *national* forum on American higher education in the nineteenth century, as shown in the Johns Hopkins University series of monographs and Ph.D. dissertations on American institutions prepared under the direction of the legendary historian Herbert Baxter Adams. Specifically, Alvin Fayette Lewis's Ph.D. dissertation on the history of higher education in Kentucky was directed by Adams as part of the series and published as a pamphlet by the U.S.

Bureau of Education in 1899.[16] Whether using the conservative or the generous estimates on college founding, it is clear that, in the first half of the nineteenth century, central Kentucky was fertile ground for building educational institutions.

Campus celebration and promotion was a lively tradition in Kentucky that gained momentum in the 1820s and hardly ended in the nineteenth century. Indeed, in 1948, the zealous mayor of Louisville, Charles Farnsley, showed that college founding and civic boosterism still had a fond place in the municipal politics of the mid-twentieth century. In celebrating his beloved university and city, he was dissatisfied with the conventional account that the university was founded in 1837. To correct this historical problem, he enlisted a staff project that sought new historical information on possible earlier founding dates. The research project evidently was fruitful as the mayor later announced that the actual founding date for Jefferson Seminary, the predecessor to the University of Louisville, was 1798, not 1837. The endurance of this historic celebration well into the twentieth century reinforces the observation that Kentucky's nineteenth-century college-building legacy was a gift that kept on giving over time.

Mayor Farnsley's enthusiastic 1948 venture to amend the historical record provides a friendly reminder to readers today that the historical documents on educational initiatives in early Kentucky warrant caution and care. It is especially important to distinguish grand proposals from fulfilled projects. One finds, for example, inspiring narratives about a "state system" of academies and schools, including mention of stable tax support. These perhaps indicated a critical mass of college-educated, well-intentioned leaders with hopes and plans for accessible schooling in the new state. However, as early as 1820, the record of state and county appropriations indicated that the plan had withered—and by 1830 it was most certainly resting in peace.

Amid this enthusiastic energy and financial uncertainty, what does stands out is the remarkable accomplishment of Transylvania University— now viewed more as a local institution to those in the Bluegrass region of Kentucky. But in its heyday it was a genuine source of *national* respect and prestige in American higher education of the nineteenth century. What explains this success story, both in its ascent and, sadly, in its later demise?

Transylvania University's Tale of Success and Excess

Transylvania marks its founding as an academic seminary as 1780 and its Virginia collegiate charter as 1798. During the early decades of the nineteenth century, Kentucky was a prosperous state, owing, not surprisingly, to its strong agricultural production, which then was joined by mercantile and commercial wealth as the state became a center of buying, selling, and transporting goods. This was fortuitous for Transylvania as it acquired what might be termed "most favored status" in state educational support. The historian James Klotter found that, by the early 1820s, the university "received 20,000 acres of land; it got one-sixth of all surveyor's fees in the state; it collected for its coffers 2 percent of all Lexington auction sales. Beyond that, the state granted it $20,000 to buy books, directed that significant portions of the profits from state-chartered banks go to it, and allowed the school to start a lottery."[17] These features formed the prelude and foundation for an exciting and nationally significant chapter in the institution's history. This started in 1818 with the arrival of a new president, Horace Holley. A native of New England educated at Yale and successful as a minister with a large congregation in Boston, Holley personified the optimistic, energetic academic builder who deliberately sought to come to Lexington and Kentucky—a region today considered to be in the South but in the early nineteenth century seen as the West. With his impeccable scholarly credentials, Holley also characterized an important religious evolution that had taken place in New England. Namely, he moved from his original Congregationalist roots and eventually became a Unitarian. This so happened to parallel the change in dominant religious affiliations that characterized Harvard during this period. Lexington, Kentucky, became the transplanted forum for this educational and religious ferment and related progressive ambitions.

According to customary measures of institutional vitality, Transylvania flourished when Horace Holley was president.[18] Its enrollments were strong, with the undergraduate college or "academic department" eventually surpassing two hundred students per year. Put into perspective, this was a larger undergraduate enrollment than that of Princeton—and did not lag much behind that of Yale or Harvard. The college was joined by a constellation of professional schools—medicine (which was attractive to large number of students from its start) and law. It received endorsements, and even some donations, from a galaxy of national heroes and leaders. Henry Clay, the transplanted Virginian who found a professional and political base in Lexington, served on Transylvania's board of trustees and, for a while, taught law. Even such esteemed national figures as Thomas Jefferson were impressed by the school's energy and its ability to enroll (and graduate) good students and future leaders. The summary of alumni for the first half of the nineteenth century included 2 U.S. vice presidents,

2 Supreme Court justices, 50 U.S. senators, 101 U.S. representatives, 36 governors, 34 ambassadors, and the president of the Confederate States of America.

Horace Holley's combination of talent, commitment, timing, and good fortune made his tenure as president of Transylvania University the epitome of the right person in the right place at the right time. His attention to academic planning and curricular innovation was fused with genuine civic charm. Quickly, he and the local Lexington leaders enjoyed mutual admiration. The state and city provided substantial, albeit transient, subsidies that allowed President Holley to recruit a distinguished faculty and to put in motion a modern curriculum. By offering a degree track that included English and did not require Latin or Greek, Holley worked at making the course of study attractive to young men who sought preparation for leadership without classical languages. From time to time, the city government made generous annual gifts to the university, including one as high as $70,000—largely earmarked for the medical school. Lexington was sufficiently prosperous and progressive as a city thriving on commerce and trade to be predisposed toward cultural events that brought together campus and community. The Gratz Park area adjacent to the campus and close to the downtown commercial district was the hub of Lexington society and intellectual life. Lexingtonians proudly referred to their city as the "Athens of the West"—and it would be reasonable to add that Transylvania University formed its cultural and educational citadel. Holley and his wife hosted events that transformed their home into a salon for Lexington's literary and artistic life. Trite but true, President and Mrs. Holley were the proverbial toast of the town.

This prodigious record of college founding connects young Kentucky, not only to an American tradition, but also to an older and overriding legacy of town-and-gown interdependence developed in cities in Europe and to Oxford and Cambridge Universities in England. So Lexington is in good company with Thomas Bender's memorable *The University and the City*.[19] Central to connecting local history to the large and old context is John D. Wright's *Transylvania: Tutor to the West*—a work that keeps gaining in respect as subsequent new generations of scholars rediscover this account of a campus and community in the Bluegrass.

The ascent of Transylvania and the simultaneous renown of President Horace Holley represented a combination of local and national prestige. The paradox (and price) of popularity was that Lexington and Transylvania came to be—and be seen as—an island community whose distinction fostered distrust and resentment outside Lexington through many counties and sections of the commonwealth of Kentucky. The historian Merle Borrowman has claimed that the literary events and artistic works associated with Horace Holley eventually offended many clergy, citizens, and legislators elsewhere in the state. Allegations of nude statuary in the Holley's home garden along with concern about book discussions of (shudder) novels accumulated to create a collective profile of Lexington and Transylvania University as tantamount to sin city. Evidently, the Lexington gentry and press remained supportive and protective of Holley's tastes and collegiate plans as local newspaper editors refused to print letters or articles criticizing "their" president and his college. Unfortunately, this safety net ended at about the city limits. After about eight years, the buffer of local support ceased to hold back the attacks from a variety of churches and rural politicians. Transylvania and Lexington were potent enough to create an island of campus and community—but this achievement could not withstand indefinitely the neglect and overt attacks of a statewide constituency with which that island was often at odds. The tipping point came with the increased factionalism and disagreements even within the Transylvania University board and faculty as the deism, secularism, and Unitarianism that flourished under Holley generated more heat than light. Holley's resignation in 1827 suspended Transylvania University's era of good feeling and high hopes.

After some lean years marked by contentious infighting among the university's board and other constituencies, Transylvania showed signs not only of survival but also of recovery, thanks in large measure to the conciliatory and energetic leadership of Henry Brascomb as president. The academic strategy included a shift to control by the Methodists, the latest in a succession of denominational sponsors, flashes of generous financial support from the city of Lexington, and, above all, a memorable record of campus construction, best recognized by the grand Morrison Hall, known as Morrison College, home of the liberal arts course of study.

How might we estimate the impact of a successful college on the life and economy of a city? In the case of Transylvania University and Lexington, the mutual gains seem to have been substantial. At high tide, Transylvania's combined enrollment in its three departments—the liberal arts college, the medical school, and the law school—probably was about six hundred students per year. Beyond tuition payments (which were relatively modest charges), students' expenditures on lodgings, meals, clothing, accessories, books, supplies, and entertainment were a boon to the shopkeepers, merchants, landlords, grocers, theater managers, and barkeeps of the central business district. And, of course, student fees transformed into salaries, which helped provide Lexington a critical mass of an educated professional elite as represented by the residence and work of professors and college presidents in the city. Despite these substantial economic contributions, Transylvania's primary contribution was to the cultural life of the community. (See, e.g., Transylvania's engagement of B. H. Latrobe, the nation's foremost architect, discussed in Patrick Snadon's essay in this volume.) Newspaper accounts and secondary sources indicate that campus and community had a shared fate owing to disasters and calamities, ranging from numerous cholera epidemics to financial scandals and economic downturns. The presidents of Transylvania worked in vain to gain sustained external funding or to maintain healthy enrollments in all three units of the university at one time.

The persistent trend, unfortunately, was that the undergraduate liberal arts college declined in enrollments, eventually dipping below fifty students per year. Meanwhile, the largely autonomous Transylvania department of medicine ascended in popularity, as measured by enrollments and M.D.'s conferred. Transylvania's endurance in Lexington ultimately suffered a big loss when the medical school faculty moved their operations to Louisville.[20] A bit later, the law school recovered from low enrollments to gain substantial student appeal. Nearby, the colleges favored by particular denominations—namely, the Presbyterian Centre College and the Baptist Georgetown College—competed with growing effectiveness for potential undergraduate students in the liberal arts course of study. Georgetown College, for example, affiliated with the Kentucky Baptist Educational Society in 1829 and acquired the right to confer the bachelor's degree. This stature as the first Baptist college west of the Alleghenies enhanced its appeal to donors and students. Despite disputes within the ranks of Baptists, its energetic young president, Rockwood Giddings, managed to increase the college's endowment to $70,000. His successor, Howard Malcom, led an ambitious capital construction plan between 1840 and 1849.[21] Georgetown College exemplified the potential appeal of a denominational college to its regional religious constituency and, thus, its ability to enroll students. The Bluegrass region of the mid-nineteenth century turned into an overbuilt and underfunded academic market.

Closely related to this keen competition for students was another dynamic in the paradox of popularity that arrested the enduring success of colleges in Kentucky. The proliferation of new colleges soon turned from initial enthusiasm and support of local boosters to a relentless competition for adequate funds and students from scarce supplies. Transylvania University had for some years enjoyed favored status both from private donors and from the legislature. Eventually, the clamor for support from a number of other Kentucky colleges, plus the failure of the state to adopt adequate, sustained funding for colleges, stretched all Kentucky colleges in attempting to maintain instruction and operation.[22]

A further complication in this worsening situation for undergraduate collegiate education was a fact of life in American society: few, if any, professions required a college degree or even professional certification or licensure. Medical schools seldom required applicants to have a high school diploma, let alone a bachelor's degree or what today would be considered a premed course of study. Furthermore, there was neither the formal regulation of or formal requirements for the practice of law or medicine; for example, the custom was for a young man literally to read law as an apprentice or clerk for a judge or an established attorney. Hence, a problem that faced all colleges nationwide was that, in the mid-nineteenth century, going to college waned as a choice exercised by late adolescents. It was a descent that would not be arrested until the 1890s. As late as 1881, for example, although the United States was home to hundreds of colleges, only seventeen of them could claim an undergraduate enrollment of more than two hundred students per year. A local note on declining enrollments was that, prior to the Civil War, Lexington suffered more than one serious economic recession and several outbreaks of cholera and other health epidemics that tended to repel enrollment at Transylvania. The upshot is that these trends tend to bring renewed emphasis on how unusual the success and prestige of Transylvania University was in the early and mid-nineteenth century. For a few decades, it was no less than a local institution with national significance. It was at the forefront of demographic and institutional change in the relatively new states of the South—a region that had a prosperous economy and strong voting power in the U.S. Senate and House of Representatives.

Beautiful Dreamers: University Builders, South by Southwest

The focus of this essay and volume is, of course, Lexington and its educational institutions. Yet this case study gains logic and significance when understood as a central piece in the puzzle of ambitious college building in the South and West. An excellent source for this perspective is from the historian Merle Borrowman's 1961 article for the *History of Education Quarterly*, in which he brought together the stories of promising, ambitious universities in the South founded during the late eighteenth century and the early nineteenth: Transylvania (or "Kentucky University"), South Carolina College, the University of Virginia, and the University of Nashville.[23] For Borrowman, the enthusiastic founding of these new institutions signaled the "false dawn" of the state university. Each rode the crest of a charismatic leader, an eager and underdeveloped region and locale, and civic pride. And each displayed a characteristic prevalent in American enterprise, both commercial and academic—namely, ambition that was overextended, suggesting that the ideas and institutions were ahead of their time. My own emphasis on this collective story is that such figures as Horace Holley at Transylvania, Thomas Jefferson and the University of Virginia, Philip Lindsley and his University of Nashville, and Thomas Cooper at South Carolina College represented beautiful dreamers who tried and failed magnificently in their grand visions for extending higher education South by Southwest.

The consideration of building colleges in the early nineteenth century brings to mind Samuel Johnson's verdict about meeting a talking dog: the amazing feature is not whether the dog talks well or poorly but that the dog talks at all. The obstacles of a frontier terrain and culture, combined with the lack of regular funding, made starting a college an adventurous undertaking. In the case of Transylvania and the University of Nashville, highly regarded scholars and educators from Harvard, Princeton, and Yale made deliberate decisions to come to the South to build new, inspiring institutions that would discard some of the baggage that was, they believed, hampering higher education in the Northeast. The primacy of religious denominations and the resultant denominational disputes constituted one syndrome they wished both to avoid and to provide attractive alternatives to. Lindsley, coming to Nashville from the College of New Jersey in Princeton, devised a plan to accomplish two simultaneous goals: first, he wished to provide families in the South and West a sound academic alternative to having to send their sons north to Harvard, Yale, or Princeton; second, he wanted to neutralize the feuding of, for example, Methodists versus Baptists versus Presbyterians. His proposed solution was to create a great secular, nondenominational university that would be supported by all constituencies and religions of greater Nashville. He made his eloquent case in his 1829 baccalaureate address:

> A principal cause of the excessive multiplication and dwarfish dimensions of Western colleges is, no doubt the diversity of religious denominations among us. Almost every sect will have its colleges, and generally one at least in each State.

Of the scores of colleges in Ohio, Kentucky, and Tennessee, all
are sectarian except two or three; and, of course few of them are what
they might and should be; and the greater part of them are mere im-
positions on the public. Why should colleges be sectarian, any more
than penitentiaries or than bank, road or canal corporations, is not
very obvious. Colleges are designed for the instruction of youth in
the learned languages—in polite literature—in the liberal arts and
sciences—and not in the dogmatical theology of any sect or party.
Why then should they be baptized with sectarian names?[24]

It was the right idea at the wrong time and place. While Lindsley's essays
on modernizing higher education gained nationwide fame, his own Nashville project floundered. He sadly discovered that parents of prospective
students, along with donors, really preferred to support the small denominational colleges of *their* choice.

Thomas Jefferson's University of Virginia, founded in 1819, is probably the best known and most revered of the innovative universities in the
South. Its classical architecture, the plans for pavilions to create an "aca-
demical village," the departure from academic conventions in the curriculum, all heralded a special place. Yet, in its early years, even Mister Jefferson was disappointed in the students' disinterest in academic exploration,
their preference for duels, and their relative indifference to serious study
involving Enlightenment philosophy and such emergent disciplines as political economy. At the same time, faculty from universities as distant as
Europe were equally unhappy with the student values and constituencies
that gained hegemony over their professorial commitments.[25] Beyond the
architecture of the Rotunda and the Lawn, the educational greatness of
the University of Virginia did not come close to fruition for years to come.

Perhaps one of the more effective of the innovative universities in the
South was South Carolina College (later renamed the University of South
Carolina) under the presidency of Thomas Cooper. Cooper, an Englishman, had been mentored by Thomas Jefferson at the University of Virginia. Cooper's strident anticlericism endeared him to the deist Jefferson
but put him in hot water with the local (and influential) clergy. When
selected as president of South Carolina College, he put into motion a
design for collegiate education that eventually shaped state and national politics. The undergraduate curriculum emphasized skills of oratory
combined with the liberal arts, including the field of political economy,
grounded in nullification theory and states' rights. South Carolina College, much like Transylvania University, became a magnet as the alma

mater of a prodigious number of young white men who would go on to serve as governors in many southern states, including Georgia, Florida, South Carolina, Alabama, and Louisiana. Cooper's South Carolina College alumni constituted a large percentage of elected officials, especially as senators and members of Congress from states in the South. The college was the crucible that led to the persuasive argumentation and oratory that characterized the South's domination of the U.S. Congress in the late 1850s by providing a strong antifederalist vote combined with advocacy for extending slavery into new western states. Despite this pedagogical success, President Cooper fell from grace in South Carolina by (once again) baiting the local ministers—a habitual practice that made him the common enemy who united clergy who otherwise were distrustful of one another.

Fiscal Fitness and Kentucky Higher Education at Midcentury

One tempting interpretation is to fault the commonwealth of Kentucky and its legislators and taxpayers for failure to provide the recurrent annual state subsidies that would have transformed Transylvania University into a genuine, enduring state university. That observation is accurate—but also calls out for balance with context from other states. Where in the antebellum United States did one find a state government that provided generous support and regular annual appropriations for its designated college or university? My own added wrinkle to the interpretation is to be persuaded by the historian John Whitehead's argument that the category of a state college versus that of a private college really did not exist in American institutional thinking until the 1870s. Until then, funding for universities was a crazy quilt of mixed sources—with no prohibition on state governments giving resources to church-related colleges. On the other hand, the bad news was that there was no guarantee that state governments would give much in the way of support to *any* college or university. The outlook for higher education in Kentucky was not bright—nor was it elsewhere. To the north, Henry Tappan stalked out of the Michigan Statehouse, angry and defeated in his quest for funding to build a great state university. In the late nineteenth century, citizens of Urbana, Illinois, really wanted their town to be the home of a state penitentiary rather than a new industrial and agricultural college. New England, the region usually hailed as the heart of great colleges and universities, gave state colleges and universities modest support—whether in 1860 or in 1960. To grasp the precarious condition and small enrollments of midwestern state universities, it is helpful to recall the historian James Axtell's reminder that, in the 1880s, such allegedly small private liberal arts colleges as Amherst, Williams, and Dartmouth each typically had larger student enrollments and library holdings than did most Midwestern state universities such as Indiana University, the University of Minnesota, or the University of Wisconsin.[26]

A possible source of financial salvation for Transylvania University and its fellow colleges in the central Kentucky of the mid-nineteenth century might have come from the federal government. Indeed, long before passage of the Morrill Act of 1862 and its funding mechanism whereby the proceeds of land sales would allow states to create programs in the agricultural and mechanical and liberal arts, drafts of the bill surfaced in Congress. And, time and time again, senators and congressmen from southern states rejected them and the expansion of federal powers and programs. Little surprise, then, that, after secession and creation of the Confederate States of America, the incumbent states of the United States approved passage of the Morrill Act. But this was too little, too late for support of antebellum higher education in Kentucky.

If public support in the form of state or perhaps federal appropriations failed to materialize as a source of stable, ample support for Transylvania University and its sister institutions in the latter half of the nineteenth century, what were the prospects for another revenue stream—namely, support by private donors? Whether by accident or by design, the historical fact was that, between 1870 and 1910, a new generation of wealthy industrialists emerged as generous donors and philanthropists who showed great interest in giving colleges and universities donations and endowments heretofore unprecedented—and probably beyond the dreams of those fortunate college presidents who were recipients. Unfortunately for the colleges of Kentucky's Bluegrass, geography mattered—and the new philanthropy was inordinately concentrated in the Northeast, Middle Atlantic, Midwest, and Pacific Coast. It meant that a financially struggling College of New Jersey could transform itself into Princeton University. The railroad fortune of Leland and Jane Stanford could found and fund a brand-new Stanford University. And, in the Midwest, the oil refinery wealth of John D. Rockefeller led to the opening of the magnificent new University of Chicago. Whereas the colleges of the South were a source of generous support and enthusiasm in the early nineteenth century, after the Civil War there were few subsidies and little philanthropy comparable to what was enjoyed in the North.[27] Commodore Vanderbilt's philanthropy dedicated to creating a great Methodist university in Nashville was perhaps the significant exception to the rule of impoverished southern higher education. When northern philanthropists and foundations did include southern education on the agenda, their primary focus was on providing basic schooling for African American children via such largesse as the Rosenwald Fund, made possible by the fortunes of the Sears Roebuck Company.[28] In the main, the historic campuses of the South were left out and left over. In Virginia, for example, the historic and once affluent and prestigious College of William and Mary failed to gain state support to restore its colonial prestige as a liberal arts college. The college president also tried in vain for years to acquire reparations from the U.S. government for damages the college physical plant suffered during the Civil War. Its only recourse was the peculiar marketing strategy of advertising itself as "the oldest and cheapest college in the South"—a heroic effort that was more inspired than effective.

Elsewhere in the South, colleges did not fare well financially. There was no counterpart to Rockefeller or Carnegie wealth to rescue and revitalize a Kentucky college in the late nineteenth century. To compound this bleak financial situation, state governments in the South had neither the resources nor the commitment to use tax revenues to put into place a comprehensive system of public schools—a neglect that meant the region's colleges and universities were unlikely to have a persistent flow of academically prepared high school graduates who then would enroll as undergraduates.[29] In sum, the characterization that the historians Carolyn B. Matalene and Katherine C. Reynolds gave to the University of South Carolina between 1880 to 1906—namely, "struggling to survive"—could be extended to almost all colleges and universities in the South, including those in Kentucky. Higher education in the South faced adversity in enrollments, tax support, and private donations until after World War I.[30]

Epilogue: Harnessing the Heritage of Campus and Community in Kentucky

What a difference a century makes! In 1910, Edwin Slosson, the editor of the *Independent* magazine, concluded a nationwide study of higher education innovation and selected fourteen institutions for inclusion in his book *Great American Universities*. No university south of the Mason-Dixon line qualified for membership in this prestigious circle. It was a dramatic contrast to the prosperity and national prominence that Transylvania University had shown in 1810.[31] Given this historical change, how best to remember this vitality of Kentucky higher education in the early nineteenth century? Was Transylvania University a meteor that lit up the sky of the Bluegrass, moving across the horizon before burning out quickly? Did the collective history of the various colleges that constituted jewels in the crown of Kentucky's Bluegrass in the first half of the nineteenth century end with the bittersweet epitaph of "opportunity lost"? As James Klotter concluded, the history of higher education in Kentucky was characterized by "promise, pessimism, and perseverance."[32]

Perhaps, however, there were also opportunities for redemption and rediscovery in the late nineteenth century and the early twentieth. Kentucky, as with almost all states, went through spurts of initiative and exhaustion after the Civil War in attempts to create an enduring, substantive array of colleges and universities. The Land Grant Acts of 1862 and 1890 brought some provision for selective funding from the federal government while at the same time allowing each state legislature ample latitude in marketing their allotment of western land sales to gain funding for state investment in useful and liberal arts education. And often overlooked is that the Morrill Acts did not restrict the creation of the so-called A&M (agriculture and mining and mechanics and military programs) to state or public institutions. The grand era of the great state university as we understand the institution today was still embryonic and evolving.

In Kentucky, for example, the original land grant programs were awarded by the legislature to what we would consider a private or independent institution—a hybrid confederation of programs known as Kentucky University. On closer inspection, its real identity was none other than what had been known as Transylvania University. Kentucky University experienced a mix of successes and failures in groping to provide varied courses of study that were attractive to students and useful to the Lexington community as well as the entire commonwealth of Kentucky. And, eventually, the state legislature rescinded its Morrill Act A&M programs housed at Kentucky University, opting instead to provide a home for them in the newly chartered Kentucky State College in Lexington—an institution that in the early twentieth century would be renamed as the now familiar and enduring University of Kentucky. The commonwealth of Kentucky also paid a price in trying to create a new A&M university owing to its insistence on racial segregation in public higher education. This was because the conditions of the 1890 land grant act set forth by the federal government allowed a state to continue its tradition of a racially exclusive all-white A&M campus so long as the land sale proceeds were then shared to provide funding for a second, separate historically black

Capitol and campus. (*Kentucky Progress Magazine*, April 1930.)

land grant college. And this was the choice Kentucky made, leading to the creation of a distinct, separate campus in Frankfort, familiar today as Kentucky State University.

These varied initiatives in the late nineteenth century in the Lexington area finally achieved one of the original goals of such luminaries of an earlier era as President Horace Holley of Transylvania University. Kolan

Morelock's *Taking the Town* reconstructs the remarkable story of how the student literary societies, debating clubs, and drama groups at Transylvania/Kentucky University and the new Kentucky State College/University of Kentucky captured the praise and participation of the Lexington gentry from about 1880 to 1917.[33] The undergraduates' presentations enjoyed sustained popularity among the public and in reviews by Lexington newspaper editors. During the Gilded Age, the collegiate jewels in the crown regained and reasserted their integral role in making Lexington once again the Athens of the West. Morelock's study warns, however, that this distinctive period ended—or, at least, changed fundamentally—after World War I. The collegiate literary culture and tradition of performing arts waned in appeal to the community as they were displaced by the popularity of college football as a spectator sport.

This is not to say that the heritage of the early nineteenth-century town and gown was altogether forfeited in the Bluegrass. Between World War I and World War II, concerted efforts by state and local governments invoked the academic legacies of the region as a key to prosperity as well as cultural vitality. A good example is the campaign of the Kentucky Progress Commission starting in 1928 to harness the commonwealth's higher education heritage to economic development. The April 1930 issue of *Kentucky Progress Magazine* showcased historic colleges as the key to energizing the state and attracting commerce and industry from elsewhere in the nation. The cover featured a highly stylized rendering of Transylvania University's "Old Morrison" as the symbol (and hope) of Kentucky's potential. Thanks to the powers of historical memory and modern techniques of public relations, once again the collegiate jewels in the crown had some sparkle.

Notes

1. Robert M. Rosenzweig with Barbara Turlington, *The Research Universities and Their Patrons* (Berkeley and Los Angeles, 1982).

2. John R. Thelin, "Research Universities," in *The Encyclopedia of American Social History*, ed. Mary Kupiec Cayton, Elliot J. Gorn, and Peter W. Williams (New York, 1992), 2537–45.

3. Daniel J. Boorstin, "The Booster College," in *The Americans: The National Experience* (New York, 1965), 152–61.

4. Herman Eschenbacher, "When Brown Was Less Than a University and Hope Was More Than a College," *Brown Alumni Monthly*, March 1978, n.p.

5. John R. Thelin, "Campus and Commonwealth: A Historical Interpretation,"

in *Higher Education in American Society*, ed. Philip G. Altbach, Robert O. Berdahl, and Patricia J. Gumport (Amherst, NY, 1994), 21–35.

6. Frederick Rudolph, *The American College and University: A History* (New York, 1962), 8.

7. Jurgen Herbst, *From Crisis to Crisis: American College Government, 1636–1819* (Cambridge, MA, 1982), 143–243.

8. John Whitehead, *The Separation of College and State: Columbia, Dartmouth, and Yale, 1776–1876* (New Haven, CT, 1973).

9. Rudolph, *The American College and University*, chap. 9.

10. Andrew F. Smith, "'The diploma pedler': Dr. John Cook Bennett and the Christian College, New Albany, Indiana," *Indiana Magazine of History* 90 (1994): 26–47.

11. Dwayne J. Cox and William J. Morison, "First among the Medical Schools of the West," in *The University of Louisville* (Lexington, 2000), 11–19.

12. Whitehead, *The Separation of College and State.*

13. James C. Klotter, "Promise, Pessimism, and Perseverance: An Overview of Higher Education History in Kentucky," *Ohio Valley History* 1 (2006): 45–60.

14. George Keller, *Academic Strategy: The Management Revolution in American Higher Education* (Baltimore, 1983), 5–8.

15. Colin B. Burke, *American Collegiate Populations: A Test of the Traditional View* (New York, 1982), esp. app. A, "Institutions in Operation, 1800–1860," 299–342.

16. Alvin Fayette Lewis, *History of Higher Education in Kentucky*, Contributions to American Educational History Series, Monograph no. 25, Circular of Information, no. 3 (Washington, DC, 1899), 3–327.

17. Klotter, "Promise, Pessimism, and Perseverance," 47.

18. John D. Wright Jr., *Transylvania: Tutor to the West* (1975; Lexington, 2006), 65–98.

19. Thomas Bender, ed., *The University and the City: From Medieval Origins to the Present* (London, 1988).

20. Wright, *Transylvania: Tutor to the West*, 145–57.

21. Megan LeMaster, *Georgetown College* (Charleston, SC, 2005), 7–8, 10–11.

22. Wright, *Transylvania: Tutor to the West*, 172–89.

23. Merle Borrowman, "The False Dawn of the State University," *History of Education Quarterly* 1 (1961): 6–22.

24. Philip Lindsley, "The Problems of the College in a Sectarian Age" (1829 baccalaureate address), in *American Higher Education: A Documentary History*, ed. Richard Hofstadter and Wilson Smith (Chicago, 1961), 232–37 (quotation 233–34).

25. Jennings L. Wagonern Jr., "Honor and Dishonor at Mr. Jefferson's University: The Antebellum Years," *History of Education Quarterly* 26 (1986): 15–17.

26. James Axtell, "The Death of the Liberal Arts College," *History of Education Quarterly* 11 (1971): 339–52.

27. Robert Bremner, *American Philanthropy*, 2nd ed. (Chicago, 1988).

28. Eric Anderson and Alfred A. Moss Jr., *Dangerous Donations: Northern Philanthropy and Southern Black Education, 1902–1930* (Columbia, MO, 1999).

29. Carolyn B. Matalene and Katherine C. Reynolds, "Struggling to Survive: The Old College from 1880 to 1906," in *Carolina Voices: Two Hundred Years of Student Experiences*, ed. Katherine B. Reynolds (Columbia, SC, 2001), 66–103.

30. Michael Dennis, *Lessons in Progress: State Universities and Progressivism in the New South, 1880–1920* (Urbana, IL, 2001).

31. Edwin Slosson, *Great American Universities* (New York, 1910).

32. Klotter, "Promise, Pessimism, and Perseverance."

33. Kolan Thomas Morelock, *Taking the Town: Collegiate and Community Culture in the Bluegrass, 1880–1917* (Lexington, 2008).

9

Horace Holley and the Struggle for Kentucky's Mind and Soul

Tom Eblen and Mollie Eblen

Among America's rising stars at the beginning of the nineteenth century, few shone more brightly than the Reverend Horace Holley. Born in 1781 to a New England merchant and a Baptist preacher's daughter, Holley graduated near the top of his class at Yale University. After abandoning a brief apprenticeship at law in New York, he returned to Yale as a theology student. He was chosen for the pulpit of Boston's Hollis Street Church in 1809 and quickly developed a reputation as one of the city's best orators. One 1811 sermon "was so overpowering, that a spontaneous acclamation burst forth from the crowd that thronged the doors of the church."[1] The Hollis Street congregation doubled in size under Holley's leadership, and a new sanctuary was built. Holley was an active member of Harvard University's board of overseers, the Boston School Committee, and "various literary, scientific and benevolent institutions," his colleague the physician Charles Caldwell later wrote. "He united the dignity of the divine with the urbanity of the gentleman."[2] Holley sat for Gilbert Stuart, the nation's leading portrait painter. Former president John Adams and his son John Quincy, the future president, were among his many admirers. John Quincy Adams would later describe Holley in his diary as "a man of genius, learning and eloquence."[3] His fame would eventually attract the attention of several members of the board of trustees of Lexington's struggling Transylvania University. Although none of them had ever met Horace Holley, he seemed to be just what they needed.[4]

Between 1775 and 1815, Lexington had grown from a pioneer blockhouse into the most important city on the western frontier. Wealth from agriculture and commerce had built a prosperous community. Lexington's leading citizens developed an interest in literature, the arts, and refined culture, and they proudly called their city the "Athens of the West." But times were changing and not for the better. During the era when goods moved by pack animals and flatboats, Lexington served as an important trading hub. Once steamboats enabled upstream navigation, business began moving to Cincinnati and Louisville. The Ohio and Mississippi Rivers became the new highways of commerce. Rapid settlement of the Northwest Territory shifted the center of western population away from Kentucky to Ohio. The sour economy that followed the post–War of 1812 boom weakened Lexington; commerce declined, and businesses failed. Civic leaders believed that the best way for the city to regain a healthy economy and preserve its stature as a city of culture and sophistication was to create a great university to provide future leaders for the growing West.[5]

Lexington had a university, but it was hardly great. In fact, Transylvania University was then little more than a grammar school.[6] The Virginia General Assembly had authorized the school's creation in 1780, but it would be another five years before classes began, irregularly, in a Presbyterian minister's cabin near Danville.[7] The school moved to Lexington in 1789 and "enjoyed a moderate degree of prosperity for a number of years; not brilliant indeed, but sound and healthy," another Presbyterian minister later acknowledged.[8] Deadly Indian attacks and meager resources— followed by religious and political disputes—led to a constant reshuffling of Transylvania's trustees, frequent changes in leadership, and mergers with other small schools.[9] Transylvania's early years were a hit-and-miss legacy of educational accomplishment, with only twenty-two graduates by 1818.[10] The school's enrollment was small, and many of its students were children. There were more than thirty private competing academies in the Bluegrass; two of them in Lexington had more students than Transylvania, and one charged fees three times higher. Critics complained that the university lacked academic excellence and the leadership capable of creating it.[11]

Presbyterian clergymen had been instrumental in Transylvania's founding, but their determination to control the institution and everything taught there caused constant conflict.[12] Most Kentuckians at the time were not especially religious. Of the state's 220,955 residents in 1800, only about 10,000 belonged to an established denomination, and only 1,880 of them were Presbyterians. Even after the Great Revival had tripled Kentucky's churchgoing population by 1803, active Christians still constituted a small minority. But that did not deter the Presbyterians, whose members included many of the state's business and political leaders.

The separation of church and state was a hot topic then, as now, but with different issues and players. Christianity in its broadest form was tacitly accepted as a positive influence on government and politics, even by many people who were not especially religious themselves. Ministers often led schools and colleges, many of which had been started to train church leaders. But what constituted "correct" Christianity was a subject of endless debate. Denominations fought bitterly over differences in doctrine, and Kentucky public opinion opposed the state sanctioning of any sect or its dogma. Baptists, still mindful of the persecution they had suffered in American colonies where the Church of England enjoyed government endorsement, were among the strongest advocates of religious liberty and the separation of church and state. Many Kentuckians suspected the Presbyterians of seeking government influence—if not outright religious establishment—and of favoring unpopular Federalist Party politics, which prompted the denomination's ministers to write several denials in the newspapers. But there was no denying the Presbyterian clergy's determination to control Transylvania, the state's official university.

Presbyterian ministers openly referred to those who did not subscribe to strict Calvinism as *infidels*, and they denounced *liberal* education that questioned their theology. Religious liberals on Transylvania's board of trustees feared that they would never attract the most talented professors and students as long as the Presbyterian-led majority continued its lackluster management of the school and restricted academic freedom. "The repressive, inhibitory, theological ethics of Calvinism were out of harmony with the realities of the society which now wished to be served by the University," Niels Henry Sonne wrote in his 1939 *Liberal Kentucky.* "It was foolish to have one's children brought up to look upon horse races and the theater as sinful, when one saw in these things true means of graceful, fashionable, and successful living."[13] Nothing would change, the liberal trustees thought, without a revolution—and a new president with enough stature and skill to transform Transylvania into the great university they envisioned.

That revolution would be led by John Bradford, an Episcopalian who had started the state's first newspaper, the *Kentucky Gazette,* in 1787 and helped form Lexington's first library in 1796. Bradford was elected as the trustees' first chairman in 1798, when Transylvania officially became Kentucky's state university, and he held the job more often than not for

This engraving appeared in *A Discourse on The Genius and Character of the Rev. Horace Holley, Ll.D.: Late President of Transylvania University*, which Holley's widow, Mary Holley, and the Transylvania University medical Professor Charles Caldwell wrote immediately after his death. The engraving was made from a portrait of Holley painted by Gilbert Stuart before Holley left Boston in 1818 to accept the Transylvania University presidency. The whereabouts of Stuart's original painting are unknown.

the next three decades. He constantly battled the religiously conservative trustees, led by the Presbyterians, who increasingly were being criticized in newspapers and the General Assembly for their management of Transylvania. After a prominent New York Presbyterian turned down the school's presidency, Bradford led the board in electing Horace Holley as president in November 1815. Less than four months later, however, the offer was rescinded—not because Holley had initially shown little interest in the job, but because the conservative trustees found out more about him.[14]

His religious awakening had come to Holley when the Great Revival reached New Haven his senior year at Yale. He became a staunch Calvinist, delivering his class's graduation speech, which he titled "The Slavery of Free-Thinking." As a graduate student in theology, he became a favorite of Yale's austere Calvinist president, the Reverend Timothy Dwight. But, between 1805 and 1808, while ministering to a Congregationalist church in Fairfield, Connecticut, that Dwight had once served, he began to share his wife's more liberal views. By the time he and his wife, Mary Austin Holley, reached Boston, Holley had become a Unitarian, and "his mind unfolded to a more extended view of Christianity," as his wife later wrote. "He saw that though one set of opinions might be right, another, in many respects different, need not of necessity be wholly wrong—they might agree in fundamentals—and that religion does not consist so much in thinking as in feeling and acting. . . . He believed the scriptures to be the rule of faith but allowed of a variety of interpretation."[15] To Kentucky's Presbyterian clergy, this philosophy made Holley little better than Satan himself.

Public opinion of Transylvania declined as the trustees, divided ever more sharply along religious lines, failed to attract an accomplished president. Legislators sympathetic to the liberals formed a committee to investigate the university and put forth a resolution demanding that the trustees appear before the House of Representatives to "show cause why they shouldn't be turned out of office." The *Gazette* published a lengthy editorial calling for the election of a liberal president of wide reputation.[16] The Reverend Robert Davidson, a Presbyterian minister, would later describe the situation this way: "The tone of sentiment among the leading men in that place had become deeply tinctured with the spirit of French infidelity. There were two parties in the Board—the friends of evangelical religion, and the open, or disguised, abettors of deism and infidelity."[17] Faced with legislators who were threatening to replace them and strong public sentiment against Presbyterian power, Transylvania's trustees narrowly elected Holley president on November 15, 1817. His position was strengthened soon afterward when the General Assembly voted overwhelmingly to replace the trustees. Rather than clergymen, the new board included prominent business and civic leaders, among them Henry Clay, John Pope, Thomas Bodley, and Robert Wickliffe. Democratic-Republicans firmly controlled Kentucky, and they viewed Holley as the kind of accomplished man of letters that Transylvania needed, despite evidence that he held Federalist Party political sympathies. At last, religious liberals seemed on the path to creating a great university based on religious tolerance and academic freedom, a university that could enhance the economy, intellectual capital, and national image of their Athens of the West.[18] Now, if only they could convince Holley to take the job.

As he set out from Boston in February 1818 to investigate this job offer, Holley did not know what he would find in Lexington. He knew little about Transylvania except that his wife's first cousin Stephen Fuller Austin, for whom the capital city of Texas would later be named, had graduated in the university's class of 1810. Mary Holley, then expecting the couple's second child, was against moving to Kentucky. She enjoyed the cultured life she and her husband led in Boston.[19] Others, however, told Holley that he would be foolish to ignore this opportunity to shape what could become the West's great university. The young minister resolved to keep an open mind. "My equilibrium is unchangeable till I have examined the place, the institution, and the circumstances for myself," he wrote to a friend, James Freeman.[20]

Holley would make the most of the months-long journey to Lexington, stopping in New York, Philadelphia, and Washington, DC. In Washington, he was entertained at the White House by President and Mrs. James Monroe and dined with John C. Calhoun, his Yale classmate who was then secretary of war and would later be vice president under John Quincy Adams and Andrew Jackson. Perhaps most important to Holley, he planned to visit Charlottesville, Virginia, and meet the sage of Monticello, Thomas Jefferson. To this end, as Holley kissed his wife and young daughter good-bye, he carried a letter of introduction from John Adams. "You will find him frank enough, candid enough, social enough, learned enough and eloquent enough. He is indeed an important Character; and if Superstition, Bigotry, Fanaticism and Intolerance will allow him to live in Kentucky, he will contribute Somewhat to the illumination of the darkest and most dismal Swamps in the Wilderness. I shall regret his removal from Boston. . . . He is one of the few who give me delight," Adams wrote to his friend Jefferson—quite an introduction from a man not known for flattery.[21] But, when Holley arrived at Monticello, Jefferson was away. It would be another six years before they met.

When Holley reached Kentucky, he was warmly received by Henry Clay and Governor Gabriel Slaughter, invited to parties and dinners, and asked to speak from many pulpits. The Presbyterian clergy were polite, but cool. In letters to Mary in May 1818, Holley painted a glowing picture of Lexington. "It was immediately known that I had arrived, and the citizens turned out in sufficient numbers to make their greeting as cordial as I could wish, and to convince me that the opposition to my appointment here is nothing," he wrote. "Everything is done that can be done to gratify me with the prospect before me." Holley's letters were masterpieces of marital salesmanship: "You will not only be contented in Lexington, but you will be pleased and delighted. . . . If I were not well convinced that we should be happy in Kentucky, I would not come. But we shall be." Holley was pleased with the annual salary of $3,000 and excited about the opportunity to create a great university. "I believe it is in my power to do more good in this region than in any other at this moment," he wrote to Mary. "My life has not been half so useful in Boston . . . as I am persuaded it will be in Lexington. . . . For the sole purpose of doing good, I would rather be at the head of this institution than at the head of any Eastern college. The field is wider, the harvest more abundant, and the grain of a most excellent quality. I may become what you call a martyr, but it is not my intention to be one."[22] The next nine years would prove them both right.

Caldwell, who would later become Holley's most ardent defender, acknowledged that Holley was not the most accomplished scholar. He did not have deep knowledge of Greek, Latin, and French. Furthermore, Caldwell wrote: "To all other modern languages, he was an entire stranger. . . . He was not himself enamoured of the study of arithmetic, mathematics, mechanics and chemistry. . . . Gifted as he was, had he eagerly and perseveringly toiled for the attainment of literary and scientific eminence, the age in which he lived . . . would have scarcely exhibited, in its galaxy of genius, a more resplendent luminary." Instead, Holley's strengths were his keen intellect, his skills as an orator and philosopher, and his social graces. People often described him as charming and handsome, despite a prematurely balding head. He had an athletic body and a melodious voice. A swift and voracious reader, he enjoyed poetry and novels as well as scholarly tomes. Because he usually spoke extemporaneously from spare notes, few of his lectures or sermons were published. Holley wrote clear prose, avoiding the flowery rhetoric popular at the time, but he published little. He was a brilliant and persuasive conversationalist. "No one could be dull or inattentive in his presence," Caldwell wrote. "Nor was it possible to be long in his company without receiving something to remember and prize."[23] In his diary, John Quincy Adams described a heated religious debate over dinner in Boston involving himself, Holley, Daniel Webster, and another man, noting: "Holley was quite a match for us all."[24] But Holley's habit of boldly expressing his opinions could make him seem arrogant.

"The only thing that diminished the charm of his society was an uncomfortable sense of inferiority, which his conversation sometimes imposed on the mind," his wife later wrote.[25] Still, Holley achieved quick success at Transylvania because of his remarkable ability to lead and inspire those who shared his values.

Holley returned to Lexington with his family in November 1818 and was welcomed with a reception in Transylvania's three-story main building, in what is now Gratz Park, and an invitation to stay at Clay's Ashland estate until his own home could be made ready. He was inaugurated on December 19, 1818, at the Episcopal church, the university chapel being too small to hold the crowd. Holley offered a prayer and delivered an address on "literature, science, morals, religion, and civil and religious liberty"—all the subjects at which he hoped Transylvania would come to excel. As he had written Mary during his first visit to Lexington: "Everything is to be done, and so much the better, as nothing is to be reformed. Almost the whole is proposed to be left to me to arrange." Holley set about making Transylvania, not only the best university in the West, but also a rival to the great universities of the East.[26]

Holley began by reorganizing Transylvania into the now-common four classes—freshmen, sophomores, juniors, and seniors—and by renovating classrooms. He took over instruction of the juniors and seniors, especially in the areas of philosophy, rhetoric, and composition. His weekly sermons in the chapel were attended by many of Lexington's influential citizens in addition to the university's faculty and students. Holley asked friends back East for books to stock Transylvania's library, and they sent their personal copies of such volumes as Faber's *Thesaurus*, Postlethwaite's *Dictionary*, and Swammerdam's *History of Insects*. When recruiting faculty, he went straight to the top, offering positions to Boston's premier surgeon, John Warren, and Yale's most famous name in the science department, Benjamin Silliman. Although they declined and Holley settled for lesser-known but still well-educated men, he had announced his ambitions for this frontier university, whose name literally meant "across the woods" in Latin. By July 1819, Holley was playing host and preaching to President Monroe and General Andrew Jackson, who visited Lexington to attend Independence Day celebrations.[27]

That same busy summer, Holley began reviving Transylvania's medical school. The well-known physician Samuel Brown had been a professor at Transylvania's early attempt at a medical school in 1799 but had left in 1806. He returned, along with Benjamin Dudley, a physician as well-known in Europe as in Kentucky. The medical school opened in November 1819 with Dudley, Brown, and four other distinguished professors. "It is confidently believed that a better medical education cannot be obtained in any school in the United States than in that of Lexington," boasted Robert Wickliffe, then chairman of Transylvania's board of trustees.[28] Holley hired the notable but eccentric botanist Constantine Rafinesque to teach the natural sciences. In time, Rafinesque would also become the head librarian and add his own notes and specimens to the university's collection.

Holley recruited Caldwell, a noted Philadelphia physician and University of Pennsylvania professor, to the medical school and, in 1821, sent him to Europe with $11,000 collected from the city and state to buy books and scientific instruments. In its first session under Holley's reorganization in 1819, the medical school had thirty-seven students. After Caldwell's European expedition, the class grew to 138. By 1823, there were twice that many medical students.

Holley also restarted Transylvania's law school, where Clay had once taught. Among the law professors he recruited were the prominent Kentuckians Jesse Bledsoe and William T. Barry, both of whom had served in the state General Assembly and the U.S. Senate and House of Representatives. Law school enrollment grew from nine students in 1821 to forty-four in 1823.[29]

As Transylvania's enrollment increased, so did its resources. By 1827, the university had a vast store of scientific instruments, many imported from France, and more than sixty-three hundred books, five-sixths of which were acquired during Holley's tenure.[30]

Holley had promised his intelligent wife a lively social life in Lexington: "Our house will be a place of resort for persons of the best minds in the region . . . for all who shall have any claims to literature, refinement, manners, music and accomplishment."[31] That is exactly what happened, first at a rented mansion on North Limestone Street, where Sayre School is now located, then at a more modest and economical home at 228 Market Street. Holley gave Transylvania students instruction in manners, and he encouraged them to bring their girlfriends to some classes and lectures.[32] "While he enriched them with knowledge, he zealously cultivated in them pure and high-toned principles of rectitude and honor and . . . imparted to them the air and polish of gentlemen," Caldwell recalled.[33]

In September 1824, Holley was finally able to visit Jefferson at Monticello. In letters to his wife and Barry, he vividly described the eighty-two-year-old former president and how he had immersed himself in planning and lobbying for support of the University of Virginia. He wrote that Jef-

This portrait of Horace Holley when he was president of Transylvania University is attributed to the great Kentucky portraitist Matthew Jouett, a Transylvania alumnus. The portrait is in Transylvania University's collection. (Photograph courtesy of Transylvania University.)

ferson asked him many questions about Transylvania, its organization and methods. Jefferson admired what Holley was doing, and he cited Transylvania as a model university. "If our legislature does not heartily push our University, we must send our children for education to Kentucky or Cambridge," Jefferson wrote to Joseph C. Cabell, a Virginia politician and ally. "The latter will return them to us as fanatics and tories, the former will keep them to add to their population. If however we are to go begging anywhere for our education, I would rather it should be to Kentucky than any other state, because she has more of the flavor of the old cask than any other."[34]

The Presbyterians never gave up hope of controlling higher education in Kentucky.[35] They petitioned the General Assembly in October 1818 for a charter to start a new school in Danville, which became Centre College.[36] Amid public opposition to plans for the state to give Centre a $30,000 endowment, legislators amended the charter to specify that "no religious doctrine peculiar to any one sect of Christians shall be inculcated by any professor in said college." But, within five years, the state had given up control of Centre to the Presbyterian Church.[37] The Presbyterian clergy also kept close watch on Transylvania. In his 1847 *History of the Presbyterian Church in the State of Kentucky*, Davidson accused Holley of forcing out two Presbyterian professors and taking over the duties of another. "To President Holley were committed the entire charge of the religious and moral instruction of the students, and the duty of preaching in the College Chapel," he wrote. "The character of these instructions from the pulpit and the chair was such as to justify the worst fears of the evangelical party." However, Holley was so successful during his first four years at Transylvania that critics kept a low profile. "The President's popularity was unbounded," Davidson acknowledged. "Even the intractable Presbyterians were reduced to silence."[38]

Holley's religious views caused little concern among the general public, at least in Lexington, and the Transylvania board had members of several denominations, including Episcopal, Methodist and Baptist.[39] "[Holley] preaches the power, goodness and mercy of God, as manifested in the flesh—he adopts no sectarian peculiarities—he extends the right hand of fellowship to all true Christians, upon all the great points of interest—in his feelings he is catholic and in our opinion he is orthodox," one newspaper editor wrote.[40] But Holley's criticism of "narrow creeds" and "illiberal thinking" grated on the Presbyterian clergy, who waited for an opportunity to attack him.[41] Holley gave them that opportunity on May 19, 1823, when, from the pulpit of Lexington's Episcopal church, he delivered a eulogy for Col. James Morrison. A Revolutionary War veteran and one of Lexington's first settlers, Morrison had become a wealthy merchant and banker. He died at age sixty-nine while on a business trip to Washington, DC.[42] Morrison was then chairman of Transylvania's trustees and the university's most generous benefactor. At Clay's urging, his will left Transylvania a huge legacy for the time: $20,000 for an endowed professorship and, on the death of his widow, nearly $50,000 more. That money was used in 1833–1834 to build Old Morrison,[43] which remains Transylvania University's administration building and appears on Lexington's city seal.

Holley's eulogy praised Morrison, accurately describing and aggressively recommending his liberal Christian views.[44] "He ordinarily attended worship in the churches of the Presbyterians, a highly respectable and pious body of Christians; but he was entirely eclectic in his principles, taking truth wherever he found it, and giving the hand of fellowship to all good men of every country and denomination," Holley said. "In this respect, he invites our imitation." He then launched into a forceful defense of liberal theology and the value of good works and a broad education—even for women—indicating that they were a preferable path to eternal salvation than strict obedience to any denomination's creed.[45] From the Presbyterian clergy's perspective, Holley "took the occasion to sneer bitterly at the bigotry of Sectarians," Davidson wrote.[46] Emboldened by success and popularity, Transylvania's young president had taken a swing at the hornets' nest. The hornets now swarmed to sting him.

Holley's eulogy for Morrison attracted much public comment, thanks to its availability in a pamphlet published by Bradford. As was common at the time, commentaries appeared in newspapers and pamphlets under pseudonyms, with one anonymous author criticizing another. Lexington's newspapers generally supported Holley, so most of the anonymous attacks on him came from pamphlets and newspapers published elsewhere. Most of the criticism is thought to have been written or instigated by the Presbyterian clergy, some of whom wrote under several pseudonyms.[47] In addition to infidelity, deism, and "irreligion," these articles repeatedly accused Holley of mismanagement of university funds.[48] The allegations prompted legislators to appoint a committee to investigate; in November 1824, the committee issued a report finding no mismanagement and heaping praise on Transylvania and its leadership.[49] Anonymous authors criticized Holley's large salary and claimed: "It is notorious that President Holley is liberal and extravagant towards the Theatre, Ball room, Lotteries yet . . . neither he, nor his family ever contribute a cent to any charitable institution whatever."[50] They complained that Holley read novels and attended parties, and some even accused him of playing cards. Critics cited as evidence of his immorality a marble statue of a naked female bust in his family's drawing room, to which Mary Holley later replied: "As if Christianity must cancel taste, case the heart in marble, extinguish in it the glow of social charity, and render it insensible to those delightful emotions, which are awakened by the innocent pleasures of life!"[51]

Holley tried to ignore the criticism, although friends, Transylvania faculty, and former students rose to his defense.[52] The attacks clearly took their toll, especially those that accused him of corrupting the minds of Transylvania's students with his religious instruction. In response, the university's trustees announced that a rotating cast of clergymen would replace Holley in the chapel pulpit each Sunday so as to expose students to "the great doctrines of our common religion."[53] The plan called for five denominations to share the duties in turn: Roman Catholics, Methodists, Presbyterians, Episcopalians, and Baptists. The Presbyterians refused to participate, citing the plan as evidence of Holley's guilt. But, in the end, Kentucky politics, rather than religion, would be Horace Holley's downfall.

Kentucky's economy had been weak since 1817. Different banking and currency systems led to a flood of paper money, excessive debt, and heated political debate about how to deal with it. Meager state support for Transylvania led to large tuition increases, opening the university to criticism that it was becoming an elite institution for the rich families of many states rather than the promising young men of Kentucky. Hard times led to general animosity toward Lexington's intellectuals and wealthy elite. That, combined with religious fundamentalism and political opportunism, made Holley an easy target. The *Argus of Western America* in Frankfort, which by 1824 was the Kentucky newspaper most willing to criticize Transylvania, accused the president of promoting the Federalist Party's beliefs, deism, and "dandyism." But the most deadly blows came from Governor Joseph Desha, whose 1825 message to the General Assembly complained that Transylvania's tuition increases excluded the poor while the president and faculty members enjoyed high salaries and extravagant lifestyles. Rather than investing in Transylvania's elite, Desha wanted to spend state money on common schools for more Kentuckians. But what he and his political allies actually did was use state education funds to build politically popular highways.[54]

Over seven years, despite a poor economy and little state financial support, Holley had transformed Transylvania from an underperforming school into one of the nation's most celebrated universities. Instead of thanking him, the governor was attacking him. Two months after Desha's rebuke, in January 1826, Holley quit. Transylvania's trustees persuaded him to stay on, but the turmoil sent shivers through Lexington. Transylvania's enrollment over the next year fell from 419 to 286, the law school was suspended, and Holley's salary was reduced by one-third. Desha again attacked Holley in his 1826 message to the General Assembly, saying that Transylvania had ceased "to unite the confidence and affections of the people."[55] By March 1827, Holley had had enough. He again submitted a letter of resignation to Bradford. While his words were affectionate, this letter is unlike other examples of his precise and measured handwriting now preserved in Transylvania's archives: it looks like the angry scrawl of a frustrated man.

In his final report to the trustees, Holley summarized his accomplishments and noted that, while Transylvania had graduated only 22 men before he arrived, his eight-year tenure had seen the graduation of 558. "This alone is, and will be considered by the candid public as a full and unanswerable refutation of the calumnies which our enemies have invented and industriously circulated," he wrote. "We are satisfied with the contrast. Are they?"[56] Those Transylvania students would go on to become some of the most influential Americans of the age, including at least eighteen U.S. senators or representatives. One of them, Jefferson Davis, would become the only president of the Confederate States of America.

"Within the walls of Transylvania the fond recollections of her polite, kind, generous, learned, accomplished and much loved President will never perish," Bradford and two other trustees replied in a letter accepting Holley's resignation. "The patronage of the Commonwealth may be withdrawn, the institution may decline, the walls themselves may be crumbled; but so long as the name remains, there will be associated with it the most affectionate remembrances that flow from mutual attachments, or have a habitation in the hearts of those who are susceptible of the emotions of gratitude."[57] The Holleys—taking their young son, Horace, but leaving behind their married daughter, Harriette—left Lexington on March 27, 1827, and were escorted out of town by a large gathering of students, faculty, friends, and admirers. "Had they known it was to be his only funeral procession, they could not have shown more sympathy and respect," his wife later wrote.[58]

By the end of 1827, Transylvania's enrollment fell to 184 students—157 medical and only 27 academic. By the Civil War, both the law and the medical schools had closed forever. The university went through four presidents after Holley's departure, including Davidson, the Presbyterian minister. "Each of these men retired, after a short period of comparative failure," Sonne wrote.[59] Many of the issues and behaviors that led to Holley's demise would echo through two centuries of Kentucky history and into today's headlines: battles over the separation of church and state, religious fundamentalism, anti-intellectualism, suspicion of elites, and the tendency of Kentucky politicians to invest in politically popular highways rather than education.

What became of Horace Holley? He traveled down the Ohio and Mississippi Rivers—"like a prisoner escaped from his fetters"—to New Orleans. He planned to gather a group of the young sons of wealthy planters and take them to Europe for six to eight years in a traveling academy based in Paris. Holley called his proposal "a Plan of Education for the few who can afford it." The venture never materialized. Holley's wife later wrote that he was persuaded to stay and plan a College of New Orleans, where he would have generous private financial support and the freedom to manage the school and determine the curriculum. Before that could happen, he became exhausted by the intense heat of the New Orleans summer. The Holleys booked passage aboard the packet ship *Louisiana* for a three-month vacation in New York. While sailing through the Gulf of Mexico, they both came down with yellow fever. Holley died on July 31, 1827, and was buried at sea. He was forty-six.[60]

Mary Holley was left virtually homeless with a young son to support. She traveled frequently in the years to come before her own death in New Orleans from yellow fever in 1846. She still had family and many friends in New England to visit as well as her daughter and grandchildren in Lexington. Most significantly, she made several lengthy trips to Texas to see her brother, Henry Austin, and cousin, Stephen F. Austin, the Transylvania graduate who became a Texan legend. She had not seen Stephen since he was a boy, but as adults they became friends and frequent correspondents. Mary became famous for writing about Texas. She published *Texas: Observations, Historical, Geographical, and Descriptive* in 1833 and a later edition, *Texas*, in 1836. She was a prominent supporter of Texas statehood; her 1844 poem "The Plea" of Texas was widely published in newspapers, and another poem was put to music as "The Texan Song of Liberty."[61]

But Mary Holley's first literary effort began just weeks after her husband's death. She felt compelled to record and defend his legacy at Transylvania. When she could not find a man to do it, she decided to do it herself. It was unlikely that learned men would take seriously any biography written by a woman—much less the subject's widow—so she partnered with Caldwell, the Transylvania medical school professor, who had written a long, rambling speech, "A Discourse on the Genius and Character of the Rev. Horace Holley, LL.D." Caldwell's speech praised Holley, but it also detailed his faults, including this telling passage: "Had President Holley been less independent in spirit, less firm and resolute in purpose, and less frank and intrepid in disclosing his sentiments, he would have been more fortunate, and Transylvania more prosperous."[62]

Mary Holley spent the early months of 1828 holed up in her daughter's Lexington home, writing a lengthy biographical appendix to Caldwell's speech. To raise money for the book's publication, she traveled to Washington and stayed with Henry and Lucretia Clay, who helped her solicit national leaders for promises to buy copies. A Boston publisher issued the book in late summer 1828 under Caldwell's name with no credit to Mary Holley, although several references in the appendix make clear the author's identity.[63] At the end of the volume, she included other notes. One was a detailed examination of how much more money other states invested in their universities than Kentucky did.[64] She also added excerpts from some of Holley's few published articles, which contained opinions about higher education that were remarkably ahead of their time. "We want, in our education, accuracy and depth; fewer declaimers and more thinkers," Holley wrote. "Our planters, farmers, merchants and the higher orders of mechanics, ought to number in their catalogues many men of letters, and particularly of science. The population of a free country like this should be extensively educated in all its departments, if we mean to secure the blessings of liberty, civil or religious."[65]

Horace Holley accomplished remarkable things during his one hundred months as president of Transylvania University. It is tempting to speculate how much more another decade or two of his leadership could have burnished the luster of the Athens of the West.

Notes

1. James Spear Loring, *The Hundred Boston Orators* (Boston, 1853), 370; John Pierpont, *A Discourse Delivered in Hollis Street Church, Boston, September 2, 1827, Occasioned by the Death of Horace Holley LL.D. Late President of Transylvania University* (Boston, 1827), 5.

2. Charles Caldwell, *Discourse on the Genius and Character of the Rev. Horace Holley, LL.D.* (Boston, 1828), 148–49. Caldwell's lengthy "discourse" makes up the first section of this book; the rest contains a biographical appendix and notes edited and largely written by Mary Austin Holley, although she is not clearly credited.

3. Charles Francis Adams, ed., *Memoirs of John Quincy Adams, Comprising Portions of His Diary from 1795 to 1848*, 12 vols. (Philadelphia, 1875), 7:323.

4. Niels Henry Sonne, *Liberal Kentucky, 1780–1828* (New York, 1939), 139.

5. Ibid., 135–36.

6. Caldwell, *Discourse*, 70.

7. John Bradford, *The Voice of the Frontier: John Bradford's Notes on Kentucky*, ed. Thomas D. Clark (Lexington, 1993), 231–34.

8. Robert Davidson, *A History of the Presbyterian Church in the State of Kentucky* (New York, 1847), 289, 297.

9. Sonne, *Liberal Kentucky*, 47–51.

10. Robert Peter and Johanna Peter, *Transylvania University: Its Origin, Rise, Decline and Fall* (Louisville, 1895), 91–92.

11. Sonne, *Liberal Kentucky*, 147–49.

12. Thomas D. Clark, *A History of Kentucky* (Lexington, 1960), 228.

13. Sonne, *Liberal Kentucky*, 13, 109–11, 137.

14. Ibid., 139–43.

15. Caldwell, *Discourse*, 117–18, 130, 134–35, 142.

16. Sonne, *Liberal Kentucky*, 151, 153; *Kentucky Gazette*, October 4, 1817.

17. Davidson, *Presbyterian Church*, 289–90, 298.

18. Sonne, *Liberal Kentucky*, 143–59; Davidson, *Presbyterian Church*, 299; Bradford, *Voice of the Frontier*, 241.

19. Rebecca Smith Lee, *Mary Austin Holley: A Biography* (Austin, 1962), 100–101.

20. Horace Holley to James Freeman, April 2, 1818, quoted in Lee, *Mary Austin Holley*, 104.

21. John Adams to Thomas Jefferson, January 28, 1818, quoted in ibid., 102.

22. Caldwell, *Discourse*, 151–62.

23. Pierpont, *Discourse*, 26; Caldwell, *Discourse*, 4–25, 28, 78, 109, 122, 143.

24. Adams, ed., *Memoirs*, 130.

25. Caldwell, *Discourse*, 27, 148.

26. John D. Wright Jr., *Transylvania: Tutor to the West* (Lexington, 1975), 65; *Kentucky Gazette*, December 25, 1818; Horace Holley to Mary Holley, May 27, 1818, quoted in Caldwell, *Discourse*, 153.

27. Lee, *Mary Austin Holley*, 118, 124; Caldwell, *Discourse*, 199; Wright, *Transylvania*, 68–69.

28. *Western Monitor*, November 16, 1819.

29. Wright, *Transylvania*, 74, 78–84, 87–92.

30. Caldwell, *Discourse*, 209.

31. Ibid., 160.

32. Sonne, *Liberal Kentucky*, 183–84.

33. Caldwell, *Discourse*, 68.

34. Horace Holley to Mary Holley, September 6, 1824, and Horace Holley to William Barry, September 5, 1824, Transylvania University Special Collections; Thomas Jefferson to Joseph C. Cabell, January 22, 1820, in *The Works of Thomas Jefferson*, ed. Paul Leicester Ford, 12 vols. (New York, 1905), 12:154–55.

35. Sonne, *Liberal Kentucky*, 196.

36. Davidson, *Presbyterian Church*, 303–4.

37. Clark, *History of Kentucky*, 233.

38. Davidson, *Presbyterian Church*, 304.

39. Sonne, *Liberal Kentucky*, 192.

40. Ibid., 186 (quoting *Commentator,* January 8, 1819).

41. Ibid., 192.

42. Horace Holley, *A Discourse Occasioned by the Death of Col. James Morrison* (Lexington, 1823), 8–12; Davidson, *Presbyterian Church*, 307–8.

43. Peter and Peter, *Transylvania University*, 135.

44. Davidson, *Presbyterian Church*, 307; Holley, *Discourse*, 19–26.

45. Holley, *Discourse*, 19–26.

46. Davidson, *Presbyterian Church*, 308.

47. Sonne, *Liberal Kentucky*, 225–26.

48. Ibid., 196–207, 213.

49. Thomas D. Carneal et al., *Report, on the Transylvania University and Lunatic Asylum* (1824), Transylvania University Special Collections.

50. Sonne, *Liberal Kentucky*, 210 (quoting *Literary Pamphleteer,* 1 [1823]: 16).

51. Caldwell, *Discourse*, 220; Sonne, *Liberal Kentucky*, 218.

52. Caldwell, *Discourse*, 11; Sonne, *Liberal Kentucky*, 215–17, 226.

53. Caldwell, *Discourse*, 230.

54. Clark, *History of Kentucky*, 221–22.

55. Sonne, *Liberal Kentucky*, 253.

56. Caldwell, *Discourse*, 211.

57. Sonne, *Liberal Kentucky*, 254–25; Horace Holley to John Bradford, March 24, 1827, Transylvania University Special Collections; Caldwell, *Discourse*, 207–11, 216–17; Davidson, *Presbyterian Church*, 315.

58. Caldwell, *Discourse*, 273; Pierpont, *Discourse*, 7.

59. Sonne, *Liberal Kentucky*, 260.

60. Pierpont, *Discourse*, 9.

61. Lee, *Mary Austin Holley*, 238–39, 244, 273–74, 331, 361–62.

62. Caldwell, *Discourse*, 72.

63. Lee, *Mary Austin Holley*, 189–94.

64. Caldwell, *Discourse*, 241–56.

65. Ibid., 257–65.

❧ 10

Living Hills
The Frontier Science of Rafinesque

Matthew F. Clarke

In November 1815, the European naturalist Constantine Samuel Rafinesque found himself shipwrecked off the coast of Connecticut, floating amid the debris of his luggage—"books, manuscripts, plates, drawings, maps, herbarium, collections, minerals, &c."[1]—an accumulation of labor that must have formed an odd collage on the surface of the tempestuous ocean. Having been driven from Europe's revolutionary climate, Rafinesque had left the Sicilian port of Palermo on July 21, aimed for the shores of America. After stopping at Gibraltar and the island of St. Michel, Rafinesque's ship was overrun by a storm only miles from the American coast. The abiding scientist quickly sought to turn his misfortunes into an opportunity by redoubling his efforts to reconstruct the *Critique des Genres* (Criticism of genera), his vainglorious attempt at reclassifying the world's plants and animals, now lost at sea. In the wake of this unfortunate accident, Rafinesque was left to fill his curios and curiosities with the untrammeled natural treasures of the American wilderness; its flora and fauna were the subjects of a larger movement to codify, by the methods and techniques of science, a national identity. Not only would this so-called naturalist lay claim to American natural history; he would also aspire to turn this great loss into a marketable thriller for the emerging intellectual elite of the new republic. "Shipwreck of a Naturalist," reads the prospectus for the memoir, will recount the harrowing "particulars of my voyage, shipwreck and losses."[2] After petitioning for support, Rafinesque would embark on a journey that ended in the unsuspecting trading entrepôt of Lexington, Kentucky, located along several key roads in the country's interior, which was undergoing an unprecedented period of

Portrait of Rafinesque as
a young man, probably by
Matthew Jouett. (Transyl-
vania University Library,
Lexington.)

growth in learning and enterprise. His presence in the merchant town
coincided with a vibrant period of culture and progress and, at the same
time, ran parallel to the evolution of American science from a hobby of
wealthy landowners to separate disciplines that were supported and organized by strong institutions.

The narrative of Lexington, Kentucky, as the "Athens of the West"
was defined by people like Rafinesque. He spent time there as the professor of natural philosophy at Transylvania University. At the same time, the
1820s and 1830s were seen as the golden age of natural philosophy. Transylvania's prominent medical, philosophical, and natural science faculty
members held international reputations, helped alter the course of early
American science, and defined its purpose within society. At the dawn of a
period of European enlightenment, the natural scientists at Transylvania
were testing the theories and speculations of the leading philosophers of
Europe against the empirical evidence (preserved in its untouched nature) found in the American frontier. In the first half of the nineteenth
century, the scientists lecturing at Transylvania made important contributions about the composition of matter, the natural classification of flora

and fauna, the idea of "infinite variety" in species, the morphology of Indian languages, and the origins of archaeology. Despite the religious sectarianism that eroded the university's progressiveness, this "lamp in the forest" made lasting and important contributions to American society at a time when scientific legitimacy was essential to the growing republic. Indeed, since science in America is "not a story of great scientific discoveries and theoretical breakthroughs but of scientific exploration of the New World,"[3] Transylvania was poised to serve as a leading agent of that exploration with its advantaged location and its supportive community. This chapter looks at the origins of this period of scientific research in Kentucky and, in particular, uses Rafinesque's interest in the archaeology of the region to demonstrate the lasting legacy of the Athens of the West and its relevance to the history of science.

Science as Democracy

Prior to the rise of western universities, science in America was limited to the few urban centers along the Eastern Seaboard—Philadelphia, New York, and Boston—and the intellectual organizations and publications that traded the currency of knowledge. Quite naturally, these institutions were created and sustained to prove that America was just as capable as Europe in the practice of science; to the leaders of these societies, their role in supporting democracy was just as important as the institutions of government and law. The success of the newly independent country depended on a vibrant scientific community to serve domestic interests such as agriculture and engineering and, abroad, to affirm the intellectual capacity of America on the international stage. Despite these efforts, the first decades of American culture were focused on the pragmatic aspects of survival and development and not necessarily on forging a high-level scientific culture. Benjamin Rush, the founding father and Pennsylvania physician, claimed: "Philosophy does not here, as in England, walk abroad in silver slippers; the physicians (who are the most general repositories of science) are chained down by the drudgery of their professions: so as to be precluded from exploring our woods and mountains. Besides, there are not men of learning enough in American as yet, to furnish the stimulus of literary fame to difficult and laborious pursuits."[4]

Rush's comments describe one of the prevailing tendencies of this incipient nation, that most scientists were first and foremost doctors, wedded to the practical application of knowledge and the need for financial security. It would not be until the early to mid-nineteenth century that science divided into autonomous specialties with enough backing to support independent research. The first true scientists of America were those European travelers, such as Chateaubriand and Bartram, who used their journeys to record and transmit the abundant natural wonders of the New World. William Bartram's *Travels through North and South Carolina*[5] best exemplifies the sort of literary account of America's natural history and, in the process, connects the early efforts of taxonomy with the English romantics and their pantheistic celebration of nature and the sublime. As one would expect, painting became an important visual tool in this process. Charles Wilson Peale, for example, used the natural world as subject matter for his primary vocation as a painter. Later, he would populate his natural history museum in Philadelphia, the country's first, with these paintings and taxonomic displays of the wildlife. Not least of these figures was Thomas Jefferson, who favored agricultural research over scientific theorization, a position that would define a generational attitude toward the relation between science and society. His own *Notes on the State of Virginia*,[6] considered by many to be the most important American book of the eighteenth century, includes not only an introduction to his political philosophy but also a catalog of his home state's plant and animal life. He uses this manuscript to refute the Comte de Buffon's theory of degeneration, an erroneous speculation by the esteemed French naturalist that says that all plants in the New World are imperfect copies of those in the Old. Jefferson's *Notes* was, in some respects, the clarion call to pick up the instruments and devices of science for the democratic project, to refute not only Buffon's theory but also the hegemony of European science in general.

But, before this could happen, America had to overcome two pressing obstacles: first, few institutions or individuals could afford to stock their libraries with the latest journals and books since most of the literature was then published in the well-oiled academic centers of Europe; second, American academics had very few opportunities to publish their discoveries domestically or to find willing sponsors for their research. Most native-born scientists relied on medicine to provide income, and many immigrant scientists in search of a pristine natural environment left for more favorable shores after some years of hapless wandering. Nonetheless, many institutions had the right mix of people and resources for science to germinate and, eventually, to thrive.

Philadelphia was the center of America's intellectual culture in the eighteenth and nineteenth centuries; home to the University of Pennsylvania (and its schools of law and medicine), the Peale Museum, the

American Philosophical Academy, the Academy of Natural Science, the Philadelphia College of Physicians, and the Franklin Institute, the former capital city thrived in its role as the leader of science and technology. New York had no shortage of resources; after a meeting of prominent citizens such as Fenimore Cooper and William Gracie, the New York Atheneum was organized to support literature and science in the emerging metropolis.[7] And, in Boston, Harvard attracted leading European scientists to hold distinguished research seats at the university, including Asa Gray and Louis Agassiz. These examples make clear that science was ultimately urban: it depended on the human and financial capital of dense cities to sustain the incipient practices of science. These centers could afford to collect and manage large libraries, they had access to printers and publishers, and they had stable audiences for public lectures and events.

Dependent on the frontier to acquire plant and animal specimens, these institutions cultivated relationships with capable settlers and organized lengthy expeditions of explorers, scientists, and artists. For example, William Maclure, the president of the Academy of Natural Sciences in Philadelphia, led, with the zoologists George Ord and Thomas Say, a geological expedition to the offshore islands of Georgia and Florida during the winter of 1817–1818. Later, in 1826, Maclure would help establish the New Harmony colony in Indiana as an outpost of Philadelphia's research interests and a home for naturalists needing lengthy time to study in the wilderness. The relation between science in situ, in the forests of the western states, and the institutional establishment in Philadelphia was, at best, tenuous. The freethinking field naturalists, most comfortable as wanderers in the tradition of the romantic poet, often clashed with the "empire builders," like Agassiz and Gray, "who used their lofty positions at Harvard to determine what became scientific 'truth' in American science."[8] As the American population moved westward and new urban agglomerations formed on the edge, new, well-stocked centers of science emerged that benefited from their proximity to the wilderness and the relative freedom of their intellectual culture.

Lexington, Kentucky, Cincinnati, Ohio, and Charleston, South Carolina, were the first cities outside the Northeast to develop as intellectual centers, each for its own reason. Charleston, the largest city in the South by 1780, became a center of scientific activity with the production of naturalists' folios, studies on yellow fever, and meteorological investigations taking place before the nineteenth century. Cincinnati, on the other hand, drew from the arrival in 1800 of the physician Daniel Drake, who used his connections to the University of Pennsylvania to develop institutions to support medical and scientific research. Lexington thrived during the presteamboat era, serving as a center of trade between East and West by means of a network of roads to Cincinnati, Virginia, the Carolinas, and Louisiana (via the Natchez Trail). Also a center of manufacture, it produced cordage and bagging from the hemp grown by its elite, landowning farmers.[9] These merchants and manufacturers were proud of their city, and they gave liberally to the cultural institutions that supported the arts and sciences. The early town leaders were surprisingly self-aware of their precociousness and used it as a branding opportunity. At a celebration for Washington's birthday at Lexington's Union Philosophical Society, a formal toast was given: "Lexington—Like the star of Bethlehem, it directs the votaries of freedom to the shrine of science."[10] And at his introductory lecture at Transylvania on November 7, 1820, Rafinesque would say: "Situated in the center of this Western Continent we shall be the central point from which the rays of Knowledge will diverge in all directions and sides." Learning must have been profitable, for the city could support upward of four newspapers, the *Kentucky Gazette*, the *Kentucky Reporter*, the *Public Advertiser*, and the *Western Monitor*, the last published by John D. Clifford until his death in 1820. The Lexington Library, established in 1795 and incorporated in 1800, had 2,573 volumes by 1815, as listed by the catalog of books published by F. Bradford, and the Athenaeum of Lexington provided access to literary journals and books for its members.[11] These examples represent a small slice of the liberal culture of Lexington, whose organizations supported music, philosophy, literature, and theater. During the first two decades of the nineteenth century, Lexington was the unequivocal capital of the American West, and, as such, it became home to a great number of dignitaries, merchants, lawyers, and politicians, a group that ranged easily over the liberal arts, following the enlightenment approach to learning. This progressive attitude had its downside, drawing vehement criticism and scorn from the religious sectarianism that dominated the frontier, led by the influential Presbyterian denomination. As the *Evangelical Record*, a Presbyterian paper, said: "The good people of Kentucky, are, like the most of the people of the United States, divided with respect to religion, into two grand divisions; viz. the infidel, and the Christian part of the community."[12] Transylvania University, the most important cog in this literary town, was a product of this religious schism, beginning its life as a seminary, and evolving into a liberal outpost of the enlightened theories of natural philosophy.[13]

Harry Toulmin's election to the presidency of Transylvania Seminary in 1794 was the first rupture between the Presbyterian-dominated board of directors and the rising liberal class. Toulmin, bearing a letter of recommendation from James Madison, gave the liberals a chance to promote the interests of their cause within the school. Chartered in 1780 by the Virginia legislature, the university, which combined with the Kentucky Academy on December 22, 1798, vacillated between the poles of theological orthodoxy and intellectual liberalism. The first decade of the nineteenth century was a period of Presbyterian control at the school, reflected in the ineffectual presidency of the Reverend James Blythe, whose administration upheld the authority of the Bible as the sole source of knowledge. He suffered from attacks by the local merchant class. At the close of the War of 1812, interest in the future of Transylvania grew rapidly, driven not only by the liberal imperative but also by the changing economic landscape of postwar America. As Lexington lost some of its prestige to Cincinnati and Louisville, a group of Jeffersonian Republicans made the claim that the town would succeed only if the conservative federalist Presbyterians were extricated from the helm of Transylvania. The efforts, led by the board of trustees, were directed to find and hire an esteemed professor from an eastern school to serve as president, whom they found in a promising graduate of Yale University, Horace Holley. As Tom Eblen and Mollie Eblen's essay in this volume makes clear, Holley's tenure marked the high point of Lexington's time as the leading outpost of natural philosophy in the country and, in many respects, the world.

The calm in the ideological storm between the years 1818 and 1826 gave rise to a surfeit of resources, professors, and scientific advances. The showpiece of the institution was its medical college, led by the indefatigable Benjamin W. Dudley, who had taken a medical degree at the University of Pennsylvania and studied further while abroad. Dudley's leadership helped convince Daniel Drake, the esteemed physician and museum director from Cincinnati, to join the faculty in 1823 (following on his visiting appointment in 1814). Possibly to an even more important effect, Charles Caldwell, an expert on yellow fever and a frequent debater of Benjamin Rush, was recruited from Philadelphia to serve as the professor of the institutes of medicine and clinical practice.[14] In a sign of the legislature's faith in the new institution, Caldwell was granted the amazing sum of $13,000 to import from Europe the best books and apparatuses for the university. The spoils represented the "finest library in medicine and natural philosophy, together with a select set of scientific apparatus, owned by any university in the nation."[15] Arguably, however, the most interesting character among this collection of Philadelphia transplants was Joseph Buchanan. Educated at Transylvania in 1804, he had later written a book, *Philosophy of Human Nature*, that brought about an international movement toward the secularization of naturalism, a feat that helped divorce the biblical theories of origin with the Enlightenment notions of the natural world. In doing so, he formulated an idea of matter that argues against the stasis of the physical world, an idea with no parallel outside the work of Leibniz. He states: "The elements of matter are capable of combining together in an infinite variety of forms which are changed into each other, like colors of the solar spectrum, by unnoticeable variations."[16] Even though the faculty of Transylvania during this period were not explicitly committed to a single theoretical framework, they shared a tendency to think of the natural world as in flux, as unstable, as mutable; it can only be speculated that this trend was a product of their environment, distanced from the oversight of eastern institutions and closer to the panoply of the American wilderness. To them, more so than to the "stale" perspective of those urbanites, both the natural world and society were evolving toward a more perfect expression of the democratic ideal that America represented.

Buchanan's *Philosophy* contributed to a movement of natural classification that organized the natural world according to the forces acting on the living species, their context, as opposed to the more traditional Linnaean view, which rigidly categorized plants and animals according to their reproductive process. Constantine Samuel Rafinesque, the beached naturalist, was the eccentric leader of this method, and, as such, he anticipated Darwin's theory of evolution.[17] While his reputation as a scientist was always tainted by error-prone methods and obvious gestures toward self-aggrandizement, he was able to work as a liminal figure in the ideologically charged environment of Lexington. Nonetheless, his pantheistic philosophy and lack of decorum would damage the reputation of both Transylvania and President Holley. Rafinesque still identified himself as a European, but he was engaged in a decidedly American endeavor. As such, he was especially free to use science as a narrative instrument to connect the dreams of the new country with the natural conditions of the frontier in which he resided.

Rafinesque's Western Monuments

Rafinesque was born in 1783 in Constantinople to a French merchant father and a German mother. Apprenticed to his father's friend in Philadelphia at an early age, he returned to Europe, to Sicily, in 1805. His love of botany and natural history developed in the hills of Sicily, secured by a financially lucrative business trading in materia medica.[18] After returning to America the second time, Rafinesque spent time in New York, developing relationships with DeWitt Clinton, the future governor of New York, and William Mitchill, the editor of the *Medical Repository*, one of the early scientific journals of importance in the New World. Even though he intended to settle in Philadelphia full-time, he decided to undertake a lengthy journey through the West to collect specimens for his library and for future publications on natural history. In 1818, he managed to secure a contract with a Pittsburgh publisher to make a map of the Ohio River from Pittsburgh to the Wabash River. With several other Frenchmen, Rafinesque purchased a flat, slow-moving boat (the better to avoid shipwrecks) and set sail down the Ohio River, collecting fish specimens, and exploring the lands beyond the Alleghenies. This work would later be published in his classic *Ichthyologia ohiensis* in 1820.[19] After staying a weekend with the esteemed naturalist John James Audubon (and being ridiculed in the now famous "Odd Fish"),[20] he stumbled on John D. Clifford, a merchant and science lover who knew Rafinesque through his voyages to Sicily. As a member of the board of trustees at Transylvania University, Clifford helped secure the wandering European a position as professor of botany and natural history. As a result, Rafinesque found himself lecturing at Transylvania without ever soliciting an appointment. For one of the first and last times, his prospects looked bright: "He could investigate the immense, bountiful Mississippi valley, and unexplored land on his map, and had a prestigious position at an institution that was the first of its kind west of the Allegheny mountains."[21] He was an intellectual opportunist (his merchant father left him with an indelible business acumen, an important aptitude in scientific endeavors), and he had on many occasions petitioned prestigious universities for teaching positions. At Transylvania, he relied on public lectures, private instruction, and independent publications for an income. His self-made mythology used the idea of genius, a stock character in the romantic idiom, to market himself to the learning-hungry community.[22] Whether teaching Greek to the wives of wealthy merchants, or giving lectures on the latest techniques of botany, or starting new literary publications, Rafinesque wholeheartedly engaged himself in the community.[23] Growing confident in his new position, he soon branched out into other methods of inquiry, such as archaeology and etymology, ones that demonstrated his ability to identify a market for his very peculiar talents.[24]

Rafinesque became enraptured by the mysteries of this new territory, its unclassified fauna, its fishes, its customs, its geography, and its his-

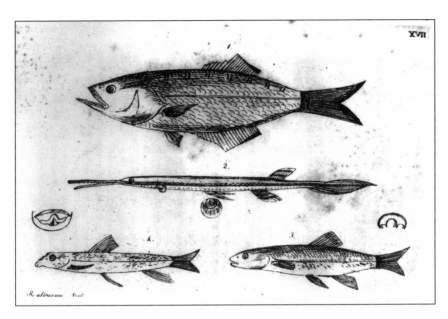

Rafinesque's drawings of three "new" genera of fish, *Pomoxis, Sarchirus,* and *Exoglossum.* (From *Journal of the Academy of Natural Sciences of Philadelphia* 1, pt. 2 [1818].)

tory. He brashly proclaimed that he would gradually identify every living creature in the country, part of a surreal plan to catalog and reproduce "the whole Animal and Vegetable kingdoms of North America." On his trips into the wilderness, he and Clifford, his frequent botanizing partner, often stumbled across oddly shaped mounds of earth that were quite obviously of human origin. In the December 1819 edition of Clifford's *Western Review,*[25] the kind of informal literary journal that typified the learned culture of Lexington, Rafinesque submitted a brief article about his intentions to study an "ancient monument or fortification, situated about two and a half miles from Lexington, in an easterly direction above the head of Hickman Creek": "I mean to survey and measure accurately the whole, taking at the same time the plan of the surrounding country, as it will be interesting to know how the Alleghawee nation built their walled towns. . . . We already know so many monuments of the civil religious, and military architecture, of that powerful nation. . . . Those known are, Towns, Villages, Temples, Avenues, Walks, Lines, Earthforts, Mark Stones, Circle of Stones, Walls, Palaces, Tumuli, Mounds, Platforms, Ditches, Council Houses, Ridges, Ascents, Steps, Aprons, Embankments, &c."[26]

Any serious research on these mounds was essentially nonexistent, save for fanciful narratives by travel writers and the occasional report in a farmers' journal; no previous scholar was as willing to use so little evidence to draw so many conclusions, and Rafinesque was criticized for projecting such an obviously western, architectural image onto these aboriginal creations. Nonetheless, he makes perfectly transparent that the monuments of the Ohio valley are just that, monuments, and that they require extensive research and should be compared to the entire canon of world architecture.

Interest in the Indian burial mounds of the Ohio valley reached a new plateau in the years 1818 and 1819, thanks mostly to three men who exchanged research on the location and descriptions of these mysterious earth forms. In 1780, when James Bowdoin had spoken to the American Academy of Arts and Sciences, he went so far as to suggest that knowledge of America's antiquities was unessential, given the "uncivilized, unprogressive, and illiterate" Indians that the colonists had encountered.[27] Not until settlers had breached the Allegheny Mountains did works of grand scale and form appear; the project of interpreting these ruins became a defining aspect of early American science. Clifford, one of those early researchers, published a series of ten letters in the *Western Review* that described, in exacting detail, how the monuments of the Ohio valley were the burial mounds of a lost "mound-builder" culture. Clifford was indebted to "text-aided archaeology" and the deductive process of building a story about civilizations past through archival texts and documents. He contemplated the broad questions of human civilization in America before the European colonists, using philology and archaeology to reconstruct the culture that erected, by his summation, temples and places of worship, likely descendants from an Asiatic tribe that moved into South and Central America before the arrival of Columbus. Rafinesque, on the other hand, was wedded to the process of relentless classification: measuring and surveying the topography of America in order to come to a full and complete understanding of the country's ancient history. In many ways, his approach to archaeology was similar to his method of natural classification and equally prolific. He stressed comparative philology and archaeology as essential tools to understand the mound builders, and he came to the conclusion that they descended from the Atalantes culture, a group that supposedly migrated across Europe and Africa on its way to America.

As Rafinesque continued his investigations, he often crossed paths with (and even provided drawings and surveys to) Caleb Atwater, a postmaster and attorney in the town of Circleville, Ohio. Named for the

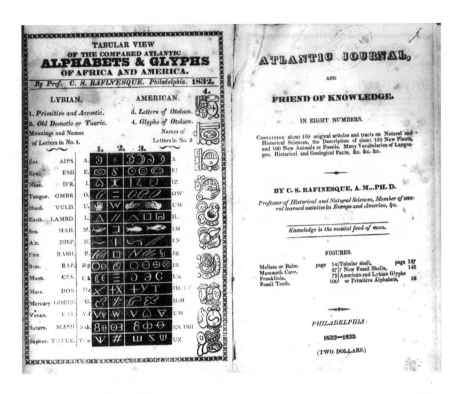

Frontispiece of Rafinesque's *Atlantic Journal* (1832–1833). The chart created by Rafinesque compares and links the languages of America and Africa. (Library Company of Philadelphia.)

shape of its well-defined and large collection of earth mounds, Circleville had become the center for eastern immigrants interested in the origins of American history. Atwater's letter on May 30, 1818, to the recently formed American Antiquarian Society announced that he had been collecting "aboriginal antiquities" for some time and offered to assist the society in its research. Isaiah Thomas, the society's president, was taken by Atwater's letter and encouraged him to pursue more surveys under the assumption that the society would publish the results. Even though Thomas denied Atwater's frequent requests for more funding, he managed to publish *Description of the Antiquities Discovered in the State of Ohio* in volume 1 of *Archaeologia americana*. The book concluded that the mounds, all of which were to be found west of the Alleghenies, were a product of a burial mound culture that had subsided some centuries before. Atwater speculated that these mounds were built by a tribe that had its origins in Hindu culture, drawing from evidence in Clifford's informal museum of antiquities, particularly the Asiatic-looking countenances on the celebrated triune vessel that he estimated to be representations of Brahma, Vishnu, and Shiva.[28] *Archaeologia americana* became the first archaeological publication in America, and it would foreshadow the beginning of the federal government's official exploration of archaeological science. For the first time, archaeology and the origins of the American Indians became leading topics of scientific research in the country, and Lexington, Kentucky, was leading the way.

By 1824, Rafinesque had already produced a self-published volume, *Ancient History; or, Annals of Kentucky*, that served as a preface to Humphrey Marshall's *History of Kentucky* and cataloged the evolution of populations across the American continent. It included "philological and ethnological tables abridged from an elaborate survey of about 500 languages and dialects, reduced to 50 mother languages."[29] He speculated that there was regular contact among people from the Ganges to the Mississippi and that their architectural culture reflected this proximity. Even though it was widely discredited, *Annals* still remained an influential study as the very first account of the ancient monuments of Kentucky; it was an introduction to Rafinesque's philosophy of humankind, grounded in a radical view of all humans as equal progeny of a single race: "The white, tawny, coppery, brown, and black varieties of mankind are connected by numerous links, and claim a common origin; they have been early divided, variously separated, and occasionally blended again."[30] His statement was considered blasphemy to polygenecism, a school of thought that held that humans were created in multiple geographic centers and evolved to their present distribution across the globe. These theories codified racism in the early republic, a scientific explanation for the presence of slavery and the mistreatment of the aboriginal Indians.[31] Rafinesque's research in philology and ethnography, considered by many to be the first example of comparative language studies, was tied directly to his interest in the burial mounds and their role in forging a national identity. He was unique in his secular attitude about the hybridity of culture; Indian monuments were rightfully compared to the ruins that dotted the landscape of his former home in Sicily and to the "Hindoo" temples of the Far East. At a time when science was exploited to justify racism and colonialism, Rafinesque abstained from holding prejudices against other cultures; his worldview was synthetic and sympathetic. After years of wandering the globe, adapting to many cultures and countries, he had developed a peculiarly tolerant, even empathetic attitude toward other races and creeds. He saw nature as the ultimate object of reverence and respect and not some anthropocentric god.

Rafinesque, the inveterate opportunist, took it on himself to capitalize on this new interest in antiquities and started his own campaign by undermining the competition. Atwater's text, Rafinesque claimed, was "animated" but "diffuse, and not always correct"; it lacked originality and was poorly arranged.[32] Already publishing articles in the *Kentucky Reporter* and the *Western Review* about western "monuments," Rafinesque courted the favor of Thomas at the American Antiquarian Society. In a letter to Thomas, republished in Rafinesque's failed journal, the *Western Minerva*, the botanist exclaimed: "The numerous monuments scattered throughout the Western States, are the principal records left us by a powerful nation, which dwelt in them at an early period, and to which I apply the name of Alleghawee, given to it by the Lennape Tribes. It is high time that these monuments should all be accurately surveyed, described and drawn, ere they disappear under the plough, or through wanton neglect. It is my intention to perform this, respecting all those of this state."[33]

"Ere they disappear under the plough" is a trope common to this early period of archaeology. Those engaged in science at this time felt that the demands of cultivation on the frontier threatened the pristine quality of the American wilderness. Since Rafinesque saw democracy as the supreme innovation of the new republic, the monuments of the West, in his view, represented the foundations of these democratic ideals. Just as the taxonomy of flora and fauna gave order and patterns to this new society, so too could ancient ruins prefigure the emergence of a new country that was rational and just. Rafinesque's scientific and literary talents helped him sell this argument, be it accurate or not.

Like the other scholars at Transylvania, Rafinesque saw America's flora and fauna as constantly changing, different, and new. What is an American? is an implicit question in his discourse, and he directed it toward the mounds on the plains of the Ohio valley. They represented, in all respects, the monuments of the country, our respective Acropolis and Agora, our temples and theaters, our forums and courts. Irrespective of their true origins, they were adaptable to their new nation, and in a carefully framed argument, using the tools of science, they could also be seen as the first monuments to a democratic culture. Just as he might classify and describe the locust tree and the Ohio catfish, so too would he describe the burial mound according to its purpose and typology. Rafinesque eloquently describes this imperative in a publication produced many years later, in Philadelphia, that drew on his experiences in Lexington: "If the annals of the Greeks and Romans had been lost, as have been those of Egypt, of Assyria and many other early empires, we should still have in the ruins and monuments of Italy, and Greece, complete evidence of the existence of those nations, their location, power and skill; nay, even of the extent of their dominion by their colonial monuments scattered from Syria to Spain, from Lybia to Britain."[34] Clearly, the European-born naturalist wanted to situate the American heritage with that of Europe and the rest of the world. By doing so, he asserted himself as an Adamic figure, a popular construction of the early literati in America, and referred to the need in America to give name and order to the natural world: "Like the biblical Adam, . . . who immediately upon naming the creatures became aware of his need of a companion, . . . so too did Americans in the early years of the republic engage in taxonomic construction as a rehearsal . . . of social and political construction."[35] The burial mounds were social and political constructions, they were directly associated with the ruins of Greece, Rome, and the historical ideals these places represented, and they were adaptable to the cause of forming a new American society.

Rafinesque must have imagined himself through the eyes of the citizens of Lexington, the intrepid lawmen and merchants, the budding intellectuals, the common hemp traders, and the artisans, a European in the context of this wilderness, part and parcel of the mythology of distant places: "a fellow citizen who drew his first breath and had his cradle in that Grecian land, the ancient seat of the Muses, Philosophy, and Liberty . . . and who finds himself thrown by human events and his free choice among you, Western Republicans!"[36] It was this voice that projected the hills of Kentucky and Ohio as specimens of a monumental project of democracy. Until then, they had been circumvallations and burial mounds, but not civic architecture: no Indian was given the agency as architect. Rafinesque was not the only such voice in the wilderness; others were learning how to talk about, measure, and describe these mounds and, in the process, were developing the first science with its origins in America.

Rafinesque recognized the need for science in the new republic and changed himself to suit its needs. One might even apply his own theories of natural deviation, or the ability of plants and animals to adapt to their context, to his own life story.[37] He represents the myth of knowledge and its arc across the Atlantic, from the shores of ancient Greece, to Italy, to Philadelphia, and, finally, to Lexington, Kentucky. Only from this international perspective is he able to see the mounds of the Ohio valley as descendants of the Roman ruins of Sicily, of the Grecian monuments at Paestum, and of the Byzantine edifices of Constantinople.

The Evolution of Science

Rafinesque's fascination with these monuments coincided with the rise of institutional science, a shift in authority that is best represented by the establishment of the Smithsonian and the inauguration of its series Contributions to Knowledge. The institution's first secretary, Joseph Henry, wanted the Smithsonian to become a center for scientific research.[38] The first edition of Contributions, *The Ancient Monuments of the Mississippi Valley*, written by Ephraim Squire and Edward Davies, drew substantially from Rafinesque's research, particularly his measurement and mapping of the burial mounds of Kentucky, but, perhaps more importantly, its title reflects the importance of Rafinesque's global attitude and his imaginative outlook. Earlier scholars like Atwater and Clifford were uncomfortable using the term *monument* to describe the strange hills and relied on ambiguous terms like *circumvallation* to describe their usage. Nonetheless, the effort by Squire and Davies to record the complete disposition of the Ohio valley's monuments was an effort guided by rationality and emotional distance. Henry instructed his researchers to avoid speculation about the origins and uses of these constructions and to rely on measurement and empirical knowledge in their work. This approach would not have found welcome ears in the intellectual climate of Lexington and Transylvania, a place where the certainty of knowledge of the world was never trusted.

The theory of matter espoused by the natural philosophers at Transylvania like Buchanan and Rafinesque held that everything is subject to change and evolution. The university and its members were subject to the same forces. In large part because of the conservative pressure of the Presbyterian sect, the liberalism of Transylvania lost the support of the community and the trustees. What is more, the economic downturn that began in the year 1817 divided the Republican Party over methods of addressing economic recovery. The schism permeated all aspects of the party's operations and resulted in a depletion of income for Transylvania. At the same time, political complaints criticized the institution as being aristocratic and elitist, with Holley as the figurehead for this collection of "wealthy" professors. The pressure from Frankfort and the community was great enough to remove Holley in 1827, along with the entire board of trustees. Sonne holds that the passage of Transylvania into sectarian control was a linchpin in the passage of Kentucky into an orthodox, Christian state; there is no doubt that the free air of liberalism that colored the Bluegrass region in the bright decade of the 1820s was stifled by the university's decline. The land grant institution down the road, which would become the University of Kentucky, would take over as the state's flagship institution of higher learning.

As eras of prosperity fade, their monuments often remain as testaments to a collective memory. When a conflagration struck Transylvania's main building in 1829, the most solid evidence of the school's golden years tumbled to the ground. On these ruins would arise new edifices, new academic buildings, a bigger campus, and new opportunities to discover in the past, the origins of the future.

Notes

1. Constantine S. Rafinesque, *Circular Address on Botany and Zoology* (Philadelphia, 1838), A3.

2. Ibid.

3. John C. Greene, *American Science in the Age of Jefferson* (Ames, IA, 1984), 3.

4. Quoted in ibid., 11.

5. William Bartram, *Travels through North and South Carolina* (Philadelphia, 1791).

6. Thomas Jefferson, *Notes on the State of Virginia* (Philadelphia, 1794).

7. *New York Times*, June 15, 1901.

8. Wayne Durrill, "Becoming Rafinesque: Market Society and Academic Reputation in the Early American Republic," *American Nineteenth Century History* 9 (2008): 127.

9. Greene, *American Science*, 120.

10. *Kentucky Reporter* (Lexington), March 7, 1825.

11. Hartley Dupre, *Rafinesque in Lexington* (Lexington, 1941), 32, 11.

12. *Evangelical Record* 2 (1813): 10.

13. For the most complete study of Transylvania's liberal heritage, see Niel Sonne's remarkable *Liberal Kentucky, 1780–1828* (New York, 1939).

14. Ash Gobar and J. Hill Hamon, *A Lamp in the Forest: Natural Philosophy in Transylvania University, 1799–1859* (Lexington, 1982), 9.

15. Ibid., 10.

16. Joseph Buchanan, *Philosophy of Human Nature* (Richmond, VA, 1812), 7.

17. Scholars have inconsistently upheld and overturned this theory, derived, in part, from Rafinesque's late epic-styled *The World; or, Instability, a Poem* (Philadelphia, 1836).

18. Rafinesque's knowledge of business informed his scientific research. For a survey of how he appropriated the acumen of a merchant and market societies, see Durrill, "Becoming Rafinesque."

19. C. S. Rafinesque, *Ichthyologia ohiensis; or, Natural History of the Fishes Inhabiting the River Ohio and Its Tributary Steams* (Lexington, 1820).

20. John James Audubon, *Audubon and His Journals* (New York, 1831), 480.

21. Leonard Warren, *Constantine Samuel Rafinesque: A Voice in the American Wilderness* (Lexington, 2004), 77.

22. Durrill, "Becoming Rafinesque," 132.

23. Despite the opportunities he was afforded in Lexington, Rafinesque was also looking for a way out, particularly to the newly formed University of Virginia. See Edwin Betts, "The Correspondence between Constantine Samuel Rafinesque and Thomas Jefferson," *Proceedings of the American Philosophical Society* 87 (1994): 368–80.

24. Among the many derisions Rafinesque faced in his time and posthumously, none were received with such hilarity as his classification of lightning.

25. John D. Clifford edited the *Western Review and Miscellaneous Magazine* and did so as a means to publish his own work in science and other branches of knowledge.

26. Rafinesque, "On a Remarkable Ancient Monument Near Lexington," *Western Review and Miscellaneous Magazine*, December 1819, 313.

27. Greene, *American Science*, 343.

28. Ibid., 366.

29. C. S. Rafinesque, *Ancient History; or, Annals of Kentucky; with a Survey of the Ancient Monuments* (Frankfort, 1824), 2.

30. Ibid., 3.

31. The scientific positions explaining the diversity of races were roughly divided into three camps: (1) the Jefferson-Morton position, in which races evolved out of several regional centers; (2) the Barton-Mitchill position, in which a land bridge over the Bering Strait distributed different races; and (3) the Maclure-Rafinesque position, in which races were infinitely ramified and the white Europeans were not the ideal type or epitome of creation.

32. [Constantine Samuel Rafinesque], review of *Archeologia americana . . .* , vol. 1, in *Western Review and Miscellaneous Magazine* 3 (1820–1821): 104.

33. *Western Minerva; or, American Annals of Knowledge and Literature* 1 (January 1820): 1.

34. Constantine Samuel Rafinesque, *The Ancient Monuments of North and South America* (Philadelphia, 1838), 4.

35. Christopher Looby, "The Constitution of Nature: Taxonomy as Politics in Jefferson, Peale, and Bartram," *Early American Literature* 22 (1987): 252–73.

36. Dupre, *Rafinesque in Lexington*, 56.

37. For a take on the scientist as someone "better understood in the broader, literary context of early American writing about the nature of America and Americans," see Jim Endersby, "'The vagaries of a Rafinesque': Imagining and Classifying American Nature," *Studies in History and Philosophy of Biological and Biomedical Sciences* 40 (2009): 168–78, 177.

38. In many ways, Henry's aspirations would prefigure the role of the federal government in the advancement of science.

✒ 11

Lexington Limners
Portrait Painters in the "Athens of the West"

Estill Curtis Pennington

At the same time Lexington was being "transformed from a rude frontier post into an attractive community of fine homes, landed estates,
and diverse manufacturing and mercantile enterprises," the lives and
works of portrait artists became a part of the dynamic popular culture
of the "Athens of the West."[1] These artists can be seen as messengers
of style, as participants in the transformation, as those who imparted to
a Transylvanian community the international tastes and aesthetic values
then current among artists and patrons in more established urban areas.
The art of portraiture is the most reciprocal form of the visual arts, primarily because of the equation it sets in motion: artists need jobs, and
sitters want a pleasing likeness, informed by the acknowledged fashion
of the day. To comprehend that fashion requires hearing the accounts set
down by contemporaries and seeing the verisimilitude of detail between
precedent and product.

First sightings of those artists are sparse in detail and concerned
with itinerant vagary. Samuel Woodson Price reports a mythic portraitist
named "West" who came across the mountains from Maryland in the late
1790s, but this artist has never been identified as Price seems to have been
confused about the family relationships of Edward West Jr., artist, inven-
tor, and entrepreneur in Lexington.[2] Similar confusion has been made
between an early settler, Richard Terrell, who was not an artist, and the
artist Richard Terrell, who appeared in Indiana in 1828.

Edward West Jr. may be regarded as the first resident limner in town.
A native of Virginia, he and his family appear in the 1790 Bourbon County
Kentucky census, prior to moving to Lexington around 1792. A silver-

smith and a miniaturist, a man "of all work, all ideas," West, recalled his contemporary Samuel McCullough, "could make a watch or a clock, or he could mend one. He could make a rifle or a gun, or he could mend one, within my recollection he could make or mend anything."[3] Two of West's sons, John Brown and William Edward, began to paint miniatures at an early age. William Edward West would go on to become one of the most famous American portraitists of the nineteenth century, even as his father nurtured several younger portrait artists in his hometown.

There was a very notable arrival in 1806, when the English landscape artist George Beck arrived and advertised in the *Kentucky Gazette* as a portrait painter.[4] Though no likenesses by him have been found, an important landscape painting of the iron furnace at Owingsville is extant. Beck, an instructor at Transylvania, also translated classic Greek and Roman poetry, which he published in the *Kentucky Gazette* of October 27 and November 3, 1806. His wife, Mary, listed as a miniaturist, is better known for having taught young ladies drawing classes in Lexington.

Another early artist, who left a dastardly legacy, was Samuel Dearborn, often said to have been the first practicing portraitist west of the mountains.[5] A native of Boston, he worked in Pittsburgh as early as 1804 and appeared in Lexington by 1809. Though somewhat competent in oil, he more energetically pursued profile painting in watercolor. Advertising his services in the *Kentucky Gazette* of May 1, 1809, he encouraged those who wish to have their portraits painted "to apply soon": "The low price which he asks for his small likenesses on paper is expected to induce many to substitute them for blank profiles [a reference to the art of the silhouette]."

Dearborn subsequently went to Frankfort, where he was involved in a violent episode evolving from a sharp rebuke on his landlady's housekeeping by a fellow boarder, Isaac Robertson, an up-and-coming bureaucrat in the government of the commonwealth. According to Love family accounts, Dearborn, on April 17, 1811, "having secured a dirk, made a cowardly attack upon Mr. Robertson, while he was seated in the garden . . . surrounded by his little children and entirely unarmed, and stabbed him savagely."[6] Later that day Robertson died. After the murder, Dearborn escaped jail and disappeared from Kentucky. Finding his way back to Boston, he changed his name to Nathaniel and produced some engraved "views of little merit."[7] He died in 1852, having gotten away with murder, but also having left behind a handful of the earliest documented profile portraits in Kentucky.

By 1808, Matthew Harris Jouett, who would become the most legendary portraitist in the history of Kentucky, had begun to paint, following some instruction from George Beck. His father, Jack Jouett, had intended him for the law. "I sent Matthew to college to make a gentleman out him," he once said, "and he has turned out to be nothing but a damned sign painter."[8] During the War of 1812, Matthew Jouett enlisted in the Third Mounted Regiment of Kentucky Volunteers, rising to the rank of captain. After the war, in 1815, he returned to Lexington and determined to become a portrait artist, in part to repay a debt of some $6,000 he assumed when a packet of pay vouchers in his possession went missing after the Battle of the River Raisin.

Jouett had shown a precocious ability to draw, especially likenesses of his fellow officers. When his initial efforts proved successful in the Lexington area, he decided to obtain further training. William Edward West, his exact contemporary, was already making a name for himself on an itinerant track from Kentucky to New Orleans, by way of Natchez, having spent some time with Thomas Sully in Philadelphia. According to family legend, Jouett set out for Philadelphia in search of the "sons of Edward West," but, when unsuccessful in finding them, he continued to Boston, where he encountered Gilbert Stuart.[9]

Renowned as the life portraitist of George Washington and other figures of the Revolution and the young republic, Stuart had settled in Boston after fleeing debts in England and Ireland. When the cantankerous, and often rude Stuart met Jouett, he told him to get at it "quickly too for I have no time to chat, Kentucky boat man."[10] Stuart always referred to Jouett as "Kentucky," in tribute to the younger artist's abilities as a raconteur, a trait for which Kentuckians of the period were much celebrated.

Jouett kept notes on his encounter with Stuart. "Rude hints & observations, from repeated Conversations with Gilbert Stuart, Esqr. In the months of July, August, September, & Oct. 1816 under whose patronage and care I was for the time" is a unique document, a much cherished, firsthand account by an impressionable student working with an established master. The young artist admired Stuart as someone with a "singular facility in conversation and powers of illustration" and indicated that he would not defame him by anything except direct quotation. Accordingly: "I hereby so acknowledge that but in two pages have I given his words."[11] It is a rambling account, punctuated with local color, and highly charged with an apprentice's deep belief in his master's ability. The remarks may be considered as offering hints on three levels: the construction and composition of a portrait beginning with the placement of the head on the picture plane, the coloration of the facial features and subsequent anatomical and background detail, and, finally, suggestions on how best to capture the character of the sitter.

Stuart informs Jouett: "There are three grand stages in a head as in an argument or plot of any sort: a beginning, middle & end: and to arrive at each of these perfect stages should be the aim of any painter." He was not a practitioner of creating a sketch in chalk or pencil on the canvas and then rendering a colored image. "In his portraits" Jouett saw "all spirited drawing & yet no outline." Instead, Stuart worked *alla prima*, directly from brush to palette to canvas, as he considered drawing "the features distinctly & carefully with chalk loss of time. All studies to be made with brush in hand. Nonsense to think of perfecting oneself in drawing before one begins to paint: When the hand is not able to execute the decisions of the mind in some shape a fastidiousness ensues, and on the heels of that disappointment & disgust . . . preserve as far as practicable the round blunt stroke in preference to the winding flirting wisping manner."

Stuart's disdain for concentric lines and the mannerist parallelisms essential to atmospheric depth and perspective are often repeated. "Avoid by all means, parallel lines whether they be parallel straight or parallel curved" for the "eye ought to be accustomed to distances & directions from point to point. More important, to give a prominent admeasurement of distances than a set of mincing curves." Color, not repetitious geometry, is the key to establishing character. "To give great perspective, give great gloom to the foreground," he advises Jouett. Deep, warm flesh tones, which Jouett constantly refers to as "peach," often characterize Stuart's painting. The older artist thought flesh "like no other substance under heaven. It has all the gaiety of a silk mercers shop without the gaudiness or glare and all the soberness of old mahogany without its deadness or sadness." An atmospheric evocation of the sitter and not a stultifying exactitude was what made a portrait great: "The true and perfect image of man is to be seen only in a misty or hazy atmosphere."

Unlike his English contemporaries, especially Thomas Gainsborough, Stuart did not believe in florid, flattering facial coloration: "Equal color upon equal surfaces produce equal effects. That in the commencement of all portraits the first idea is an indistinct mass of light & shadows, or the character of the person as seen in the heel of the evening in the gray of the morning, or at a distance too great to discriminate features with exactness. That in every object there is one light, one shadow & one reflection, and that tis from a judicious entering into & departing from either of them that mark the harmony of a painting."

Martha Scott Bibb (1815–1825), by Matthew Harris Jouett, ca.
1820, oil on canvas, 27½ × 22½ inches. (Filson Historical Society,
1995.13.1.)

Jouett faithfully records the layout of Stuart's palette and makes a
drawing of the artist's board. But, in reviewing both artists' work, it seems
as though the best advice Stuart offered to Jouett concerned the final
touches: "Always use spirits of turpentine in your white drapery. It assists
to evaporate the oil & leaves the white a standing white, & free from the
yellowness occasioned by the oil." This practice Jouett bought to Kentucky, giving many of his works a brilliantly delicate quality heightened

by the painterly presence of a floating piece of lace or a frothy jabot. It is this "standing white" that distinguishes his finest portraits in the period 1815–1825.

As to character, Stuart advised: "Consult truth rather than fancy; & without reason to systematize & control the fervor of the imagination." That done, "our paintings will be like our dreams when they come to be examined coolly & philosophically—fancy without reason & good taste like declamation without sense, or a fine voice and good words & fine gestures without common reason or common arrangement." Never intimidated by a sitter, Stuart advised Jouett to be "decisive in your drawing, seize with firmness your idea and put it down with vigor," disdaining the "folly of attending too closely to the mere mechanical processes of the art." If this is the goal, then "the person should be so portrayed as to be read like the Bible without notes."

Having some sense that Jouett would return to Kentucky and make his living as a painter of head and shoulder works intended for the home, Stuart warns against "too much attention to background detail" as it "detracts from the establishment of a firm character . . . all background material should serve the purpose of dating . . . etc." Character derives from close observation, from an awareness of the individual's place in the natural world: "The great danger of a man becoming a mannerist from a too little care to the studies of nature. A blind adherence to any one man's style calculated to fetter the mind & the hand." An artist must learn to look: "In all nature whether of animate or inanimate there is abundance of character. Or why expands the soul at the sight of old trees & rocks swept over by the raging flood. One should never design his picture other than his imagination approves. It often happens that an attitude singularly *necessary & proper* is sacrificed to one that is more easy to the hand. No man can meet his fancy, but tis a good rule not [to] be contented to treat a subject but as it deserves."

Giving a sitter, especially a sitter of note, a proper sense of character depends on the placement on the picture plane. Concerning this, Jouett offers a *"reflection of mine:* In painting great public characters be sure to have them elevated above you—this opens the countenance & gives a grandeur to the figure Another advantage in having your sitters elevated when the pictures are hung[:] the same view seems to be had of them, that is by giving an elevation to the sitter you suit the picture to the height in hanging, and the perspective is agreeable. I thus note them that I may not forget to think and act for myself." Stuart's portraits and the compositional format Jouett derived from them have a strong frontality, which places the sitter high on the canvas, close to the picture plane, and in a pose directed to engage the viewer. In attitude, they reflect the forthright manner of the neoclassic age, the age of reason, the age when the individual rights of man were being affirmed. Stuart was not disposed to flattery, nor was Jouett.

Matthew Harris Jouett returned to Lexington and became the most successful portraitist in the commonwealth, much in demand, and highly productive. He painted many of the most important political and social figures of the day, including Henry Clay, Governor Isaac Shelby, and various members of the Crittenden, Todd, Breckinridge, and Brown families. Many of his adult subjects project an alert sense of the moment in which they have paused to meet the artist's gaze. Later art historians have also admired his images of children, who seem to be both innocent and quietly aware of the artist's presence. In what proved to be the last decade of his life, Jouett also nurtured a group of artists who had settled in Lexington and emulated his affection for the Stuart style, depicting their subjects in what the Philadelphia artist John Neagle called "spoon fashion."[12] Joseph Henry Bush, Asa Park, Alexander Bradford, John Grimes, Louis Morgan, and the younger artist Oliver Frazer were all legatees of his stylistic formulations. Given certain similarities of detail in their approach to compositional format and coloration, they may deserve to be called the Kentucky school. That school may be characterized by the high placement of the sitter, the absence of background features, and a high-gloss attention to costume detail.

Jouett came down with "bilous fever" in the late summer of 1827 and died, not quite forty, just one year before his old master, Gilbert Stuart, died in Boston. A later biographer would describe Jouett as having "conquered the Bluegrass."[13] His obituary notice in the *Lexington Reporter* of August 17, 1827, reported him as "an artist of rare genius and of considerable celebrity. As a father, husband, friend, and citizen his death is deeply lamented, for in all these relations he occupied an elevated and enviable station in our society." Doubtless, his celebrated abilities as a raconteur entertained his numerous sitters to the last.

By that time, William Edward West had been absent from Lexington for seven years and was not to return again, except for brief visits to his family. Yet his life and exploits generated an oral history expounding the heights to which a local limner could aspire. Having charmed sitters on his itinerancy from Philadelphia to Lexington to New Orleans, he departed for Italy in 1820 in order to study at the Florence Academy. Like Jouett, West was also called "Kentucky" for his ability to regale an audience with

George Noel Gordon, sixth Lord Byron (1788–1824), by William Edward West, ca. 1830, oil on canvas, 30 × 25 inches, variant of the original portrait of 1822. (Bluegrass Trust for Historic Preservation, John Hunt Morgan House, Lexington, on extended loan from the National Trust for Historic Preservation.)

the saga of a sitting. And, like Jouett, he left behind a firsthand account of his encounter with one of the defining figures of his age. Nothing he ever did gained him greater notoriety than his encounter with Lord Byron in 1822. According to West, George K. Bruen of New York approached him to paint the romantic poet for the American Academy.[14] West created a dewy-eyed image of Byron, curly head held high, reaching forth from the planar field with a gently curving hand that demonstrated the skills in flesh tones the artist had recently acquired.

Considering subsequent events, the encounter with Byron was indeed fateful. It turned out to be Byron's last life sitting, and it occurred near the time his fellow English romantic poet Percy Shelley drowned while visiting him. Byron left Italy for Greece, where he would die in 1824. West moved on to Paris and London with the portrait, which he used as a calling card to gain access to wealthy sitters. The Byronic image became part of West's European baggage; he kept the picture for the rest of his life, making copies at times to keep his creditors at bay. One of those variants is on display at the Hunt Morgan House on Gratz Park in Lexington, placed there in an effort to ensure that the artist's masterpiece remains on display in his native city.

Joseph Henry Bush came to the attention of Jouett in 1814, and, with the financial aid of Henry Clay, he journeyed to Philadelphia for study with Thomas Sully, remaining in that city until 1817. After Stuart's death, Sully, and his vividly romantic style, became the benchmark for American portraiture. Bush was his principal legatee in Kentucky, especially seen in the charming portraits he painted of his family in Lexington. Sully's brief *Hints to Young Painters*, though spare, offered a counterpoint to Stuart's instructions. He writes of the importance of acquiring "the power to draw from memory the human figure in any position. This being attained, painting will be easily acquired; without this power, the painter will be frequently perplexed and liable to error. A knowledge of perspective is requisite." Sully deemed this knowledge essential to the process of grasping the character of the subject and rendering that subject sympathetically with a technical accuracy that begins at the time of the first sitting: "When the person calls on you to make arrangements for the intended portrait, observe the general manner, etc., so that you may determine the attitude you had best adopt."[15]

Comparing and contrasting the recorded remarks of Sully and Stuart give insight into the stylistic shift that was then transforming American portraiture from the forthright perspective of the young republic into the romantic expressionism of a rapidly expanding nation, increasingly obsessed with heroic individualism. Stuart prompted Jouett to paint from nature, observing character as he went. Sully advised adopting attitudes. Stuart had little interest in flattering his subjects, while Sully's reputation as a portraitist comes from doing just that, albeit with a masterful warmth of color and painterly detail. Though perhaps simplistic, these stylistic concerns offer two dialectics of taste, manifest in the emerging careers of Bush and his slightly younger Lexington contemporary Oliver Frazer.

While in Philadelphia, Bush wrote to Clay that he was "engag[e]d in painting some large pictures to exhibit in the western County which, I am induced to believe will pay very well" as they had been "very highly complimented by Mr. Sully."[16] On his return to Lexington, he exhibited two works in Jouett's gallery, located in a building owned by Henry Clay and formerly known as the Kentucky Hotel, across from the Fayette County Courthouse on Short Street. The *Kentucky Gazette* of July 10, 1818, called the attention of the "lovers of fine arts and the friends of native genius" to the "exhibition of two pictures by a Kentucky artist . . . the one a Virgin Mary with the infants Christ and St. John, the other a Sleeping Venus *as large as life*." Any doubt about taste in the Athens of the West can be assuaged by the assurance that "these pictures are eminently worthy of the examination of the most refined and critical connoisseurs." The painting of Mary and the infants was a copy of Raphael's *Madonna of the Chair* in the Uffizi Gallery, while the nude is possibly Titian's famous *Venus of Urbino*. The Raphael copy survives in family hands, and, while the fate of the life-size nude is unknown, it could well have found its way to a place of honor over the bar of a local watering hole, from whence it slipped into oblivion. The *Gazette* notice highly recommends Bush to the "patronage and liberality of the community" in the hope that he might "persevere in his studies with more vigor in distant schools" in order to "confer honor upon his native state." After this date, Bush moved to Louisville—perhaps in acknowledgment of Jouett's ascendancy—where he enjoyed the patronage of the William and George Rogers Clark family.

Asa Park had also worked in Boston with Gilbert Stuart. A native of Massachusetts, he appeared in Lexington in 1816, as documented by an announcement in the November 10, 1816, *Lexington Reporter* that he "has taken a room on the corner of Main and Limestone Streets" and "flatters himself [that] by giving satisfaction, which he feels confident of doing, he may not suffer the want of encouragement." He also declares that he "is from Boston under the patronage of the celebrated Stuart and Penniman," which means that he was almost certainly there at the same time as Jouett, an intriguing coincidence perpetuating a Boston-Lexington aesthetic relation.

John Ritto Penniman's activities in Boston during the first quarter of the nineteenth century assured his reputation as one of the most "inventive . . . and versatile ornamental painters" of the era.[17] Though well regarded as a portraitist, he had an ability to create popular panoramas and history paintings, especially his monumental depiction of the conflagration of the Boston Exchange coffeehouse in 1819. From Penniman, Park could have learned the skills required to produce clear semiotic images, broadly outlined, and cast with a visual immediacy that drew even the least-discerning eye. Park's advertisement of his services as a sign painter, as well as a portraitist, documents the need experienced by many early portrait painters to rely on their abilities as decorative painters to pay the bills between commissions.

As a portraitist, Penniman was a classic New England plain painter, an artist whose concern with accuracy resulted in a proto–photographic realism dependent on a highly linear approach to facial modeling and contouring. It may have been from Penniman or Stuart that Park learned the technique of placing the subject high on the planar field, usually in the upper-left or -right quadrant, and very forward toward the picture plane. Penniman's portrait of Henry Nolen (Worcester, Massachusetts, Museum of Art) offers an interesting comparison to Park's work as both have a boldness of anatomical detail and a flat, vivid coloration that has more in common with sign painting than with high art portraiture.

As Park is not thought to have appeared in Lexington until the autumn of 1816, he could have met Jouett in Boston during those months. Jouett was known to have bragged that there was good money to be made painting portraits in Kentucky, where the demand for representation far exceeded the pool of talent. Perhaps the acquaintance and the opportunity inspired the move west, although Park's discreet connections in the Order of Free Masons may also have been at play. Park's few known works exhibit the same ability to create a "standing white" in the delicate quality of a floating piece of white lace or a frothy white jabot as may be seen in Jouett. Indeed, so similar are some of the works by these artists that misattribution of autograph may have occurred in amateur record keeping, a circumstance further compounded by Jouett's enormous popularity during the colonial revival era of the late nineteenth century.

Yet Park's portraits differ from those works of Jouett in two very distinct ways. Park's subjects are cast in an attenuated anatomical format, separated by a large space between the arm/shoulder and the edge of the planar field. Jouett's subjects occupy the entire planar field in more careful proportions top to bottom and left to right. Furthermore, Jouett's sitters invariably engage the viewer with their eyes. Park's sitters have rather glassy eyes and seem to be gazing at a distant object off right rather than at the viewer, a convention more in keeping with the semiotics of a well-versed sign painter than with an insightful portraitist striving to be true to Stuart's teachings on character and equal placement of light and shadow.

Park's masterpiece, the full-length portrait of George Washington, also gives signs of a versatile and inventive ornamental artist, even as it asks several demanding questions.[18] To create his monumental portrait in the American grand manner, Park may well have used several existing print sources for the composition and facial likeness. The most obvious source is Stuart's iconic "Lansdowne" Washington, engraved by James Heath in England in 1800, and widely distributed in the United States. In this work, the president is to be seen full length, his right arm extended in a gesture of friendship, his left held down by his side, sword in hand, his legs slightly turned from the planar field, and his knees bent in counterpoint to the picture plane. Not only does Park echo this pose, but Washington's open field jacket, buttoned waistcoat, and frilled jabot are all reminiscent of Stuart's work. Park alters Washington's civilian attire as seen in Stuart to a fanciful military uniform, which may have been partially inspired by the prints after works by John Trumbull and Charles Wilson Peale. Ironically, the uniform's coloration is almost exactly that of the Windsor uniform in buff and blue designed by King George III for himself and his minions.

The print by Thomas Chessman after Trumbull's *Washington at Trenton* may account for the pronounced epaulettes as well as the equine imagery of Washington holding a horse by the reins. Park's horse has a most docile and servile gaze, rather like that of an allegorical white beast preparing to ride on in majesty. The stance of the horse does echo poses in Van Dyck portraits of King Charles I (H.M. the Queen, the Royal Collection) and in an imaginative historical painting, *Washington at the Passage of the Delaware* (Museum of Fine Arts, Boston), painted by Thomas Sully and engraved by John Doggett in 1825.

While in Lexington, Park became closely associated with the family of the inventor/silversmith Edward West (also a Mason), the father of William Edward, then working in the Deep South. He made several trips to other central Kentucky towns, including Danville. Park seems to have left Lexington for Cincinnati in 1820 but is again noted in Lexington in 1825. For Lafayette's visit that year, he made a large transparency of an eagle rampant, which hung in a prominent archway between the dancing and banqueting halls of the Grand Masonic Lodge. Newspaper accounts indicate that he closed his studio there on April 1, 1826, and died the following year.

George Washington (1732–1799), by Asa Park (1790–1827), oil on canvas, 84 × 60 inches, ca. 1825. (Georgetown College, Georgetown, Kentucky.)

Levi Prewitt (1799–1880), by Alexander Bradford (1791–1827), 1825, oil on canvas, 32 × 27 inches. (Collection of Robert Kirkpatrick, Millersburg, Kentucky.)

Alexander Bradford was a member of an accomplished family that settled in central Kentucky in the late eighteenth century. His kinsman John Bradford operated the first printing press in Kentucky. Little is known of his career except for one remarkable commission. Martha Chandler Prewitt, a widow living on the Walnut Hill road near the Clark/Fayette border, hired him to paint her entire family in 1825, following the death of her husband, of whom she had no likeness. Bradford was to paint her eight sons, a daughter, two daughters-in-law, and herself. He spent an entire year on the project, in residence with Mrs. Prewitt.

Anna Barrow (1808–1864), by John Grimes (1799–1837), nineteenth century, oil on canvas, 23½ × 21 inches. (Collection of the Speed Museum, Louisville, 1942.1.37.)

These portraits have a bold frontality and strong modeling reminiscent of A. H. Corwine, whom Bradford may have encountered in Cincinnati. His work has also been mistakenly identified as being by Jouett. Edna Talbott Whitley made the observation that, "because he was but three years younger than Jouett," Bradford "is not apt to have been his pupil." "Since they lived but a few miles apart and their life spans correspond so closely, it is probable that their work has been somewhat confused."[19] Bradford also died in 1827.

John Grimes, often written of as a waif who just appeared in Lexington in the early 1820s, was more likely to have been from a Dayton family, and, while losing both his parents at an early age, he does seem to have retained a connection with their siblings. When he arrived in Lexington in the early 1820s, he came to the attention of Thomas Grant, the proprietor of a paint and tobacco shop on Cheapside in Lexington, who gave him a job and became a foster father to him. Grimes met Jouett in that shop. Jouett was so impressed by the young man's talent at drawing that he took him on as a student.[20]

Grimes assisted Jouett in an ambitious project to paint a monumental *Three Marys* (archdiocese of Louisville) after A. Carracci. After Jouett's death, Grimes moved to Nashville, Tennessee, where he secured the patronage of Felix Grundy, the local congressman who had also served on the Kentucky Supreme Court. He developed tuberculosis around 1835 and returned to Lexington to die in the home of his adoptive family, the Thomas Grants, in 1837.

Astonishingly, in the space of three years, 1827–1830, the Kentucky school was dispersed. Jouett, Park, and Bradford died. Like Jouett, Joseph Henry Bush pursued a seasonal itinerancy in the Deep South but after 1830 was identified as Louisville's resident portraitist. Between 1828, when Oliver Frazer departed for study in Philadelphia, and 1834, when he returned from study in France, there was no resident portrait artist in the city. Central Kentucky never again had a native school of resident portrait artists who attracted the same attention as Jouett's generation, and, after 1834, the field was left entirely to Frazer and several notable itinerants of national reputation drawn to Lexington by the prominence of Henry Clay.

Oliver Frazer was the first Kentucky artist to study abroad. Both Frazer's father and his paternal uncle were successful silversmiths, first in Paris, Kentucky, and then in Lexington. After his father's early death, the young Frazer received sufficient support from his uncle to enable him to pursue a career in art. Following some study with Jouett, he made the obligatory trip to Philadelphia to study with Thomas Sully, in 1828, but found little joy in the City of Brotherly Love. "The people are much more selfish than with us; if you lived here three months you would see the difference between this place and Kentucky; selfishness is handed down from father to son," he wrote home.[21] His frequent lament that he was not allowed to draw from life indicates a romantic affection for the real thing, as opposed to classical statuary.

Opinions, and strong ones, were always one of Frazer's noted personality traits. While in Philadelphia, he saw the work of Washington Allston, which "fell short of my expectations," even as they "looked like life in comparison" to early portraits by Benjamin West. Prior to departing for Europe, he did pay one last homage to early American portraiture by copying Stuart's full-length portrait of Washington for the Kentucky capitol building, assisted by William S. Shackelford. In May 1834, he sailed for France. On his arrival in Paris, he sought instruction in the ateliers of Baron Gros and Thomas Couture and made the acquaintance of the young artists G. P. A. Healey and James De Veaux, who would become a resident portraitist in Charleston, South Carolina. While professing no great affection for French portraiture in the neoclassic taste, he did admire the realism of Horace Vernet's battle paintings at the palace of Versailles. He was so moved that he "could scarcely persuade myself that I did not see a real battle."[22]

While in Europe, Frazer visited museums and galleries in France, Switzerland, Belgium, Germany, and England. Through the auspices of Charles Robert Leslie, the American history painter, he drew copies of Old Master works in English collections. Rembrandt, Titian, and Van Dyck were his noted favorites. His copy of a Titian Madonna and child, commissioned by Richard Higgins of Lexington, still hangs in the parish hall of Christ Church Cathedral.

On his return to Kentucky in 1838, Frazer established a studio in Lexington and became the last permanent resident portraitist in the Kentucky tradition. He also married Martha Bell Mitchell, Margaret Allen Jouett's niece, in that same year.

Well connected, he was soon receiving multiple commissions from the political and social establishment of the Inner Bluegrass. He became the house favorite of the Henry Clay family, painting several portraits of the famous politician. In later years, the artist's eyesight began to fail, with the result that some of the works from the period have a slightly dim, murky appearance, giving them a vague, romantic cast.

Henry Clay's presidential aspirations attracted the last group of noted portrait painters to Lexington during the antebellum period. While president, Andrew Jackson had opposed a national banking system, ignored or defied Supreme Court decisions, and vetoed congressional legislation. His opposition to public works projects particularly irked Clay, long a champion of the "American System," which promoted internal improvements to the national system of roads, canals, railroads, and harbors to better travel and trade routes and increase the general prosperity. The

Martha Bell Mitchell (1816–1903) with Fanny Frazer (1846–1878) and Nancy Oliver Frazer (1848–1917), by Oliver Frazer (1808–1864), 1849, oil on canvas, 27½ × 22 inches. (Collection of Mack and Sharon Cox, Richmond, Kentucky.)

new Whig Party formalized that opposition to Jackson's policies, and Clay led it. In late 1839, the financial crises plaguing Martin Van Buren's administration prompted Clay to seek the Whig Party nomination for the presidency. Whig policies were particularly important to the western movement springing from Kentucky and the Ohio River valley. But Clay lost the 1840 nomination to William Henry Harrison, whose early death put John Tyler into office. Tyler proved to be no more receptive to Clay's policies than previous administrations, prompting Clay to make one of his periodic retirements to his home, Ashland, in Lexington. By 1842, he was again ready to run and plotting his strategy, which this time involved one of the first makeovers in American political history. A series of portraits painted in the 1840s redefined Clay's image, elevating him from the common fray, and turning him into the "sage of Ashland," an eminently electable presidential candidate. The first, and most successful, of those efforts came about in 1842 when the Whigs of Philadelphia commissioned John Neagle to paint a full-length portrait of him.

Neagle, who had visited Kentucky twenty years earlier, journeyed to Lexington in 1842, staying at Ashland for several months, making sketches for the work. Completed in 1843, the full-length portrait is one of the most celebrated American works in the grand manner. Clay, immaculate in black suit and tie, stands erect, head turned slightly left, while his hands graciously gesture down right toward a globe swathed in the folds of the stars and stripes. On that globe we see Latin America, a reference to Clay's interest in the emerging new nations in the Western Hemisphere. Foreground details include an anvil and a shuttle, industry's tools. In the background, a cow and a plow stand on a shore beyond which a distant sailing ship recedes. The "harmonious juxtaposition" of these symbolic elements of Whig prosperity is "meant to suggest a state of peaceful, productive economic cooperation."[23] An allegory well received, the portrait enjoyed success in Kentucky and elsewhere. When John Sartain engraved it in 1843, it became the best-known image of Clay as the election of 1844 loomed. The *Frankfort Commonwealth* of June 6, 1843, called it "a complete masterpiece, a most perfect likeness, embodying, with the highest and most truthful effect in the full action and animation of debate, the dignity and majesty of the intellectual greatness of the subject."

Far from grand, but just as critical to the image change, the Nashville miniaturist John Wood Dodge created a "portrait in small" of Clay, an allegorically intimate rendition in the genteel tradition. Dodge visited Lexington in 1843 and painted Clay seated beneath a tree at Ashland, a favorite dog at his feet, and a placid idyllic landscape in the background. Dodge, a miniaturist noted for detail and vivid coloration, likely intended his work to be the prototype for an engraving. One, issued by H. S. Sadd in 1843, "formed a substantial contribution to the campaign" that "promoted the image of Clay as the 'Sage of Ashland.'"[24]

Although Clay successfully pursued the Whig nomination for president in 1844, these works of art in print form did not redeem his image sufficiently enough to secure him the highest office in the land. Yet once again, he lost the presidency. But even in defeat he remained a figure of national importance and continued to be sought out by ambitious portrait artists as a sitter. In 1845, G. P. A. Healy, a portraitist with a marked flair for the dramatic, happened to be in a highly historic position: he went to Ashland in June to paint Clay, having just left the deathbed of Clay's great nemesis Andrew Jackson. As told by Healy, after their last encounter, the artist, having accomplished all he could do in this final sitting, prepared to take Jackson's leave. Yet, according to Healy's *Reminiscences*, old Hickory asked him to stay: "Please come in. I wish it." And so Healey was there to hear the last words: "Why do you weep for me? I am in the hands of the Lord, who is about to release me. You should rejoice that my sufferings are at an end." With this news, Healy arrived at Ashland, where he found that the "contrast was great in every respect. Instead of tears, suffering, of death, I found happiness, luxury and joyous life."[25] Healy had been commissioned by King Louis Philippe of France to paint a series of portraits of famous American men for the palace of Versailles, as Clay knew. The painter's report of the encounter portrays a sitter far more rustic than the wise sage of the previous years. The worn look Clay wears may have been the result of his tweaking Healy, saying: "You are an indifferent courtier; though you come to us from the French King's presence, you have not spoken to me of my livestock. Don't you know that I am prouder of my cows and sheep than of my best speeches?"[26]

Implicit in Healy's jovial account is an undercurrent of unease between the two men. Clay challenged Healey on the integrity of Andrew Jackson's faith, and Healey replied: "[If] General Jackson was not sincere, then I do not know the meaning of the word." The Great Compromiser also exasperated the portraitist by constantly interrupting sittings for meetings with political cronies who dropped by. But Healey was complimentary about the hospitality, remarking on seeing his first minstrel show, and flattering Mrs. Clay about her hospitality and ability to keep her husband's legendary temper at bay. The portrait proved to be a standard head-and-shoulders type. Though the two men parted in peace, Clay had little further interest in sitting for Healy. When the artist visited Washington in later years, he sent a card in to Clay's office, only to hear him exclaim, "What! Another?" seemingly unaware that Healey was within earshot. But, on Healey's entering, Clay playfully remarked: "I thought you were with the King!" So ended the encounter from which one critic

Henry Clay (1777–1852), by George Peter Alexander Healy (1813–1894), 1845, oil on canvas, 30 × 25 inches. (National Portrait Gallery, Smithsonian Institution, Washington, DC, NPG.65.44.)

said that Healey "had made of Jackson an old lion" and of Clay "an old fox."[27]

The 1850s saw the rise of photography as an alternative, and radically different, form of taking a likeness. By 1852, James Mullen had established a photographic studio in Lexington to which numbers of the local citizenry would flock to have a much less expensive memorial image made. The day of the flourishing local portrait painter had ended, leaving behind a body of work that subsequent generations of antiquarians converted from "reasonable likenesses" to iconic material culture venerated

as the focal point for ancestral worship of the pioneer generation, implying documentary proof of an inherent social order. This has caused much
confusion in recent times about the value of portraiture.

In certain circles, there has always been a disparaging view of portraiture as a fashion-driven, ephemeral, or applied branch of the arts whose
subservience to taste seemingly limits the genius of application. Such observers see portraits as commodities rather than as objects with an aesthetic value informed by the climate of taste in which they were created.
For some, art historical interest in an object can have the effect of elevating a portrait to the position of a historical document. Portraits are not
historical documents, nor are they photographs; they are *representations* of
someone who once was.

How, then, can we adjust the lens through which we might now be
able to *see* these objects as products of messengers of style, mindful of the
metaphoric construct we invoke when we speak of the Athens of the West.
Ancient Athens was both a locale and a crossroads, an urban culture where
Plato's philosophy of inherency jousted with Aristotle's phenomenologi-
cal observations, where country met city in the marketplace, and, most
importantly, where vastly different ideologies swirled in the individual
stoas of the larger agora. Antebellum Lexington was also alive with ideas,
especially among the community of portrait artists who varied in talent,
training, and impact.

Jouett and Frazer studied with master artists with international reputations. Both those artists returned to Lexington with abilities that far
exceed the limitations of the condescending contemporary label *regional
artist*. Nor should the works of the lesser-known painters Park, Bradford,
and Grimes be held hostage to some ongoing cultural reconstruction that
views a national body of art from a rigidly northeastern point of view. It
should be recalled that this body of material culture reflects the complex
relationship between sitter and subject, ill served by current revisionist
notions of portraits as luxury items, in the parlance of a recent commentator on Jouett's work.[28] Luxury is in the eye of the beholder, and, by
their lights, the "desire of the pioneers to be reproduced on a flat surface,
whether from vanity or not, was natural then as now, and for its gratification they would then as now make personal sacrifices."[29] Portraiture is at
once memorial and mimetic, an artifact "understood to act as a bridge
between the mental and physical worlds, between past and present."[30]

As limners illuminate, this account of these varied artists' activities in
Lexington sheds light on the particular distinction of place and the tender
concerns of its inhabitants. For while "death may deprive us of a beloved

associate or a dear friend . . . the painter cheats, in some measure, the fell destroyer" and preserves "a perfect presentment of those whom, living we so fondly loved, and whose memories, in death we so dearly cherish."[31]

Notes

1. John D. Wright Jr., "Lexington," in *The Kentucky Encyclopedia*, ed. John E. Kleber (Lexington, 1992), 549.

2. Samuel Woodson Price, *Old Masters of the Bluegrass* (Louisville, 1902), 4.

3. Marion Mulligan Ross, "Story of West, Painter," *Lexington Leader*, May 1, 1921, Sunday supplement.

4. Edna Talbott Whitley, *Kentucky Ante-Bellum Portraiture* (n.p., [1956]), 629.

5. William Dunlap, *History of the Rise and Progress of the Arts of Design in the United States* (New York, 1969), 226.

6. Curatorial Files: Samuel Dearborn, Filson Historical Society, Louisville.

7. Dunlap, *Arts of Design*, 227.

8. William Barrow Floyd, *Jouett-Bush-Frazer: Early Kentucky Artists* (Lexington, 1968), 4.

9. Whitley, *Kentucky Ante-Bellum Portraiture*, 703.

10. John Hill Morgan, *Gilbert Stuart and His Pupils* (New York, 1939), 55.

11. The text taken for Jouett's account of painting with Stuart is from Floyd, *Jouett-Bush-Frazer*, 169. In an oral history interview conducted by the author on June 27, 1981, Floyd stated that he had personal knowledge of the manuscript, at one time in the possession of the family, with whose current generation he had contact, but that it was lost. This manuscript is one of the great missing treasures of primary material in American art studies, its actual fate a subject of considerable speculation. Here is the most likely scenario: it is first reported to exist by Charles Henry Hart in a series of articles he published on Jouett in *Harper's* magazine in May 1899. Hart had been in contact with Richard Jouett Menefee, the keeper of his grandfather's heritage, to secure a Jouett work of the Chicago World's Fair in 1893 and, by oral history, is reported to have lent Hart several documents at that time that were not returned after Menefee's death in that same year. It is next reported to have been in the possession of John Hill Morgan of New York, who published it as an appendix to his *Gilbert Stuart and His Pupils*. Morgan states that Hart bought the manuscript from Mrs. Richard H. Menefee, the artist's daughter (which is open to question, considering the veneration with which she and her son held the portraitist), and that Hart's widow sold it to the collector Harry MacNeil Bland of New York. Bland allowed Morgan access to the manuscript. There is reference to a typescript in the Frick Art Reference Library.

12. John Neagle, November 15, 1842, Filson Historical Society.

13. E. A. Jonas, *Matthew Harris Jouett, Kentucky Portrait Painter (1787–1827)* (Louisville, 1938), 69.

14. Estill Curtis Pennington, *William Edward West, Kentucky Painter* (Washington, DC, 1985), 17.

15. Thomas Sully, *Hints to Young Painters* (New York, 1965), 6.

16. James Hopkins et al., eds., *Papers of Henry Clay*, 10 vols. and suppl. (Lexington, 1959–1992), 1:359–60.

17. Dunlap, *Arts of Design*, 215.

18. See Estill Curtis Pennington, "The Larger World of Asa Park, Portrait Painter," in *A Boston Painter in Kentucky, Asa Park (1796–1827)* (Georgetown, KY, 2006). Questions concerning the portrait center on when was it painted. It is currently dated ca. 1815. If painted before 1817, it would have had to have been painted in Boston and brought to Kentucky, which, considering the stress of travel, seems unlikely. Could it have been painted in the spring of 1825, as part of the preparations for decorating the Grand Masonic Lodge in Lexington for the visit of the Marquis de Lafayette in May of that year for which Park is known to have been the artist? John Penniman, a Mason, introduced Park to the Rite. Lafayette was made a Mason by George Washington, the Grand Master Mason of America. Many of the leading political and military figures of the day in Kentucky were Masons, including members of the Clay, Breckinridge, Howard, and Ward families. What better tribute could be placed in a Masonic hall than a portrait of its greatest American hero, the father of his country, by a Free Mason?

19. Whitley, *Kentucky Ante-Bellum Portraiture*, 634.

20. Price, *Old Masters*, 111.

21. Oliver Frazer to James Frazer, Philadelphia, June 1828, Frazer, Redd and Whitcomb Papers, University of Kentucky Special Collections.

22. Quoted in Floyd, *Jouett-Bush-Frazer*, 132.

23. Robert Torchia, *John Neagle, Philadelphia Portrait Painter* (Philadelphia, 1989), 60.

24. Clifford Amyx, "The Painters of Henry Clay as 'the Sage of Ashland,'" *Kentucky Review*, Spring 1988, 73.

25. George Peter Alexander Healy, *Reminiscences of a Portrait Painter* (New York, 1970), 146.

26. Ibid.

27. Shearer West, *Portraiture* (London, 2004), 53.

28. Scott Erbus, "Portrait of Asa Blanchard," in *Highlights from the Permanent Collection* (Louisville, 2007), 115.

29. Price, *Old Masters*, 3.

30. Marcia Pointon, *Hanging the Head: Portraiture and Social Formation in Eighteenth-Century England* (New Haven, CT, 1993), 237.

31. *New Orleans Times-Picayune*, February 13, 1842.

✺ 12

Public Music Making, Concert Life, and Composition in Kentucky during the Early National Period

Nikos Pappas

The time is 6:30 P.M. on November 12, 1817. The doors have just closed to the assembly room in Sanford Keen's tavern located on the southeast corner of Main Street and Limestone, with the audience eagerly waiting to hear the newest virtuoso to grace the Kentucky stage. For the past week, the *Kentucky Reporter* had praised the playing of Lexington's most recent resident violinist, the Bohemian emigrant Anthony Philip Heinrich, in his post as soloist and member of Lexington's professional theater orchestra, part of Samuel Drake's company.[1] Now, Heinrich, with the assistance of the local keyboardist, musical proprietor, and music teacher John C. Wenzel, Samuel Drake's son Alexander, the actor and singer Francis Blissett, members of the orchestra, and amateur musicians of Lexington, would present a "grand concert of vocal and instrumental music" (see opposite page).

The program would include music in choral, orchestral, chamber, and solo mediums following a model of English concert programming extending back to the seventeenth century. Although the types of pieces on the concert program remained typical for the early nineteenth century, this concert has become legendary, solely through the programming of a "SIM-FONIA con Minuetto" by Ludwig van Beethoven (1770–1827), this being the first performance of a Beethoven symphony in Kentucky and the third in the United States.[2]

Despite the appearance of Beethoven's symphony on the roster, the other programming choices provide much more valuable and suggestive information about Lexington's cultural and concert life than this single celebrated work. The composers represented include Ludwig van Beethoven, John Danby (1757–1798),[3] Wolfgang Amadeus Mozart

264

GRAND CONCERT

OF VOCAL AND INSTRUMENTAL MUSIC,

Under the direction of A. P. HEINRICH,

ASSISTED BY THE PRINCIPAL PROFESSORS AND AMATEURS,

At Mess. Keene & Lanphear's Assembly Room,

On Wednesday Evening, Nov. 12,

* * *

PART 1st.

SINFONIA con Minuetto. .	*Beethoven.*	Full Band
GLEE – "When Sappho tuned"		Mess. S. Drake, Blisset, and an Amateur
ADAGIO con Sordini e Violino Obligato	*Mozart.*	Full Orchestra
SONG – "The Anchor-Smiths"	*Dibdin.*	Mr. Blisset
DUETTO Concertante, due Vi - Olini	*Viotti.*	Mess. S. Drake and Heinrich
CATCH – "Ah! How Sophia," alias, "A House on Fire"		Mess. Blisset, Alex. Drake, & an Amateur
Solo Violino con Variazioni	*Fiorillo.*	Mr. Heinrich
RONDO	*Pleyel.*	Full Band

PART 2d.

GRAND OVERTURE	*Gyrowetz.*	Full Orchestra
SONG – "From blood stain'd plains of glory"		Mr. S. Drake
The celebrated Concerto Violino	*Giornovichi.*	Mr. Heinrich
CHEERFUL GLEE – "Sigh no more, Ladies"		Mess. Blissett, Drake, and Amateurs
OVERTURE TO LODOISKA, followed by the Queen of Prussia's Waltz, on two Piano Fortes	*Kreutzer. & Himmel*	Mess. Wenzel & Heinrich
COMIC SONG – "The Auctioneer"		Mr. Alexander Drake
CATCH – "It was you that kiss'd the pretty girl"		Mess. S. Drake, Blisset, & A. Drake
FINALE	*Haydn.*	Full Band

* * * * * * * * *

Doors to be opened at 6 o'clock, and performance to commence at half past 6. Tickets of Admission, ONE DOLLAR each, to be had at the several Book-Stores, at Mess. Keene & Lanphear's Bar, and at Mr. Wenzel's Music Store.

Anthony Philip Heinrich, program broadsheet in musical scrapbook. (Rare Books Collection, Library of Congress.)

(1756–1791), Charles Dibdin (1745–1814), Giovanni Battista Viotti (1755–1824), John Wall Callcott (1766–1821),[4] Frederigo Fiorillo (1755–after 1823), Ignace Joseph Pleyel (1757–1831), Adalbert Gyrowetz (1763–1850), Giovani Giornovichi (1747–1804), Richard John Samuel Stevens

(1757–1837),[5] Rodolphe Kreutzer (1766–1831), Friedrich Heinrich Himmel (1765–1814), and Franz Josef Haydn (1732–1809). At first glance, they would, on the basis of the ethnic origins of their names, appear to constitute a grouping of composers emanating from England, Austria, Germany, and Italy. However, the compositions themselves overwhelmingly originate from musicians associated with the London stage of the 1780s and 1790s (Danby, Dibdin, Viotti, Callcott, Fiorillo, Pleyel, Gyrowetz, Stevens, Haydn),[6] with France (Giornovichi, Kreutzer) and Austria (Mozart, Beethoven) following a distant second, and Prussia (Himmel) bringing up the rear.

Further, twelve of the fourteen composers were born within twenty years of each other (Haydn and Beethoven being the exceptions), eight of these being alive at the date of this performance and two others recently deceased (within the past three years). As with much of the United States, the concertgoing public of Lexington remained thoroughly modern in its taste for secular music. Somewhat atypical for Kentucky and the rest of the United States, however, Heinrich assembled a selection of pieces composed solely between 1785 and 1801, with nothing more current than the Himmel and Beethoven works. Thus, Heinrich as impresario programmed an entirely modern concert, albeit slightly dated, in his efforts to appeal to Lexington audiences. More typical of theatrical presentations than secular concerts in Kentucky during the early national period,[7] especially as far as secular vocal music is concerned, his selections followed accepted trends in programming found on concert programs throughout the Ohio River valley.

Finally, this concert reveals much information concerning the intended social hierarchy of the audience expected to fill the house. For instance, the audience attended a performance that largely involved *theater* musicians in the *ballroom* of a *tavern*. As a result, this concert would not have appealed to the evangelical population of Lexington. Keen and Lanphear's Assembly Room, also known as Keen's Ball Room, was located in Sanford Keen's tavern, the meeting place of Kentucky's first Jockey Club and Henry Clay's Junto, a prominent debating society in Lexington.[8] As the most prestigious meeting place in Lexington, Keene's tavern served as the site to host a banquet for the visiting dignitary President James Monroe in 1819. Finally, Heinrich's assistant in the concert, John C. Wenzel, onetime organist at Christ Church Episcopal, sold fine London-made pianos out of his music store. The audience would surely have recognized the status of the event on the basis of its performers, location, and venue. In sum, this event was designed to appeal, not to the lower- to lower-middle-class citizens of Lexington, but instead to those with both disposable income and connections to high society.

During its period of nascent cultural activity (1790–1830), Lexington remains distinctive, compared with other cities in the West, in terms of both nature of activities and number of concerts and theatrical performances. Although, in his preface to Carden's book, James Ramage considered Lexington's concert life "unimpressive" when seen alongside urban centers on the Eastern Seaboard, notably Boston, this assessment is not entirely fair or relevant in understanding cultural activity throughout the Ohio River valley. Joy Carden herself presented the best argument for understanding Lexington's importance in the creation of a viable concert scene during the early national period.[9] Boston, founded in 1630, did not engender a cultural environment to support public concerts until 1729, almost one hundred years later.[10] Lexington, founded in 1775, sponsored its first dramatic performance in 1790[11] and its first public concert in 1805.[12] From this vantage, Lexington's transition from urban frontier to urban metropolis remains unparalleled in comparison with any American city of its time. That it could support regular amateur and professional concerts within thirty years of its inception testifies both to its wealth (in terms of disposable income) and to its self-image as a prestigious cultural center, despite the comparative paucity of public music making in comparison with older established cities.

However, the act of public performance involved more than an act of simple music making. Instead, it constituted a ritual of status, education, and refinement. To grasp the act of performing music from this vantage involves understanding the milieu of both the greater American cultural climate and those forces that shaped local and regional trends of composition and performance. Exploring first the general musical climate of the Eastern Seaboard, and then focusing on public performance and composition in Lexington, explains much.

Professional Musical Culture in the Early National United States

Unique to this time period, the professional musical culture of the early national United States was most influenced by English musical conventions, despite the presence of Continental-born German, Italian, and French musicians. As Donald W. Krummel stated, "London's domination was complete," especially during the latter part of the early national period.[13] Although London may have served as the ultimate model for

American professional activity, the United States did not remain one unified and unvarying block of expression. Instead, American professional activity remained tied to several regional centers, reflecting, not only a prevailing British musical diaspora, but also the distinctive cultural and social features of the major urban centers of the New England, Middle Atlantic, and southern states. For Kentucky musicians, the influence of the Middle Atlantic cities Philadelphia and Baltimore, and perhaps Richmond, Virginia, provided the main sphere for cultural influence as well as the geographic area from which most Ohio valley professional musicians launched their American careers. Thus, musicians in Kentucky reflected in a series of outward-extending arcs the musical taste of the commonwealth, musical trends of the West centered in the Ohio River valley, patterns of cultural influence from the Middle Atlantic and Chesapeake Bay, and, finally, the general aesthetic of the United States.

However, before discussing these patterns of cultural influence, an examination of the British musical diaspora will provide the foundation for understanding America's professional musical culture. The predominance of the English musical style within American performance practice resulted, not just from the proliferating English mainstream culture in the United States, but also from the musical-societal conventions found in Great Britain throughout the Hanoverian period (ca. 1700–1840), as argued by Nicholas Temperley.[14] More so than in other European countries, musicians in Great Britain moved in two basic musical worlds: the aristocracy and the middle-class public. With the strength of the middle class throughout much of England, musicians did not have to eke out a living only through royal or ecclesiastical patronage, as on the Continent. Indeed, for most British-born musicians, the middle class afforded the only viable means of employment and monetary gain because of England's elitist bias toward Continental-born musicians.

In documenting musical practice, scholars have tended to overlook the music of the middle classes for two reasons. Most important, popularly based music could not afford to be avant-garde; it had to state the current fashionable expressions of the middle classes. As a result, composers of middle-class music reflected societal contexts, as opposed to the elite group, which created a reactionary musical expression. Not only did popular musicians have to produce music that incorporated newer, fashionable trends, but their music had to retain basic familiar elements, thereby pleasing a larger musical audience. In effect, the "great man" theory (the theory that only famous composers wrote music worthy of modern performance) neatly excised any musicians' contributions outside the sphere of mainstream private and ecclesiastical patronage because any popular-music-oriented composer would have to please rather than challenge his audience.

The second reason for an apparent neglect of popular music before the twentieth century stems from its supposed inferior craftsmanship and construction, in comparison with the elitist music circles. If, say, an opera, such as one by Jean-Jacques Rousseau (1712–1778) or Thomas Augustine Arne (1710–1778), contains more simple songs than one by high-classic composers such as Wolfgang Amadeus Mozart or Franz Josef Haydn, then it is often seen as naive or underdeveloped in comparison to the later advancements of Viennese classicism. Because modern standards of quality classical music stem from a nineteenth-century German aesthetic of motivic development and counterpoint, scholars have simply overlooked a musical style outside this Teutonic ideal because it does not correspond with these principles of or values in composition. As a result, the music of Great Britain (1700–1840) and, subsequently, the United States (1780–1840) demands a revision of attitude and deserves a fresh evaluation within the context of its own aesthetic ideals.

In addition, comparison of professional early national music with contemporary developments in Great Britain serves only as a foundation for an understanding of American classicism. This phenomenon becomes particularly apparent in the realm of orchestral music. While England provided the stylistic model for early national practice, musicians in the United States contributed their own unique developments to symphonic composition, as heard in the overture-symphonies written by the early national period emigrant composers John Christopher Moller (1755–1803), Rayner Taylor (1747–1825), and John Bray (1782–1822) on the Eastern Seaboard and Anthony Phillip Heinrich (1781–1861) and William Cumming Peters (1805–1866) in the Ohio River valley. Further, the societal structure of Great Britain's middle class differed greatly from that of its American counterpart because the middle class of the United States dominated both the common and the elite musical circles. In England, native musicians by default found themselves confined to a lower musical caste because of that country's elitist attitude toward Continental composers, particularly the Italians, Germans, and Viennese. Likewise, any European composer active in the United States, regardless of ethnic background, would have received greater approbation because of America's own reticence to honor native efforts within professional circles. As a result, the British composers active in the United States earned greater respect and social standing than would have been possible in Europe.

The musical culture of early national America differed from that of most other places in Europe because the British middle-class style became the elite style of music in the United States. While most English musicians could only hope for a contract with the Covent Garden theater in London, immigrants to early national America soon found themselves leading and directing a society's musical climate and aesthetic. However, this societal elevation did not change the British method of composition; it only exposed the strengths and flexibility of the English style within another societal setting. As in Great Britain, where the popular nature of the native British musical culture sought to keep abreast of current stylistic developments while still producing works with a sense of the familiar, in the United States musicians simply transferred this compositional approach through an identical methodology. American classical music incorporated the fashionable musical elements of contemporary Europe while producing music that catered to the desires of a uniquely American audience. Both this rise in musical status and a deluge of foreign musicians to the United States in the last decade of the eighteenth century partly explain the philosophic ideal behind early national professional music.

Using a traditional British approach to composition and instruction, immigrant composers in the United States created an American form of classical music that could have existed only within the societal context of early national America. For professional musicians in the United States, popular music was the classical music within society. Consequently, one type of music had to serve both an intellectual and an uneducated audience. In theory, the music had to remain simple enough that the untutored listener could understand it, but it also had to employ a high degree of sophistication in order to satisfy the learned musician and gentleman. This desire to appeal to a broad audience also found economic expression by an anonymous writer in the *Philadelphia Federal Gazette* on December 24, 1792. As a subscriber to a concert series, he believed that, "in such situations, the music should be smooth and affecting, the songs artless and rural, borrowed chiefly from scenes of country life; so the rich man may feel a species of delight in transporting himself a moment from the splendours that usually surround him, to scenes of tranquil and unambitious ease; and the poor man consoles himself to think that some of the most flattering views of life are to be drawn from the situation of those who, like himself, are treading only the humbler walks of life."[15] Instead of separate musical classes, as in Great Britain, the United States had one; the previously underprivileged immigrant British composer suddenly became a young nation's leading musician. Though mirroring the intellectual literature of the early national period, illustrated by the writings of James Fenimore Cooper[16] and Michel-Guillaume Jean de Crèvecoeur (naturalized on emigration as J. Hector St. John de Crèvecoeur),[17] its practical execution varied greatly, as seen in the implied status-based hierarchy of Heinrich's 1817 program.

That the musicians could so readily adapt to the musical climate of the United States reveals the true strength of the early national composer and his musical standards. In terms of versatility, quality, and adherence to a national style, early national musicians remain unsurpassed in their ability to create a national aesthetic separate from the tastes of other English-speaking countries as well as Continental Europe. In sum, professional musical style in the United States developed as a combination of mainstream European culture with uniquely American characteristics, creating a formative, national professional musical practice.

Concert Music in the American West: Amateur and Professional

Professional early national musical activity in the American West occurred in several arenas of performance: the theater, the ball, and the formal concert. Of these venues, the theater remained the most egalitarian because its audience comprised all social classes, including sire, slave, and servants; the others appealed more to the elitist and fashion-conscious middling classes. Not surprisingly, professional and concert life in Kentucky developed first in the area of the state that saw the greatest influx of these classes of Americans to the West: Lexington, Frankfort, and, at a slightly later period, Louisville.

In terms of professional performances, Kentucky can claim many firsts, both musical and dramatic. On April 26, 1790, the first public dramatic performance in the West took place at the then Transylvania Seminary in Lexington, though the pieces performed remain unidentified. The first known performance of a musical play occurred on September 30, 1797, in Washington (near Maysville), with the afterpiece *The Padlock* by Charles Dibdin, one of the leading English middle-class opera composers in Great Britain.[18] The earliest-documented concert given in the American West took place on May 22, 1805, in Bradley's Long Room in Lexington. Finally, the earliest-known western orchestra provided the accompaniment to the Kentucky Music Society's concert on November 21, 1805, again in Lexington.[19] Lexington's initiatives in the realm of dramatic, concert, and orchestral performance reflect the establishment of a society devoted to leisure, learning, and higher culture. This phenomenon stands in stark contrast to a survival-based frontier culture found throughout most of the emerging West and often associated with Kentucky during this time.

Two Ohio River Valley Composers: Anthony Philip Heinrich and William Cumming Peters

The nature of performance and the taste of early national audiences both in the Eastern Seaboard and in Lexington indicate that several trends of cultural influence permeated programming choice. Performers and audiences displayed a preference for music largely originating from the London stage, exhibiting a model of concert activity based on British precedent, both from the United Kingdom and within its greater diaspora, including the United States. Despite the presence of German, French, Italian, British, and Russian performers in the West, all subscribed to a prevailing English-dominated musical and performative aesthetic. Instrumental music constituted a more international base of expression, including works by composers from Central and Western Europe, ranging from Czech-speaking lands to the British Isles. In stark contrast, vocal music remained thoroughly and almost exclusively English in popular taste. However, one element was missing from this discussion: the original artistic creations of musicians active in the Ohio River valley. Although not seen with the program of Anthony Phillip Heinrich, American music constituted a significant portion of programmed repertory, with works by itinerant performers forming the largest portion of these compositions. At the same time, almost all the active professionals in the West were immigrants to the United States.

Programming trends by impresarios met the aesthetic preference of the public. Therefore, it should follow that compositional methods would mirror this same process. Although this is to some degree accurate, this process does not account for the additional complexity of incorporating the aesthetic of the United States. The American-composed repertory instead drew its inspiration and stylistic mannerisms from the ethnic origin of the composer, his personal professional musical experience, and his personal aesthetic, besides the music having to meet the strictures demanded by the public. Further, though the United States was a part of the British diaspora, it was not the United Kingdom. It had its own national aesthetic, adapted from British practice, but unique unto itself. As a result, most professional musicians attempted to meet the receptive demands of an American audience while at the same time expressing this through music shaped by personal experience and American popular taste. Because of the vital role that theatrical performance occupied in its viability for employment, many professional American composers wrote music influenced by dramatic musical conventions, expressed through compositional cultural traits found in their pieces.

Two composers in particular stand out among the approximately dozen or so professional musicians active in the West: Anthony Philip Heinrich and William Cumming Peters. Though both immigrated to the United States, becoming professional musicians, their respective backgrounds could not have been more diverse. Peters came from a musical family, becoming professionally active in his late teenage years. Heinrich became a professional musician only after he lost his livelihood, fortune, and family. Peters was born in isolated southwestern England along the southern coast, separated not only from London but also from other important cultural cities in western England, such as Bath and Bristol. Heinrich, though born in a small village in Bohemia, traveled often to Vienna and Prague, important musical centers at the beginning of the Age of Revolutions. Heinrich grew up in affluence, Peters in a middle-class family. Despite such differences in background, both drew on a similar compositional repertory for inspiration and influence in their own works. An analysis of compositional influence reveals how these effects found expression, illustrating once again the complex operative of aesthetic present in programming choices by impresarios in the Ohio River valley.

Anthony Philip Heinrich

Anthony Philip Heinrich was born on March 11, 1781, in Schönbüchel in Bohemia.[20] In his youth, he became endeared to his uncle, a wealthy merchant specializing in Viennese crystal, operating this business both in Bohemia and in Austria. At the age of twenty, he inherited his uncle's business and sought to expand its operations to a wider market. In 1805, he came to Boston to find purveyors for his crystal and linen. In this year, Heinrich also met his future wife, "an American Lady of superior personal and mental endowments."[21] They later married, sometime around the year 1810. Returning to Bohemia, the couple had a daughter, Antonia, but childbirth left Heinrich's wife in extremely poor health. Fearing her imminent death, she requested to see her parents one final time. Leaving the daughter in the care of a relative, "Joseph Hladèck, residing on the domains of Prince Lichtestein, at Grund, near Rumburg,"[22] Heinrich came back to the United States with his wife in 1814. She did die, and, soon after, the Austrian financial crash and Bonaparte's destruction of Vienna left Heinrich penniless and stranded in the United States. In 1817, at the age of thirty-six, he decided to become a professional musician, presumably because of early training on the violin and piano.

Like many musicians, Heinrich first found employment as a theater musician, accepting a post in Pittsburgh. On his arrival there, he found the theater closed and himself again without employment. Probably through the encouragement of either the Drake family or Francis Blissett, he came to Kentucky, landing first at Maysville, and then walking to Lexington. Soon after he arrived, he performed the famous Lexington concert discussed earlier in this essay. Shortly thereafter, he followed the Drakes to Frankfort and Louisville, performing as the director of the theater orchestra.

In 1818, Heinrich became seriously ill with scarlet fever, finding respite in a log house outside Bardstown. While recovering, he began to compose music initially through improvisations on the violin. As his reputation as a composer spread, local figures commissioned him to provide music for numerous patriotic events in Bardstown, including songs with texts by Kentucky poets.[23] From 1818 to 1820, he composed dozens of pieces for piano, violin, chamber ensemble, orchestra, band, and voice. He published this magnum opus as *The Dawning of Music in Kentucky; or, The Pleasures of Harmony in the Solitudes of Nature* in 1820, the work representing his first blossoming as a composer. In 1823, he moved first to Boston, then to London, and then to New York, where he died at the age of eighty in 1861.

In his development as a composer, Heinrich quickly sought to become, not just a Bohemian resident of the United States, but an American, absorbing the ebullient rhetoric of the early national period. Recognizing that the United States and American music in general were still in an embryonic stage of development, he addressed these issues, as well as the handicap of being self-tutored in the art of composition, in the preface to *The Dawning of Music in Kentucky:*

> The many and severe animadversions, so long and repeatedly cast on the talent for Music in the Country, has been one of the chief motives of the Author, in the exercise of his abilities; and should he be able, by this effort, to create but one single *Star* in the *West,* no one would ever be more proud than himself, to be called an *American Musician.* He however is fully aware of the dangers which, at the present day, attend talent on the crowded and difficult road of

eminence; but fears of just criticism, by *Competent Masters*, should never retard the enthusiasm of genius, when ambitious of producing works more lasting than the too many *Butterfly-effusions* of the present age. He, therefore, relying on the candour of the Public, will rest confident, that justice will be done, by due comparisons with the works of other Authors (celebrated for their merit, especially as regards Instrumental *execution*) but who have never, like him, been thrown, as it were, by *discordant events*, far from the emporiums of musical science, into the isolated wilds of nature, where he invoked his Muse, tutored *only* by ALMA MATER.[24]

In terms of his approach to composition, Heinrich stood between the classical and the romantic periods. From one perspective, following the philosophical writings of Rousseau he sought inspiration in a place that many Europeans would have considered outside the realm of civilization. Here, in an uninhibited state, he created music from the pure inspiration of solitude and not from the corrupting influence of society. From another perspective, his preoccupation with American nationalism, combined with the self-portrait of an artist thrown against the winds of fate and cast into the wilderness where the power of the environment gave power to tonal expression, empowered his art with romantic and supernatural or gothic elements.

Heinrich's music from the Kentucky period displays traits illustrative of his cultural background as well as personal mannerisms evident in many of his pieces. As a native of Bohemia, Heinrich wrote several songs following compositional techniques of Central Europe. *Hail! to Kentucky*, presumably composed during his stay in Bardstown, declares his sentiments for his adopted country. While the vocal part presents the same music for each verse, the keyboard part consists of a theme and variations format for each successive verse, after the style of *Lied* composition associated with German composers of the early nineteenth century, including Beethoven and Karl Friedrich Zelter. While not common among composers in the United States, this German style of song composition found favor among some German emigrant composers, such as Carl Meinecke in Baltimore.

Conversely, Heinrich also wrote pieces in a characteristically American structural format that contain Bohemian musical references. *Marcia di Ballo*, originally used as an overture to a ball given by Major James Smiley (1758–1829) of Bardstown, follows an American form for orchestral composition with a march for the first movement and a rondo with an extended coda based on the *Yankee Doodle* theme. As compared with the

This image shows Heinrich recuperating from a long illness, a period when he became inspired by the (at least to his eyes) seeming wilderness of Bardstown, Kentucky, symbolized by the log house. An African American banjo player visited him during his recovery, and a friendship developed between the two. The shabby attire suggests that Heinrich is depicted as a hermit. A parody of the European court composer, this Heinrich demonstrates his artistic romantic authenticity through the inspirations of poverty, exoticism, and the wilderness, powerful symbols of the nineteenth century. However, the setting for his waste-land is not a remote, uninhabited desert but rather a domestic farm filled with cows, agricultural implements, and neighbors. (The image is taken from "The Log House," in *The Sylviad; or, Minstrelsy of Nature in the Wilds of N. America* [Boston, 1823, 1825–1826].)

other pieces, this overture incorporates elements from both Heinrich's homeland and his adopted country. The opening to the march presents a type of fanfare common in Bohemian music beginning with the orchestral suites of the Czech composer Heinrich Ignaz von Biber (1644–1704). Jux-taposed with this Bohemian-Austrian device are the recurring variations on *Yankee Doodle* found in the rondo.

Elements of Heinrich's own eccentricities can be found scattered throughout his pieces. Of these works, *La Buona Mattina: A Sonata for the Piano Forte* offers several examples. As stated in the Italian opening of the song, Heinrich asks the audience to "accept the offering of the poor son of Orpheus" by a composer living in forests and caverns and only "inspired by the sounds of nature." Here, as in many of Heinrich's writings, the concept of Rousseau's noble savage comes to the forefront of his identity (Heinrich also called himself the log cabin composer), presaging the "log cabin" politicians of the post-Jackson period as well as the Walden Pond theosophy of Henry Thoreau and the transcendentalists. Heinrich wrote only one composition in this form, but it reveals several of his compositional quirks. First, the piano sonata opens with a song; second, each movement is in a different key (D major–D minor–B♭ major); and, third, the first movement resembles a sonata only in that it alternates between melodic passages and animated transitory passages, as opposed to presenting thematic and motivic unity for its construction. It certainly is not a light morning entertainment.

William Cumming Peters

William Cumming Peters was born March 10, 1805, in Modbury, County Devonshire, England.[25] The eldest son of William Smalling Peters, an amateur musician and teacher, William Cumming, along with the entire Peters family, immigrated to the New World, initially to Canada, and then later to Troy, New York. He first received training on the clarinet, presumably from his father, as well as instruction on the piano and organ. By 1827, Peters, then living in Pittsburgh, advertised his services as a "Professor of Music." While in Pittsburgh, Peters taught band and keyboard instruments, held a post as organist at Trinity Episcopal Cathedral, and served as teacher and arranger-composer for the Harmony Society, a German communal association under the leadership of George F. Rapp. Between 1827 and 1831, he provided approximately fifty orchestrations, compositions, and arrangements for the Harmony Society orchestra.

Peters moved to Louisville sometime between 1830 and 1832. Again advertising his services as a "Professor of Music," he operated a music store, offered lessons, concertized, and composed pieces for various organizations in Louisville and surrounding areas. He also converted to Roman Catholicism and became the organist and choir director at St. Louis Catholic Church in Louisville from at least 1843 through 1849.[26] Finally, he became the first printer and the second publisher of engraved sheet music in Kentucky through his Louisville firm of Peters and Webb, beginning ca. 1839.[27] Peters would later move to Baltimore and then Cincinnati, where he died in 1866, though he continued to operate his business in Louisville up to the time of the Civil War.

Like Heinrich, Peters expressed concern for the progress and development of American music. However, his enthusiasm for American composers embraced a much different set of cultural mores and a different understanding of American culture. On his arrival in Baltimore, Peters initiated the publication of the *Baltimore Olio*, a musical periodical in which he expressed his views of American music and musicians.[28] For Peters, music in the United States by the year 1850 had not developed into anything uniquely American but was on its way: "There are elements at work among us, which if fostered and encouraged, will evolve, if we mistake not, a national music, as strongly and broadly marked as that of Scotland, Switzerland or any other country."[29] Peters could not offer any direct advice as to the place from which it would spring, geographically or culturally speaking, though he had his theories. Responding to an essay in the *Cincinnati Columbian* with regard to the evolution of "national music," he could not "agree with the writer in supposing that we are to find it in the American Negro. We shall probably be somewhat indebted to the writers of Negro Melodies [blackface minstrelsy], but we have yet to see the first melody written by an American Negro."[30]

In one sense, he adopted the same stance as Heinrich, believing that American music had yet to receive equal merit as European, given the lack of training available to many American musicians. From another perspective, he could not have been further from Heinrich's belief that America should draw inspiration from its native peoples, its African American population and their performative traditions, and the wilds of the romantic, American landscape. Heinrich gazed at the broad vista of American experience, Peters the polite world of the drawing room, creating an indoor-outdoor duality of inspiration. Peters expressed strictures of contrivance and control; Heinrich became subsumed by his passions. Though Peters respected Heinrich as one of America's formative composers, he certainly found him eccentric. In the second number of the *Baltimore Olio*, an individual identified only as "H." contributed a biographical essay about Heinrich that voiced a sentiment most likely shared by Peters: "There he [Heinrich] sought the aid of music, to give a charm to the solitude that surrounded him, and composed an eccentric piece entitled 'The Dawning of Music in Kentucky.' This production gives some idea of the loneliness of his hermitage, and the pianoforte told of rats gnawing the logs, the howling of wolves, and the groaning of lofty pine trees as they waved to the stormy winds."[31] Peters's compositions display the same popular influences found in Heinrich's music, though expressed in a much less romantic and passionate tonal rhetoric.

Peters's music also betrays his British heritage and his knowledge of the popular music then heard on the Eastern Seaboard. Several compositions and a number of arrangements survive from his Pittsburgh and early Louisville periods (1827–1833). Most of the orchestral arrangements and instrumental compositions from this time are in the form of functional dance music, including waltzes, quadrilles, hop waltzes, gallopades, and military marches. *A Favorite German Waltz* (1833), a known Kentucky composition, was either composed or arranged by Peters. The holograph score, located in the archives of the Harmony Society in Economy, Pennsylvania, includes the location and date of this composition. This waltz demonstrates Peters's use of the sigh motives commonly associated with the *Empfindsamer stil* of early classical composers in Europe, particularly in Germany and in Great Britain. This waltz is also the earliest piece of orchestral music to survive in its original orchestral format from Kentucky. *The Queen of Prussia's Favorite Waltz* was originally composed by Friedrich Heinrich Himmel (1765–1814), court composer to Friedrich Wilhelm II of Prussia and his successor, Friedrich Wilhelm III, piano instructor to Queen Luise, and known for his operas and *Singspiel. The Queen of Prussia's Favorite Waltz* was one of the most popular waltzes published in federalist America, issued from various publishing houses in Philadelphia and Baltimore. The orchestration dates from Peters's Pittsburgh period and was completed from one of these sheet music imprints.

Peters also wrote a few pieces in more extended forms, including his *Symphonie, Composed & Arranged & Dedicated to the Economy Band, by their Friend* (1831). Because of the lack of substantial information on Peters's move from Pittsburgh to Louisville, it is uncertain whether this piece was composed for the Harmonists while he was in Pittsburgh or after his move to Louisville. In any case, this "symphonie" represents his only example in this genre, and its format requires some explanation. American composers before 1825 composed overture-symphonies in two basic formats: a three-movement fast-slow-fast form descending from Italian practice and a two-movement form with a first movement in binary form, such as a march or some other dance, followed by a rondo second movement. The two-movement American symphony, as expected, descends from British practice (through an adaption of the French overture split into two separate movements, such as that for *The Beggar's Opera*, by John

Christopher Pepusch) but was modified by professional American musicians for the wants of American audiences for melodic presentation over motivic development.

In the case of Peters's symphonie, the influences expressed in the piece remain obscure. The first movement, a waltz, betrays two main influences: (1) the opening section of the overture to the opera *Le calife de Bagdad*, by François-Adrien Boieldieu (1775–1834), with its structure and violin cadenza and (2) a waltz composed by the Pittsburgh attorney Charles von Bonnhorst (1776–1844), the legal representative of the Harmony Society and the composer of approximately fifty pieces of dance music for the Harmonist orchestra, from which the opening melodic theme was lifted. Peters would later take a quadrille composed by Bonnhorst and use it as his own composition in a set of quadrilles, *The Corncracker Quadrilles*, that he published ca. 1840. The second movement rondo bears a strong melodic and rhythmic similarity to theater overtures composed by Thomas Cooke, the musical director of the Crow Street Theater Royal in Dublin, ca. 1800–1815, most notably his *Ella Rosenberg* overture, composed in 1803. Finally, the rhythmic format of the theme to the rondo follows the rhythms of a traditional English hornpipe, illustrating a British cultural mannerism within an American form of symphony.

American concert culture and its social, musical conventions drew overwhelmingly from British precedents. The repertory, vocal and instrumental, was shaped by pieces composed for, and mostly written in, London. Despite the presence of a wide proliferation of foreign-born musicians active in the United States from France, Italy, Germany, Austria, and the Czech Republic, America's musical climate did not foster a concert scene that reflected this wide array of ethnic composition during the early national period. All musicians, regardless of cultural background, adapted to the American scene by combining a British-influenced national style with the American penchant for simplicity of form, emphasis on melodic presentation, and the presentation of national melodies, drawing largely from theatrical musical conventions of the late eighteenth century and the early nineteenth. Not until the passing of the early national period did a change in cultural influence shift away from a predominantly British practice to follow the romantic mannerisms of Italian opera and Teutonic orchestration and symphonic style.

The narrow strictures found within American music and concert programming can in part be attributed to the relationship between audiences and performers. While performers chose the pieces that appeared on their programs, the range of material remained within the jurisdiction of the audience. Audiences demanded a narrow range of repertory, based on perceived notions of refinement and taste. At this time, more than in any other period in American history, concert culture and its elite society was governed by a thoroughly British diaspora. As a result, taste was governed by the audience's direct exposure to London's musical sphere or an indirect perception based on print culture and oral dissemination. Performers had no choice but to cater to these demands. Without a social network, such as a musicians' union, to guarantee a base payment for services rendered, a musician's only basis for monetary success lay in his ability to perform *to* his audience and its aesthetic. Only with the changing taste of middle-class London, and, subsequently, America's Eastern Seaboard urban centers such as Philadelphia, New York, and Baltimore, could professional musicians begin to emerge from these limitations.

Nevertheless, within this narrow breadth of musical style and cultural influence, musical culture in the United States followed its own regional trends in programming, performance, and composition. All favored British-dominated performance traditions but drew on different American regional urban centers in the East. Thus, the social arenas that governed musical life and its identity encompassed a series of outward-extending arcs of influence involving city, state, region, and nation. Evidence for this phenomenon appears in programming trends, professional activity, performance mode, and composition.

Finally, concerts followed a basic unvaried method of construction designed to appeal to a limited class/range of individuals. Restricted not just in composition choice, performers shaped their concerts after a tradition of concert programming extending back to the seventeenth and eighteenth centuries. Similarly to the liturgy of an Episcopalian church service, concerts constituted a ritualistic enactment of status, education, and economy. Programs followed a litany of composition order. Composition choice drew from specific, predetermined repertories. Professional standing determined concert venue and performance mode. The venue itself indicated the class standing of its attendees. Despite the democratic sentiment voiced by many in the United States at this time, concert life remained elitist. However, these cultural endeavors bespeak greatly of the efforts of its community, reflecting their concerns and desire to promote the arts in an effort to further nineteenth-century concepts of cultural progress and its social advancement on the national stage.

Too often, cultural activity focuses on the perceived nexus of America's urban population. Because of long-standing cultural traditions and their establishment along the Eastern Seaboard, scholars have tended to study Boston, Philadelphia, New York City, and, perhaps, Charleston, to the exclusion of important population centers in the interior of the country. Kentucky poses a challenge to this assessment as the artifacts of elitist culture became manifest throughout the Bluegrass area within a quarter century of initial settlement. In particular, Kentucky musicians performed a Beethoven symphony before any of this composer's orchestral works received premieres in New York City, Boston, Baltimore, Charleston, and many other important cities along the coast.

Though frontier conditions did exist in areas of Kentucky concurrently with the presence of refined culture in the central part of the state, these appurtenances should not be unexpected as they became part of the necessary trappings of an urban frontier. In its efforts to replicate perceived notions of urban culture, residents attempted to put into place items associated with high society, be they operatic or orchestral performances, the establishment of institutions of higher learning, or the commission of neoclassic architectural designs from the professional architect Benjamin Latrobe. Functioning primarily as an instrument of cultural reception, Lexington's importance in the history of American concert culture lies not just in the chronological establishment of these cultural objects. Instead, residents of the state considered them important enough within this urban frontier to promote and establish them as essential instruments of society. Older cities are expected to have had these institutions. Lexington, a town founded as a log-palisaded fort in 1775, is not supposed to have offered theater and opera by the 1790s. Focusing solely on these long-established cities fails to show, not only how quickly residents arrived in the early trans-Appalachian West, but also how rapidly its commodifications proved essential to the western experience. From this vantage, Lexington remains unparalleled in the story it narrates of the early western urban frontier.

Notes

A remarkable recording was made during the symposium from which this collection of essays is drawn: it contains performances by soloists and a twenty-piece symphony orchestra of music composed in antebellum Kentucky, much of it not heard since the Civil War. It is available at www.kentuckypress.com.

1. "An AMATEUR notices with pleasure, that the music at the theatre has been greatly improved by the acquisition to the band of one of the first Violin performers in America. On Monday evening last, we heard with exquisite delight the finest *Solo* ever performed on that instrument in our Orchestra. The gentleman is a stranger, but

intends to reside in this place, if properly encouraged in his profession. His extraordinary skill and talents cannot fail to attract the attention of persons of taste; such will be pleased to learn that he intends offering a public concert next week." *Kentucky Reporter* (Lexington), November 5, 1817.

2. Joy Carden, *Music in Lexington Before 1840* (Lexington, 1980), 8–12.

3. "'When Sappho Tuned.' Glee." A glee is an English type of part song that comes out of the Italian madrigal.

4. "'Ah! How Sophia,' alias 'A House on Fire.' Catch." A catch is a type of round.

5. "'Sigh No More, Ladies.' Cheerful Glee."

6. The non-English composers represented in this circle traveled to England mostly through the motivation and activities of Johann Peter Salomon (1745–1815), a violinist and concert impresario in London beginning in 1781.

7. West T. Hill Jr., *The Theatre in Early Kentucky, 1790–1820* (Lexington, 1971), app., 171–92. This appendix contains a record of all known theatrical performances within the parameters given in the text.

8. Carden, *Music in Lexington*, 35.

9. Ibid., 31. In spite of small inaccuracies of fact, her points remain sound and valid.

10. "This is to give notice, that there will be a consort of musick performed on sundry instruments, at the dancing school in King-Street, on Tuesday the 18th instant, at six a clock in the evening, and that tickets for the same will be delivered out at seven shillings and six pence each ticket, at the places following, viz. at Mr. Luke Vardy's at the Royal Exchange, at Mrs. Meer's at the Sun Tavern near the dock, and at the place of performance. N.B. No person to be admitted after six." *Boston Gazette*, February 10, 1729. See also H. Joseph Butler, "Harpsichord Lessons in the New World: Peter Pelham and the Manuscript of 1744," *Early Keyboard Journal* 12 (1994): 40.

11. Hill, *Theatre in Early Kentucky*, 9. This performance was reviewed in the *Kentucky Gazette* of April 26, 1790, though it took place on April 10.

12. "SACRED MUSIC. At the request of several respectable persons, a gentleman lately arrived in this town, (from England) in conjunction with MR. GREEN of Lexington, purposes giving a *Concert of Sacred Music*, interspersed with pieces on the Piano Forte, at Mr. Bradley's Long Room, on the evening of Thursday the 22nd of May at half past 7 o'clock." *Kentucky Gazette*, May 21, 1805.

13. Donald W. Krummel, "Philadelphia Music Engraving and Publishing" (Ph.D. diss., University of Michigan, 1958), 17.

14. Nicholas Temperley, *Bound for America* (Urbana, IL, 2003), 201: "But in German-speaking Europe, composers made most of their living from the cultivated aristocracy, where fine art-music was most appreciated and composers were encouraged to develop their highest talents. Britain was more democratic than Germany and Austria; it had a wealthy middle class, largely independent of the nobility, which encouraged simpler and more obvious musical effects."

15. Quoted in Oscar G. Sonneck, *Early Concert-Life in America (1731–1800)* (Leipzig, 1907), 88.

16. "I have never seen a nation so much alike in my life, as the people of the United States, and what is more, they are not only like each other, but they are remarkably like that which common sense tells them they ought to resemble. . . . In short, it is not possible to conceive a state of society in which more of the attributes of plain good sense, or fewer of the artificial absurdities of life, are to be found, than here. There is no costume for the peasant (there is scarcely a peasant at all,) no wig for the judge, no baton for the general, no diadem for the chief magistrate." James Fenimore Cooper, *Notions of the Americans Picked Up by a Traveling Bachelor* (1828), in *The Harper American Literature*, ed. Donald McQuade, 2 vols. (New York, 1994), 1:916.

17. "[America] is not composed, as in Europe, of great lords who possess everything, and of a herd of people who have nothing. Here are no aristocratical families, no courts, no kings, no bishops, no ecclesiastical dominion, no invisible power giving to a few a very visible one; no great manufacturers employing thousands, no great refinements of luxury. The rich and the poor are not so far removed from each other as they are in Europe." J. Hector St. John de Crèvecoeur, *Letters from an American Farmer* (1782; London, 1940), 39–40.

18. Hill, *Theatre in Early Kentucky*, 9. This performance was advertised in the *Washington Mirror* of September 30, 1797, for performance on October 12.

19. *Kentucky Gazette*, November 21, 1805. Also discussed in Carden, *Music in Lexington*, 36–38.

20. William Treat Upton, *Anthony Philip Heinrich: A Nineteenth-Century Composer in America* (New York, 1939), chap. 1. All the succeeding biographical information about Heinrich will be taken from chaps. 1 and 2 of this volume.

21. Anthony Philip Heinrich, *The Dawning of Music in Kentucky; or, The Pleasures of Harmony in the Solitudes of Nature* (Philadelphia, 1820), 218.

22. Ibid.

23. Peter William Grayson, Esq. (1788–1838), of Bardstown and James R. Black, Esq., of Shelbyville. Grayson was later involved in the founding of Texas, serving as a delegate to the Texas Consultation from the Goliad District (1835), as attorney general for the Republic of Texas (1836–1837), and as a candidate for the presidency of the Republic of Texas (1838). Ibid., 11, 67, 181; Anthony Philip Heinrich, *The Western Minstrel: A Collection of Original, Moral, Patriotic, & Sentimental Songs, for the Voice & Piano Forte, Interspersed with Airs, Waltzes, &c.* (Philadelphia, 1820), 14.

24. Heinrich, *Dawning of Music in Kentucky*, 3.

25. Richard D. Wetzel, *"Oh! Sing No More That Gentle Song": The Musical Life and Times of William Cumming Peters (1805–66)* (Warren, MI, 2000), chap. 2.

26. Wetzel, *"Oh! Sing No More That Gentle Song,"* 250–51. This volume includes several citations from the Louisville periodical the *Catholic Advocate and Journal of Useful Literature, and General Intelligence* listing Peters's activities with the cathedral, including the installation of an organ in 1843–1844 and an inaugural concert for this instrument in the cathedral on February 20, 1844. The *Catholic Advocate* was edited by "A Clergyman" and operated from some point in the 1830s through 1849.

27. John Goodman, the first publisher of engraved sheet music in the Ohio River

valley, operated a cabinet shop in Frankfort, Kentucky, ca. 1800–1806. He issued at least two songs, mostly likely engraved and printed by John Aitken of Philadelphia (a determination based on engraving style), "Sandy & Jenny" by James Sanderson and "A Rosy Cheek." See Reuben T. Durrett Collection on Kentucky and the Ohio River Valley, Special Collections Research Center, University of Chicago Library. Digital facsimiles of both pieces can be found on the American Memory page of the Library of Congress Web site (http://memory.loc.gov) in "The First American West: The Ohio River Valley, 1750–1820" collection.

28. The journal's full title was *The Baltimore Olio, and American Musical Gazette: A Monthly Parlor Companion for the Ladies, Devoted Chiefly to Music, the Arts, and Musical Intelligence Generally.*

29. "Our Course," *Baltimore Olio* 1, no. 1 (1850): 1.

30. "National Music," *Baltimore Olio* 1, no. 2 (1850): 9.

31. H., "Biographical Sketch: Anthony Philip Heinrich," *Baltimore Olio* 1, no. 2 (1850): 11.

℀ 13

Benjamin Henry Latrobe and Neoclassical Lexington

Patrick Snadon

In assessing Kentucky's position within the culture of early nineteenth-century America, it is useful to focus on the work of Benjamin Henry Latrobe, the country's most avant-garde architect of the federal period. Latrobe (b. 1764 in England of an English father and an American mother; d. 1820 in New Orleans) received formal training in both architecture and engineering in London and emigrated in 1796 to the United States, where he became one of the nation's earliest professional architects. Made surveyor of public buildings in 1803 by President Thomas Jefferson, he carried on the design and construction of the already-begun president's house and the U.S. Capitol Building in Washington in addition to such commissions as the Baltimore Cathedral and numerous other public buildings and residences. Latrobe must be considered the first American architect of international stature and is credited with establishing the American architectural profession, where before his arrival buildings had been produced mainly by nonprofessional gentlemen-amateurs or by builder-designers.

Latrobe practiced primarily within an East Coast corridor, beginning in Richmond, Virginia, then working in Philadelphia, Washington, and Baltimore. Surprisingly, the architect's work included eight projects in the new state of Kentucky. Those projects were designed between ca. 1802 and 1817, with six in Lexington, at that time the state's major city, and one each in Frankfort and Newport.[1] This seems an amazingly high number of designs for a region so far from Latrobe's eastern practice. Of the eight Kentucky projects, five were built, based in some form on Latrobe's designs, while three remained on paper. Latrobe's substantial architectural presence in Kentucky suggests how highly early nineteenth-century Kentuckians valued progressive architecture; in some instances, his architectural patrons in the New West seemed more adventurous than those in the already more tradition-bound states of the East. His Kentucky clients tended to be prominent figures like Henry Clay and John Pope, influential on the national as well as the regional political scene. Latrobe perhaps sensed fewer inhibitions in his Kentucky clients and may have hoped that the developing West could potentially be a *tabula rasa*, or blank slate, on which he could write his most advanced architectural theories. He may also, as the first professional architect of note in the United States, have had a vision of introducing the architectural profession to the New West through his commissions and influential clients. In fact, he did so, not only through his projects, but also through a professional genealogy of his pupils and their pupils, who eventually led the way to a full-fledged architectural profession in Kentucky.

While Latrobe's western projects contributed significantly to this important new region, at the same time they stretched his newly established professional practices nearly to the breaking point owing to the great distances involved and the difficulties in communication and transportation. The architect was able neither to visit the sites nor to supervise the construction of these western buildings, nor was he able to send supervisors in his stead, as he sometimes did for his eastern projects. Nevertheless, he optimistically attempted to control the design and construction processes by meeting with his clients in the East (principally Washington, DC, where Clay and Pope, e.g., served in the U.S. Congress), by exchanging letters with them, by corresponding with the local builders whom they hired, and by attempting to deliver professional drawings and specifications in carefully timed sequences during construction. All this had mixed results. Sometimes his designs and instructions were received and followed; sometimes they were received but modified by the clients or their builders; sometimes his documents miscarried or arrived late; and sometimes he himself became confused or fell behind the construction schedule.

Of Latrobe's eight Kentucky projects, only five are documented in the nationwide Latrobe Papers Project (published 1976–1994), which suggests that the architect's body of works is larger than we yet know.[2] His Kentucky projects signaled the importance of this emerging region and reflected the overall range of his work, from ambitious but unbuilt projects to modest but elegant ones, with some of his Kentucky commissions being among the best designs of his career.

Lexington's Form and Development

It is useful to discuss briefly the form of early Lexington, which created the context for most of Latrobe's western projects. While the town was termed the "Athens of the West," its topography little resembled its storied classical counterpart. Lexington began in 1779 as a wilderness fortress, on a fork of Elkhorn Creek, which came to be called the Town Branch. Although too small to be navigable, the stream provided an abundant water supply. The Town Branch ran from east to west, through a small plain between two slopes, that to the south with a steeper elevation, that to the north with a more gradual rise. A plat was drawn in 1780 (revised in 1817) laying out a town "commons" of 165 feet in width, on the plain along the stream, surrounded by a regular grid of "in-lots" that constituted a downtown of six blocks running east-west, parallel to the stream, and three blocks running north-south, on the shallow plain. Several blocks of gridded, five-acre "out-lots" were created north and south of this inner grid, with the greatest number of out-lots climbing the more gradual slope to the north. The central feature of the downtown grid was the courthouse square.[3] John Lutz's 1835 "Plan of the City of Lexington" records the city as it had extended itself by this date.

From this early plan, Lexington developed five distinct sectors. The central portion of the early grid, laid out along the Town Branch, became the downtown, containing a mixture of commercial, institutional, and residential buildings. The sector immediately north of downtown developed as a combined residential-educational quadrant. Transylvania Seminary, chartered in 1780, had, by 1793, permanently located on out-lot 6, between Second and Third Streets, north of downtown. It gained university status in 1799 and provided one of the main ingredients in the cultural milieu that gave Lexington its "Athenian" character.[4]

The eastern quadrant of the town, from a distance of about half a mile to three miles from the city center, developed as an arc of neoclassical suburban villas and genteel farms.[5] These elegant residences housed the elite of antebellum Lexington and occupied the clean, upstream portion of the Town Branch. With serendipitous symbolism, this eastern "villa quadrant" represented, like a sunrise, the ascent of Lexington's national influence through the political, social, and economic leaders who created these elite houses. Major local and national figures, including Henry Clay and John Pope, built their residences in this sector of the developing city.

Lexington's southern quadrant was destined for connections with agriculture and the deeper South. The originally platted out-lots south of

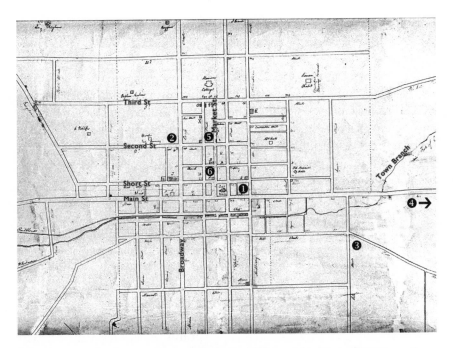

Detail of central portion of John Lutz's 1835 "Plan of the City of Lexington" (University of Kentucky, Special Collections Library). Latrobe's buildings and projects in Lexington: (1) First Kentucky Bank, ca. 1803–1804, northeast corner Main Street and Bank (now Wrenn) Alley; (2) First Presbyterian Church, 1807, southwest corner Broadway and Second Street; (3) Pope Villa, 1810–1813; (4) Ashland, ca. 1812–1814, Richmond Road; (5) Transylvania University (unbuilt project), 1812, between Mill and Market and Second and Third Streets (now Gratz Park); (6) Henry Clay houses, shops, tenements, 1813–1814, northwest corner Short and Market Streets.

downtown occupied a ridge atop the steep slope above the Town Branch, beyond which stretched rich, Bluegrass farmland. By the early 1850s, the Kentucky Agricultural and Mechanical Society and the Maxwell Springs Fair Association had established themselves on this shelf of land, with agricultural fairgrounds and racetracks.[6]

Lexington's western quadrant lay downstream of the Town Branch, which, though polluted as it flowed through downtown, could be harnessed for power. This area developed as the manufacturing sector of the city.[7] This industrial area may have been viewed as a visual liability and potential health problem as, in the 1840s, Lexington's leadership created the new Lexington Cemetery, with its lovely, naturalistic landscape, to the west of the town. This may have been a conscious attempt to screen the city from its downstream, manufacturing sector. The location of the new cemetery proved more apt than its planners realized: the early nineteenth-century political and social leaders who built their villas in the town's eastern quadrant and gave rise to Lexington's importance ended their careers in the lovely cemetery, signaling the sunset of Lexington's national influence. Henry Clay's interment there in 1852 represented the loss of Kentucky's most Periclean figure and the end of Lexington's golden age.

Lexington achieved its economic apex in the second decade of the nineteenth century; after that, the introduction of steam-powered boats to western rivers such as the Ohio and the Mississippi (an engineering development to which Latrobe contributed) meant that the inland city lagged behind rival river towns such as Cincinnati and Louisville.[8] Still, Lexington's visionary leadership, rich agricultural base, progressive institutions, and accumulated cultural capital maintained its national influence for another two decades.

In the broadest of brushstrokes, then, Lexington reached its zenith in the first and second decades of the nineteenth century and developed in five distinct sectors: a commercial, institutional, and residential downtown; an educational sector to the north; a sector of suburban villas and landholding gentry to the east; an agricultural sector to the south; and a manufacturing sector to the west, eventually screened by the intervening landscape of the picturesque Lexington Cemetery. Between 1802 and 1814, the town's period of greatest growth, Latrobe designed projects for three of the five sectors of the city: a bank, a church, and townhouses for downtown, two villas on the east, and plans for Transylvania University on the north. These Lexington projects, plus an armory commissioned by the state legislature at Frankfort and a residence at Newport, constitute Latrobe's eight Kentucky projects—an impressive selection of commercial, religious, educational, government, and domestic building types. These projects have never before been considered as a group and deserve analysis both individually and for the collective light they throw on Kentucky's progressive attitudes and rising importance in the West and the nation.

First Kentucky Bank, Lexington, ca. 1803–1804

Latrobe's earliest western project was for the First Kentucky Bank (formerly at 53 East Main St.) in Lexington, created for the Kentucky Insurance Company, and chartered by the state legislature in 1802. The bank

Benjamin Henry Latrobe, facade of the Bank of
Pennsylvania, Philadelphia, 1798–1801. (Engrav-
ing from Owen Biddle, *Young Carpenter's Assistant*
[Philadelphia, 1805]. University of Kentucky, Special
Collections Library.)

was built, apparently to Latrobe's designs, though it disappeared in the
later nineteenth century.

No Latrobe drawings for the bank survive, nor is it mentioned in his
papers.[9] But the early Lexington settler and merchant William A. Leavy
discussed the bank in his "Memoir of Lexington and Its Vicinity" (written
ca. 1841) and stated: "The edifice was a handsome one for a Bank, and
cost the Directors for the plan alone of a Washington City or Baltimore
Architect Latrobe two or three hundred dollars."[10] In 1802, Latrobe still
resided in Philadelphia, where, between 1798 and 1801, he had designed
and built the Bank of Pennsylvania, a monumental Greco-Roman-style
building of fire-resistant, vaulted masonry construction—his major commission to date in the United States. His Philadelphia bank took the form

of a Greek Ionic temple with amphiprostyle porticos (at either end) and a low Roman dome emerging at the roofline over the circular, two-story central banking hall.

The Philadelphia bank surely gave rise to the Lexington commission, although the Kentucky bank cannot have been as elaborate as its eastern counterpart. Unlike the Bank of Pennsylvania, which had a prominent corner site, the Lexington bank sat within its block and had only 28½ feet of street frontage.[11] Few visual sources remain to document the Lexington building: one is John Lutz's 1835 "Plan of the City of Lexington," which shows the building's outline as a shaded square, labeled *C*, located on Main Street (immediately east of Wrenn Alley, formerly Bank Alley) in the block to the east of the courthouse square. A second visual source is the 1857 "View of the City of Lexington, Ky.," a bird's-eye map that, albeit with little detail, shows the Main Street facade of the bank building.[12] It appears to have been a three-bay, two-story structure, set back somewhat from the sidewalk, unlike its neighboring buildings, which were built to the sidewalk's edge. The shallow space, or forecourt, between the sidewalk and the set-back bank facade appears to have been covered over by a single-story, four-columned portico or colonnade with a flat roof or one with a very shallow slope. Above this colonnade rose the second story with three tall windows; above that was an attic story with smaller windows. We cannot know what designs Latrobe sent to Kentucky or how they fared at the hands of the local builders. But, given the constraints of the site, the outlines of the bank as depicted in the 1857 bird's-eye view seem to conform to Latrobe's practices. In both public buildings and urban residences, he preferred to set his structures back somewhat from the front line of the lot and, thus, to contrast with the surrounding buildings, which usually sat directly at the sidewalk. This he did in several urban buildings, such as the Bank of Pennsylvania and Waln House in Philadelphia and a design for a house for the Tayloe family in Washington, DC.

Like other "banking houses" of the period, the Lexington bank probably contained residential quarters for the banker or clerks on the second story. The banking rooms on the first story were likely of masonry-vaulted, fire-resistant construction; those of the residence above were probably not. In this regard, the Lexington bank may have resembled Latrobe's Louisiana State Bank in New Orleans (designed in 1820, completed in 1822 after the architect's death), except that the vaulting of the first-floor banking chambers of the Lexington building would not have been as complex as those of the later, New Orleans bank. Like the Lexington bank, the

↑
Latrobe's building

Detail of ca. 1857 bird's-eye "View of the City of Lexington." Lithograph by Middleton, Wallace & Co., Cincinnati, showing Latrobe's First Kentucky Bank at the lower right, in the block west of the Courthouse Square. (University of Kentucky, Special Collections Library.)

New Orleans bank was a simple rectangle in plan (approximately 40 feet wide × 60 feet long; the Lexington bank was approximately 28 feet wide × perhaps 40 or 50 feet long). Unlike the New Orleans bank, however, which occupies a corner site and fills its lot to the sidewalk, the Lexington bank, with its middle-of-the-block site, set-back facade, and street-level colonnade, may have resembled the central three bays of Latrobe's design for the Tayloe family's townhouse in Washington, DC, of ca. 1796–1799—a building closer in date to the Lexington bank than Latrobe's later New Orleans bank.[13]

Latrobe's Lexington bank building lasted slightly over half a century. The Kentucky Insurance Company, which owned it, failed in 1818; by 1825, the building had become a subscription library.[14] It was replaced sometime after the middle of the nineteenth century by a harness and saddle works and store, a three-story, four-bay brick building with a cast-iron storefront and shop windows at street level that dated from the early 1860s. This building sat at the edge of the sidewalk, so its facade cannot

South (front) elevation of John Tayloe House (unexecuted design) by Latrobe, ca. 1796–1799, for an unknown site in Washington, DC. The three central bays and portico of this house may have resembled Latrobe's design for the First Kentucky Bank, Lexington, ca. 1803–1804. (Library of Congress, Division of Prints and Photographs.)

have been a remodeling of Latrobe's setback bank building, although it is possible that the new store facade was built at the sidewalk and that portions of the earlier structure survived behind it.[15]

First Presbyterian Church, Lexington, 1807

Latrobe's second Kentucky project was a church in downtown Lexington. The architect's drawings apparently arrived late and were not used, though his written specifications arrived earlier and may have somewhat influenced the final form of the church as it was built at the southwest corner of Broadway and Second Streets. The building is no longer extant, though Latrobe's preliminary designs for it do remain.

In 1807, the architect made a sheet of drawings, containing a plan with a partial section, of a church or meetinghouse for the First Presbyterian Church congregation. The architect's drawings survive in the University of Kentucky Special Collections Library; neither the project nor the drawings are recorded in the Latrobe Papers.[16] Although unsigned,

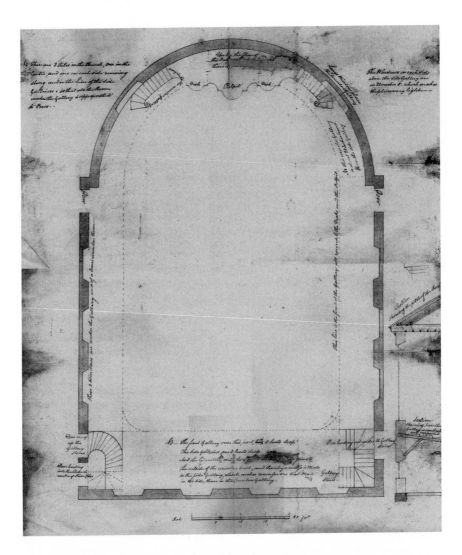

Latrobe's plan and partial section drawing of the First Presbyterian Church, Lexington, 1807. Although unsigned by Latrobe, this sheet of drawings is annotated in his handwriting. The partial section drawing is in the lower-right-hand portion of the sheet. (University of Kentucky, Special Collections Library.)

the sheet of drawings is clearly annotated in Latrobe's handwriting, and on the reverse is written by Andrew McCalla, an early Lexington settler, apothecary, and community leader, "A Plan of a meeting House drawn by Mr. Latrobe of Phil.a and presented as a compliment to the first presbyterian congregation in Lexington Kentuck[y]," procured by my father at my request in the year 1807."[17] No further drawings by Latrobe for the church survive, and the extensive notations by the architect on this sheet imply that it may have been the only drawings he sent, in order to elicit preliminary approval or suggestions from the building committee before preparing further drawings.

The plan consists of a square, approximately sixty feet to a side, with a half-circular apse appended to it, making the overall dimensions of the building approximately sixty feet wide by ninety feet deep. The apse contained a raised pulpit and reading desks. A shallow gallery, supported by a combined bracket-and-cantilever system, encircles the interior. The plan and section, along with Latrobe's notations, allow for a hypothetical reconstruction of his intended front and side elevations. It is a simple edifice, showing Latrobe's preference for pure geometries and bold forms. A belt course, corresponding to the gallery inside, divides the exterior horizontally into unequal parts, with large arched windows above, at the gallery level, and small semicircular windows below, at least in the sides. A gable roof creates a front pediment. Entrance is lateral, through twin doorways in the sides under the gallery stairs, in the front corners of the plan. The lack of a central, front entrance makes this plan unique among Latrobe's known church designs. The front elevation may have been blank below the belt course at street level, or it may have contained semicircular windows below, as in the sides. Latrobe's notations are unclear on this point. A third door, on the left-hand side, provides exterior access directly to the gallery; it may have accommodated enslaved or free African Americans. Two further doors occur in the sides near the apse. The plan is a fusion of a centralized meetinghouse type—focused on preaching—with a longitudinal basilica-type church, a synthesis of centralized and longitudinal types with which Latrobe was experimenting on a grander scale in his contemporary Baltimore Cathedral (1805–1820). The architect's only pure, centralized church plan was for the later St. John's Church, in Washington, DC, of 1815–1817; it is an equilateral Greek cross of a similar size to the proposed Lexington church. But the Lexington church, with its combined square and half-circle plan, its unusual side entrances, and its unequal division between larger upper windows and smaller lower ones (predicting the facade of the Pope Villa [see below]) is unique among Latrobe's designs, while its bold forms are a fitting reflection of the plainness and simplicity of the Presbyterian faith.

Like other of Latrobe's distant projects, the little Calvinist meetinghouse was destined to be built in a more conservative form. Latrobe's

Hypothetical reconstructions of front and side elevations of Latrobe's intended designs for the First Presbyterian Church, Lexington, 1807, from the architect's drawings in University of Kentucky, Special Collections Library. Latrobe's drawings are unclear whether he intended the front facade to have the small, semicircular windows in the lower story, hence the alternative reconstructions. (Patrick Snadon/Thomas Williams.)

drawings arrived too late, and another, more traditional meetinghouse was built instead. Three drawings—probably by the local builders—survive of this substitute project.[18] One is a cross section labeled (again by Andrew McCalla on the reverse) "plan of the Meeting house erected . . . in the year 1807 before Mr. Latrobe's plans arrived." It is a basic section drawing, with deep galleries supported on columns, as opposed to Latrobe's shallower galleries supported on his bracket-and-cantilever system, which would not have interrupted audience members' lines of vision to the pulpit, as would the columns. The section drawing also shows lower-story windows of greater height than the upper ones, yielding a more conventional exterior than Latrobe's, with its smaller windows below and larger above. On the end wall of the section drawing is shown an elevated pulpit; a gable roof with a king-post truss spans the whole. Schematic floor plans, seemingly related to this drawing, show the layout of pews and aisles on both the ground floor and the gallery level of the church. The pew layouts

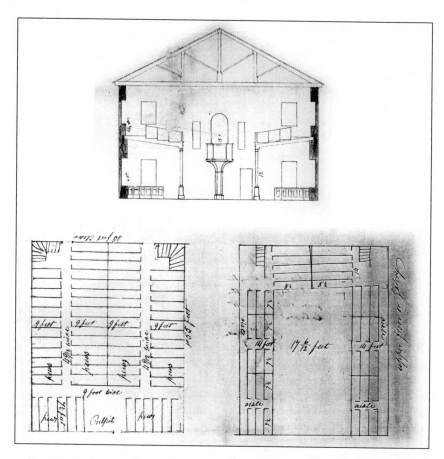

Floor plans (first floor and gallery level) and section drawing of the First Presbyterian Church, Lexington, presumably as designed and constructed in 1807 by the builders Gaugh and Hedrington. (University of Kentucky, Special Collections Library.)

are similar to those proposed by Latrobe in the notations on his plan, with a double row of box pews in the center, flanked by two aisles, with two side rows of pews under the galleries. The stairs to the galleries are in the front corners of the plan, like Latrobe's, but the twin entrances are in the front of the building rather than on the sides, as in Latrobe's plan. The overall dimensions of the final plans were approximately fifty feet wide by sixty feet deep, nearly the dimensions of Latrobe's plan minus his half-circular apse. Presumably, the final building corresponded with these later plans. The resulting church, with its multistage wooden cupola, appears in both an 1850 view and an 1857 bird's-eye view of Lexington, at the southwest corner of Broadway and Second Street.

Accompanying the drawings is a three-page estimate of costs and materials in Latrobe's hand; at the end of it is an addendum of items in another hand, made by the local builders, who identify themselves as "Gaugh and Hedrington" (Gaugh is probably the early Lexington builder Michael Gaugh).[19] This suggests that Latrobe's materials list and cost estimate did arrive, perhaps accompanied by a (now lost) letter describing his designs, in time to be employed in the construction process. Latrobe's specifications and possible written description of his designs may, thus, have influenced the rough dimensions of the building and its general interior layout of pews, aisles, galleries, and pulpit, but without his semicircular apse, his unusual side entries, or his radical window arrangement. Latrobe perhaps had some influence on the final building, but it was significantly more conservative in its design than his proposals. This building was demolished in 1857 and replaced by a new Presbyterian church; the Broadway Christian Church (which dates from 1916) now occupies the site.

The Pope Villa, Lexington, 1810–1813

While Latrobe's First Bank of Kentucky disappeared a few decades after its appearance and his designs for the First Presbyterian Church remained largely on paper, his third project for Lexington, the Pope Villa, survives and is the most avant-garde house designed in America in the federal period. By the early nineteenth century, Latrobe had theorized what he called a *rational house* for America on the basis of his observations of environmental factors and social life (which he called *climate and manners*) in the new republic. His theories for rethinking the American house were so radical, however, that he found few clients willing to patronize them. The Popes proved to be the most progressive residential clients of Latrobe's career. Their Lexington house represents the fullest realization of the architect's domestic planning theories and is one of the most exceptional buildings in America of its date.[20]

The clients were John and Eliza Pope. Pope was a Kentucky lawyer and U.S. senator whom Latrobe met in Washington and with whom he worked on a major proposal for "internal improvements," a system of roads and canals linking the eastern and western states; Eliza Pope was a sophisticated woman raised in London and the younger sister of Louisa Catherine (Johnson) Adams, the wife of John Quincy Adams. The daring character of the Pope Villa is surely due in part to Eliza Pope, whom

Latrobe credited as a collaborator in the design process, saying of the final plans: "I should be glad to explain them to Mrs. Pope to whose ideas I have endeavored to conform them, very much to the improvement of the taste and convenience of the building."[21] The Pope Villa is documented through both surviving letters and drawings by Latrobe, and much new information has emerged about it since a fire of 1987 and its subsequent restoration by the Blue Grass Trust for Historic Preservation.[22]

The Popes chose a ten-acre site overlooking the Town Branch, approximately a mile east of downtown. Their house was among the earliest of the residences that eventually constituted the arc of suburban villas east of the town. It conforms to virtually all Latrobe's rational house theories and constitutes an extremely adventurous act of architectural patronage. The house is a simple and handsome square block with a hipped roof. Its first story is essentially a ground-level service basement, with the principal public rooms located on the second story above. This functional division is clear in Latrobe's surviving elevation drawing, which shows smaller windows on the first floor, with larger windows above, and a central triple window in the second story, with single side windows. The architect offered two options: a villa of either two or three stories; the clients chose the two-story version. In Latrobe's floor plans, and in the house as built, the second story contained three great triple windows that, indeed, more effectively denoted the location of the public rooms. The first story—the ground-level service "basement"—contained Pope's office and Mrs. Pope's household parlor in front, with an internalized kitchen, "wash house–bake house," and servants' rooms across the back, constituting what the French called a concealed service *degagement*, and eliminating the need for the standard, rear service ell, which Latrobe criticized as inefficient and visually destructive of both the external composition of the house and views from it.

Latrobe felt that, in the American climate, with its frequent rain, ice, and snow, exterior stairs were dangerous; thus, for environmental reasons, he preferred to eliminate the partially submerged basement and exterior stairs of the standard American house of the period so that visitors entered at ground level and climbed to the second story public rooms via a protected interior stair. At the Pope Villa, this public stair (on the left) is balanced by a concealed service stair (on the right), thus avoiding the standard American central stair hall, which Latrobe derided as at once a "turnpike" and a "common sewer," through which everyone, whether family, visitors, or servants, male or female, sick or well, passed and through which the dirty laundry, chamber pots, etc. were carried.[23]

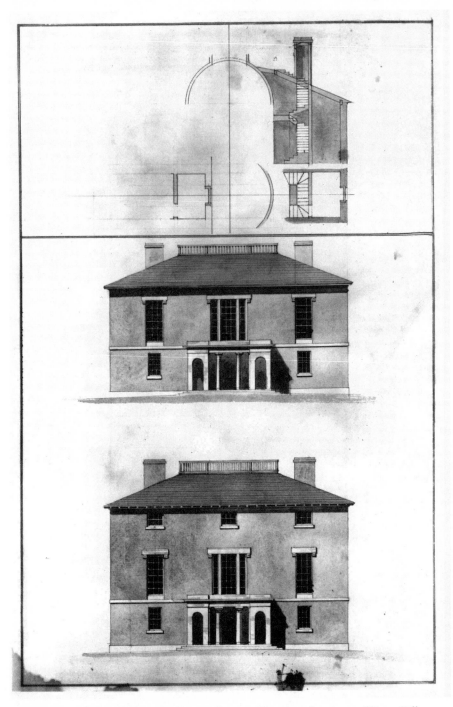

Pages 301–303: Latrobe, elevations, plans, and section drawings of Pope Villa, Lexington, all ca. 1811. (Library of Congress, Division of Prints and Photographs.)

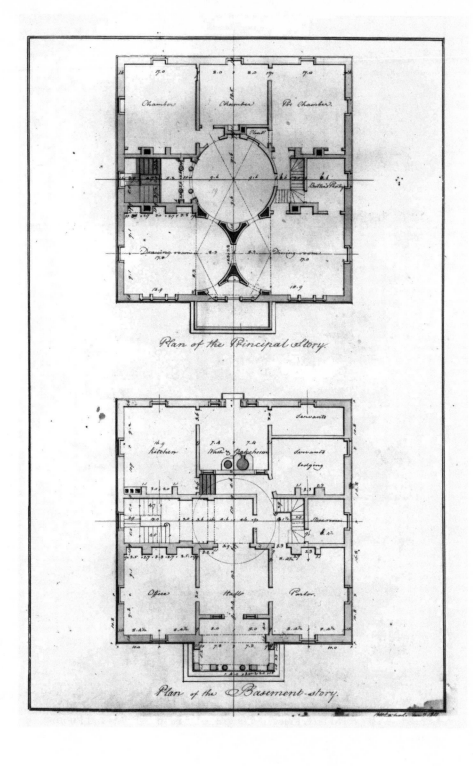

Plan of the Principal Story.

Plan of the Basement-story.

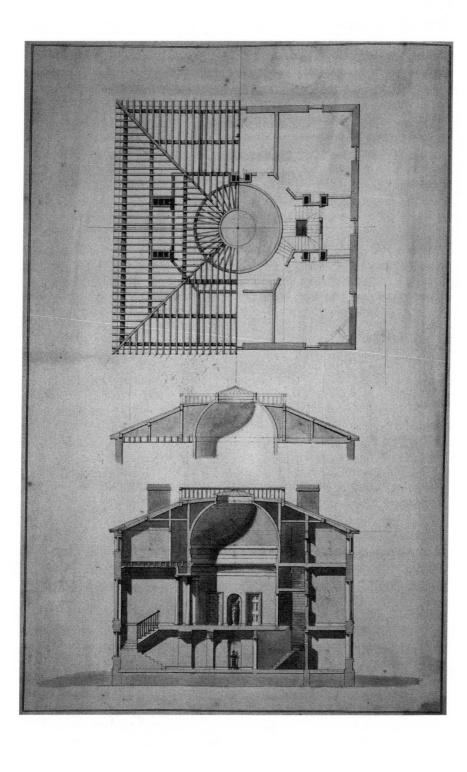

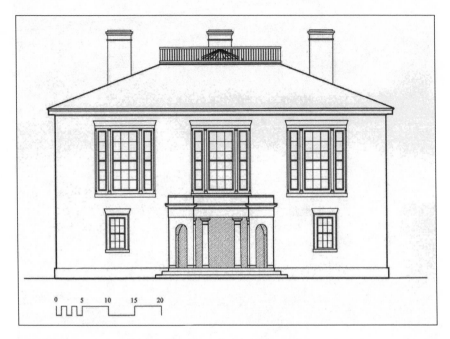

Hypothetical reconstruction of the facade of Pope Villa as built, ca. 1811–1812. (Patrick Snadon/Thomas Williams.)

On the second story of the Pope Villa, the main stair rose into a dramatic, central, top-lit rotunda, reminiscent of the sixteenth-century Italian architect Andrea Palladio's renowned Villa Rotonda at Vicenza. Latrobe's rotunda, however, communicated via twin diagonal axes with the back-to-back basilica-form drawing and dining rooms in the front of the house, while three bedchambers arrayed themselves across the rear. The public spaces of dining room, drawing room, and rotunda constitute a compact "circuit" of three public rooms that Latrobe recommended as best for "entertaining company": they would have served, respectively, for dining, conversation and card playing, and music and dancing.[24]

In addition to being a rational house (and a *rotunda villa*), the Pope Villa exemplifies another of Latrobe's domestic achievements: it is what he called a *scenery* house; that is, the asymmetrical route from the entry, through the low, rectilinear spaces of the first story, up to the surprise of the top-lit rotunda and the high, curvilinear rooms of the second story, constitutes a dramatic visual and spatial experience, with constantly changing scenic views and contrasts of light and shadow. Latrobe derived his theories of spatial sequencing and interior scenery from the landscape principles of English naturalistic or picturesque parks; it even seems that, like the small revived historic buildings in picturesque gardens, he included tiny pieces of "antique architecture" within the picturesque sequence of the Pope Villa. The interpenetrating entry corresponds to a small Greek prostyle temple, the rotunda is an embedded circular Roman temple or "Pantheon," and the drawing room/dining room suite constitutes a pair of half basilicas.

In summary, Latrobe's rational and scenery houses, as exemplified in the Pope Villa, departed in radical ways from the standard American houses of the period. First, rather than locating the public rooms on a first story above a raised basement with exterior stairs, the Pope Villa had a ground-level entry into a low first story, with the major public rooms in the second story above, accessed by an internal stair. Second, rather than a standard, rear ell wing with kitchen and service rooms, the Pope Villa's kitchen and services were concealed within the block of the house, at the rear of the first story. Third, unlike standard American houses, in which the plans of the first and second stories were similar, if not identical, and that were organized around a central stair hall, the Pope Villa plans differed dramatically from first to second story, and the central hall has given way to side stairs that form part of a picturesque sequence of differently shaped spaces and surprise-filled visual events. Altogether, the Pope Villa is theoretically and spatially the most sophisticated house designed in federal-period America.

Latrobe intended to control the building of the villa from Washington through working drawings and letters carefully timed to give the local contractor only the information necessary for each phase of construction (so that neither builder nor clients would be tempted to deviate from his plans). He wrote to the Popes' Lexington builder, Asa Wilgus: "Sir, I shall send you from time to time working drawings of every part of the roof and the rest of the carpentry. If I were near you, much less drawing and writing would answer the purpose, but as I shall probably never see Mr. Pope's house, it is necessary that my house on paper and yours in solid work should go up exactly alike."[25] However, Latrobe's system worked less smoothly than he had anticipated.

The Popes took a preliminary set of floor plans and a front elevation back to Lexington for estimates. The price apparently shocked Senator Pope, for he told Latrobe that he was "considering other projects."[26] Nonetheless, perhaps at Eliza Pope's urging, the Popes decided to continue, and they and their builder began the house with only Latrobe's floor plans and front elevation drawing. They carried the house up nearly

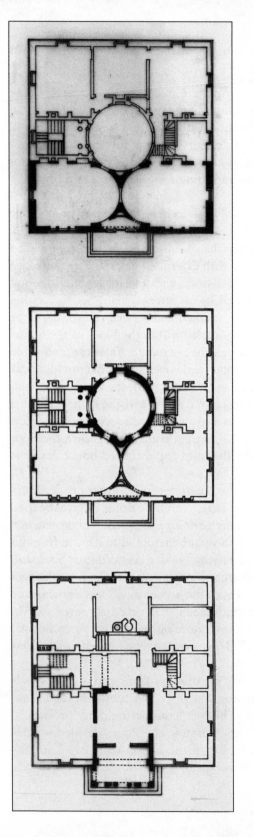

"Antique temples" embedded within the Pope Villa plans. (Patrick Snadon/Lejla Vujicic.)

The Pope Villa facade as restored by the Blue Grass Trust for Historic Preservation. (Photograph by Scott Heisey, 2005.)

to the roof and realized that the complexities of framing around the dome required further information. Mrs. Pope, then in Washington, visited Latrobe and requested help. Latrobe sent Pope a scolding letter, expressing his surprise and displeasure: "I regret exceedingly that you have actually proceeded to build without the necessary drawings and that it is highly probable that your house never will be in point of cheapness or elegance what I intended."[27] However, Latrobe did send on the requisite drawings, and, although the Popes and their builder deviated in some ways (such as the locations of the front windows and much of the interior detailing, which is more delicate and ornamental than Latrobe would have sanctioned), the house is still Latrobe's most rational house for America and exhibits all his avant-garde spatial distributions and sequences.

Later owners, however, strove to eradicate Latrobe's rational house planning. By the 1840s, the house had gained both a rear kitchen ell and the central hall that Latrobe so loathed, and an 1860s Italianate villa remodeling increased the size and number of first floor windows while decreasing the size of those on the second story in order to make the first story look like the principal floor and, thus, turn Latrobe's upside-down rational house upright. In the early twentieth century, the house was divided into apartments, ten in number by 1987, when it suffered a disastrous fire. Since then, the Blue Grass Trust for Historic Preservation has been carrying out careful research and restoration.

Latrobe's unusual planning and spatial sequencing at the Pope Villa had only limited regional influence (few people were privy to it, and later owners gradually eradicated it), but the triple-windowed facade was highly influential, affecting the development of central Kentucky country houses for several decades to come.[28] Beyond its regional context, however, the Pope Villa is among the most important buildings created in federal-period America. It is the best surviving example of Latrobe's domestic planning theories, with which he aimed to create a new, American house type and show the world how the citizens of a new, democratic republic might live. It is, in this respect, a building of international significance.

Designs for Henry Clay: Ashland, Transylvania University, Clay Townhouses

Ashland, Lexington, ca. 1811–1814

Almost contemporary with his work for the Popes, Latrobe executed a series of designs for Pope's political rival, Henry Clay. Unquestionably the greatest politician and leader that Lexington produced, Clay served almost continuously in either the U.S. House of Representatives or the Senate from 1806 until his death in 1852, was U.S. secretary of state, and came near to being elected president. The first designs that Latrobe produced for Clay and his wife, Lucretia, were for their country house, Ashland. Situated approximately two miles from downtown Lexington, Ashland was one of the outermost of the arc of suburban villas and country estates that surrounded the city to the east.

In the 1950s, the architectural historian Clay Lancaster discovered Latrobe's plans of 1812–1813 for the wings of Ashland.[29] In its final form, Ashland was a grand five-part composition with an earlier, two-story central block to which Latrobe's wings were added. Current views of the house show it after a complete 1850s rebuilding by Clay's son, James B. Clay, but reportedly with the same floor plan and similar massing as the original house—but with an infusion of mid-Victorian Italianate details. Because the 1812 sketch plan of the wings shows the central block of the

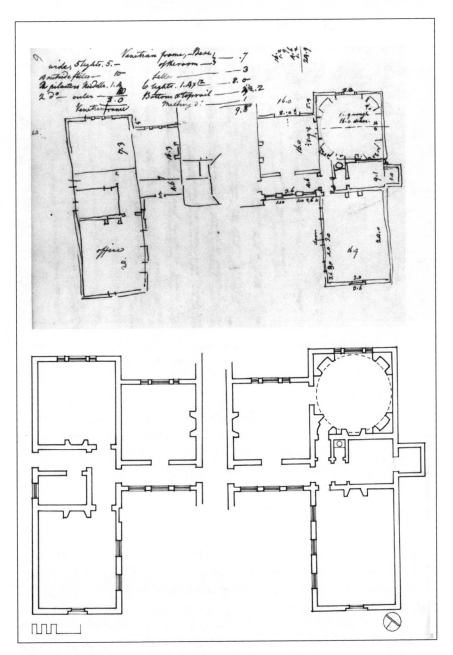

Latrobe sketch plans, ca. 1812, for the wings of Ashland, the Henry and Lucretia Clay House, Lexington. (Latrobe Letterbooks, Maryland Historical Society, Baltimore. Redrawing of the wing plans [below] by Michael Fazio.)

Ashland, photograph of the west (entrance) front showing the house as rebuilt, ca. 1852–1856, by the Clays' son, James B. Clay, and his architect, Thomas Lewinski, but with floor plans and massing similar to the original house. (Patrick Snadon.)

house only in a schematic form (but one that does acknowledge its octagonal entry), Lancaster and others assumed that Latrobe added the wings to a preexisting house with which he was unfamiliar. But a review of all the evidence suggests that he had a hand in designing the earlier central block as well.

Latrobe and Clay worked closely together in Washington, DC, in 1811–1812 on a remodeling of the House of Representatives chamber in the U.S. Capitol Building, specifically to improve its acoustics, while Latrobe was architect of the Capitol and Clay was speaker of the House.[30] The Latrobes and the Clays were friends and frequently dined together. During this time, Clay was building the central block of Ashland. No Latrobe drawings or letters survive for the central block (this does not seem unusual since Clay and Latrobe could have consulted about it in Washington and Clay have taken the drawings with him to Lexington). A later Latrobe letter to Clay of 1813, about the subsequent wings, contains a second sketch plan (unknown to Lancaster) that shows the staircase and octagonal dining room of the main house.[31] Taken together, these two sketch plans suggest that Latrobe did indeed know the room distribution of the Ashland central block, especially its most unique feature, the tangentially related octagons of the entrance hall and dining room. Both

Ashland, photograph of the east (garden) front showing the house as rebuilt, ca. 1852–1856, by the Clays' son, James B. Clay, and his architect, Thomas Lewinski, but with floor plans and massing similar to the original house. (Patrick Snadon.)

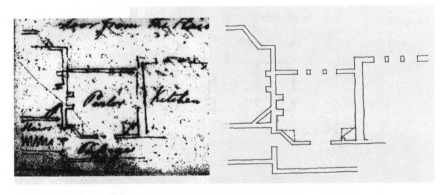

Latrobe, sketch plan of Ashland's south wing, included in a letter from Latrobe to Henry Clay of September 5, 1813. (Latrobe Letterbooks, Maryland Historical Society, Baltimore. Redrawing of wing plan by Michael Fazio.)

these sketches, plus the close relationship of Latrobe and Clay in 1811–1812, suggest that Latrobe designed the earlier central block as well as the later wings of Ashland. The planning of the central block (as reflected in the 1850s rebuilding) reinforces this hypothesis.

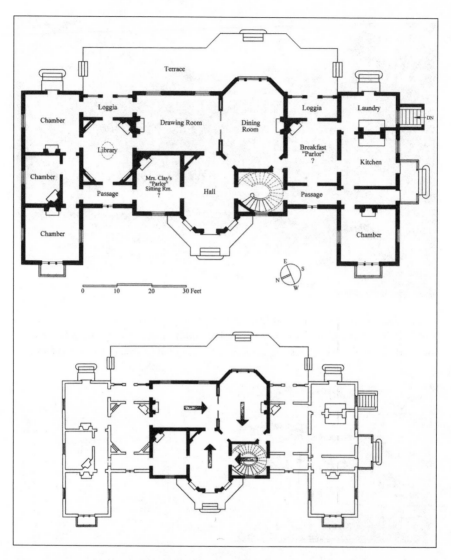

Plan of Ashland after 1850s rebuilding by James B. Clay and the architect Thomas Lewinski; below, diagram of Ashland plan showing the tangentially revolving, or pinwheeling circuit of public rooms in the central block, typical of Latrobe's domestic planning. (Patrick Snadon/Thomas Williams.)

The protruding octagonal entrance of Ashland resembles Latrobe's Markoe House in Philadelphia (1807–1811), while the unusual, pinwheeling circuit of main rooms resembles the planning that Latrobe learned from his mentor, the London architect S. P. Cockerell, and that he sub-

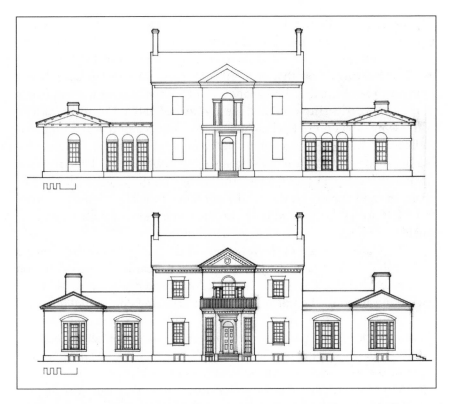

Ashland, hypothetical reconstructions of the west (entrance) front with the ca. 1812–1813 wings as Latrobe planned them (above) and the combined west front and wings as constructed by the Clays and their local builder (below). Latrobe designed the wings to have small arched windows on the west (above), with triple windows on the east; the Clays reversed this, building the triple windows on the west front instead (below). (Patrick Snadon/Michael Fazio.)

sequently employed in American residences such as the Pennock House in Richmond and Decatur House in Washington.[32] This sort of diagonal scenery planning was previously unknown in Kentucky (and was also uncharacteristic of Thomas Lewinski, the architect who rebuilt Ashland in the 1850s). A puzzling feature of the plan is the asymmetrical, canted bay on the garden front of the house; this may have resulted from some modifications to the plans by Clay and his builders. Certainly, if Latrobe designed the central block of Ashland, Clay's local builder, John Fisher, gave the exterior of the house rather old-fashioned, almost Georgian proportions and details.[33]

It is unclear whether the Clays originally conceived of Ashland as having wings or whether they added them to the scheme as the house progressed. Latrobe's documented sketch plans and letters of 1812–1813 regarding the wings show that he intended for the west, or entrance, fronts of them to have small arched windows and for the east, or garden, fronts to have large, tripartite windows. He also intended that the north (or left-hand) wing contain the kitchen and service rooms and that the south (or right-hand) wing contain a library, bedchamber, and nursery. Clay and his builder made significant modifications to Latrobe's plans. They reversed the functions of the wings (placing the kitchen on the south, with the bed-chambers and nursery on the north) and flipped the elevations from front to back (putting the large windows on the western, entrance front and the smaller windows on the eastern, garden front).

The Clays' reversal of the functions of the wings was perhaps owing to Latrobe's lack of familiarity with the site. An earlier house existed on the estate when the Clays purchased it. This earlier house possibly faced Richmond Road to the north, with its service wing and outbuildings arrayed behind it to the south.[34] When the Clays built the central block of their new house, they perhaps incorporated the older building into it—or at least kept the existing service axis to the south—but put the entrance front of the new house on the west. If this (probably) preexisting service axis to the south were unknown to Latrobe, it would explain why he proposed putting the kitchen on the north—which he always preferred so that the kitchen and its associated service spaces could buffer the main rooms from the cold, northern exposure. But the existence of an older axis of services to the south of the site would explain why the Clays preferred locating the new kitchen on that side; this ultimately resulted in their placing the kitchen on the southern, or warmest, exposure and the bedchambers and nursery on the northern, or coldest, exposure—an uncomfortable contravention of Latrobe's environmental theories.

The Clays' second change to Latrobe's designs, the reversed location of the larger windows from the east, or garden front, to the west, or entrance front, was probably owing to their misunderstanding of the country house planning traditions in which Latrobe worked. In British neo-Palladian country houses, which, like Ashland, had lateral wings, the opposing, long elevations, rather than being front and back, were of equal importance, the facade toward the road or approach being the entrance front—often with a more closed and private character—and the opposite facade being the garden front, facing the park with larger windows and more openness to the landscape. By designing the smaller windows of Ashland's wings on the west, or entrance front, with the larger windows on the east, or garden front, Latrobe intended for the house to conform to this tradition. Kentucky houses, however (and American vernacular houses generally), had only one principal facade—the entrance front—while the opposite facade was a back, often with an asymmetrical, kitchen-service ell, a service yard, and an axis of service outbuildings, none of which encouraged large windows and views from the public rooms. One senses that at Ashland, even with its services located laterally to the south, the Clays never quite understood the concept of a dual-fronted house, one with a more closed entrance front and an opposing, more open garden front. Hence, they placed the larger windows of the wings on the entrance front, contrary to Latrobe's plans.

These accumulating changes increasingly confused Latrobe, who finally wrote on September 5, 1813: "I confess myself a little at a loss on the subject of the wing[s] of your house."[35] The architect was out of the loop but still attempting to be helpful and to control the design process from Washington. That the Clays sought plans from Latrobe but then so freely modified them indicates the complex interactions between a prominent—but absent—architect, his clients, and their local builder. Clay was famous for crafting political compromises; the design process for Ashland seems consistent with these proclivities.

Despite the alterations to Latrobe's plans, however, Ashland represented a major contribution to domestic planning in Kentucky. Although less radical than the extraordinary two-story scenery route at the Pope Villa, the tangentially related octagons of the Ashland plan formed an impressive circuit of public rooms with diagonal, scenery vistas and circulation, making the spatial relations of its interiors advanced for America. While both Ashland and the Pope Villa were executed with a regional palette of details by the clients and their local builders, the houses displayed spatial sequences that were among the most sophisticated of Latrobe's domestic work. This elevates both Lexington houses to a position of national and even international importance within the early nineteenth-century neoclassical movement.

Designs for Transylvania University, Lexington, 1812

With Ashland still under construction, Henry Clay in 1812 requested plans of Latrobe for a new building for Transylvania University in Lexington. Clay was a staunch supporter of Transylvania and served on its board of trustees as his political career and time in Lexington allowed. Chartered in 1780, the school became the earliest institution of higher learning in the trans-Appalachian West. Latrobe's drawings for Transylvania are lost, and his building was never built; however, his letters to Clay describe his plans in such detail that it is possible to hypothetically reconstruct his intended building from the letters alone.

In the spring of 1812, the university trustees began to consider the erection of a new building on the university's approximately 160 × 300–foot site, which occupied a town out-lot in the northern quadrant of the city between Second and Third Streets and Mill and Market Streets (now the site of Gratz Park). John Wesley Hunt, a trustee, addressed a letter to Clay (then in Washington) requesting a plan. Although Hunt's letter does not survive, Clay's response of May 9, 1812, does. Clay wrote to Hunt that he had contacted Latrobe "to engage him to execute his promise."[36] This suggests that Latrobe had already agreed to furnish Clay with plans for the proposed university building, free of charge, as the architect consistently waived his fees for educational and religious institutions. Clay's letter urged the trustees to refrain from building "until they have a judicious design prepared by some architect," and he went on to criticize "the miserable building put up for a Court House in Lexington [in 1806, drawn by David Sutton and built by the local contractors Hallett M. Winslow and Luther Stephens]—the disgrace of the town and the derision of everybody," which, he stated, "ought to admonish us to proceed with more discretion in our public edifices."[37] Clay was anxious to raise the quality of public buildings in Lexington, and his work with Latrobe on both the U.S. Capitol Building and his own Ashland had persuaded him of the value of consulting a professional architect.

Clay passed the Transylvania trustees' request for designs on to Latrobe, evidently accompanied by a list of their requirements for the new building. By 1812, Latrobe had already been involved in the design of five or six colleges.[38] The architect responded promptly to Clay, in a letter of May 15, 1812, in which he reacted to the trustees' request and their proposed budget.[39] Although the trustees' letter and requirements do not survive, it is clear from Latrobe's two subsequent letters to Clay that they envisioned a building with five "recitation rooms" (lecture-classrooms), a "hall for public exhibition" (a large auditorium for public lectures) that could accommodate two hundred people, a dining room for the students, a suite of three rooms for a steward and his family, and fifteen student lodging rooms to accommodate between thirty and forty students.[40] This meant that either two or three students shared a room, which Latrobe

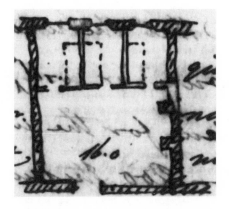

Latrobe's sketch of the "Princeton system" of lodging students in cells partitioned from within a larger room, included in a letter from Latrobe to Henry Clay of May 15, 1812. (Latrobe Letterbooks, Maryland Historical Society, Baltimore.)

compared to the systems at Princeton University in New Jersey (for which he had remodeled Nassau Hall in 1802–1805) and Dickenson College at Carlisle, Pennsylvania (for which he had designed a building in 1803). The alternative to this system was to house the students in large, open dormitories where they slept, with common study rooms elsewhere in the building. In his letter of May 15, 1812, Latrobe included a sketch of the "Princeton system" of lodging, which included three small sleeping and study cells for individual students, partitioned from within the larger room, the remaining space of which gave the students a common sitting room with a fireplace or stove.[41]

Having ascertained the trustees' desires, Latrobe quickly composed plans, which he transmitted to Clay on June 24, 1812.[42] The architect's drawings are lost, but the letter that accompanied them survives and is so detailed that it is possible to hypothesize the building he envisioned. It had a U-shaped plan, with its main front to the south, toward downtown Lexington, and two subsidiary wings to the northeast and northwest, creating a three-sided entrance courtyard open to the north; its east-west dimensions were controlled by the approximately 160-foot width of the college lot. The building resembled Latrobe's earlier college designs and exhibited his rational theories of planning and composition (many of which he had already employed in the Pope Villa, discussed above). The main rooms faced south, with a ten-foot-wide circulation corridor on the north. This conformed to Latrobe's theories of environmental orientation by giving the principal rooms the best exposure while locating halls and passageways to the north in order to buffer the southern rooms from the cold. Another of Latrobe's environmental theories dictated the avoidance of exterior staircases, which he felt were dangerous in the American cli-

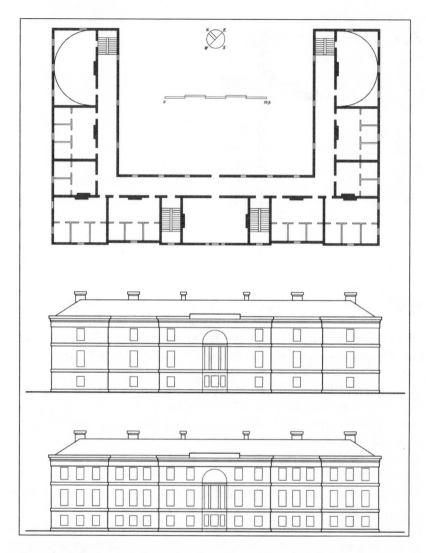

Hypothetical plan and alternative elevations of Latrobe's designs for Transylvania University, Lexington, reconstructed from descriptions in his letter to Henry Clay of June 24, 1812. (Patrick Snadon and Jose Kozan, Virtual Grounds, LLC.)

mate. In his designs for the Transylvania building (as at the Pope Villa), he created a low service story (or basement), its entry at ground level with access to the main, upper stories via protected, interior stairs. The ground story was to contain the main dining hall, in the center of the south wing, with the kitchen, pantries, and storage rooms to the northwest and other service rooms and three rooms for the steward and his family on the northeast.

On the principal, or second, story, Latrobe placed a "recitation room" (large classroom) in the center of the south wing (above the ground-story dining room). He located two large semicircular lecture halls, thirty-six feet in diameter, in the east and west wings. These auditoriums had "rising" seats (today called *sloped seating*) that also occupied the lower (ground) story; each auditorium could accommodate audiences of two hundred or more people.

The students' rooms were distributed four to each corner of the building and were partitioned into either two or three individual student study and sleeping cells, for a combined total of sixteen rooms, with forty-four student cells, on the two upper stories. The students' rooms were eighteen feet deep by either sixteen or twenty-four feet wide, depending on the number of student cells; the individual cells were approximately eight feet square. The third story was almost identical to the second story, except that over the semicircular lecture halls in the east and west wings were rectangular meeting rooms for student societies (literary, oratorical, and debating societies).[43] These could also be used as classrooms if needed. All the stories had circulation corridors to the north. The locations of the stairs and the exact distribution of the students' rooms are conjectural, but, given the description in Latrobe's detailed letter of June 24, 1812, the building as he designed it must be similar to this hypothetical plan.[44]

From this plan and Latrobe's letters, alternative elevations can also be hypothesized for his south, or primary front. The building was to be of brick with stone or marble trim; Latrobe described the ground story as being nine feet high, while the two upper stories were each to be twelve feet high. The fascia, or entablature, of the third story began immediately above the windows, making that story appear somewhat lower than it actually was so that the second, or principal, story presented the greatest apparent height on the exterior. The upper wall was to be terminated by a "blocking course" or parapet, which would have partially concealed the roof. Of the alternative, hypothetical elevations, the first has seventeen window bays, assuming that each student's study-sleeping cell had its individual window (as in Latrobe's sketch plan). However, all the student cells in a given room may have shared a single window, meaning that the partition walls that separated them were perhaps intended to rise only six or eight feet in height (rather than rising fully to the twelve-foot ceiling height), thus sharing light over the tops of the partitions.[45] This system would yield a front of only seven or nine window bays—the second elevation—which better conforms to Latrobe's general preferences for broad, planar wall surfaces with fewer windows.

The Transylvania trustees had hoped to erect their new building for between $15,000 and $18,000. Latrobe, however, made it clear to them that any building that would provide the accommodation they required could not be built for less than $30,000–$32,000.[46] Realizing that he was thus sending plans for a building almost twice as expensive as the trustees anticipated, Latrobe proposed two alternative strategies: first, that each of the rooms in his proposed building could be reduced in size by a few feet, for an overall savings of $2,000–$3,000; second, that expenses might be postponed by constructing only the central (south) block of his building or the south block plus the west wing, thus deferring construction of one or both wings until a later date.

A note appears in the university minutes on July 27, 1812, regarding payment of postage for Latrobe's plans, so we know that they arrived in Lexington.[47] But the trustees set Latrobe's plans aside. The reasons may have been both financial and political. Not only did Latrobe's plans exceed the expected cost, but the War of 1812 with Britain had begun to upset the national equilibrium. Henry Clay supported this war (indeed, was known as one of the War Hawks), while others on the national and local levels did not. Senator John Pope opposed the war (which ultimately cost him his Senate seat); Transylvania's acting president, James Blythe, also opposed it.[48] Thus, Latrobe's plans, promoted by Clay, may have raised objections from Blythe. The trustees considered other plans, but not until 1816 did they actually begin a new edifice, one designed by the Lexington builder-architect Matthew Kennedy. It was completed in 1818.[49]

Kennedy's new building differed significantly from that proposed by Latrobe. Latrobe's U-shaped plan had distributed its functions and spaces by environmental orientation and had a well-lighted northern corridor, a ground-level entry and service story, and internal stairs up to the principal story above. By contrast, Kennedy's building was a single block, with no attempt to orient spaces and functions according to environmental forces, with dark, internal halls, and with a partially submerged basement and external stairs up to the first, or principal, story.[50] Latrobe's exterior had a broad and simple horizontality, with a few compositional elements repeated for combined monumentality of character and economy of construction; by contrast, Kennedy's facade had a complex, fragmented, and vertical composition, with seven different window and door configurations and a busy roofline climaxed by a wooden cupola in a fussy, Georgian-baroque

Transylvania University main building, Lexington, designed by Matthew Kennedy, 1816–1818. (Engraved view published in *Discourse on . . . Horace Holley* [Boston, 1828]. Transylvania University.)

style, by that time a century or more out of date. As Latrobe had closely predicted in 1812, the completed building cost $30,000.

Latrobe's designs for Transylvania University incorporated his most progressive and rational theories of planning and composition and represented his mature thinking about architecture for educational institutions.[51] Had his designs been executed, they would have given Transylvania one of the most advanced university buildings in America and a handsome, modern addition to Lexington's architectural landscape.

Clay Townhouses, Tenements, and Shops, Lexington, 1813–1814

A year after the designs for Transylvania University, Henry Clay requested of Latrobe designs for a group of urban townhouses and tenement houses, some with shops at street level, in downtown Lexington. These buildings were built in some form to Latrobe's design. While they have long since disappeared, the surviving letters between Latrobe and Clay, along with meager visual records, do give some sense of their arrangement.[52]

On May 4, 1813, Clay agreed to purchase from the Lexington innkeeper John Keiser a property at the northwest corner of the intersection of Short and Market Streets. It was a desirable site as the courthouse square lay diagonally to the southeast. The property fronted 66 ²/₃ feet from east to west on Short Street and ran north along Market Street to an east-west alley that bisected the center of the block. The parcel contained three existing brick houses, one apparently fronting on Short Street at the western boundary of the site, a second and larger one at the corner of Short and Market Streets, operating as a tavern, with another brick house that Keiser was then building, apparently north along Market Street, with a small frame house adjacent to it.[53]

In a letter of August 15, 1813, Latrobe acknowledged receiving a plan of the site from Clay that included the locations and dimensions of the existing buildings; the architect also requested that Clay send elevation drawings of the existing buildings so that he could integrate his new buildings with them.[54] On August 24, 1813, Latrobe forwarded to Clay in Lexington an overall ground plan, which included floor plans for five or six new, in-fill townhouses between the existing buildings on the site. Then, on September 17, 1813, Clay contracted with the Lexington builders Robert Grinstead and Allen Davis to execute the brick- and stonework for the new buildings.[55] In October 1813, Latrobe moved from Washington to Pittsburgh to supervise the construction of Ohio River steamboats in partnership with Robert Fulton—a development that ultimately allowed river cities such as Louisville and Cincinnati to challenge Lexington's leadership in the West.

Clay's builders were evidently preparing to construct the new townhouses or had already begun them when, on January 16, 1814, Latrobe wrote to Clay from Pittsburgh acknowledging questions that Clay had sent in a letter of January 11, 1814 (not found).[56] In response to Clay's questions, he discussed the reasons for his overall arrangement of the new houses fronting on Short and Market Streets, with their rear yards and privies in the center of the block, and described how a passageway might be created from the street into the center of the block through one of the existing brick houses (probably one of those fronting on Market St.) by partitioning its ten-foot-wide entry-stair hall into a smaller, six-foot-six-inch-wide hall, leaving room for a three-foot-wide passage from the sidewalk through to the center of the block. He made a small sketch of this proposed modification in the margin of the letter to Clay. Of all Latrobe's drawings for Clay's project, this tiny sketch is the only one to survive.

The letter to Clay suggests that Latrobe had designed three tenements, each ten feet wide, to in-fill between the two existing buildings on Short Street, with two or three more houses of greater width, destined for individual families, along Market Street. Clay apparently intended the new buildings on Short Street to accommodate shops below and residenc-

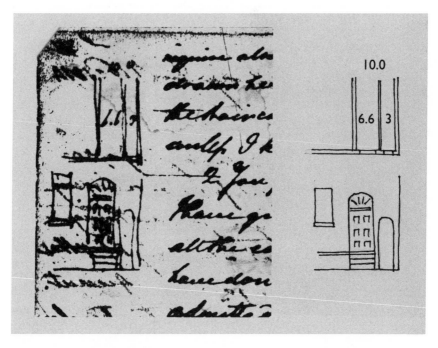

Latrobe sketch of a new door and passage (from Market St.?) through into center of block, Henry Clay houses, shops, and tenement buildings, on the northwest corner of Short and Market Streets, Lexington, from a letter by Latrobe to Henry Clay of January 16, 1814. (Latrobe Letterbooks, Maryland Historical Society, Baltimore. Redrawing by Patrick Snadon.)

es above. Latrobe designed as one possible option a continuous, one-story colonnade over the sidewalk for the Short Street fronts. Clay must have questioned the utility of this feature, for Latrobe wrote: "The front you like least is the Collonade. Your fears lest there should be a want of light are not, I believe, well founded & if they were, it would be a recommendation to Shop Keepers, who prefer a very moderate amount of Light as more favorable to the appearance of their goods."[57]

Latrobe's proposed colonnade related the Clay townhouses to the front of his First Kentucky Bank, two blocks to the east (ca. 1803–1804, discussed above), except that the bank facade was set back so that its colonnade covered, not the sidewalk, but its recessed forecourt. Clay's buildings undoubtedly extended to the edge of the sidewalk, for Latrobe mentioned that, in Philadelphia, regulations allowed such colonnades over sidewalks to a depth of four feet six inches. Although the architect couched his de-

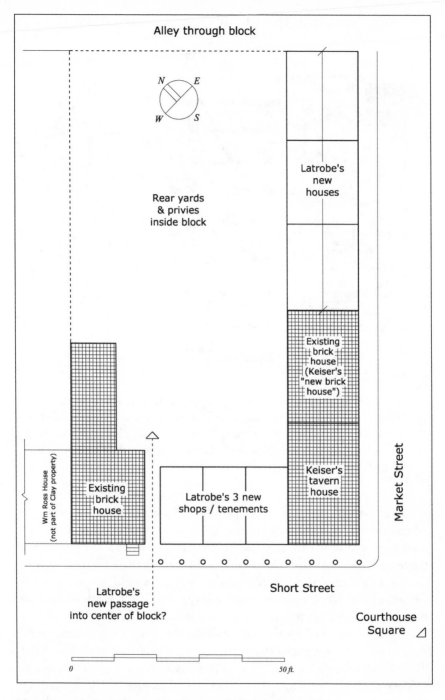

Hypothetical plan of Latrobe's 1813–1814 designs for in-fill houses, shops, and tenements for Henry Clay, northwest corner of Short and Market Streets, Lexington. (Patrick Snadon.)

fense of the colonnade in practical terms, one suspects that he intended it to give his in-fill shops and townhouses—perhaps the entire half block along Short Street and all its disparate buildings—a more unified appearance. Such a continuous colonnade over the sidewalk, spanning multiple buildings, would have introduced a new urban feature to Lexington. A schematic plan of Latrobe's project can be hypothesized.

How Latrobe's plans and advice affected the building process is unknown. Clay soon departed for Europe on his diplomatic mission to negotiate a peace treaty with Britain, and the completion of the Lexington buildings devolved on Clay's relative, John Watkins, with whom Latrobe exchanged letters in May and June 1814, and to whom he sent further drawings. Visually unifying all the buildings—old and new—preoccupied Latrobe, and he stressed to Watkins that the fascias, or entablatures, of all the buildings along Market Street needed to be made to run in one, continuous horizontal line.[58]

Despite Latrobe's move to Pittsburgh, Clay's departure for Europe, and the vicissitudes of posting drawings over long distances, Latrobe seems to have remained involved with the design of this urban ensemble of buildings through its completion in the summer of 1814. Because of its location near the courthouse square, this desirable site experienced rapid redevelopment. By ca. 1832, the Bank of the United States had completed a large building on the northwest corner of Short and Market Streets, fronting on Short Street (where Keiser's tavernhouse had been), with its attached banker's residence adjacent to the west, along Short Street.[59] This building, in an early Greek Revival style, may either have replaced or have incorporated Clay's earlier row of buildings. After the demise of the Bank of the United States in the mid-1830s, the Northern Bank of Kentucky occupied the building and, in 1889, demolished the older bank edifice and whatever might have remained of the Clay-Latrobe townhouses to build a large, new bank building that still survives at the corner of Short and Market Streets and covers much of Clay's original site.[60]

Henry Clay proved an enthusiastic advocate of Latrobe's talents. In addition to working with the architect on the Capitol Building in Washington, he personally commissioned him to design significant portions of his Lexington house, Ashland, and a group of shops and houses for his downtown site, an urban ensemble unique both to Latrobe and to Lexington. Clay further attempted to make Latrobe the architect for a major new building at Transylvania University, a visionary endeavor that failed.

With Clay's Lexington projects nearing completion, Latrobe wrote, on January 4, 1814, an interesting letter to his Kentucky patron: "Dear Sir, By the papers I observe that the State house of your State at Frankfort is burnt down. I am so ambitious as to wish to design a new one for the State & as I shall go down the Ohio in May in my steam boat to Louisville, & probably ride over to Lexington and Frankfort, I might perhaps find thro' your means, the gratification of my ambition."[61]

The first Kentucky Statehouse (built in 1793–1794) had burned in 1813. It is tantalizing to imagine what Latrobe might have designed to replace it. Although involved for years in building the U.S. Capitol, Latrobe never had the opportunity to design a state capitol. Had he received this commission, it might have altered the course of Kentucky, and American, architecture. However, his steamboat-building enterprises ended in financial disaster for him, and he failed to make his planned trip down the Ohio from Pittsburgh to Kentucky. Instead, the Lexington builder-architect Matthew Kennedy, who also designed the new Transylvania University building rather than Latrobe, built the second Kentucky Statehouse, between 1814 and 1816.[62]

Designs for a Kentucky State Armory, 1817

Despite missing the opportunity to design a new statehouse at Frankfort, Latrobe soon received a commission to design another major public building for Kentucky. The architect's old friend and client John Pope, whose villa Latrobe had designed in 1810–1811 (discussed above), requested him to design a government armory for the state. Latrobe's drawings for the armory complex reached Kentucky but have not been found; his letters, however, give hints of its design. No part of the project seems to have been built.

Pope had, as a U.S. senator in 1812, voted against the war with Britain; this proved such a controversial action with his Kentucky constituents that he returned to Lexington in 1813 on the expiration of his senate term without attempting another run. In 1816, on the death of Kentucky governor George Madison, Lieutenant Governor Gabriel Slaughter became acting governor and appointed Pope his secretary of state—an unpopular decision with the Kentucky citizenry and many members of the General Assembly. Latrobe, on the failure of his steamboat-building endeavors in Pittsburgh in 1815, had returned to Washington to rebuild the U.S. Capitol after its burning by the British in the war.

The Kentucky House of Representatives requested Slaughter in 1817 to procure plans for an armory "for the manufacturing of such a quantity of arms as may be requisite to supply the militia of this state," along with estimates of its cost and suggestions as to an appropriate site.[63] Slaughter passed the request on to Secretary of State Pope, who, on October 19, 1817, wrote to Latrobe requesting information and designs. Pope's letter is lost, but Latrobe's reply, dated November 3, 1817, survives.[64] On November 20, 1817, Latrobe sent Pope three sheets of drawings for the complex: a ground-floor plan, a principal- (or second-) floor plan, and three elevations of the buildings, accompanied by a letter.[65] Latrobe encountered great difficulties in his second tenure as architect of the U.S. Capitol; ironically, this was the very day that he submitted his resignation.

In his designs for the Kentucky armory, Latrobe consulted his colleague Col. George Bomford of the U.S. Army Ordnance Department, who advised him on the latest developments in arms manufacture, which were toward industrial machinery to create standardized armaments with interchangeable parts. Latrobe's plans for the Kentucky armory contained multiple buildings grouped around a courtyard or "square" of 120 × 136 feet (though the architect stated that the plans might be reduced to enclose a yard of only 80 × 120 feet). Latrobe estimated that the armory would employ a hundred workmen and could produce forty-eight hundred firearms per year. In addition to the manufacturing shops, he included a residence for a live-in superintendent and his family and a gate lodge for a guard or porter. The workers, he felt, could live in a village near the facility. He stated that his plans were for a water-powered plant but that he was making an alternative drawing, to be mailed shortly, adapting the complex for a steam engine, which he preferred as a more reliable power source. Latrobe estimated the cost for the buildings to be between $65,000 and $75,000, with an additional $25,000 for equipment and machinery, bringing the estimated total cost for the complex to around $100,000. As the state had not yet chosen a site, Latrobe's plans were not made for a specific location.[66]

Latrobe had designed an armory in 1798 for Virginia, but it remained unbuilt, and no drawings survive.[67] Closer in time, though not identical in function, were his designs of 1814 for the U.S. Allegheny Arsenal in Pittsburgh.[68] While this complex functioned for the storing rather than the manufacture of arms, it consisted, like Latrobe's Kentucky armory project, of multiple buildings arranged around a central yard. To accommodate the weight of the ordnance, and for purposes of fireproofing, the Pittsburgh buildings were of masonry-vaulted structure. The plans consisted of a regularly spaced grid of square columns from which sprang groined vaults to support the floors. This rational, modular structure expressed itself on the exterior in regular, arched windows, the architectural equivalent of the standardized manufacturing methods that Latrobe recommended. Latrobe articulated the Pittsburgh arsenal with only essential structural and functional elements; even the small, circular temple atop the roof functioned as a ventilation cupola. His designs for the Kentucky armory would likely have conformed to these utilitarian principles.

On December 19, 1817, John Pope presented Latrobe's plans to the Kentucky legislature.[69] At that date, no decision had yet been reached about the power source (water vs. steam) or the site, though both Frankfort and Louisville were considered. The legislators subsequently sent Latrobe $300 for his drawings.[70]

Latrobe's design would have introduced advanced industrial methods and a structurally and functionally rational architecture for this early western factory complex. However, it seems unlikely that any portion of his project was built. In 1825, the Kentucky legislature expressed a desire that the federal government might construct an armory near Louisville, along the newly chartered Portland Canal, which was to be built around the Falls of the Ohio.[71] Kentucky evidently still had no official armory at that date, but by their resolution the legislators acknowledged that the industrial impetus within the state was shifting to Louisville.

General James and Keturah Taylor Mansion, Newport, 1817–1819

Latrobe's final Kentucky project consisted of designs for a house for General James Taylor and his wife, Keturah, in Newport, on the Ohio River opposite Cincinnati. The dates of this commission, following the introduction of steamboats to the Ohio River, further signaled the shifting of regional influence away from Lexington and central Kentucky to the nearby river cities of Cincinnati and Louisville. The commission is known only through a letter from Latrobe to the clients (undocumented by the Latrobe Papers Project); none of Latrobe's drawings for the house survive. The original house was completed in ca. 1819 but burned in 1842 and was rebuilt. No visual sources remain to document the appearance of the early house, though the rebuilt house may follow its general outline, foundations, and composition.

Taylor, a second cousin to President James Madison and first cousin to President Zachary Taylor, became one of northern Kentucky's wealthi-

Latrobe elevation and ground-floor plan drawings for Allegheny Arsenal complex, Pittsburgh, Pennsylvania, 1814. The Pittsburgh buildings may have resembled Latrobe's lost designs for a Kentucky State Armory of 1817. (Library of Congress, Division of Prints and Photographs.)

est land speculators and businessmen. He played a key role in the development of Newport and lobbied successfully for a new federal arsenal to be built there.[72] It is unclear how Latrobe and Taylor met, but they had many mutual friends, including Thomas Jefferson, James and Dolley Madison, and Henry Clay.

A single surviving letter of February 27, 1817, reveals that Latrobe was designing a house for the Taylors. The letter evidently accompanied drawings (not found) as the architect wrote to Taylor: "Pray say to your Lady, that she must cut and carve the plan as she would a Turkey, and take or reject the whole or a part. I am at her service, knowing once exactly what she wishes, to the very verge of my talents."[73] The lack of further information about the designs is unfortunate, but this passage provides significant insights into Latrobe's interaction with his clients, particularly his desire for their participation in the design process. His graphic use of the metaphor of carving to describe the development of a plan also makes clear his expectation that the female partner in a set of married clients would, or at least could, take a major role in a domestic commission.

The Taylors may or may not have followed Latrobe's plans as they continued to solicit other designs. In 1818, Taylor wrote to James Madison, in Virginia, that he was preparing to build and asked whether Madison or Dolley Madison could procure for him plans of a house in the neighborhood of their own Montpelier that he had seen and admired.[74] It is possible that the Taylors used Latrobe's plans or modified them to incorporate features of other houses they liked or that they built to other designs entirely. However, it seems probable that Latrobe's drawings did influence the final design.

The Taylors completed their house in ca. 1819 and called it Bellevue for its hilltop site and extensive views of the Ohio River. Although no visual records remain of this early house, evidence suggests that, when the Taylors rebuilt it after the fire of 1842, they may have followed the footprint—perhaps even have reused foundations and other materials—from the earlier house.[75] The post-1842 house survives (with later nineteenth-century alterations); it has a central block of three bays with a slightly outset center, a shallow, one-story portico, a low, hipped roof, and symmetrical wings adjoining it on the sides. This general composition resembles certain of Latrobe's domestic designs, such as that of the Harvie-Gamble House in Richmond, Virginia (ca. 1798–1800).[76] This suggests that Latrobe's design may have influenced the form of the Taylors' 1817–1819 house and that this early house may then have influenced the composition of the house as rebuilt after the 1842 fire. If this is the case, the process resembled that of Henry Clay's Ashland, where the earlier house by Latrobe influenced the rebuilt house of 1852.

Conclusion

Of Latrobe's eight designs for Kentucky, four were for public buildings (a bank, a church, a college, and an armory), while four were domestic (the Pope Villa, Ashland, Clay's townhouses, and the Taylor Mansion). Of the domestic commissions, all were built, some—like the Pope Villa—quite faithfully to Latrobe's designs. Of the public commissions, only one—the bank—was built. This may be explained by the greater size, expense, and complexity of public projects (clients consisting of boards, building committees, legislatures, etc.), while domestic projects are smaller and private, commissioned by individuals or families. But the higher rate of success of Latrobe's Kentucky domestic projects suggests that individual clients, such as the Popes and the Clays, were more progressive than their general, Kentucky context. Also, the domestic clients knew Latrobe personally and had seen his public works (the Popes and the Clays had resided in Washington, for example), while the individuals composing the committees and boards for the public projects had probably neither met the architect nor seen his completed public buildings.

Some of the advanced architectural ideas that Latrobe strove to introduce to Kentucky remained on paper, some were confined to the individual buildings by him that were built, and some had a wider impact. At the Pope Villa, for example, his giant triple windows seemed to influence later Kentucky buildings. The Shaker architect Micajah Burnett introduced multiple triple windows in his Trustee's Office and Guest House at Pleasant Hill (1839–1841), and central Kentucky architects of the 1840s–1850s, such as Thomas Lewinski and John McMurtry, used triple windows so liberally in their domestic facades that the resulting houses constitute a unique Bluegrass Greek Revival villa type.[77] However, perhaps Latrobe's greatest contribution to Kentucky architecture came through his pupils and the resulting establishment of the architectural profession in the state.

In the first half of the nineteenth century, one learned architecture through apprenticeship, by studying and working with a practicing architect. Latrobe was the first architect in America to train students in an organized fashion; among his numerous pupils, William Strickland and Robert Mills were most important. They, in turn, trained pupils, and the resulting genealogy contributed largely to creating the American architectural profession. Of Latrobe's pupils, Strickland's line was most influential for Kentucky.[78] Strickland (1788–1854) studied with Latrobe from ca. 1803 to 1805. Among Strickland's pupils was Gideon Shryock of Kentucky (1802–1880); thus, Latrobe's professional grandchild. The son of the Lexington builder Mathias Shryock, Gideon studied with Strickland in Philadelphia for approximately a year, in 1823–1824; part of the young Kentuckian's training consisted of observing important buildings in Philadelphia and the East, and the impact of Latrobe's buildings on Shryock seems as great as the influence of his mentor, Strickland.

Latrobe had introduced Greek Revivalism to America in such examples as the Bank of Pennsylvania, an adaptation of a Greek temple. But he had always, for functional reasons, combined Grecian forms with Roman structure and spaces, such as arches, vaults, and domes, and had progressively distilled his neoclassicism to create what he considered an appropriately simple and economical American style. Latrobe's pupils moved toward a more literal and archaeological Greek Revival, with giant, columned porticos on the exteriors of their buildings, a development that Latrobe had initiated but then largely discarded in favor of a more restrained and original neoclassicism. However, the later, more exaggerated replication of Grecian forms proved popular with Americans, who fancied themselves the inheritors of ancient Greek democratic culture.

Shryock returned to Kentucky to design many of the state's most important buildings, including the Kentucky Statehouse in Frankfort (1827–1830), the first Grecian-derived, temple-form capitol building in the nation, and Morrison College at Transylvania University (1830–1835), which, with its bold, Greek Doric portico atop an artificial acropolis of steps and antepodia, gave effective physical form to Lexington's Athenian self-image. Both were projects that Latrobe had desired but failed to achieve. Shryock introduced Strickland's more literal Greek Revival style in his exteriors, while his spatial sequences and sophisticated vaulted and domed interiors acknowledged the lessons he learned from Latrobe's buildings. Shryock was Kentucky's first professionally trained architect, and he himself trained numerous pupils, including his younger brothers, Montgomery and Cincinnatus Shryock, his son Charles, and the Lexington builders John McMurtry and George Weigart, thus greatly contributing to the establishment of the profession in Kentucky. Part of Latrobe's legacy to the state was, thus, architectural professionalism, as represented by Shryock, who garnered the kind of monumental public commissions

Kentucky Statehouse, Frankfort, by Gideon Shryock, 1827–1830. Shryock trained under Latrobe's pupil William Strickland, and his buildings show Latrobe's influence.

Morrison College, Transylvania University, Lexington, by Shryock, 1830–1835, perhaps the ultimate building in the construction of Lexington's Athenian image.

that Latrobe had missed and trained a further generation of Kentucky architects.

In the first two decades of the nineteenth century, Lexington's burgeoning economy resulted in numerous commissions by the nation's most famous architect, Benjamin Henry Latrobe. Despite the vicissitudes attending his Kentucky projects, they form an important group of designs and buildings that exhibited Kentucky's social and political leaders to be in a highly progressive posture architecturally and aesthetically. The survival of the Pope Villa, the most sophisticated domestic design of Latrobe's career, is an exceptional stroke of luck for both the state and the nation. It is a stunning physical reminder that federal-period Kentucky could be at the leading edge of the new republic, not only geographically, but also in terms of ideas.

Notes

I wish to dedicate this essay to the memory of Dorothy Crutcher, who recognized in Lexington's classical past one of its great assets for the future, and who was instrumental in saving Latrobe's Pope Villa for posterity. I thank Dr. Daniel Rowland for his longtime encouragement and support of my Latrobe scholarship, his lifetime commitment to the restoration of the Pope Villa, and his valuable suggestions and patience in the development of this essay. Thanks also to Edith Bingham for reading drafts and making excellent suggestions, to my colleague Michael Fazio for advice and drawings, and to Jose Kozan of Virtual Grounds, LLC, for much assistance with digital images. Finally, my gratitude to Dr. James D. Birchfield, whose expertise and assistance are invaluable to anyone attempting to write on the history of Lexington and central Kentucky. He has helped me in numerous ways, including providing ideas and research, locating and evaluating sources, and reading drafts and making suggestions.

1. Adena, the Thomas and Eleanor Worthington House at Chillicothe, Ohio, of 1805–1807, is a ninth western project by Latrobe, geographically near his Kentucky works. The family conformed to the pattern for Latrobe's most important western clients: he met them in Washington, where Worthington was a U.S. senator from Ohio, and he and Latrobe collaborated on schemes for "internal improvements." Worthington, the main advocate of Ohio statehood, later became governor of the state; in 1805, when Latrobe designed Adena, Chillicothe was the capitol of Ohio. The Worthingtons knew Latrobe's important Kentucky clients, including John and Eliza Pope and Henry and Lucretia Clay, who stayed at Adena on journeys between Lexington and Washington, DC.

2. The Latrobe Papers Project publications cited in this essay are Edward C. Carter and Thomas E. Jeffrey, eds., *The Papers of Benjamin Henry Latrobe Microform*

Edition, Guide, and Index (Clifton, NJ, 1976) (hereafter *BHL Microform*), a microfiche edition of all known Latrobe documents; Edward C. Carter, ed., *The Virginia Journals of Benjamin Henry Latrobe*, 3 vols. (New Haven, CT, 1977) (hereafter *Journals of BHL*), Latrobe's personal journals, in the Maryland Historical Society; John C. Van Horne et al., eds., *The Correspondence and Miscellaneous Papers of Benjamin Henry Latrobe*, vol. 1, *1784–1804*, vol. 2, *1805–1810*, vol. 3, *1811–1820* (New Haven, CT, 1984–1988) (hereafter *Correspondence of BHL*), a selection of Latrobe's letters to and from clients, friends, and family and other papers, with some small sketches reproduced from the letters; and Jeffrey A. Cohen and Charles E. Brownell, eds., *The Architectural Drawings of Benjamin Henry Latrobe, Parts 1 and 2* (New Haven, CT, 1994) (hereafter *Architectural Drawings of BHL*), Latrobe's known architectural drawings (as of 1994) with commentary by the editors. A volume of Latrobe's engineering drawings (Darwin H. Stapleton, ed., *The Engineering Drawings of Benjamin Henry Latrobe* [New Haven, CT, 1980]) has also appeared, but none of these applies to Latrobe's Kentucky projects.

3. Clay Lancaster, "Planning the First Two Towns in Central Kentucky: Harrodsburg and Lexington," *Kentucky Review* 9 (1989): 10–13; John D. Wright Jr., *Lexington: Heart of the Bluegrass* (Lexington, 1982), 3–5.

4. Wright, *Lexington*, 17.

5. For specific accounts of these suburban villas, see Clay Lancaster, *Ante Bellum Houses of the Bluegrass: The Development of Residential Architecture in Fayette County* (Lexington, 1961), esp. chaps. 5–7 and the accompanying map. See also Clay Lancaster, *Ante Bellum Suburban Villas and Rural Residences of Fayette County Kentucky* (Lexington, 1955).

6. Clay Lancaster, *Antebellum Architecture of Kentucky* (Lexington, 1991), 264.

7. Short Street and the Western Suburb eventually housed a community of artisans and workers west of downtown, though the most dramatic of the manufacturing establishments in this western sector were the large woolen factory, paper mill, and workers' housing complex that constituted Manchester (named after the English industrial city), the development of the New Englanders James and Thomas Prentiss who arrived in Lexington in 1805. The Prentisses' industrial endeavors subsequently failed in 1818. Wright, *Lexington*, 24.

8. For the general history of western cities in the region, see Richard C. Wade, *The Urban Frontier: The Rise of Western Cities, 1790–1830* (1959; Urbana, IL, 1996).

9. As no drawings are known for the bank building and it is not mentioned in any of Latrobe's surviving letters or papers, it consequently does not appear in the Latrobe Papers Project. The bank and other of Latrobe's Kentucky projects are discussed in William B. Scott Jr., "Greek Revival Architecture in Kentucky," *Southern Quarterly* 26 (1987): 102. See also William B. Scott Jr., *A History of the Profession of Architecture in Kentucky* (Louisville, 1987), 7–8. Relying on Scott's research, Mills Lane also discussed some of Latrobe's Kentucky projects in *Architecture of the Old South: Kentucky and Tennessee* (Savannah, GA, 1993), 59–62.

10. William [A.] Leavy, "Memoir of Lexington and Its Vicinity," *Register of the Kentucky Historical Society* 41, no. 134 (1943): 57. Regarding the dating of the building,

the act to incorporate the Kentucky Insurance Co., which operated the bank, was approved by the state legislature on December 16, 1802; Leavy stated that the building was erected in 1803 (ibid.); a notice in the *Kentucky Gazette* of April 24, 1804, implies that it was nearing completion but not yet occupied. Thanks to Dr. James D. Birchfield for these references. Some later accounts call it the Kentucky Insurance Building and claim that its banking privileges resulted only from a cleverly worded clause in the Kentucky Insurance Co. charter. See G. W. Ranck, *Guide to Lexington, Kentucky*, 2nd ed. (1884; Lexington, 1974), 69. Ranck's account does not mention Latrobe. Later sources mention the bank's connection with Latrobe, but all apparently rely on Leavy for their information. See Rexford Newcomb, *Architecture in Old Kentucky* (Urbana, IL, 1953), 53.

11. An 1825 deed describes the lot as being 28½ feet in width (fronting on Main St.) and 108 feet in depth (running north along Bank Alley). Deed, July 10, 1825, between James Haggin and his wife, Hetty, to the Sharers of the Lexington Library, Fayette County Deed Book X, 327, Fayette County Courthouse, Lexington. (The Lexington Library later acquired the building. See n. 14 below.) Thanks to Dr. James D. Birchfield for this reference. The depth of the building would have been less than that of the lot and would probably have included an enclosed rear court or garden behind (as was the case with Latrobe's earlier Bank of Pennsylvania in Philadelphia and his later Louisiana State Bank in New Orleans).

12. John Lutz, "Plan of the City of Lexington" (1835); "View of the City of Lexington, Ky.," color lithograph by Middleton, Wallace & Co. (Cincinnati, [ca. 1857]). Both maps are now in Special Collections, University of Kentucky Library. Thanks to Dr. James D. Birchfield for calling to my attention the location of the bank building on the first map and providing detailed images from both maps.

13. On Latrobe's designs for the Tayloe House, see *Architectural Drawings of BHL*, 1:114–26.

14. The bank's charter expired in 1818, and it failed financially under the direction of James Prentiss. See also n. 7 above. On Prentiss and the collapse of the bank, see *Kentucky Gazette*, February 14, 1818, and March 6, 1818. Thanks to Dr. James D. Birchfield for these references. In ca. 1823–1825, the Lexington Library Co. acquired the building for its use. Leavy, "Memoir of Lexington," 56–57. See also n. 11 above.

15. Latrobe's bank building apparently disappeared—either demolished or subsumed within the later building—sometime between 1860 and 1864. In 1860, the harness and saddle makers John P. Tingle and Thomas Quinn purchased the property (Fayette County Deed Book 36, p. 316 [August 8, 1860], Fayette County Courthouse); in the 1859–1860 Lexington City Directory, Tingle and Quinn saddlers are listed on Mulberry (Limestone) St.; in the 1864–1865 City Directory, the firm had become Tingle and (Butler F.) Thompson and is located on the site of Latrobe's former bank building (now 53 Main St.). A *carte-de-visite* photograph of the Tingle and Thompson building exists in Special Collections, University of Kentucky Library. It shows a few feet of the west side wall of the new building, toward the adjacent alley, with three irregularly placed iron bolt-ends for tie-rods, which suggests that the brick front

and upper stories of the 1860s building may have been added on to Latrobe's earlier building and have required tie-rods to stabilize the additional masonry. Thanks to Dr. James D. Birchfield for the deed reference and for calling my attention to this early photograph. The firm subsequently became the Thompson and Boyd saddle works. For a description and views of the building under Thompson and Boyd, see Ranck, *Guide to Lexington*, 69; and Bettie L. Kerr and John D. Wright Jr., *Lexington: A Century in Photographs* (Lexington, 1984), 98. Newcomb (*Architecture in Old Kentucky*, 53) also suggests that the Tingle/Thompson/Boyd building may have contained portions of the earlier Latrobe building. This 1860s building was replaced by yet another commercial building in the early twentieth century (the Hay Hardware Co., as shown in the 1920 Asa Chinn downtown survey photograph of this block). The site is now a parking lot.

16. Drawings labeled "Plan of a Meetinghouse by Mr. Latrobe, 1807," First Presbyterian Church Archives, Special Collections, University of Kentucky Library. Thanks to Dr. James D. Birchfield for helping locate, interpret, and reproduce these drawings and the associated drawings and documents in nn. 18 and 19 below. Although the Presbyterian church project is not included in the Latrobe Papers volumes, it is mentioned in Scott, "Greek Revival Architecture in Kentucky," 102, and *A History of the Profession of Architecture in Kentucky*, 7–8.

17. On Andrew McCalla, see Wright, *Lexington*, 12 (which states that McCalla is a subscriber to a pew in the Episcopal church), 18, 29, 59.

18. Drawings labeled "Plan of Meetinghouse," First Presbyterian Church Archives. The section drawing is labeled specifically "an end view of the plan of the first Presbyterian Meeting House of brick with a cupola, put up on the year 1807."

19. "An Estimate of the Work & Materials session House of First Presbyterian Church Lex-Ky," Special Collections, University of Kentucky Library. The builder Michael Gaugh (1778–1855) arrived in Lexington from Maryland and was closely associated with the builder Mathias Shryock (who married Gaugh's sister). See Lancaster, *Ante Bellum Houses of the Bluegrass*, 29–30.

20. This discussion of the Pope Villa is a distillation of a more thorough account of it published in Michael W. Fazio and Patrick A. Snadon, *The Domestic Architecture of Benjamin Henry Latrobe* (Baltimore, 2006), 389–446. For a more complete discussion of Latrobe's rational house theories, see ibid., 183–91, 528–44.

21. Benjamin Henry Latrobe to John Pope, January 3, 1811, Latrobe Letterbooks, Maryland Historical Society, Baltimore (*BHL Microform*, 82/A8).

22. Three sheets of drawings by Latrobe for the Pope Villa (that containing the floor plans is dated 1811) survive in the Library of Congress, Division of Prints and Photographs. See *Architectural Drawings of BHL*, 2:529–38. Six letters from Latrobe to the Popes and their Lexington builder survive in the Latrobe Letterbooks. See *BHL Microform*, 82/A8 (January 3, 1811), 82/G9 (January 18, 1811 [also in *Correspondence of BHL*, 3:10–13]), 83/D7 (January 30, 1811), 88/C12 (July 28, 1811), and 93/B4 (December 9, 1811), all BHL to John Pope, and 84/B8, 84/B12, Latrobe letter and bill of scantling (estimate for wooden elements of the house) to Asa Wilgus, the Pope's

Lexington builder. Files on the Pope Villa restoration are in Special Collections, University of Kentucky Library, and at the Blue Grass Trust for Historic Preservation, Lexington.

23. Latrobe to William Waln (of Philadelphia), March 26, 1805, Latrobe Letterbooks (*Correspondence of BHL*, 2:36).

24. Ibid.

25. Latrobe to Asa Wilgus, March 1, 1811, Latrobe Letterbooks (*BHL Microform*, 84/B8).

26. Latrobe to John Pope, July 28, 1811, Latrobe Letterbooks (*BHL Microform*, 88/C12).

27. Ibid.

28. Latrobe's Pope Villa plans seem to have influenced a few grand federal-period houses in Kentucky, especially the diagonal vistas from its rotunda into its drawing and dining rooms (part of Latrobe's scenery). This "double-diagonal" view reappears in the John Wesley Hunt (Hunt-Morgan) House and the Bodley-Bullock House in Lexington and Elmwood in Ludlow, Kentucky. See Lancaster, *Antebellum Architecture of Kentucky*, 131–34, 152–56. By contrast, the Pope Villa's giant triple windows become a standard feature in later, Greek Revival–style villas in central Kentucky. See n. 77 below.

29. Talbot Hamlin, *Benjamin Henry Latrobe* (New York, 1955), 381–82. Hamlin credits Lancaster with the discovery of Latrobe's Ashland plans. See also Lancaster, *Ante Bellum Houses of the Bluegrass*, 56–57, 137–39, and *Antebellum Architecture of Kentucky*, 126–27, 299–301. Latrobe's sketch plan of the Ashland wings is interleafed in the pages of a letter from Latrobe to Henry Clay regarding Latrobe's and Clay's work on the U.S. Capitol rather than Ashland. See Latrobe to Henry Clay, June 29, 1812, *BHL Microform*, 100/A13 (also in James F. Hopkins ed., *The Papers of Henry Clay*, 10 vols. and suppl. [Lexington, 1959–1992], 1:684). Clay and Latrobe were both in Washington, and the location of the Ashland wings sketch plan at this point in Latrobe's Letterbooks suggests that he and Clay had been working together on both the Capitol and plans for Ashland. Latrobe's sketch is also reproduced and discussed in *Architectural Drawings of BHL*, 2:335–36. For a more detailed account of Latrobe's work on Ashland, see Fazio and Snadon, *The Domestic Architecture of Benjamin Henry Latrobe*, 655–66.

30. Latrobe's first documented correspondence with Clay is Latrobe to Henry Clay, December 11, 1811, in *BHL Microform*, 93/B9 (also in Hopkins, ed., *Papers of Henry Clay*, 1:599–600). The content is personal rather than architectural, but the letter implies previous acquaintance. On Latrobe's and Clay's work on the U.S. Capitol, see Latrobe to Robert Wright, December 22, 1811 (in *Correspondence of BHL*, 3:205 [also in *BHL Microform*, 93/D12]), in which Latrobe mentions conferring with "the Speaker" (of the House of Representatives, i.e., Clay).

31. Latrobe to Henry Clay, September 5, 1813, in *BHL Microform*, 112/E3 (also in Hopkins, ed., *Papers of Henry Clay*, 1:823, but with the sketch plan omitted).

32. See Fazio and Snadon, *The Domestic Architecture of Benjamin Henry Latrobe*, 30–33 (Cockerell's planning), 211–21 (Pennock House), 481–508 (Decatur House).

33. Latrobe designed one house with an asymmetrical bay (see ibid., 237–39) and other houses with twin, symmetrical bays on either garden or entrance fronts (see ibid., 255–63 [Harvie-Gamble House, Richmond, Virginia], 292–300 [Riversdale, Maryland], and 635–40 [Clifton, Richmond, Virginia]). The Clays' builder, John Fisher, was of a prominent Lexington family of builders, originally from Maryland (see ibid., 665n). John Fisher to Henry Clay, account for a wing of Ashland, September 10, 1813, in Hopkins, ed., *Papers of Henry Clay*, 1:824.

34. Clay purchased the Ashland estate "lately occupied by Elisha Winters," apparently through the agents Thomas Bodley and Cuthbert Banks, on September 13, 1804, though the final deeds were recorded only on October 13, 1811. See Hopkins, ed., *Papers of Henry Clay*, 1:148–49; and Fayette County Deed Book D, p. 120, Fayette County Court House. See also Richard Laverne Troutman, "Henry Clay and His Ashland Estate," *Filson Club History Quarterly* 30 (1956): 159–60; and C. Frank Dunn, "Old Houses of Lexington," 2 vols. (n.d., typescript, available in the Kentucky Room of the Lexington Public Library), 1:16–24. This earlier house may have faced north, toward Richmond Rd. See "Survey of Meadows at Ashland," July 16, 1807, in Hopkins, ed., *Papers of Henry Clay*, 1:299.

35. Latrobe to Henry Clay, September 5, 1813 (n. 31 above). Also mentioning the design of Ashland are Latrobe to Henry Clay, August 15, 1813, in *BHL Microform*, 112/A13 (also in Hopkins, ed., *Papers of Henry Clay*, 1:818–19), and Latrobe to Henry Clay, January 16, 1814, in *BHL Microform*, 114/C12 (also in Hopkins, ed., *Papers of Henry Clay*, 1:851–52).

36. Henry Clay to John Wesley Hunt, May 9, 1812, in Hopkins, ed., *Papers of Henry Clay*, 1:652–53. Although Hunt's letter does not survive, Latrobe mentioned its date as being April 15, 1812, in one of his later letters: Latrobe to Henry Clay, June 24, 1812, in *Correspondence of BHL*, 3:320 (also in Hopkins, ed., *Papers of Henry Clay*, 1:678–83).

37. Henry Clay to John Wesley Hunt, May 9, 1812 (n. 36 above). On the Fayette County Courthouse, which Clay criticized, see Lancaster, *Antebellum Architecture of Kentucky*, 127–28.

38. In 1800, Latrobe had made designs for a national military academy (site unknown). Also in 1800, he redesigned a building for the University of Pennsylvania in Philadelphia (to which he later added a medical hall). In 1802, he rebuilt Nassau Hall at Princeton University after a fire (and in 1803–1804 added smaller, flanking buildings to it). Also in 1802, he submitted a design for South Carolina College (unbuilt). In 1803, he designed Dickinson College in Carlisle, Pennsylvania (surviving). See Paul Venable Turner, *Campus: An American Planning Tradition* (Cambridge, MA, 1984), 62–67; and *Architectural Drawings of BHL*, 1:259–68 (national military academy), 2:424–31 (Dickinson College).

39. Latrobe to Henry Clay, May 15, 1812, in *Correspondence of BHL*, 3:292–94 (also in Hopkins, ed., *Papers of Henry Clay*, 1:655–56). (In *The Papers of Henry Clay*, the date is given as May 16, 1812, but I have used the May 15 date given in *The Correspondence of BHL*.)

40. Latrobe to Henry Clay, June 24, 1812 (n. 36 above).

41. Latrobe to Henry Clay, May 15, 1812 (n. 39 above).

42. Latrobe to Henry Clay, June 24, 1812 (n. 36 above).

43. Ibid. On the early student literary societies at Transylvania, see John D. Wright Jr., *Transylvania: Tutor to the West* (Lexington, 1980), 292–94.

44. In his June 24, 1812, letter (n. 36 above), Latrobe describes the now-lost plans that he sent with the letter, then details how reductions in the dimensions of the plans might save some expense. The reconstructed plans are based on his descriptions; the general rules of which are as follows: (1) The building is symmetrical and of three stories, with a frontal block to the south and two wings to the north. (2) The south front is approximately 160 feet wide in order to fit the site. (3) The building contains sixteen lodging rooms housing forty-four students, with twelve rooms partitioned into three student cells, each eight feet square, and four rooms partitioned into two student cells of the same dimensions. This implies four rooms in each corner of the building, housing eleven students, in two stories, for a total of forty-four students on the two upper stories. The hypothetical, reconstructed plans meet all these criteria; however, I cannot make them agree with every point in Latrobe's letter. There are three unresolved points: (1) Latrobe states that, in reducing the plans, the student cells could each be shortened by a foot in width (from eight by eight feet to eight by seven feet), which would save ten feet in the overall length of the main block (five feet on each end) and five feet in the length of each wing. This implies five student cells in each direction (for a total of forty rather than forty-four students); I cannot resolve this contradiction with my reconstructed plans as forty-four student cells require six cells in one direction and five in another. (2) I have assumed that the fireplaces are all on the short, cross walls of the plan rather than parallel with the long walls (so that the chimneys could be corbelled in the attic to emerge perpendicular to and centered on the roof ridges); however, Latrobe states that the common area of the student rooms is ten feet deep but that the "chimney jaumbs [*sic*] project 1 ft. 2 inches into it, leaving 8 ft. 10 in the front." This implies that the chimneys run parallel with the long dimensions of the wings, which would make for difficulties in construction of the chimneys and roofs. (3) Finally, in the first story, or the basement-service story, Latrobe states that "the three rooms next to the Kitchen may be thrown in to one for a dining room"; this would be difficult given the locations of bearing walls and chimneys, which I have hypothesized on the upper stories. Excepting these three problems, my hypothetical plans agree with all the other statements in Latrobe's letter. His letter specifies neither the length of the east and west wings nor the locations of the staircases within the building; in my plans, these elements are speculative.

45. While the sketch plan in Latrobe's May 15, 1812, letter (n. 39 above) implies separate windows for each student cell, a statement in his June 24, 1812, letter (n. 36 above) suggests that the larger student rooms (those of twenty-four feet in width) might eventually be adapted to accommodate four, rather than three, student cells, implying that the partition walls were of light, temporary construction (perhaps of wood or plaster and lath) that could be easily rearranged irrespective of the permanent win-

dow configuration of the outer wall. This system was probably employed in Latrobe's 1803 designs for the Dickinson College building, where multiple student study/sleeping cells must originally have shared a single window per room. For Latrobe's surviving plans for Dickenson College, see *Architectural Drawings of BHL*, 2:424–31.

46. Latrobe to Henry Clay, June 24, 1812 (n. 36 above).

47. Transylvania University Minute Book 1, p. 104 (July 27, 1812), Transylvania University Archives. See Lancaster, *Antebellum Architecture of Kentucky*, 128, 325n.

48. Wright, *Transylvania*, 57–59.

49. Lancaster, *Antebellum Architecture of Kentucky*, 128–30, 173–74.

50. Ibid., 129. For Kennedy's plan for an alternative design, which must have been near his floor plan for the building as built, see ibid., 174 (fig. 9.31).

51. Following the designs for Transylvania, Latrobe designed only one further university building: an 1816 proposal (unbuilt) for a "National University" on the mall in Washington, DC. Like the Transylvania designs, it was for a three-sided courtyard scheme, but it was developed only schematically. See *Architectural Drawings of BHL*, 2:671–76.

52. An earlier version of this account can be found in Fazio and Snadon, *The Domestic Architecture of Benjamin Henry Latrobe*, 667–69.

53. "Agreement with John Keiser," May 4, 1813, in Hopkins, ed., *Papers of Henry Clay*, 1:795–96. Clay subsequently rented the existing house at the west end of the property on Short Street and Keiser's new house and the small wooden house adjacent to it, both on Market Street, back to Keiser and to his sister Elizabeth. See "Rental Agreement with John Keiser," September 3, 1813, in ibid., 822–23; and "Rental Agreement with Elizabeth Keiser," September 22, 1813, in ibid., 826–27.

54. Latrobe to Henry Clay, August 15, 1813 (n. 35 above).

55. Latrobe to Henry Clay, August 24, 1813, in Hopkins, ed., *Papers of Henry Clay*, 1:820 (also in *BHL Microform*, 112/C9). See also Latrobe to Henry Clay, September 5, 1813 (n. 31 above); and "Agreement with Grinstead and Davis," September 17, 1813, in Hopkins, ed., *Papers of Henry Clay*, 1:825. Grinstead and Davis were by profession bricklayers; the amount of the contract was $1,600. See also "Agreement with Robert Grinstead and Allen Davis" (May 4, 1813, in ibid., 794–95), a contract for $3,000 that may also relate to these houses.

56. Latrobe to Henry Clay, January 16, 1814/C12 (n. 35 above).

57. Ibid.

58. Latrobe to John Watkins, May 28, June 9, 1814, in *BHL Microform*, 117/D8, 118/B5. In his May 28 letter, Latrobe acknowledged a letter from Watkins of May 2 (not found) and stated that he had transmitted to Watkins a packet of drawings in March that evidently miscarried. With his June 9 letter, he transmitted to Watkins copies of one or more of the previously lost drawings (but not including full working drawings). Of the duplicated drawing(s), Latrobe stated: "The design accords with that finally adopted by Mr. Clay, the range of shops that form the row being laid down [probably on Short St.]. I should be glad if the appearance of the houses on Market can be so made as nearly as possible to that at the other end, in order that the whole

front may possess a unity of design, but it is essentially necessary that the fascia below the upper windows should be 23 feet above the water table" (Latrobe to John Watkins, June 9, 1814). Clay had given John Watkins power of attorney to act for him on October 12, 1813 (Hopkins, ed., *Papers of Henry Clay*, 1:833).

59. See Ranck, *Guide to Lexington*, 29. As early as 1830, Clay had urged the banker Nicholas Biddle to construct a building for a new Lexington branch of the Bank of the United States. Clay to Nicholas Biddle, September 13, 1830, in *Papers of Henry Clay*, 8:265. Clay then sold the Short and Market Street lot to the Bank of the United States in 1831 for $7,000. Fayette County Deed Book 7, pp. 387–88, Fayette County Courthouse. Thanks to James D. Birchfield for this reference.

60. On the 1889 Northern Bank of Kentucky building, see Clay Lancaster, *Vestiges of the Venerable City: A Chronicle of Lexington, Kentucky* (Lexington, 1978), 136, 243.

61. Latrobe to Henry Clay, January 4, 1814, in Hopkins, ed., *Papers of Henry Clay*, 1:848–49 (also in *BHL Microform*, 114/B10).

62. On Matthew Kennedy's building for the second Kentucky Statehouse, see Lancaster, *Antebellum Architecture of Kentucky*, 76, 327n. Perhaps in disappointment over the failure of several of his public projects for Kentucky, Latrobe recorded a scurrilous verse about the state (*Journals of BHL*, 3:273–74 [March 30, 1819]). His only actual visit to Kentucky occurred in March 1820, on his last voyage to New Orleans (where he died September 3). He and his family traveled down the Ohio River by steamboat from Cincinnati to Louisville from March 12 to March 14 and remained in Louisville from March 14 to March 24 (*Journals of BHL*, 3:335). Mrs. Latrobe described the journey in a letter and remarked that, through letters of introduction from Henry Clay, they were entertained by Louisville society, which she found characterized by "ostentatious grandeur." Mary Elizabeth Latrobe to Catherine Smith, April 18, 1820, in Samuel Wilson Jr., *Impressions Respecting New Orleans by Benjamin Henry Boneval Latrobe* (New York, 1951), 180.

63. *Journal of the House of Representatives of the Commonwealth of Kentucky, 1816–17* (Frankfort, 1817), 254. Thanks to John Downs for this reference.

64. Latrobe to John Pope, November 3, 1817, in *BHL Microform*, 138/G13. See also ibid., 139/B3 (probable cover sheet for the letter, with calculations of numbers of workers in the proposed armory).

65. Latrobe to John Pope, November 20, 1817, in *Correspondence of BHL*, 3:965–68. For a summary of Latrobe's letter, see Hamlin, *Latrobe*, 479.

66. Latrobe to John Pope, November 20, 1817 (n. 65 above).

67. Latrobe to Joseph Perkin, November 7, 1798, in *Correspondence of BHL*, 1:99n.

68. *Architectural Drawings of BHL*, 2:568–77. See also Fazio and Snadon, *The Domestic Architecture of Benjamin Henry Latrobe*, 447–51.

69. *Journal of the House of Representatives of the Commonwealth of Kentucky, 1816–17*, 76 (December 19, 1817). Thanks to John Downs for this reference.

70. *Acts Passed at the First Session of the Twenty-sixth General Assembly of the Commonwealth of Kentucky* (Frankfort, 1818), 573. Thanks to Scott Walters for this reference.

71. *Acts Passed at the First Session of the Thirty-third General Assembly for the Commonwealth of Kentucky* (Frankfort, 1825), 280. Thanks to Scott Walters for this reference. More research is needed in Kentucky State records regarding the fate of Latrobe's armory designs.

72. Robert C. Vitz, "General James Taylor and the Beginnings of Newport, Kentucky," *Filson Club History Quarterly* 50 (1976): 353–68.

73. Latrobe to Gen. James Taylor, February 27, 1817, General James Taylor Collection, Kentucky Historical Society, Frankfort (not included in the Latrobe Papers Project). For a more detailed account of the Taylor Mansion, with a photograph of the post-1842, rebuilt house, see Fazio and Snadon, *The Domestic Architecture of Benjamin Henry Latrobe*, 680–84.

74. James Taylor to James Madison, November 7, 1818, James Madison Papers, Library of Congress, Washington, DC, quoted in *Register of the Kentucky Historical Society* 34 (1936): 327–28. The Virginia house of which Taylor requested plans was probably Redlands, the Robert Carter House, Albemarle County, completed in 1813. See Lane, *Architecture of the Old South: Kentucky and Tennessee*, 62. On Redlands, see K. Edward Lay, *The Architecture of Jefferson County: Charlottesville and Albemarle County, Virginia* (Charlottesville, VA, 2000), 140–41.

75. The Taylor House burned March 13, 1842. See "Fire at Newport," *Cincinnati Gazette*, March 14, 1842. See also "Fire in Newport," *Licking Valley Register* (Covington, KY), March 19, 1842. On the surviving, post-1842 house, see Walter E. Langsam and Mary Cronin, "Bellevue (General James Taylor House)," National Register of Historic Places Inventory nomination form, October 1975, copy in the files of the Kentucky Heritage Council, State Historic Preservation Office, Frankfort. See also Walter E. Langsam, *Great Houses of the Queen City: Two Hundred Years of Historic and Contemporary Architecture and Interiors in Cincinnati and Northern Kentucky* (Cincinnati, 1997), 24–25.

76. For the Harvie-Gamble House, see *Architectural Drawings of BHL*, 1:155–61.

77. Whereas at the Pope Villa Latrobe had indicated his rational planning of major public spaces by triple windows in the second story only, later Kentucky designers used them indiscriminately on both first and second stories. For the Shakertown trustees' building, see Lancaster, *Antebellum Architecture of Kentucky*, 96–97. See also Lewinski's Mansfield (1845–1846), Lexington, and two-story villas of this type (ibid., 216–17, 224–31).

78. The Strickland line includes some of America's most famous architects, into the twentieth century. For example, Latrobe trained Strickland, who trained Thomas U. Walter, who trained Richard Morris Hunt, who trained Frank Furness, who trained Louis Sullivan, who trained Frank Lloyd Wright. Roxanne Kuter Williamson, *American Architects and the Mechanics of Fame* (Austin, TX, 1991) 3, 80–92.

Afterword

D r. Thomas Clark, Kentucky's historian laureate, was 101 in 2005 when he said in an interview: "A community without a sense of history is no community at all."

Now that's of course a theme we could reflect on for a lifetime, but I think I know what he meant. For it was just a few years earlier, when we were working together on a project to preserve Shakertown, that Dr. Clark suggested that a deep exploration of Lexington's history—our city—could create a kind of shared mental space both to reflect on our contemporary condition and to inform our thinking of the future.

Now, to be sure, we all know that an excessive preoccupation with fixed ideas about our past can be a dangerous business. In fact, Tom Clark knew that better perhaps than most of us and would often say that history is fluid and moving and engaging; it is not stationary. The lessons we gain from our contemporary lens on the past will not be the same lessons our grandchildren take from the same periods in our history. They may translate the past in new and revised ways. But it is the reflection itself that is so worthwhile as we consider today's Lexington and our future.

Reading these essays, we can gnash our teeth at the tragic undermining of Transylvania College, which in the early nineteenth century was on its way to being the Harvard of the West, educating the best and brightest in America's new frontier, but lost its footing owing to a much too tempting and convenient closed mindedness, or what Dr. Clark referred to often as a "comfortable and persistent anti-intellectualism."

We can bemoan the triumph of riverine trade in the nineteenth century and ponder a different world in which the Ohio River dipped slightly more to the south. And we can wistfully nod our heads at Henry Clay's admonition that public buildings reflect the values and ambitions of a sophisticated city and not its momentary budget concerns. I cringed when I read that he failed to convince Transylvania to employ, for a new building, the innovative architectural imagination of Benjamin Henry Latrobe, a friend of Clay's and the chief architect of the Capitol Building in Washington and Clay's own Ashland estate.

But missed opportunities, either natural by way of Lady Luck or manmade, do not define us. It is our history of seizing opportunities that has made Lexington a great American city and that points the way forward. We have seized the opportunity that our limestone-infused bluegrass has created in building Lexington into the horse capital of the world. We have boldly undertaken to protect those farms with one of the nation's first urban-service boundaries, a decision that has hemmed in the sprawl that has weakened so many other communities. And we have chosen to invest in our great universities, creating a center for culture and learning that is the envy of cities many times our size.

These are the decisions of a people aspiring to the heights of Athens. It is in the blood of our people to continue along the ambitious road that Henry Clay set us on 180 years ago.

But today we face steep challenges that are just as great as a lack of river access in the early nineteenth century. Our antiquated tax and financing systems impair our ability to build the sort of new infrastructure that fully realizes the quality of life—with its educational, cultural, and economic dimensions—to which we aspire.

And many questions exist today about the educational investments we are making and whether we are properly training the workforce of the future by arming our youths with the problem-solving skills and creativity required to thrive in a globally competitive economy.

This anthology asks us, Do we still have the capacity to engage these kinds of multigenerational issues, to achieve the level of foresight that men like Henry Clay and our founding fathers seemed consistently to possess?

Thankfully, the remarkable contributors to this book, coming at our history from so many thoughtful and informed points of view, have given us a rare chance to work on these questions. They have given us the opportunity to study and reflect on our history, to let their well-chosen stories act as ingredients in a slow-cooking exercise, so that in our own minds we can search for the big ideas that will sharply improve our future.

When I remember my talks with Dr. Clark in Shakertown, as we took on the task of rescuing the village from a steep decline in tourism, the choices we faced were stark. Do we create a curatorial museum of Shaker life, setting in amber a fascinating society that had all but vanished? Or do we take the remarkable history of the Shakers, along with the extraordinary architecture and landscape, and weave it together to create a place for creative, reflective thinking? By then, Dr. Clark was in his early nineties. He was stooped but agile of mind and spirit, still speaking in complete sentences, perfectly almost, without split infinitives or even dangling participles.

With his persuasive intellect and the purest sense of history, Dr. Clark cautioned us to remember that the study of the past is designed to shape our future, to adapt and change. "The real lesson of the Shakers," he said, "is that they didn't adapt, they didn't adjust. That's what we need to remember."

Dr. Clark drove us to consider a new Shakertown, not as a curio of the past, but as a reinvented place where history-fueled contemplation could spark new ideas, perspectives, and ventures. And that is the same promise held in this book—that these thoughtful essays exploring Lexington's past will inspire readers to reimagine and reinvent Lexington's future.

Jim Gray

Contributors

Stephen Aron is professor of history at the University of California, Los Angeles, and chair of the Institute for the Study of the American West at the Autry National Center. He is the author of *How the West Was Lost: The Transformation of Kentucky from Daniel Boone to Henry Clay* (1996) and *American Confluence: The Missouri Frontier from Borderland to Border State* (2006) and coauthor of *Worlds Together, Worlds Apart: A History of the World from the Beginnings of Humankind to the Present* (3rd ed., 2011).

Shearer Davis Bowman received his Ph.D. from the University of California, Berkeley, and subsequently taught at Hampden-Sydney College, the University of Texas at Austin, Berea College, and the University of Kentucky before his death in 2009. He authored two well-received comparative studies, *Masters and Lords: Mid-Nineteenth Century U.S. Planters and Prussian Junkers* (1993) and *At the Precipice: Americans North and South during the Secession Crisis* (2010), as well as numerous articles and reviews.

Matthew F. Clarke is a master's candidate in architecture and urban policy at Princeton University. His senior thesis as a Gaines Fellow at the University of Kentucky, "Voices of Home in Bluegrass-Aspendale" (2007), traced the shifting role of the Bluegrass-Aspendale housing project in Lexington's social fabric. Currently, he is researching the economic development of Vieques, Puerto Rico, and the regional infrastructure of New Jersey.

Mollie Eblen is the public relations associate at Transylvania University in Lexington. She holds degrees in English and library science from the University of Kentucky.

Tom Eblen is a columnist and the former managing editor of the *Lexington Herald-Leader*. A Lexington native, he previously was a writer and editor for the Associated Press and the *Atlanta Journal-Constitution*.

Randolph Hollingsworth is assistant provost in the Division of Undergraduate Education at the University of Kentucky. She also serves as an adjunct assistant professor in the History Department and a faculty affiliate with Gender and Women's Studies at the University of Kentucky. While much of her research has focused on conservative thought and U.S. women's history in the South, her most recent work has focused on contemporary issues regarding open educational resources and Kentucky women's history in the civil rights era. She is currently working on a manuscript on the history of women in Kentucky.

James C. Klotter, the state historian of Kentucky and a professor of history at Georgetown College, is the author or editor of some dozen and a half books. They include *The Breckinridges of Kentucky* (1986) and *Kentucky Justice, Southern Honor, and American Manhood*, Southern Biography Series (2003). Previously, he served as the executive director of the Kentucky Historical Society.

Nikos Pappas of Lexington, Kentucky, has a wide range of musical interests both as a performer and as a scholar. A Ph.D. candidate at the University of Kentucky, he has been involved in documentary film scores, the creation of a traditional music archive, and work for presidential libraries and projects, including those of James Monroe and Abraham Lincoln. His research has garnered awards from the American Musicological Society, the American Council of Learned Societies, and the American Bibliographic Society.

Estill Curtis Pennington has served in curatorial capacities for the Archives of American Art, the National Portrait Gallery, the Lauren Rogers Museum of Art, the New Orleans Museum of Art, and the Morris Museum of Art. His publications include *Kentucky: The Master Painters from the Frontier Era to the Great Depression* (2008) and *Lessons in Likeness: Portrait Painters in Kentucky and the Ohio River Valley, 1802–1920* (2011).

Daniel Rowland is associate professor of history at the University of Kentucky, specializing in the political thought of early modern Russia.

He is a former director of the Gaines Center for the Humanities at the University of Kentucky, which sponsored the symposium on which the present volume is based, and has been a community activist in Lexington for almost forty years.

Gerald L. Smith is associate professor of history at the University of Kentucky. He is the author of *A Black Educator in the Segregated South: Kentucky's Rufus B. Atwood* (1988). He is currently working on a general history of African Americans in Kentucky and serving as the general co-editor of the Kentucky African American encyclopedia.

Patrick Snadon is an associate professor in the School of Architecture and Interior Design at the University of Cincinnati. He has authored and coauthored articles and books on American architecture and interiors, including *The Domestic Architecture of Benjamin Henry Latrobe* (2006, with Michael Fazio), which received the 2008 Hitchcock Book Award from the Society of Architectural Historians. He has engaged in historic preservation work for many years, including assisting in the restorations of two Latrobe buildings, the Pope Villa in Lexington and Decatur House in Washington, DC. He is currently researching modernism in Cincinnati and has coauthored a guidebook, *50 from the 50s: Modern Architecture and Interiors in Cincinnati* (2008).

John R. Thelin is a professor at the University of Kentucky. He is the author of *A History of American Higher Education* (2004). In 2005, he teamed up with Sharon Thelin on the Kentucky Humanities Council project "Town and Gown in Kentucky: Campus and Community in the Commonwealth." He is the coauthor, with Amy E. Wells, of "Universities of the South," in *The New Encyclopedia of Southern Culture*.

Maryjean Wall is the author of *How Kentucky Became Southern: A Tale of Outlaws, Horse Thieves, Gamblers, and Breeders* (2010). She was the longtime horseracing writer for the *Lexington Herald-Leader* and teaches American history at the university level. She has won multiple awards for her writing. She earned her Ph.D. in history from the University of Kentucky in 2010.

Mark V. Wetherington was born in Tifton, Georgia. Earning his Ph.D. in history in 1985 at the University of Tennessee, he served as the director of the East Tennessee Historical Society, the South Carolina Historical Society in Charleston, and, presently, the Filson Historical Society, Louisville. His first book, *The New South Comes to Wiregrass Georgia, 1860–1910* (1994), won the American Historical Association's Herbert Feis book award in 1995. His second book, *Plain Folk's Fight: The Civil War and Reconstruction in Piney Woods Georgia*, appeared in 2005. He has also served as an adjunct history professor at the University of Tennessee and the University of Louisville.

Index